Further Praise for David Levering Lewis's

THE IMPROBABLE
WENDELL WILLKIE

"[David Levering] Lewis, the Pulitzer Prize–winning biographer of W. E. B. Du Bois, offers an insightful, compelling portrait of this political neophyte from the Midwest. . . . In our own polarized age, Wendell Willkie serves as a poignant reminder of what can happen when a political leader steps up to do what is right, defying his party and putting the interests of his country and its people ahead of ambition and partisan advantage."   —Lynne Olson, *New York Times Book Review*

"[An] insightful, disciplined biography. . . . In Mr. Lewis's telling, Willkie emerges as the kind of figure who is missing on the political stage today: the classical liberal, who stands for individual rights at home and will fight tyranny abroad."   —Amity Shlaes, *Wall Street Journal*

"The freshest dimension to Lewis's biography comes from the lifetime of scholarship in African-American history which he brings to bear on Willkie's domestic civil-rights efforts—terrain on which he was well out in front of Franklin, and perhaps even Eleanor, Roosevelt. . . . Lewis brings the now largely unknown Willkie to a new generation. . . . The book largely succeeds, suggesting a figure—again, like Reagan—both sunnily approachable and weirdly elusive; one who seems to require imaginative projections."   —Thomas Mallon, *The New Yorker*

"A nuanced, deeply researched account of Willkie, who despite his loss to the Democratic incumbent, Franklin D. Roosevelt, was arguably one of the most consequential public figures of the 20th century. . . . Much as Willkie was a godsend to the country, so too is David Levering Lewis for offering us this instructive story of courage and bipartisanship at a time when both are in very short supply." —Richard Moe, *American Scholar*

"Two-time Pulitzer Prize–winning biographer Lewis . . . breathes new life into the onetime Republican standard bearer and now historical footnote. . . . [Lewis's] swift, thoughtful biography makes clear Willkie's importance in WWII-era America and his lasting impact on domestic and international policies."   —*Publishers Weekly*

"Only the formidably erudite David Levering Lewis, the Voltaire of American letters, could remedy our misunderstanding of a neglected treasure like Wendell Willkie, while touting a vibrant liberalism that lifts us beyond the self-defeating narcissism of our social morass to a soaring vision of American politics."

—Michael Eric Dyson, author of *What Truth Sounds Like*

"The story of a dynamic political outsider who mounted a formidable challenge to Franklin D. Roosevelt for the presidency. . . . A thoroughly researched biography of a remarkable figure." —*Kirkus Reviews*

"Meticulously researched and brilliantly written. . . . Lewis, one of our nation's most gifted historians, rightfully elevates the devalued Willkie to high-minded, Mount Rushmore–statesman status. This is American history at its absolute finest!"

—Douglas Brinkley, author of *Rightful Heritage*

"At a time when our political system seems alarmingly immoral and rudderless, David Levering Lewis offers a powerful reminder of practical bipartisanship, visionary internationalism, and committed civil liberties and civil rights."

—Katrina vanden Heuvel, editor and publisher, *Nation*

"Regaling politics aficionados with details about how Willkie became GOP's candidate, Lewis also offers a lively account of Willkie's record-setting campaign. Though defeated, Willkie earned the reelected FDR's favor and carried out wartime inspection trips until he died suddenly, in 1944, and faded from history. Crediting Willkie with advocacy of civil rights and world peace, Lewis delivers a thoroughly researched and discerning portrait that will reestablish Willkie's political significance." —*Booklist*

"This engrossing and enlightening appraisal by a master biographer shows why and how Wendell Willkie mattered. We gain virtuoso access to a thoughtful leader who demonstrated that effective political opposition need not descend into coarse demagoguery or shrill combat."

—Ira Katznelson, author of *Fear Itself*

"Readers will delight in Lewis's sparkling prose and eagerly turn the pages as Willkie is explained in his many dimensions—a man for all seasons and a timely reminder of the ordinary decency and inspired commitments that have occasionally animated American politics and politicians."

—David Mayers, author of *America and the Postwar World*

THE IMPROBABLE

WENDELL

WILLKIE

THE IMPROBABLE
WENDELL WILLKIE

THE BUSINESSMAN WHO SAVED
THE REPUBLICAN PARTY AND HIS
COUNTRY, AND CONCEIVED
A NEW WORLD ORDER

DAVID LEVERING LEWIS

LIVERIGHT PUBLISHING CORPORATION
A Division of W. W. Norton & Company
Independent Publishers Since 1923

All rights reserved
Printed in the United States of America
First published as a Liveright paperback 2019

For information about permission to reproduce selections from this book,
write to Permissions, Liveright Publishing Corporation, a division of
W. W. Norton & Company, Inc., 500 Fifth Avenue, New York, NY 10110

For information about special discounts for bulk purchases, please contact
W. W. Norton Special Sales at specialsales@wwnorton.com or 800-233-4830

Frontispiece: Courtesy the Lilly Library, Indiana University, Bloomington, Indiana

Manufacturing by LSC Communications, Harrisonburg
Book design by JAMdesign
Production manager: Julia Druskin

Library of Congress Cataloging-in-Publication Data

Names: Lewis, David L., 1936– author.
Title: The improbable Wendell Willkie : the businessman who saved the Republican
Party and his country, and conceived a new world order / David Levering Lewis.
Description: First edition. | New York : Liveright Publishing Corporation, a Division of
W. W. Norton and Company, 2018. | Includes bibliographical references and index.
Identifiers: LCCN 2018013302 | ISBN 9780871404572 (hardcover)
Subjects: LCSH: Willkie, Wendell L. (Wendell Lewis), 1892–1944. | Politicians—United
States—Biography. | Presidential candidates—United States—Biography. | United
States—Politics and government—1933–1945.
Classification: LCC E748.W7 L48 2018 | DDC 324.2092 [B]—dc23
LC record available at https://lccn.loc.gov/2018013302

ISBN 978-1-63149-625-7 pbk.

Liveright Publishing Corporation, 500 Fifth Avenue, New York, N.Y. 10110
www.wwnorton.com

W. W. Norton & Company Ltd., 15 Carlisle Street, London W1D 3BS

1 2 3 4 5 6 7 8 9 0

TO NATALIE,
may hers be one world

CONTENTS

PREFACE

Wendell Lewis Willkie (1892–1944) was one of the most exciting, intellectually able, and authentically transformational figures to stride the twentieth-century American political landscape. In an era of well-merited disgrace, Willkie served up the American business community's most reasoned, politically effective, and judicially nimble defense against government regulation of the free-market economy. Wendell Willkie baited and debated Franklin Roosevelt, whose imperious sense of self-indispensability was turning his office into an imperial presidency, he warned with cracker-barrel farsightedness. His presidential campaign against Roosevelt was one of the toughest and bitterest (and most disorganized); after which, in defeat, he insisted that his party set a new standard of bipartisanship in Washington. He managed to outwit the isolationist leadership of the party (Herbert Hoover, Robert Taft, and Arthur Vandenberg) and engineer grudging recognition by the party platform of a qualified internationalism.

Lewis Wendell Willkie (at age twenty-five, he chose not to correct a US army clerk's transposition of his name) was a dynamic work in progress, a principled egoist who seldom allowed conventions to stand in his way. By age forty-two, this

bear of a German American lawyer from Elwood, Indiana, presided over Commonwealth & Southern, the nation's second- or
third-largest private utility holding company. After a five-year
judicial slugfest in agile defense of free-market electricity against
the Tennessee Valley Authority (TVA), he wrenched a 1939 monetary settlement from the US Treasury equivalent to 1.3 billion
contemporary dollars.

Wendell Willkie was certainly one of the most unexpected, if
not unlikely, candidates for the presidency from a major national
party. He was more unexpected than William Jennings Bryan and
only somewhat less unlikely than Barack Hussein Obama. The
reaction of one New York GOP committeeman spoke volumes.
When asked by a major contributor to pitch Willkie's candidacy
to the clubhouse party loyalists, a dismayed Kenneth Simpson
listed the difficulties:

> They'll ask me, "Willkie, who's Willkie?" And I'll tell them
> he's president of the Commonwealth and Southern . . . .
> And I will explain that it isn't a railroad, it's a public utility
> holding company. Then they will look at me sadly and say,
> "Ken, we always have thought you were a little erratic, but
> now we know you are just plain crazy." And that would be
> without my even getting to mention that he's a Democrat.

In *The Powers That Be,* an exposé of the print media's capacity to manipulate public opinion, historian David Halberstam
leant credence to the accusation that Willkie's political career was
invented by a cabal of rich newspaper and magazine publishers
educated at elite eastern institutions (e.g., Henry Luce, Ogden
Mills Reid, Gardner and John Cowles). Yet Wendell's democratic
convictions were authentic. His well-publicized conflict with New
Deal economic policies elicited plaudits from big business, yet his
conception of responsible markets was more compatible with John
Maynard Keynes's than with Adam Smith's.

Wendell's farm-boy haircut, hayseed manners, and sartorial indifference bespoke common-man straightforwardness—"grass-roots
stuff," said a wary FDR. But this businessman-turned-politician

possessed a supple intellect, a remarkable fund of knowledge, and a concealed disdain for parochial ideas. Indeed, he was constantly to surprise many admirers and bitterly disappoint more than a few intimates who mistook Willkie's small-town Hoosier origins and big business success as the sum of the inner man.

Wendell, a registered Democrat only six months earlier, captured the 1940 Republican presidential nomination in a media blitz of news publications, radio, film, and experimental television new to the nation. He unnerved Franklin Roosevelt in his bid for an unprecedented third term, and he won an unexpectedly large popular vote. He imported British notions of "the loyal opposition" into American politics after his defeat, forging the bipartisanship that made Roosevelt's foreign policy possible and United States' entry into World War II a certainty.

With the war's outcome far from decided in 1942, Wendell lifted off that August on a round-the-world goodwill mission in a prototype B-24 with the blessings of FDR. Leader of his party, he took the principles of the Atlantic Charter seriously, dismaying Charles de Gaulle in Damascus and evoking Winston Churchill's memorable House of Commons retort regarding Egypt and India. He gave the boy shah of Iran his first ride in a plane. He saw Beirut and Baghdad as distinguished world ambassador by day and adventurous student of their cultural character by night. He debated the virtues of private enterprise with Stalin. Geopolitics dictated that Wendell Willkie extoll the staying-power of Chiang Kai-shek's Kuomintang, despite the regime's metastasizing corruption. Sex and ambition dictated the tempestuous bonding of the ardent American visitor and the "last empress," Madame Chiang Kai-shek.

One World, a visionary credo based on the famous, round-the-world wartime inspection tour, written with Irita Van Doren, literary book editor of the *New York Herald Tribune* and Wendell's intellectual muse and lover, sold one million copies in seven weeks; two million by the end of 1943, its first year. "No book in the history of book publishing has been bought by so many people so quickly," Simon & Schuster's press release boasted. Nor garnered more distinguished praise, with Clifton Fadiman and

Walter Lippmann, seconded by Indiana legends Theodore Dreiser and Booth Tarkington, as a book whose author, said Tarkington, had "personally experienced the small roundness of the 20th century world." *One World* foresaw the promise and peril for the postwar United States as a beacon of democracy in a world of decaying empires, rising plebeian expectations, vast Middle East oil deposits, and flammable Islam. The extraordinary impact in its many translations of *One World* was potent enough to nurture an international movement for the betterment of the world's peoples.

A party leader whose rank-and-file was puzzled and appalled by many of his positions, Wendell defended the civil liberties of ideological pariahs (fascists and communists) in mass circulation magazines. He argued and won the landmark 1943 immigration case of *Schneiderman v. US* before the US Supreme Court. His espousal of full civil rights for colored Americans was unequaled among contenders for national office. His 1940 defeat by Roosevelt was in large part due to the fact that his progressive platform was almost a validation of his opponent's achievements. Wendell accepted the need to regulate the "force of free enterprise," espoused "collective bargaining for labor, federal regulation of interstate utilities, securities markets and banking and defended pensions, old-age benefits and unemployment allowances."

"Greatly, as the old guard lords . . . hated Roosevelt," a sympathetic Democrat wrote, "they had come to hate Willkie even more." Fired up by the old-time party religion, they assembled without him on Mackinac Island, Michigan, in the summer of 1943, drew up a new covenant half-heartedly inspired by him, then commanded their leader to renounce his ways and embrace the hallowed orthodoxy on pain of ostracism. Still official leader of his party, Wendell announced his presidential campaign on February 2, 1944. The candidate made the notable pledge to appoint a person of color to his cabinet or to the Supreme Court and to use the full power of his office to end institutionalized racism. He was the first party leader to address the annual convention of the NAACP.

Wendell Willkie sauntered away from a crushing repudiation of a second presidential run in the 1944 Wisconsin GOP primary—after which there is credible evidence of secret discussions with FDR for a realignment of the frequently dysfunctional two-party system.

Had he taken better care of himself and curtailed the consumption of scotch, he would almost certainly have continued to exercise a significant role in the unfolding drama of postwar politics in America. Alive, five years or so more, there would have been many more pages in the history books. Perhaps a page relating one of the more intriguing collaborations in twentieth-century American civil rights. The leader of the Republican party traveled twice to Hollywood with NAACP executive secretary Walter White in 1942 and 1943 in his capacity as chairman of the Twentieth Century-Fox board of directors to mobilize the film industry for a paced and smarter and more positive presentation of blacks in film. His Emergency Committee of the Entertainment Industry was the model for Hollywood support of civil rights activism twenty years later. He and NAACP head Walter White were planning a coauthored book on race relations shortly before Willkie's fatal coronary. Because black lives mattered greatly to him, the NAACP named its national headquarters building on New York's Fifth Avenue after Willkie.

Willkie's sudden, unnecessary death in October 1944 came on the crest of domestic and international celebrity that surpassed his exceptional accomplishments as the GOP's formidable presidential candidate in 1940. Dead, in his prime, at fifty-two, Willkie's prominence quickly dwindled from a notable profile in Irving Stone's *They Also Ran* to that of a once significant public figure about whom little is readily recalled. Taking the long view, however, Wendell Willkie's actual legacy to the postwar politics of the nation was decisive. The Republican Party's formal acceptance of foreign-policy bipartisanship, achieved by Willkie the year before his death, emerged as a controlling postwar doctrine. GOP House Minority Leader Joseph Martin judged this to be "Wendell Willkie's monument." Paradoxically, the party that disavowed its maverick standard-bearer entered the postwar world partially and grudgingly better adjusted to deal with complex international challenges because of its temporary and unanticipated capture by an extraordinary internationalist.

"He was a godsend to this country when we needed him most," FDR insisted. As a final judgment on his unique partner, the president's words were fitting. Harold Ickes's "barefoot Wall Street lawyer" and Clare Boothe Luce's "global Abraham Lincoln" may have wanted Americans to remember the admonition from his posthumous essay collection, *An American Program*: "Whatever we do at home constitutes foreign policy. And whatever we do abroad constitutes domestic policy. This is the great new political fact." John Gunther, the renowned global investigator, praised Willkie as "one of the most . . . forward-looking Americans of this—or any—time," praise shy of hyperbole when one weighs the geopolitical prescience of *One World* against today's lethal reality of the West versus the rest:

> *It all added up to the conviction* [Willkie understood] *that these newly awakened people will be followers of some extremist leader in this generation if their new hunger for education and opportunity for a release from old restrictive religious and governmental practice is not met by their own rulers and their foreign overlords. . . . Again and again I was asked: does America intend to support a system by which our politics are controlled by foreigners, however indirectly, because we happen to be strategic points on the military roads and trade routes of the world? . . . . If we fail to help reform, the result will be of necessity either the complete withdrawal of outside powers with a complete loss of democratic influence or complete military occupation and control of the countries by those outside powers.*

David Levering Lewis
New York City and Stanfordville, New York
2018

THE IMPROBABLE
WENDELL
WILLKIE

CHAPTER 1

ELWOOD, AUGUST 17, 1940

Callaway Park acceptance speech, August 17, 1940. *Courtesy the Lilly Library, Indiana University, Bloomington, Indiana.*

An iconic photo preserves the event, the last of its kind in the campaign history of the American presidency. The Republican Party's 1940 nominee for the presidency of the United States came home to Elwood, Indiana, to accept his party's nomination. The heat was historic, too, that Saturday afternoon, August 17. The thermometer in front of the Elwood five and dime registered 98 degrees in the shade as the Republican nominee's line of Lincoln automobiles rolled down South Anderson Street flanked both sides by five growling police Harley Davidsons. *Time* magazine reported 102 degrees. Marcia Davenport, Mozart's first American biographer and bemused New York witness to history unfolding in an unlikely place, "personally saw a thermometer on somebody's porch that read 112." Even a few of the locals accustomed to the smack-down summer heat of the Indiana heartland had been strongly inclined to stay home that day, especially a sizable number of Democrats. Minus the bedridden and newborn, though, Elwoodians came to see the tall, dark-haired man with the piercing blue eyes who stood waving a white boater from the rear seat of a gleaming Lincoln Continental Cabriolet: Wendell Lewis Willkie, born among them forty-eight years ago.[1]

Photographer J. D. Collins, on the flatbed truck ahead of the cortege, captured one of the most dynamic images in the history of presidential campaigning: a buoyant and beaming ship's prow of a Willkie sailing into a sea of thousands of exhilarated admirers. Seated with the nominee were Cora Wilk and Edith Willkie, Wendell Willkie's pouter-pigeon mother-in-law and his pert wife in her white platter of a "good luck" hat. Son Philip rode up front, proud, Ivy League precocious, and twenty-one next December. They looked the picture of a first-family ideal. Wedged between Philip Willkie and the driver was Congressman Joseph Martin, the new house minority leader and new chair of the Republican National Committee. Martin's duty that day, in keeping with the practice of the times, was the formal presentation of the official nomination document. To look at the beaming Joe Martin, one would have supposed the veteran Massachusetts politician was having the time of his life as he rolled past several elephants, inflated and live, along the flag-bedecked route and saw national pole-sitting champion Alvin "Shipwreck" Kelly hoisted at a corner.[2]

The procession had left Elwood's quaint old Nikel Plate Railroad Station on schedule at 12:30 p.m. A five-hundred-strong American Legion honor guard from Akron, Ohio, along with the Indiana University marching band, stepped out front to the rousing strains of "Back Home in Indiana," the unofficial state song. A sedan with "Press/Association" on its windscreen and two security men on board followed the lead car; then a second sedan carrying Indiana Congressman Charles Halleck, an early Willkie supporter who had placed Willkie's name in nomination before the Republican National Convention in Philadelphia. A third and fourth Cabriolet followed with Elwood's mayor and Indiana University's emeritus president, a Catholic and a Protestant prelate, and several important state and local businessmen and attorneys. There would never be another day like this one in a town whose major spectacle was the annual Miss Tomato Festival.[3]

Seven weeks earlier in Philadelphia, after five of the most unlikely convention days in its history, the Republican Party had nominated Wall Street attorney, utility company president, and, until recently, registered Democrat Wendell Lewis Willkie as its candidate for the presidency of the United States. Willkie was an overnight political sensation who had never held elective office and who, when he announced his candidacy that May, had had a Gallup handicap of 3 percent. Political neophyte and director of a billion-dollar corporation, Wendell Willkie might have seemed a decidedly problematic standard-bearer to appeal to an electorate unforgettably described four years earlier by Franklin Roosevelt as "ill-housed, ill-clad, ill-nourished," and whose improved circumstances since then were due to the aristocratic architect of the New Deal, now seeking an unprecedented third term in the White House.

Somehow, though, the Republican nominee inspired enthusiasm well beyond partisan bounds. Partly, it was the nominee's personality. Wendell Willkie's career epitomized rugged individualism; his Midwestern twang, unbuttoned affability, and radiant self-confidence seemed to strike a chord equally with the store clerk as with the banker. His record of success in business was just shy of fabulous, almost a decade of unbroken profit-taking of his giant corporation, Commonwealth & Southern, straight through the Great Depression. Partly, his appeal came from a cresting enthusiasm for a political reset. The GOP's stunning congressional gains in the 1938 off-year elections had revealed a large swath of the electorate grown weary of New Deal regulation and experimentation. Middle-class professionals disillusioned by years of tepid economic recovery were ready to give laissez-faire economics another try.

In May, Willkie had been a far-fetched, if exciting, presidential speculation.[4] By July, many veteran political observers said the presidency was his to lose. Already, there were "Democrats for Willkie" appalled by Roosevelt's third-term arrogance. "Nothing so extraordinary has ever happened in politics," Interior Secretary Harold Ickes told FDR in private. In public, Ickes lampooned the Republican contender as just a "simple barefoot Wall Street lawyer," but an early-August Gallup poll predicted a Willkie victory if the election were held that month.[5] Willkie was certainly one the most unexpected, if not unlikely, candidates for the presidency ever to come from a major national party. After all, he entered the Republican Party as a Wilsonian Democrat. Willkie was more unexpected than even "Cross of Gold" William Jennings Bryan in 1896 and only somewhat less unlikely than would be "Audacity of Hope" Barack Hussein Obama in 2008.

In *The Powers That Be,* an exposé of the print media's capacity to manipulate public opinion, the paragon journalist David Halberstam leant credence to the accusation that Willkie's political career had been invented by a cabal of rich newspaper and magazine publishers educated at elite eastern institutions. To be sure, his well-publicized conflict with New Deal economic policies elicited plaudits from big business, yet his conception of responsible markets was actually a precocious anticipation of the theory of countervailing powers advanced a decade later by economist John Kenneth Galbraith.[6] This businessman-turned-politician was constantly to surprise many admirers and bitterly disappoint more than a few intimates who mistook Willkie's small-town Hoosier origins and big-business success as the sum of the inner man.

Even before his debut as a serious presidential contender, Willkie's May 1938 founders' day address at Indiana University ("The Meaning of True Liberalism") could have put politicians of both the Far Left and Far Right on notice. The fact is the liberal attempts "the most difficult thing in the world," the returning alum insisted— "namely, to strike a true balance between the rights of the individual and the needs of society. He is like a man rowing a boat who when the boat swings to the right, pulls on the left, and when it swings to the left, pulls on the right." Booth Tarkington, vintage Hoosier novelist and two-time Pulitzer Prize winner, summed up Willkie neatly:

"in a word, a man as American as the courthouse yard in the square of an Indiana county seat."[7]

Yet, this quintessential Hoosier had lived in a grand apartment on New York's Fifth Avenue since 1930. Faithful to his simple Indiana roots, however, Willkie liked to surprise friends by revealing that he kept his Manhattan apartment door unlocked, just as the family home had never been locked when he was a boy growing up in Elwood. Scarcely a man or woman in Elwood, Mayor George Bonham included, could have guessed that the Republican National Committee would choose their down-at-the-heels town known for a tomato canning industry as the site from which to launch its 1940 presidential campaign. A third of the town's people were on the federal and state relief rolls. It had as many Democrats as Republicans, and a significant number of Elwoodians favored the politics of the Ku Klux Klan or the revolving old-age pension scheme of California physician Francis Townsend.

The fact that some twenty years had passed since the nominee had bothered to visit his birthplace made Elwood's people all the more astonished, and a fair number suspicious and even resentful that August day. That he was known to be an absentee landlord of five farms in Rushville, a prosperous township fifty-five miles southeast of Elwood, added to the sour feelings.[8] Indeed, his national campaign headquarters was located in Rushville with all that that meant for infusions of cash diverted there from Elwood's merchants. Many years later, some of the locals were still heard to say, "He came to use us"—that powerful outsiders had dusted off and bunting-ed up their unremarkable little town as a hayseed stage set for one of the most ambitiously scripted national contests ever mounted. Rumors spread of a brand-new stone monument over Willkie's parents' Elwood gravesite, a story that would occasion White House mirth when Labor Secretary Frances Perkins shared it with Franklin Roosevelt.[9]

The facts of what became "Willkie Day" were somewhat at variance with local memory, however. Elwood had scrambled smartly to get ready for their one-day unsolicited honor. It had mattered not a whit that the Republican National Committee offered the municipality neither money nor organizational talent.

The Elwood Notification Nomination Committee sprang to life under the competent parenting of Hoosier businessman Homer Capehart. Two years earlier, Capehart, a moon-faced Wurlitzer Music Company vice president dubbed "father of the juke box," had organized a "Cornfield Conference" attended by some 20,000 Republicans on his 120-acre farm in Daviess County, Indiana. Capehart's generous checkbook and briefcase of pledges from Cornfield conferees permitted the scaling up of the Notification Nomination Committee's planning to accommodate as many as 150,000-plus attendees and 30,000 parking places. A cantankerous Democrat owned one of the two cornfields needed for the car park. "The price was fantastic, $12,000," Capehart was known to sputter long after his service to Elwood's native son had helped Capehart win a seat in the US Senate.[10] By the time the nomination-day preparations were ready on Friday evening, August 16, Elwoodians discovered they were participants in an amazing spectacle that not even Homer Capehart's careful planning had fully anticipated.

When the combined Elwood constabulary, State Police, and law officers from adjacent states closed the town to vehicular traffic at precisely 10 p.m. on Friday night as planned, a veritable flotilla of some 30,000 cars with license plates from every state in the union was parked free on 160 acres of cleared cornfields; 15,000 more in a special area; another 11,000 on Elwood streets or in pay garages. The *Chicago Tribune*'s air-borne reporter filed a rhapsodic description of seamless traffic circulation worthy of the human cardiovascular system. "Coming in on route 28 . . . at a rate of about 1,500 cars an hour. No blockade visible," he reported. By one count, 45,000 passengers had arrived from all points of the Midwest and beyond on forty-five special Pennsylvania railroad trains. Thousands more came on two special bus lines.[11] With thirty years of experience as a food handler for large crowds, Chicago's Archie Rose estimated thirty tons of frankfurters, ten tons of hamburger meat, and 18,000 ice cream specialities, most of it ready and waiting in refrigerated trucks in the city park. As Elwood closed itself Friday night, the *Tribune* carried a discordant squib about Elwood's only hotel, the forty-eight-room

Sidwell ("sleep well at the Sidwell"): "The Sidwell hotel ran out of ice at 10 o'clock tonight. It hopes to get more."[12]

There was ceremony and pageantry on a stunning scale on appropriately called "Willkie Day," the next day. "WELCOME HOME, WENDELL Willkie," loudspeakers blared, as the self-assured politician reached out to shake so many hands that the driver was afraid the stop-and-go speed might cause the vapor lock for which the twelve-cylinder Lincoln engines were notorious. The original nomination-day plan had called for Elwood's famous son to deliver his acceptance speech from the steps of Central High School, the backdrop inspiration of Yale man Russell Davenport, Willkie's self-appointed political guru, recent *Fortune* magazine editor, and the gifted Marcia Davenport's husband.[13] Eight years earlier, Franklin Roosevelt had made a dramatic departure from long-held tradition by flying to the Democratic convention in Chicago to announce a "new deal" for America. In well-advertised contrast to Roosevelt, Willkie decided this scalding Saturday in 1940 to follow tradition and present himself to the electorate from a place epitomizing the virtues of small-town America. The nominee intended to boast of pride in traditions, "not in change for the mere sake of overthrowing precedents."[14] His homecoming message from Middle America was intended to serve notice that the politics of big government and the economics of class resentment spawned by the New Deal were destined for repudiation.

When "Willkie Day" came, however, the speech from the steps of Central High School (whose front portal was crowned by the proud inscription, "The Hope of Our Country") was no longer the centerpiece in the nomination production. Capehart's planning committee had persuaded Willkie to give his address from an elevated wooden platform erected in Callaway Park at the northern edge of the town. But Central High School's location was still too important as a photographic prop to eliminate. The sentimental prop nearly proved disastrous, however, when Willkie's driver forgot his instructions to veer off and drive behind the school. Instead, the car was finally forced to a stop as it wedged deeper into the uproarious sea of humanity on Main Street. *Time*'s description of the moment was frightening: "stuck solidly for 15 minutes, in a temperature of 102°; only Wendell Willkie's 220 lb. kept him from being pulled from the car by handshakers." To hear Joe Martin, the situation became an adulatory maelstrom of panic with Willkie flailing his arms "like pinwheels" until a flying police wedge extracted the party and forced a channel to the rear entrance of the high school.[15] Nearly overcome by the heat, the nominee collapsed into a chair and needed a cigarette and several minutes to recover before reappearing at the stanchion of national radio network microphones on the school steps. Willkie, impatient to reach Callaway Park, waved his boater and paid tribute to his old teachers and classmates. With that, the nominee and his party were shouldered by quick-acting Hoosier policemen over and through the flowing mass of celebrants into the lead vehicle for the final gamut to the park.[16]

Callaway Park, a forty-acre retreat bequeathed to the people of Elwood by a wealthy local family, had become gateway to a two-day phenomenon, thanks to Homer Capehart's bipartisan team—a metropolitan mirage that materialized as a city second in size only to Indianapolis virtually overnight. Twice as many Americans came to hear Wendell Willkie in Elwood than had filled Philadelphia's Franklin Field four years earlier to hear FDR deliver his acceptance speech. Three times as many, vouched *Time* magazine, than had listened in 1936 to Alf Landon, the GOP's ill-fated Kansas-bred presidential contender. "GUESSES VARY ON ELWOOD CROWD, 125,000 TO 300,000," the *Chicago Tribune* exuberated on August 18.[17] Twenty-three Augusts passed until an agglomeration of Americans would assemble in numbers equal to Elwood's Willkie Day.

On that August day in 1963 the great crowd at the Lincoln Memorial would be black as well as white. Although dark faces didn't stand out in extant mainstream newspaper photos of seemingly endless rows of white faces in Callaway Park, major black newspapers—*Chicago Defender, Philadelphia Tribune, Amsterdam News*—sported photos of proud, well-heeled African Americans wilting along with the rest of the Republicans in the park. The cause that brought well over 150,000 men and women together in Elwood in 1940 was not at all dissimilar to the 1963

March on Washington for Jobs and Freedom: to protest what many believed was a perversion of American ideals that had gone on far too long.[18]

Thunderous acclamation drowned out "Back Home in Indiana" as Willkie, clad in a blue suit and tie, strode up the platform ramp in Callaway Park, smile radiant, white boater aloft, all trace of fluster from the high school detour gone. *Life* magazine apotheosized the moment: "This is the pageant of American politics, of America's eternal Main Street hailing its ascendant son."[19] On the platform, rows of seated dignitaries awaited the nominee, among them Minnesota's wunderkind Governor Harold Stassen and Ohio's chagrined Senator Robert Taft, son of President William Howard Taft, who had been odds-on favorite going into the convention at Philadelphia. An introvert of martinet self-discipline and inflexible political convictions, Taft abided Willkie's victory as the fluke of bad timing during the convention's next to last day. Some senatorial colleagues said that Taft's was the finest mind in Washington, "until it was made up." In Taft, Wendell Willkie saw the incorruptible leader of the misguided isolationist wing of the party it was his mission to reform.[20] Both men talked together in animated fraternity for the benefit of the press and the image of GOP solidarity until the invocation delivered by Indiana University's emeritus president silenced them and perhaps a quarter-million others. "God Bless America" followed opera singer John Charles Thomas's "The Star Spangled Banner," after which Charles Abraham Halleck of Indiana's second district introduced RNC chair Martin, who rose to present the official nomination notification to the GOP standard bearer.[21]

Because Joe Martin was a politician's politician, he found himself more than a little concerned about his party's presidential choice by the time Willkie Day arrived. Although "heartened by the spectacular size of the crowd," Martin admitted later that "everything else that happened that day" filled him with discouragement. First came dismay over the nomination acceptance speech Willkie forgot in Rushville, necessitating its last-minute delivery by police motorcycle. When Martin saw the speech written in "ordinary pica type," he was flabbergasted. "Where's your reading copy?" he asked, only to hear, "This is it," from the nominee. "Not the way we do it in Washington," an annoyed Martin rejoined.[22] In fact, Martin had spent the period after the Philadelphia convention entreating Willkie to provide a draft of his acceptance speech. It would have been instructive to have had time to give it more than a quick read, Martin remembered thinking as he rose to present the nominee.

Martin's speech, bringing "the enthusiastic greetings of the great Republican party," fit the expectant mood of the great assembly. His party had met the grave challenge of the present. It had provided the nation with a man "preeminently qualified" to lead the forces of liberty and constitutional government. That man was acclaimed by "independents, Jeffersonian Democrats, progressives, liberals, and Republicans alike," Martin shouted over rolling applause. All abhorred the failed record of the last four years, the drift "toward bankruptcy, inflation, and perhaps war." Against an administration frankly claiming that "unemployment and distress had come to stay," against an administration whose "lust for power" would abrogate the "revered tradition" of the two-term presidency—"a step which may well lead to dictatorship"—the American people were ready to choose Wendell Willkie, Martin soared to a finale.[23] The three o'clock sun bore down on the great crowd in Callaway Park as it gave Willkie a stentorian, ten-minute ovation.

But Joe Martin had primed the crowd for what it would not get that afternoon—a red meat speech. Some said Wendell's speech was a failure. Sam Pryor, Pan American Airlines vice president and Willkie loyalist, thought so, as did Russell Davenport's wife, Marcia, who called the "whole thing . . . hell—the journey, the crowds, the blasting heat, the noise, . . . The speech which was not good." Joe Martin believed the speech should have been more confrontational. The fiercely Republican *Chicago Tribune* praised it as a worthy statement of principles, but it reported few memorable phrases.[24] A widespread impression formed later that the candidate had been nearly undone by the heat, the humidity, the almost dangerous jostling at the high school, and the tiny font in which his acceptance speech was typed. True, Willkie read his speech poorly, and he knew he had. He never found a satisfactory register of voice and pace of delivery. He landed repeatedly either before or after pauses and exclamation points clearly marked in his text. For a public figure whose boyhood hero was William Jennings Bryan and who proclaimed his presidential campaign a "crusade," the Callaway Park oratory seemed almost puzzlingly subpar. Puzzling, because Willkie's debating prowess and command of prose were major components of his lightning emergence in national politics as a major contender. Millions of radio listeners had heard him demolish FDR's solicitor general and future Supreme Court justice, Robert H. Jackson, in a memorable 1938 Town Hall of the Air clash over the constitutionality of government interference with business.[25]

William Jennings Bryan, he of the silver voice, would have met the fervent expectations of the day, or the Roosevelt at Osawatomie, and undoubtedly the Roosevelt at the 1932 Democratic convention—veteran politicians all, unlike Wendell Willkie the novice with a steep learning curve. After years of Roosevelt the Svengali, a majority of Americans had come to expect a high bar for presidential speech-making. *Time* diagnosed the problem accurately. Noting that Willkie's radio speeches had been formal and stiff, it decided that the nominee "was at his best when he pushed aside the microphone and talked with an unforced intimacy to the living people he could see before him." He was a debater, not an orator.[26] Willkie made his debut before ten million radio listeners and a quarter-million pilgrims as a political amateur with no experience of the hustings. Even so, not many weeks afterward, the nomination acceptance speech achieved generally much higher marks from objective observers willing to accord Wendell's text its appropriate gravitas, if not kudos for oratory, such as the much respected Scripps-Howard columnist, Raymond Clapper. "Not many major political utterances in modern times have rung with such courage," insisted Clapper.[27]

Wendell began his acceptance address on a high note of ethical duty by sharing the "political philosophy" that he said was in his heart. He told the Callaway host that he represented "a sacred cause" that was nothing less than "the preservation of American democracy," a cause in which party labels would no longer govern the movement he was pledged to lead. That was the true meaning of his mandate, he declared, "the nomination by the Republicans of a liberal Democrat who changed his party affiliation because he found democracy in the Republican party and not in the New Deal." He claimed that the GOP leadership in Congress and the party organization embraced his concept of politics above party. Robert Taft, Joe Martin, the governors of Ohio, Connecticut, Minnesota, and ranking RNC officers looked on in presumed corroboration as Callaway Park gave this line a rousing cheer and ten million listened over the radio broadcast networks. Pledging to go forward from Elwood "as into a crusade," he needed the help of all Americans: Republican, Democrat, Independent; Jew, Catholic, Protestant; "people of every color, creed, and race."[28]

His Elwood was "the story of America," then, Willkie said. Its simple democratic values of hard work, instilling of principles, and recognition of merit had made him what he had become. His parents and he had more reasons to feel even stronger about American ideals than most, he said, because both his father's and mother's people had come to the Midwest fired by ideals of liberty and justice brought from Germany after the failed revolutions of 1848. Joe Martin remembered wincing at mention of German bloodlines while the Battle of Britain was raging. Willkie pressed on to say that once again "people are being oppressed in Europe," and he cited the "barbarous and worse than medieval persecution of the Jews," calling it "the most tragic in human history." Their plight served as a terrible example to the people of Elwood of the failure of Europe's liberal democracies. Some in Callaway Park that day must also have remembered their dismay a year before when President Roosevelt denied asylum to more than nine hundred Jewish passengers aboard the German ocean liner *St. Louis*. "We have been sitting as spectators to a great tragedy," Willkie cried, a tale of principles betrayed and self-defense neglected. When European democracies promoted the distribution of wealth over the priority of production, they had opened the way for Hitler.[29]

As Wendell's words ricocheted through the American heartland, the Battle of Britain was in the fourth day of the furious

German aerial onslaught that would continue well into September. Elwood's sky remained azure blue on Willkie Day, but the endgame for civilization being played out over the British Isles weighed on the minds of people in Callaway Park and of free people everywhere. Eleven weeks earlier had come news of the once-magnificent French army's capitulation to Hitler's generals in the forest of Compiegne. Now, twenty-five years after the war to end war, the great unmentionable of the hour was the war's meaning for Elwood and the rest of America. Involvement in the European war was a prospect that evoked such ethnic divisiveness in the national melting pot and such visceral abhorrence among old-line isolationists that both the Democratic and Republican Parties professed a scrupulous commitment to the neutrality of the United States. Both parties called for a strong national defense, but Republicans were opposed to national conscription. Wendell was careful to honor the dogma of American neutrality in foreign wars, yet he hinted at a conditional neutrality that astute journalists such as Raymond Clapper of the Scripps-Howard chain were certain to notice.[30]

Wendell's neutrality was not the rock-solid stuff of the Republican Party everyman. For that reason, the candidate refused to ask the American people to put their faith in him "without recording [his] conviction that some form of selective service is the only democratic way in which to secure the trained and competent manpower we need for national defense." "Only the strong can be free," Wendell shouted, "and only the productive can be strong!" Neither Martin nor Taft was pleased to hear these words from their new leader, words Martin would surely have wanted edited from the speech. Still, as the Callaway crowd shouted and whistled, the candidate had given his campaign its mantra now. "Free men are the strongest men," and only the productive were strong.[31] Only by reaffirming our faith in the regenerative powers of free enterprise would the democracies triumph. Only if Americans accepted the "toil and sweat" of a great effort would the people of Elwood be spared the "blood and tears" inflicted by fate upon Winston Churchill's people. To understand the stakes of war in Europe meant refusing to be drawn into the war, but also the readiness and resources to determine its outcome if necessary. Franklin Roosevelt was culpable on both counts, he charged. Unless something were done soon about the nation's defenses, 130 million Americans would find themselves at risk from a defense system the New Deal had so far proved itself powerless to create anywhere "except on paper"—and, Wendell claimed, after spending "sixty billion dollars."[32]

Elwood's native son scoffed at claims that he was an opponent of liberalism because of his former connection to a large corporation. He had fought for many of the reforms of the elder Robert La Follette, Theodore Roosevelt, and Woodrow Wilson "before another Roosevelt adopted—and distorted—liberalism." He had learned his liberalism "right here at home" in Elwood where large industrial family fortunes, amassed during the last century, acquired too much power over the community. And by 1929, Wendell charged, the concentration of private power had gone "further than it should ever go in a democracy." He embraced the regulation of the "forces of free enterprise," opposed business monopolies, and believed in collective bargaining, social security, unemployment insurance, and minimum wages. His was the intelligent businessman's long-overdue synthesis of the New Deal at its best and the liberated market economy at its most productive. Finally, his was a liberalism whose predicate was a belief in a United States whose horizon had "no limit."[33] A formula to make the rich less rich didn't "really distribute wealth," Wendell Willkie declaimed. "It distributes poverty." Callaway Park roared assent.

The great crowd had sagged and surged over and again as the perspiring hope of the Grand Old Party sagged and surged through the last traditional nomination acceptance speech that a presidential candidate would give outside a convention hall. Exerting himself for the concluding salvo both he and the crowd knew was rhetorically and psychologically mandatory, Wendell threw down the gauntlet to the Jovian occupant in the White House, charging that FDR's New Deal would lead America, "like France, to the end of the road . . . to economic disintegration and dictatorship." This was a serious charge, nor was it "lightly made," he declaimed. The president had stated that he had neither "time nor the inclination" for "purely political debate." Well, he had no interest in such debate, either, insisted Wendell. But he believed that face-to-face debate was "justly honored among our political traditions." He proposed that he and Roosevelt appear on public platforms together in various parts of the country to debate the fundamental issues. At last the crowd heard the kind of pugilistic charge it wanted to hear, Henry Luce's *Time* applauded: "Thousands jumped to their feet, drowned out the band, shouted for ten minutes."

Following this rousing finale, the Willkies dined with a prominent Elwood family after the Callaway Park proceedings. They departed for Rushville, the campaign's headquarters, shortly before seven that evening. The man in the White House too busy to debate his opponent claimed not to have listened to the speech. Asked his opinion of Willkie a few days later, however, the president told radio commentator and gossip columnist Walter Winchell, "He's grass-roots stuff. The people believe every word he says." FDR suspected he was going to have "a heck of a fight on our hands with him."[34]

Twenty-five days after the candidate's triumph at Elwood, "The Pioneer," the twelve-car Willkie Special, loaded with Republican governors, Chamber of Commerce notables, and much of the national press corps, would steam out of Rushville on a grueling seven-week, whistle-stop campaign the length and breadth of the United States. Boater aloft, new blue suit rumpled, a smiling Wendell Willkie, brushing back a forelock and shouting from the caboose, pledged that he was going to talk to the people "in simple, direct Indiana speech."[35]

CHAPTER 2

"GRASS-ROOTS STUFF"

Boyhood home, Elwood, Indiana. *From the "Community Album" of the Allen County Public Library, Fort Wayne, Indiana.*

"We have exposed Willkie as a turncoat," Joseph Goebbels gloated. US newspapers had devoted "big coverage" to the Nazi propaganda minister's publicity coup. A few days before the 1940 US presidential election results, Goebbels predicted that the Republican contender's German origins (the "same goes for émigré Germans") would keep the United States out of the war. Instead, after his loss to Franklin Roosevelt, not only did Wendell Willkie praise Great Britain's defense of the humanitarian ideals menaced by German aggression, he infuriated Goebbels by claiming that his ancestors had abandoned their homeland for the promise of freedoms long since smothered by Prussian autocracy and now extinguished in the Third Reich. Embarrassed that his Führer had been "right in his judgment" about Wendell, the "swine and super-interventionist," the propaganda minister concocted a scheme to expose the Willkies as frauds.[1] On the morning of March 12, 1941, four months after the election, foreign correspondents from the *Herald Tribune* and *New York Times*, together with members of the press from other neutral countries, were called to the old Saxon town of Aschersleben for an unusual ministry briefing.[2]

Aschersleben, historic, sleepy, and ingrown, lay ninety-eight miles southwest of Berlin in the foothills of the Harz mountains. It was the bucolic birthplace of Joseph Wilhelm Willecke or Willcke, Wendell's paternal grandfather, born January 22, 1826. The town had been shaken out of its medieval repose in 1936 by construction of a huge Luftwaffe fuselage production facility for the Stuka dive-bomber, the screaming aerial predator of the Nazi *blitzkrieg*. Buchenwald concentration camp annex, Aschersleben's most recent addition, was an architectural insult housing slave laborers and lying far enough back from the town to escape the curiosity of the arriving journalists. A preening Doctor Goebbels presided while ministry staffers distributed folders purportedly containing Joseph Willcke's vital statistics.

The documents, the Reichsminister boasted, proved conclusively that a bad business deal involving a clever Jew explained why Joseph had left Germany aboard the *Bavaria* for the United States in August 1860. Joseph's widowed mother was said to have compromised her son's prospects for a sufficient living when she unexpectedly sold the family copper smithy to a scheming Bernhard Gerson. So much, then, sneered Goebbels, for the lie of grandfather Willcke's flight from Prussian persecution after claiming a "small part" in the pivotal 1848 Revolution.[3] To the diminutive propaganda minister's considerable satisfaction, the *New York Times* promptly reported that Joseph Willcke's departure for America after the 1848 Revolution may not after all have been due to politics.

That same week, however, the *Times* printed the opinion of a noted Austrian economist and recent political refugee dismissing the Nazis as "poor historians." Ludwig von Mises pointed out that the political outlook in Prussia in the 1860s was dark enough "to make the friends of liberty despair of the future." The reigning king, Frederick William IV, remembered in history for refusing his people's offer of an imperial crown, had been hopelessly insane for a number of years and not expected to live much longer. The king's brother ruled in his place and bore the sobriquet "Cartridge Prince" because his artillery had cleared the Berlin barricades at point-blank range during the 1848 upheaval.[4] Of some two thousand workers, craftsmen, and university students who stood their ground before the prince's troops, more than two hundred had been slaughtered on March 18—one of the bloodiest days in those rolling continental challenges to European monarchy begun that February with the establishment in Paris of a Republic. What had been limned at first as "the springtime of the peoples" became a season of class warfare, divisive nationalisms, and unworkable idealisms, ending in the long European winter of reactionary restoration. A regime of asphyxiating political repression and omnipresent police surveillance clamped down over the German states, and with it the outmigration of many of the best, brightest, and boldest of an entire generation, the "Forty-Eighters"—among them, one Joseph Wilhelm Willcke.[5]

Joseph Willcke sailed with uncanny timing from Hamburg not six months before the "Cartridge Prince" ascended the Prussian throne on January 2, 1861, as Kaiser Wilhelm I. Otto von Bismarck's immediate appointment as minister-president assured the consolidation of royal autocracy and the militarization of society in a Germany united under Bismarck's "iron" chancellorship and Prussian rule.[6] Grandfather Willcke departed just as the wave of Forty-Eighters arriving before the American Civil War ended: men such as archetypal Carl Schurz and his fellow freedom fighter Johan von Willich, whose liberal political and religious ideals were proscribed after 1848. We have no way of knowing if, as his descendants believed, twenty-two-year-old Joseph was among the workers, craftsmen, and university students who battled Prussian fusiliers in Aachen, Halle, or one of the other nearby cities in 1848. In any case, the quest for freedom and opportunity that carried Wendell Willkie's ancestor from the Aschersleben dead end to an American start-over was certainly vintage 1848.[7]

Fort Wayne, Indiana, was in a second population boom after completion of the Pittsburgh, Fort Wayne and Chicago Railway in 1854. The city was named after its founder, "Mad" Anthony Wayne, the Revolutionary War general who slew the Miami Indians at the battle of Fallen Timbers in 1790. When Joseph Willcke saw Fort Wayne in 1860, it still called itself "Summit City" because it was the highest point along the Wabash and Erie Canal. The city's rapid growth was now fed by the railway, much of that increase coming from German immigrants like the Willckes. Joseph quickly sized up the family prospects for settlement in the Midwest on this first trip. Satisfied that Fort Wayne offered more than the ancestral hollow, he returned almost immediately to Aschersleben to bring Minna Mathilda Breitschuh and their two children, Paul and Herman, to America sometime in 1861.[8] This second departure from Prussia would be Joseph's farewell to Germany and the old spelling of Willcke.

The Willkie family's American narrative began at Castle Garden, New York City's frenetic pre–Ellis Island immigration port, with the frightened first impression of four-year-old Herman Francis, Joseph's second son, alarmed at seeing Union Army soldiers marching in the streets. An annoyed Prussian soldier, stumbling over little Herman at play, had once beaten the boy on the family's front doorstep. Herman's parents explained that these were "the good soldiers" fighting for "the people and not the king." Reassured by this Castle Garden experience, Herman Francis began the psychological journey from Old Europe to Exceptional America on the way to the farm his father had purchased ten miles outside Fort Wayne.[9]

The Willkies' early Indiana years were undeniably hard. No overbearing Prussians in Fort Wayne, but not much more prosperity found there than in Aschersleben. Minna Mathilda bore Joseph five more children in steady succession. One, Francis, a natural politician it seems, found his way to the sketchy Indiana settlement that became Elwood. Minna died shortly after delivering her last child early in the next decade. Meanwhile, Joseph discovered he was ill suited for farming, and the locals remembered him spending much of his time reading history and philosophy, or playing the accordion, while a son-in-law raised the crops and managed the livestock. Bookish Joseph's example had a decided influence on the temperament young Herman carried into studious adulthood.[10] Although the record from Herman's early years is a blank, one might be sketched in with plausible speculations about resourcefulness, persistence, and professional ambition. Family legend recalls the *McGuffey Readers* in an adolescence almost surely dominated by self-help strategy.

In Herman's mid-twenties there is a year of college at Valparaiso (discouragingly known as "the poor man's college"), paid for with $111.50 scraped together from odd jobs and digging drainage ditches. He completed several courses at Taylor College soon thereafter, doggedly capped off by more coursework at Fort Wayne College where, at age twenty-seven in 1884, he finally earned a normal degree in teaching.[11] By then, a credentialed Herman Willkie had traded his family's Catholic faith for Methodism and impressed enough leading locals in and around Fort Wayne that he was appointed superintendent of public schools in Milford, a newly incorporated township in northeastern Indiana. He arrived there as another ambitious newcomer was preparing to meet her first grammar school class. Henrietta Trisch had just completed studies at Terra Haute Normal School. She and Herman were the same age, German Americans from similar ideological traditions, and both endowed with a temperamental restlessness that would set them apart from their neighbors. But Henrietta would be the dominant one in the marriage performed that same year, 1885, in the parlor of the president of Fort Wayne College. Aristocracy breeds difference, which Henrietta's family and close friends speculated was the reason for her serene willfulness. Her maternal bloodlines flowed from minor nobility.

Joseph Willcke's part in the Revolution of 1848 was rather speculative. Not so, that of Herman Willkie's wife's paternal lineage. Henrietta Trisch's mother was the daughter of Jacob von Hessen-Lois, an ennobled and prosperous member of Hamburg's merchant class and a political conspirator. "The last person you would expect to find among the revolutionists," a contemporary later recalled. The forces of order were more discerning, nevertheless, and when Jacob learned that his collaboration with Hamburg's republican conspirators had been exposed, he fled with wife and children by North Sea boat to England.[12] From the little that is known of the Hessen-Lois's life in England after 1848, an inference of coping gentility in reduced circumstances seems reasonable. With the poise of her class and fluency in English, one of the daughters, Julia Ann Dorothea Katherine, became self-supporting in her late teens and soon made her way to the United States as lady-in-waiting and traveling companion of a wealthy family. Less than five years after her family's escape from Hamburg, Julia Ann met and married Lewis Trisch, the son of a prosperous Warsaw, Indiana, wagon-maker and newspaper man.

The Indiana Trisches were originally Treusches from Erbach in Hessen-Darmstadt and, like the Willckes in Saxony-Anhalt, were merely skilled craftsmen—wagon-makers—who had had the good political sense to sail to North America in 1830 after the July deposition of the last French Bourbon, Charles X, sent alarming tremors under the Concert of Europe's delicately balanced power relationships. Johan Ludwig, the Treusch patriarch, tried blacksmithing in Baltimore and farming in Pennsylvania and Ohio, before settling permanently in Warsaw, Indiana, then an unincorporated settlement near four freshwater lakes, sometime in the late 1840s. By then, the family name had changed and its fortunes begun to improve. Treusch became Trisch and Johan Ludwig, helped by his oldest son, Lewis, would eventually amass a small fortune during the Civil War from the manufacture of wagon wheels for the Union Army.

When Lewis Trisch met the daughter of Jacob von Hessen-Lois sometime in 1851, he was a strapping twenty-two-year-old and probably the most eligible bachelor in Warsaw. Julia von Hessen-Lois, a year or so older than Lewis, would have been a significant presence in a town where the arrival of a stylish, well-educated, single woman of noble origins was most unexpected. In short order, eligibility and presence resulted in the matrimonial union in 1852 of Lewis Trisch and Julia von Hessen-Lois, Wendell Willkie's aristocratic maternal grandmother.[13] The following year, the year before the polarizing Kansas-Nebraska Act, the couple left Warsaw, heading by wagon train to a new life at Fort Dodge in the fractious Kansas territory. Starting out newly wed in "Bleeding Kansas" invited challenges, large and lethal, for an antislavery couple. Nor was scrofulous Fort Dodge, deep in angry Cheyenne Indian country and only fitfully garrisoned by the US Army, a place to raise a family. Free-soilers and pro-slavers skirmished in the neighborhood, and the year after Lewis and Julia threw in the towel and headed back to Warsaw with two children in 1854, John Brown rode into Osawatomie with sons and a wagonload of Sharps rifles ("Beecher's Bibles") on a holy mission to purge Kansas of ungodly slavery defenders.[14]

Lewis left Julia a wealthy woman when he died in 1873.[15] The Trisch family had prospered considerably from the Civil War partly instigated by John Brown's martyrdom. Daughters Jennie and Henrietta and the two sons had received solid secondary educations preparing them for professional careers. Julia Trisch *née* von Hessen-Lois would live on in Willkie family history as an ancestral wonder of almost mythic uniqueness. She embraced the predestinarian tenets of Presbyterianism in widowhood, after which her darkly draped figure was to be seen profiled on the flat horizons of Indiana and Kansas as, buggy-ensconced and whip coiled, she brought a stern gospel to unsaved corn-growers and hog raisers.[16] Circuit-riding Julia captivated generations of admiring Willkies. Her daughters were cut from the same proto-feminist cloth. Jennie, the older sibling, became one of the country's rare female physicians before the turn of the century. Herman's Henrietta would declare herself emancipated from childbearing when number six, Charlotte, arrived, after which she promptly qualified for the practice of law before the Indiana bar. Her children would insist that she had been Indiana's first female lawyer, which she was not, but Henrietta and Herman enjoyed the distinction of becoming the state's first husband and wife law partnership.[17]

The union of Herman Willkie and Henrietta Trisch was almost certain to make for the special family life beginning in earnest in summer 1888 when they left the little Wabash River settlement of Lagro for Elwood, one of Indiana's overnight boom-towns. They were now four; little Julia, their firstborn, was almost three; Robert, a future army officer, one year old. At thirty-one, a relatively young age for the position, Herman had been offered Elwood's public school superintendency, an exciting opportunity for professional and family advancement. Younger brother Francis ("Frank," who spelled his name minus an "i"), future mayoral candidate and perennial dabbler in the town's affairs, had lobbied successfully for Herman's appointment.[18] Fifty-two years later, when Herman and Henrietta's third son would choose the town as the stage set for his presidential nomination acceptance speech, Elwood's promise as a late-nineteenth-century piston in America's ongoing industrialization was remembered, if at all, as yet another chapter in the wanton exploitation of natural resources.

Unbridled optimism reigned in 1888, however, one year after Elwood's fabulous takeoff was literally fueled by the gas atop which it sat: what was believed to be the largest natural gas field in the world at that time. The discovery "signaled the end of the slow-paced agricultural life of east-central Indiana," two recent students of the state noted. The town's population hurtled from 2,300 toward 15,000, its industrial base from blacksmithies and a flax mill to the American Tin Plate Company, the country's biggest tin plate mill. Along with Pittsburgh Plate Glass, the town boasted some forty industries with a capitalization of $7.5 million and a labor force of 3,735 in less than a decade.[19] Accordingly, Elwood town became an incorporated city in 1891, elected its first mayor (its richest citizen), and stretched its seams to accommodate the sizable in-migration of English, Welsh, and German skilled laborers and larger numbers of unskilled Slavs and Southern Europeans drawn in by the huge tin plate factory. Natural gas fed the furnaces and heated the steam boilers of light industries at giveaway prices or, unbelievably, no cost at all. Geysers of ignited gas ("flambeaux," Hoosiers called them) now, almost magically, lit up Elwood's newly paved streets night and day, lined miles of Pennsylvania Railroad tracks in permanent advertisement of local opportunity, while they bathed the countryside for miles around in an ethereal glow of auburn permanence. State natural gas supervisor E. T. Jordan's 1891 warning of declining pressure went unheeded.[20]

The Willkies and Elwood grew *pari-passus*: second son Herman Frederick ("Fred") arrived after Robert in 1890. Herman Willkie abandoned the unstructured way things had been done in the old brick schoolhouse by classifying the students by grades, a then-uncommon innovation that sounded the death knell of the one-room schoolhouse. The institution of a two-year high school course followed, even as Herman, handling algebra, arithmetic, and Latin classes, must have carried the lion's share of the teaching. On September 25, 1890, Elwood's innovating school superintendent was admitted to the Indiana bar, and resignation as superintendent took effect almost immediately. Among his new roles was that of the town cultural caretaker, in which he mobilized respectable opinion behind incorporation of an Elwood library association as a necessary first step to the successful emplacement of one of Andrew Carnegie's public libraries. On the low side of culture, Herman was a leader in the movement to contain, if not abolish, the thumping red-light district with its "forty-odd poolrooms and bordellos" now a vestige of a more uncouth frontier lifestyle. His regard for the law entailed high moral standards. He and Henrietta hewed to a sin-conscious Methodism that forbade dancing, gambling, and alcoholic intemperance. Herman's public denunciations of gambling and booze often irritated Elwood's large Catholic population. Years later, their third son would explain to surprised New York socialites supporting his presidential candidature, "I was brought up in a home so strict about dancing that I never learned to dance a step."[21]

On the other hand, a respect for individual liberty ought to have been inherited from the three ancestral branches, and, indeed, Herman proved to be both moral crusader and professional realist. His representation of a saloon-keeper and counseling of a successful madam's investments obliged him to justify himself to a dubious Henrietta on the grounds that if he turned down clients because of their business he'd not "be living up to professional standards." In fact, owners of houses of prostitution and saloons tried Herman and Henrietta's convictions less than the squabbles and character attacks of their co-religionists. Herman served his fellow Methodists as lawyer and treasurer in order to see the brick church building to completion. Eventually, however, he and Henrietta would leave the Methodists for Julia Trisch's Presbyterians.[22]

Lewis Trisch's healthy, big grandson arrived on February 18, 1892, four days before George Washington's birth date and six days past Abe Lincoln's. "Lewis" honored Henrietta's father. "Wendell" was Henrietta's tribute to Oliver Wendell Holmes Sr., author of *The Autocrat of the Breakfast Table*.[23] At that time and in that place and for one year more to the week, the material circumstances of Lewis Wendell's birth would remain propitious. In the classic tradition of Americans intending to do well by doing good, Herman had ventured rather ambitiously into real estate by financing the construction of some two hundred modest houses for factory workers and their families. As a generous step further, Herman guaranteed the workers' bank loans, a risk he calculated as reasonable, given Elwood's housing demands. It would have taken an almost perverse restraint had Wendell's father resisted the business opportunities in Elwood's superheated environment. Trolley cars clanged down and up Anderson Street's steel tracks, powered by the new Electric Street Railway Company. The imposing DeHority and Heck Opera House anchored the intersection at Anderson and South A streets. Nineteenth Street dressed up in Queen Anne mansions owned by the likes of Callaways, DeHoritys, and Heckses. Largely thanks to Herman's role on the education board, a fine specimen of Indiana Romanesque neared completion: Elwood's first full-fledged public high school.[24]

When they celebrated Lewis's first birthday, the Willkie family would have had every reason to believe it was riding a wave of local prosperity as certain as the Gilded Age strength of the national economy. The American economy, however, commenced its collapse on February 23, 1893, five days after little Lewis's first birthday, when the overextended Philadelphia and Reading Railroad declared bankruptcy, followed in a chain reaction by the failure of the Northern Pacific, Union Pacific, and the Atchison, Topeka & Santa Fe Railroads. The shuttering of more than six hundred domestic banks followed in May. Sixteen thousand businesses abruptly shuttered, causing the unemployment of three million Americans in a labor force of fifteen million. George Pullman demanded his employees take a 28 percent wage cut. Daniel Reid's tin trust insisted on a similar take-it-or-leave-it deal from Elwood's Amalgamated Association of Iron, Steel and Tin Workers. In the judgment of progressive historian Howard Zinn, "the year 1893 saw the biggest economic crisis in the country's history."[25] It was in truth so bad that soup kitchens sprouted like kudzu, destitute families bartered chopped wood for food, and many women were reported to prostitute themselves. President Cleveland—a serious man and the sole Democrat since the Civil War to occupy the White House (twice, 1885, 1893)—managed congressional repeal of the Sherman Silver Purchase Act: the belief was that the United States' bimetallic currency (too much silver in the gold dollar) had caused overexpansion and inflation. Grover Cleveland's hard currency deflationary cure set the stage for a face-off between business and labor, money and democracy, unrivaled until the Great Depression of 1932.[26]

The country's shaken middle classes reckoned with life savings vanished in the banking meltdown and demands from creditors that easy-credit indebtedness be paid off in gold dollars, even as the economy continued its contraction deep into 1896. It was a financial predicament exactly describing Herman Willkie's: a total of $25,000 owed to five banks; two hundred houses that not even a dozen worker families could now afford to buy and maybe only dozens could rent. The Elwood *Free Press* quoted his admission, "I am having a more extensive practice . . . than I can handle." Fact was, he was broke. Indebtedness was galling enough; allegations in the local press of Herman's cheating a business partner and absconding and arrest in Mississippi on charges of check forgery were the epitome of family disgrace. In truth, Herman's eventual success in obtaining loans among German contacts in the Southwest had been irresponsibly reported in the local newspapers.[27] Lewis was probably too young to understand much about his father's misrepresentation in the local *Free Press* and Anderson *Herald*, but family debt and family politics were some of Lewis's earliest memories.

The Willkies were silver Democrats, fierce partisans of the youngest candidate in US history to lead a major political party, William Jennings Bryan, the nominee whose "Cross of Gold" speech had stampeded the 1896 Democratic convention, the candidate whose speech was his platform—free silver at 16 ounces to 1 ounce gold in the US dollar. To get down to hard pan, Bryan's campaign threatened to yoke together farmers south and west with laborers north and east behind a platform that reformed the nation's monetary system and sharply reduced business's protective tariff. In one of the most unusual electoral arrangements in US history, Bryan's ticket offered dual vice-presidential options: either a fire-breathing Populist from Georgia, Tom Watson, or a respectable Democratic banker from Maine, Arthur Sewall. Mobilized and united, the alarmed chieftains of the great banks and giant trusts launched William McKinley's high-tariff, hard-currency Republicans on an ocean of money. The 1896 presidential campaign was one of history's fiercest and certainly most decisive campaigns between 1860 and 1932.[28]

The two older Willkie boys, with their little brother heartily joining in, shouted, "Free silver for freedom and Bryan!" and down with the trusts! The neighbor boys bellowed, "McKinley rides a white horse and Bryan rides a mule. McKinley's going to the White House and Bryan is a fool." But when Herman stumped for Bryan, sometimes with Lewis on his shoulders, there was no doubting who could make the best case for popular democracy, soft money, and low tariffs.[29] Nevertheless, big business swept to lopsided victory with 51 percent of the electorate and a consolidating agenda for a realigned American order in which plutocracy was only to be superficially mitigated by genteel progressivism that channeled civil service reform and municipal reform. The battle had gone badly for their side, but Herman was convinced that the forces of popular democracy would ultimately win the war.

Meanwhile, he took pains to ensure that the baleful consequences of an unfettered capitalism were well understood in the Willkie household. Lewis learned early that his father's professional services were available on the merits of the complaint regardless of the power of the opposing side. No complimentary railroad passes to compromise independent Herman Willkie. No tub-thumping of empire in the Willkie household when the Stars and Stripes were hoisted over Manila Bay in 1898 at the end of the Spanish-American War. When the US Marines all but exterminated Emilio Aguinaldo's Filipino freedom fighters, Willkies ridiculed Kipling's mawkish "The White Man's Burden" in jocose verses made up round the dinner table. Willkies hadn't fled Prussian militarism only to end up as new American jingoists, an unlikely eventuality, in any case, that old Joseph Wilhelm's funeral served poignantly to derogate. The family train ride to his grandfather's Fort Wayne interment was four-year-old Lewis's first train ride and an unforgettable reinforcement of his sense of being a living link in a chain of proud, liberty-loving Forty Eighters, one of whom would someday be worthy of denunciation by Hitler's minister of propaganda.[30]

William Jennings Bryan, the gospel of populism made handsome flesh, barnstormed through Elwood on his second presidential quest, and Willkies, front and center cheering him on, were by then sufficiently prosperous and prominent to lodge the Great Commoner in their new three-story home on fashionable Nineteenth Street. The family's straitened economics had improved with the general business upswing under the McKinley administration's hard-currency policies. Also, Herman's clever solution for those albatross houses had reduced family debt considerably: he sold them to local farmers to use as stables.[31] For eight-year-old Lewis, increasingly called by his middle name, the lasting memory of Bryan's overnight October visit was of his father's argumentative forcefulness and of the charismatic presidential candidate's evangelical cast of mind.

In family lore, with them listening in out of sight past midnight, Wendell and his brothers remember their father urging the candidate to play down "free silver" ("a dead issue") and emphasize the evils of America's new imperial adventures instead. Bryan was being mocked in some parts of the country as "the Cowardly Lion" for his waffling over imperialism (distinguishing good imperialism from bad)—an issue upon which Herman, like old Forty-Eighter Senator Carl Schurz of Missouri, gave no ground.

Herman's insistence was likely intended to harden his guest's convictions that late evening. Three months earlier in an eloquent address in Indianapolis—"Imperialism: Flag of Empire"—Bryan, after several exasperating iterations, had finally seemed to renounce his imperialistic temptations.[32] In justice to their guest, the Great Commoner's performance in Elwood was full throttle progressive, offering something for each of the party's fractious components. He roasted the trusts (a battle "between plutocracy and democracy"), denounced Philippine annexation, and pledged a silver-based economy guaranteed to lift debtors out of debt.

The family's reputation as eccentrics extended well beyond its progressive politics and sectarian frictions. After she qualified to practice law in 1897, Henrietta no longer paid much attention to conventional household matters. "Possessed of more than ordinary educational advantages," as the respectful *Daily Record* noted, Henrietta was described as "an accomplished scholar" who speaks several languages "with ease," besides being "an accomplished musician" with laurels in "the musical world." If, as is more than likely, she read Charlotte Perkins Gilman's new *Women and Economics* the following year, Henrietta would have seen her domestic and professional ideals validated by a foundational text of feminism. She plunged into the law as she had her china painting, quilting, knitting, and Chautauqua reading program. She not only assisted Herman, she opposed him in court more than once, and once, Elwoodians claimed, she won. She was Elwood's first woman to smoke cigarettes in public. She was large, imperious, aristocratic. Her children found her disciplined drive, her reach for perfection, her "indomitable will," as they said later, awesome, and so said the epitaph they would place on her gravestone: "She was driven by an indomitable will."[33]

The hands-on mothering of four strapping boys and little Charlotte fell to oldest sibling Julia until she left for college. The result was that neighbors increasingly regarded the Willkie homestead ("crazy Willkies") as the site of some uncommon if not weird experiment in domestic living. Meals were taken opportunistically at a long table in the basement where siblings fed from a large pot on the coal-fired stove, and usually with commotion and controversy. "If discussion developed, or a book was waiting to be read," one bemused housewife recounted, unwashed dishes stacked up high.[34] The floors above filled up with books (eventually, more than six thousand, as Wendell remembered) ordered by both parents on the Chautauqua and University of Chicago extension programs. Parents and books fed a freewheeling disputatiousness on politics, free trade, socialism, religion, and the evils of empire. Herman regularly woke his brood with quotes from Shakespeare, addresses from Athens or Rome, or famous dates or verses they were expected to identify or complete. Responsibilities came early. Wendell drove Mrs. DeHority's cow and held a newspaper route, obligatory for growing American males.[35]

Standing up for your rights was quintessential Willkie, as when ten-year-old Wendell bridled at being castigated by a neighbor startled out of his noonday nap from a baseball thrown through a parlor window. He was going home "and read up in [his] father's law books," Master Wendell warned the Elwood elder. "We'll see what can be done when an innocent person has been wrongly accused."[36] His independent reading led to a few risky do-it-yourself projects with the LTOM ("Little Turds of Misery") club members. The summer scheme to follow Duck Creek into the White River into the Wabash, then into the Ohio and down the Mississippi with buddy Earl McCarel, was typical of his Tom Sawyer teens. The Mississippi exploration foundered on Wabash mud banks and too much enthusiasm for biographies about the Sieur de La Salle, the explorer who claimed the Mississippi River for France. This was just the sort of independent mindset and learning by doing that Herman encouraged in his boys, all of whom were expected to earn pocket money in the town and defray their upkeep during summers living from their wits roaming the country.

The "crazy Willkies" practiced learning by doing on Nineteenth Street at about the time such progressive notions were being formalized by John Dewey, George Herbert Mead, and other philosophical pragmatists.[37] A wide latitude for freewheeling development had its problems, however. Wendell finished his first year at Washington High School in fall of 1906 with a run of mediocre grades—passes in Latin, algebra, American history, and composition—that caused the usually tolerant Herman and Henrietta to send the fourteen-year-old to rigorous Culver Military Academy for the summer. A hang-dog Wendell in military uniform looks out of a school photo. Culver's Spartan discipline was "misery," the results positive. Wendell's second year at Washington reassured his parents and surprised the LTOM cadre.[38] Looking back some thirty years for Elwood turning points to explain Willkie the presidential phenomenon, syndicated columnists and party publicists cited the influence of an English teacher fresh from the new University of Chicago. "A little red headed Irishman . . . that fixed that boy up," LTOM-er Calvin Sizemore recalled. Philip Carleton Bing "started preaching to get to work and that kid went to town."[39] The first and only recorded time he did so, classmates remember Wendell playing on the football team during his second year. Innate intelligence and "Pat" Bing's ministrations propelled Wendell through an impressive record of Gs and Es during Washington High's last two years.

Along the way were those self-financed summers his father believed were character-building. In summer 1908, Wendell stayed home to work at the Amalgamated Association of Iron, Steel, and Tin Workers ("the AA") plant, once the biggest tin factory in the country. By then, the Elwood factory was an outlier whose skilled craftsmen had struggled to keep a living wage and scintilla of autonomy ever since their bloody defeat at Andrew Carnegie's Homestead plant sixteen years earlier. Some eight thousand Amalgamated Association members held on in Elwood and elsewhere working longer hours for less pay at the virtual sufferance of the implacable US Steel Corporation.[40] Wendell's job of "catcher"—someone grappling a bar of molten tin long enough to place it on a conveyor—was one of the industry's riskiest, so physically demanding that even experienced workers had to be relieved after fifteen minutes on the line. Antiunion policies and consolidating automation foretold the inevitable demise of Elwood's "old-fashioned" skilled craft laborers. Tall, sturdy, manly, self-assured, by force of sheer determination the sixteen-year-old shared his fellow workers' Darwinian rigors until the end of summer.[41]

Prodigal wastage of their natural resource was an even greater misfortune to the people of Elwood than the policies of the Leviathan steel trust. Two years after US Steel's 1901 incorporation, what had been America's largest gas vein collapsed almost as suddenly as it had surged sixteen years earlier. In Elwood, it was as if the first decade of the twentieth century halted in mid-flow, then steadily fizzled with a final gasp. Industries departed overnight. Those that remained became virtual husks. People who could leave, left.[42] Until the gas boom bust of 1903, the Willkie family had regained solid economic footing after the Panic of 1893. Seven years later, house proud and prominent, Herman and Henrietta had hosted the Democratic Party's presidential candidate. When their youngest son worked the summer at Amalgamated Tin Plate, however, the family's declining prosperity placed the Willkies in the ranks of the town's unaffluent genteel, notwithstanding the large house on North-Nineteenth, the law partnership of Anderson Street, combative civic activism, and political prominence. With Julia, Robert, and Fred away at college, the money Wendell could earn the last summer of high school mattered.

He and Paul Harmon, a dropout from Washington High, rode the rails to Aberdeen, South Dakota, counting on ready hires in the booming economy set off by the federal government's land grant policy. A dishwashing stint opened up a position as manager of a hotel for drunks and shiftless workers. It earned Wendell a $300 grubstake he invested in a machine to make cement blocks. If he had his father's scheme of ready housing for workers in mind, his luck was even worse than Herman's because cement supplies were nonexistent. Unshaken, he surfaced as a hand on a Montana ranch, then moved on rather quickly to Wyoming when relations with the rancher's daughter aroused her father's suspicions. Driving wagons of sightseers through Yellowstone Park, Wendell could have earned twice more than what he lost with the cement machine, had he not been fired after losing control of the team.[43] He came home at the end of August 1909, a sunburnt, possibly post-virginal seventeen with money toward a year at college just as his unconventional father agreed to represent the workers at Amalgamated Tin Plate against the steel trust's local minions.

The fight against management's open shop policy carried on through Wendell's final high school semester and beyond his first year at Indiana University. Herman's personal courage and professional integrity in guiding Elwood's striking laborers were the demotic stuff of the American everyman mythos Frank Capra's films would propagate a quarter century later. More than those anti-imperialist family doggerels recited at dinner, or routine parental parlor talk about righting wrongs in Robber Baron America, or the memory of Bryan as family guest, it was Herman Willkie as Clarence Darrow—civil liberties champion of an age—that permanently framed Wendell's values. Although the golden-voiced tribune expressed sympathy for their cause when Herman brought along Wendell to plead the case in person in Chicago, Darrow's terms were beyond the union's means: a $20,000 commission and $1,000 per diem. Faced with a positive strike vote, even though he warned the leadership of poor chances for success, Herman volunteered as sole counsel for $25 a day.

His father embarrassed the high-powered corporation lawyers and argued successfully in federal district court for repeal of the company's strike injunction, and Wendell discovered that court victories could lead to physical challenges. Three decades later he recalled how two local strikebreakers, burly Harry and Dave Rogers, ambushed Herman near the railroad tracks, intent on "teaching him" a lesson. In a Hoosier version of the Showdown at the OK Corral, Herman gave as good as he got and Wendell pitched in as Willkies and Rogerses, flailing and kicking, rolled onto the tracks as a train approached and people shouted encouragement to both sides until the police separated them just as the locomotive braked only feet away. Herman continued serving tirelessly the cause while the townspeople gradually turned against the strike that the Elwood *Daily Record* decided was "in the way of our future."[44] The tin plate workers' struggle for respect and living wages stuttered like the town's natural gas supply and finally succumbed to the open shop "way of the future" as a US Steel subsidiary. In mythology, Americans are supposed to favor underdogs. In reality, as Wendell was learning, underdogs generally lose.

In Wendell's case, reaching adulthood as the youngest son of an influential family of modest means imparted a certain social insightfulness as a participant/observer of the town's disparate ethnicities, sharp class distinctions, and sectarian ill will. Racial bigotry was rife in Indiana, a state as congenial to the Ku Klux Klan as Mississippi, but the enforced absence of any African Americans in the town rendered the prejudice mostly a silent factor in the daily lives of Elwood's citizens. No "nigger Jim" ever belonged to the LTOM Tom Sawyers, none roamed summers with the Willkie boys. Herman was on record opposing the Ku Klux Klan on principle, but Wendell's thoughts about black people were a few years away.[45] But awareness of religious and ethnic tensions came early with his parents' fed-up departure from Methodism for Presbyterianism and Herman's vocal disapproval of the local Catholics' alcohol indulgence. Class distinctions, or the narcissism of small differences, manifested themselves in one Gwyneth Harry's rejection by the local high school sorority. The Harrys were Welsh, Episcopalian, and socially ambitious. Gwyneth was Wendell's first love in his junior year. She was a sparkling-eyed brunette who affected slightly British speech, exuded personality, and sang a beautiful high soprano in the church choir. But she was still snubbed by several rich families' daughters for whom the Welsh population was regarded as socially inferior.[46]

Wendell took Gwyneth's humiliation to heart and not only loudly denounced Greek-letter exclusivity, he resigned the presidency of elite Beta Phi Sigma, the considerable distinction to which his fellows had elected him his junior year. Whether or not, as one biographer believes, Woodrow Wilson's highly publicized attempt to reform Princeton's socially exclusive "eating clubs" influenced Gwyneth's impressionable suitor, the speculation is a plausible one.[47] Wendell did more. He left the Methodists for the Episcopalians and the vicarious pleasure of Gwyneth's choral prominence. Wendell's religious disaffiliation was of finer stuff than that of the sixteenth-century Protestant prince who famously said, as he altered French history, that Paris was "well worth a mass." Still, its romantic impulsivity set the stage for future decisions in which personal considerations trumped declared principles and institutional fidelity. Indeed, Gwyneth would test his principles again when their social circumstances paradoxically reversed themselves. Hardly had Wendell arrived at Indiana's flagship Bloomington campus in January 1910, when an imperious Gwyneth, tapped by a sorority her first year at Butler University in Indianapolis, decided that fraternity membership ought be an important part of their relationship.[48]

The demands from the person at Butler University made for anxiety, even as IU's *Daily Student* portentously headlined "ANOTHER WILKIE [sic] ARRIVES," the significance of which Wendell would lose no time or opportunity fulfilling during his fast-paced four years.[49] Most of his Bloomington contemporaries would recall an unkempt, ubiquitous extrovert who favored red shirts and whose scholarly curiosity had seemed insatiable and whose run of successful challenges to Greek letter society primacy was rewarded with well-merited service on several key student bodies. He moved in with Julia and Fred off campus, the former finishing graduate studies and teaching high school, the latter a senior-year science major. Julia's continuing mother-hen role advantaged his experience with professors known for their mentoring. To Lillian Gay Berry, Wendell said years afterward, he owed his appreciation of the classics and much of what emotional maturity he possessed.

Maturity would be a long work in progress. Ambition was manifest campus-wide from the outset. Verbal fluency earned freshman-year placement on the debating team. Behind-the-scenes politicking rallied the independents, split the Greek letter voting bloc, and gained the sophomore class presidency for Wendell's Elwood chum, Paul Harmon. Another divide-and-conquer alliance put Beta Theta Pi man and future state governor, Paul McNutt, and Willkie's independents in charge of the Indiana Union, whose control of the student center enabled it to dominate the campus's cultural life.[50] The same strategy worked for the takeover of the Jackson Club (campus Democrats) by the independents.

A one-man campaign for a radical addition to the social-science curriculum distinguished Wendell's junior year. He returned to campus that year fired up from summer readings of Herbert Spencer and more substantively of Edward Bellamy's utopian novel

Looking Backward, 2000–1887, a socialist fantasy whose sales matched Harriet Beecher Stowe's *Uncle Tom's Cabin*, and his posthumous 1898 economics text, *Equality*. First, he petitioned bemused professors for support of a course on socialism, before finally accepting the challenge of the economics department's chairman: "Drum up ten [interested] students." Wendell buttonholed "almost everyone in the university" to find the critical ten, he would say of his notable coup bringing *Das Kapital* and socialist party founder John Spargo's *History of Socialism* to Bloomington. "No wonder they thought of me as a socialist." Much later, as a wiser and wilier public figure, he philosophized that "a man who is not something of a socialist before he is forty has no heart," adding exculpatorily, "any man who still is a socialist after forty has no head."[51]

The university librarian rendered a wide-eyed verdict on this Class of 1913 scholar-politician. Dr. Jenkins couldn't see "how Wendell does it. He leads his classes, is in the midst of every campus activity, and causes the faculty endless trouble; yet he is more widely read than any other boy" Jenkins said he'd ever known.[52] For all the deserved encomia of professors and peers, Wendell's final year at Indiana was personally stressful. Although success had mostly followed success, notwithstanding a miscalculation costing his otherwise carefully orchestrated attempt to capture the undergraduate yearbook editorship, Wendell found himself consistently wrong-footed at Butler University. Literally. Gwyneth's patience with his inability to dance had finally worn thin. Rather than take lessons or at least improvise a serviceable two-step, Wendell insisted on substituting interesting conversation while the music played on. She certainly appreciated his devotion, the letters he walked miles to mail her during summer jobs in Texas or the Dakotas. Older brother Robert mentions roses and chocolates sent from IU to Butler, depleting his brother's savings. Still, his well-known Greek letter opposition, compounded by dance-floor allergy and sartorial indifference, detracted from Gwyneth's sense of status whenever he visited.

She conspired with his wealthy Elwood classmate George DeHority to persuade Wendell to join a proper fraternity, admiration for Woodrow Wilson notwithstanding. His agony was existential. He was a "unorganized man," Wendell confessed to a mate, and he was "proud of it." But if he didn't join, he'd lose "my girl." Gwyneth proved well worth a fraternity—prestigious Beta Theta Pi—but Wendell held out until the last semester at Indiana, then sent her his fraternity pin along with an exalted declaration that sounds more like a plea. His life was "dedicated" to Gwyneth. "In thee I have put my trust. Let me never be confounded."[53] Prospects for their relationship were much better when the newly minted frat man departed IU's then compact campus of handsome limestone buildings in June 1913. Even so, at least temporarily, theirs would have to be a long-distance relationship.

With a B-plus cumulative average distributed across history, law, and an impressive range of other courses, Wendell headed for Coffeyville, Kansas, on the Oklahoma border. Law school would wait until there was money enough from teaching history and coaching debating and basketball teams for Coffeyville High School.[54] James A. Woodburn, chair of the department and future historian of Indiana University, thought Wendell had just the right qualities for the profession. A strong reference letter to an acquaintance on the Coffeyville Board of Education sufficed. The town had advanced some distance from its rough, dusty frontier days on the edge of Oklahoma Indian Territory. It guarded annually the proud memory of the October day in 1892 when the outlaw Dalton Gang raided the town's bank and died in a blaze of gunfire, killing them, the U.S. Marshal, and three citizens. The Coffeyville awaiting Wendell Willkie was now a major center for the manufacture of glass and bricks and the owner of a brand-new high school.

CHAPTER 3

PUERTO RICO TO
COMMONWEALTH & SOUTHERN

Lieutenant Willkie, USA, 1918. *Courtesy the Lilly Library, Indiana University, Bloomington, Indiana.*

When the time came for good-byes, Coffeyville High School's entire student body went to the train station to wish their popular teacher good luck. Wendell had been an instant favorite from the day Principal P. Y. Kennedy introduced their new history teacher before the full assembly. The lanky Hoosier with the rebellious mop of hair and barely enough years for a convincing show of authority projected a devilish energy and infectious love of learning that captivated almost instantly. His first year, then, had been quite a success story. Wendell had organized a high school branch of the YMCA and reshaped the debating team into a statewide contender. Coffeyville High won the 1914 state basketball championship, an achievement all the more remarkable because few Elwoodians recalled Coach Willkie ever participating in organized sports.

A game Coffeyville High didn't win may still be famous in the town's lore. An eleventh-hour challenge from Oklahoma's Bartlesville High to substitute for another team (lodging and travel covered) sent Coach Willkie and five players in a rented van hurtling over dirt roads one night, only to meet a proud Bartlesville football team! Prospective attorney Willkie's forceful advocacy recovered the cost of the van. Twenty-five years later, Professor Willkie's animated history lectures were still fresh in the minds of some former students who wrote admiringly to the GOP presidential candidate. Never to be forgotten after all those years, wrote one of them, "your description of England's defeat of the Spanish Armada." Wendell read that another believed he was the best teacher she ever had. He lifted "the whole school more than [he] realized. . . . So all these years [she] wondered what became of you. We all thought you were going to the top."[1]

Another year in Kansas was supposed to earn Wendell just enough scrimped and saved money for a terminal year of law school at Bloomington. Then came brother Fred's news at the beginning of the fall term of a position in Puerto Rico at three times the high school salary. Wendell's Coffeyville leave-taking followed soon thereafter on that bittersweet day in early November 1914. Fred Willkie was a chemist with Fajardo, one of the American sugar trusts dominating the economic life of the Spanish Caribbean. The job requirements weren't onerous, a quick chemistry refresher course was sufficient, said Fred, and the Puerto Rico archipelago offered some of the most beautiful scenery under the Stars and Stripes. If any memories of those family dinner-table deprecations of imperialism troubled Wendell—Herman's impatience with Bryan's waffling over the Spanish-American War, say—his father's apparent acquiescence in Fred's position with Fajardo may have eased Wendell's concerns.

In any case, with more than enough money for law school tuition in play and hasty preparations underway for a special six-week chemistry infusion at Oberlin College, there was neither temporal or intellectual space for Wendell to assess the submerged reality of Puerto Rico's de jure appropriation by the United States. For all intents and purposes the former Spanish colony was now a dependency of the US Navy, its all-too-brief experiment in self-governance arbitrarily terminated after the 1898 Treaty of Paris. Wendell arrived at Oberlin for the chemistry upgrade only a few weeks before academically challenged little brother Ed was expelled on an administratively wrong-headed smoking charge, a family embarrassment shortly mitigated by Ed's admission to Annapolis Naval Academy, thanks to Herman's Indianapolis political contacts.[2]

Wendell sailed through organic chemistry and sailed for San Juan just after the New Year, 1915. The experience would mark him for life. Puerto Rico was an exposure in technicolor quite unlike life in white in Elwood, Bloomington, and Indianapolis. He would live in a sea of mostly brown-skinned people. The Fajardo Sugar Refinery and its twenty-six thousand acres lay across the eastern end of the archipelago, about ten miles from Laguna Grande, the magnificent inlet whose rare bioluminosity had petrified its seventeenth-century Spanish discoverers. Scenic, salubrious Fajardo *municipio* at the foot of Cap San Juan—with its iridescent white buildings and imposing old rust-colored church—seemed an exceedingly fortunate place to pass six slow-paced, profitable months until Wendell enrolled in law school and resolved the long-distance relationship with the demanding Gwyneth. He found his Oberlin chemistry more than adequate to the company's requirements.

After the first month, the laboratory routine and the long hours bored him, as did, predictably, the round of staid Fajardo staff dinners and formal occasions when the new American overlords mixed with the island's old Hispanic aristocracy. And absent from all these talkative, usually rum-lubricated gatherings, Wendell soon realized, was any talk of local politics, of the conditions of ordinary people, or of the evolving American stewardship of Puerto Rico. A quarter-century ahead, while on a remarkable global observation mission, it would come to him that he began learning on that beautiful Caribbean island how to see and hear the obscured, un-interrogated conditions of those who survived beneath the surfaces on which powerful, prosperous, cultured people glided as by right. "One subject the Puerto Ricans never would discuss," he would tell a future biographer, was the state of the "submerged nine-tenths of the population." Fred said it was a mystery how hundreds of thousands of field workers subsisted on thirty cents a day for six months during the growing season, and nothing afterward. Wendell heard it said that Puerto Rico under the Stars and Stripes was like "old wine in new casks"—paternalism in a democratic container. He began riding about much of the island on horseback to see conditions for himself.[3]

The American imperial project had shattered the Puerto Rican dream of national liberation, alienated the educated elites, and smothered the island's fledgling institutions under a simulacrum of self-governance. "Puerto Rico is not forgotten, and we mean to have it," Senator Henry Cabot Lodge had reassured Vice President and fellow imperialist Theodore Roosevelt as the "splendid little war" with Spain concluded. Puerto Rico made a convenient stepping-stone to a Panama Canal likely acquired someday soon from France. Idealistic William Jennings Bryan's benign imperialism destined to uplift and democratize its wards now had no place in Admiral Alfred Thayer Mahan's grandiose US naval geopolitics and Henry Havemeyer and John Searles's leviathan sugar trust exploitations.[4]

The year before the fortunate assistant chemist's arrival, Puerto Rico's popularly elected House of Delegates had voted unanimously for independence, only to be told that their decision was "unconstitutional" under the 1900 Foraker Act passed by the US Congress. "A new form of underdevelopment took hold," Cesar Ayala, the indispensable student of the period, declares. "Gigantic US-owned sugar mills invaded all the islands, transforming the scale and organization of cane agriculture and sugar production everywhere," essentially, corporate servitude replaced plantation slavery.[5] Five years after Wendell's return to the mainland, flush with expense money, Fajardo would achieve such economic leverage, together with a hand full of American-financed Caribbean trusts, that it controlled a third of the global sugar market. A pittance of the profits made from Puerto Rico's sugar cane by Fajardo, Aguirre, South Porto Rico, and United Porto Rico stayed on the drained archipelago, the bulk absconded to North America.[6]

Straying from his Fajardo bubble to places unfamiliar or even unwelcoming to *Yanquis*, Wendell began to see the outlines of Puerto Rico's future as an informal colony of the North American behemoth. His frequent equestrian companion was an atypical local, Raffael Vevy, well-connected and subversively talkative, who stripped away the cant of Spanish paternalism and hypocrisy of American uplift.[7] The old colonial road was a slave labor feat carved from mountain rock and hacked through dense forest up the spine of the archipelago. Spectacular views and abundant flora and fauna notwithstanding, it occurred to Wendell as he rode with Vevy that they were trotting over the bones of the slaves. Even though slavery had officially ended on the island thirty-odd years before, as far as Wendell could tell, the descendants were not much better off than their slave ancestors. Malaria wracked the quinine-deprived poor with such intensity that a veteran of the cane workers' struggles, speaking of conditions rife during Wendell's brief stay, recalled that you could walk into any house "and always find someone shivering and fevered and vomiting, especially among the children," he added.[8] This man, one Don Taso, hailed from barrio Santa Isabel in the south where some of the harshest aspects of the North American occupation existed. Its *jibaros* (mixed Taino, Negro, and Spanish rural people) supplied recruits for the smoldering resistance to the tightening sugar regime imposed by Wendell's compatriots.

Suddenly, one day, as Wendell and a plantation manager rode and chatted, a fugitive *jibaro* scampered from the cane break across their path. Without slowing his horse or stopping the conversation, the manager missed the man's neck but severed the shoulder with his machete. The casual violence of the atrocity stunned Wendell Willkie to such an emotional depth that he often spoke years later of how it expanded his values. This Puerto Rican experience kept him from "thinking like a typical millionaire," even after becoming one himself, as he told Gardner Cowles, a millionaire friend and backer of his presidential candidacy.[9] The IU undergraduate who recruited enough students for a class on socialism empathized with the *jibaros*. He even derived a certain schadenfreude from the malaise they caused among the island's Hispanic grandees and North American overlords, but he also took away from the experience a redoubled appreciation about the limits of popular protest and the counterproductive consequences of rapacious capitalism when he left for home and law school at Indiana University in July 1915. Puerto Rico was Wendell's valuable introduction to brown people in the white empyrean.

Gwyneth had lived happily married in California twenty-five years when the annoying national press came calling after Wendell captured the 1940 GOP presidential nomination. Finally, a tad exasperated, she told them, "We both felt that it had gone on too long." By the time Wendell enrolled in law school that fall, he must have shared her feelings, although he might have appreciated the irony of being able to live cheaply in the Beta Theta Pi fraternity house thanks to Gwyneth's Greek-Letter imperative.[10] He began classes that September as a senior with enough pre-law credits to be reasonably assured of earning his diploma in a single, disciplined year. He and three fraternity brothers adopted a study plan of reading one book a night.[11] Outwardly easygoing self-assurance and a proclivity for organizing made for peer popularity. Wendell's classmates elected him Class Day speaker after less than two months on campus. The school publication, *Student*, noted his required Moot Court presentation and participation in one or more of the year's sixteen debates. Academic earnestness coupled with ebullient intellectual curiosity impressed the professors. All of this made for the accolade of "best all round student" and Indiana Law School's 1916 graduation gift of a 42-volume legal encyclopedia.

And Wendell almost ruined it all with a sensational Class Day oration that shocked faculty, university officials, distinguished legislators, and even members of the Indiana Supreme Court, several of whom arrived unexpectedly to hear his presentation.[12] The "best all round student" Class Day speaker seems to have expected a chorus of cheers from colluding classmates. Instead, their silence and expressions of feigned surprise left him deflated, alarmed. He had only himself and President Woodrow Wilson to blame for his predicament. Wendell's Greek Letter animus in high school and college owed more to Wilson's dogged efforts as Princeton's president to demote the importance of the college's exclusive eating clubs than Gwyneth Harry had been able to abide. The charismatic statesman-politician Wendell now admired more than William Jennings Bryan was in a furious run for reelection to a second term just as IU's "best all round student" completed his final law requirements. No text of the speaker's exact words survived the indignant irruptions of that day, but IU President William Lowe Bryan said years afterward that he would never forget Wendell Willkie's Class Day address on the eve of his law class commencement. "He made the most radical speech you ever heard."[13]

Very possibly, Wendell's controversial speech may have been called "The New Freedom," but, whether it was or not, its tone and content were almost certainly inspired by the twenty-eighth president's 1912 "New Freedom" campaign platform and *New Freedom* book the following year. On that voracious diet of a book a night, not only would Wendell have immersed himself in the literature of Wilsonian reform, avidly digesting the president's *New Freedom* with its eloquent summons to sweeping reform, top to bottom, but, given Herman's crusading bent, his son was bound to have been caught up in the high stakes of the 1916 election. Sadly, absent that enthusiasm was any recorded awareness of Wilson's bone-deep negrophobia. Four more years of Wilson would consolidate the legislative building blocks that all but set up the modern governance of the United States. It is also conjecturally relevant to note the rough coincidence of Wendell's graduation address with the controversial Supreme Court confirmation of Louis Brandeis, Wilson's ideological muse and the first Jewish justice. Brandeis's *Other People's Money, and How the Bankers Use It* hardly escaped Wendell's list of nightly readings. That book's progressive pragmatism was a major factor in the New Freedom's Clayton Anti-Trust Act, Federal Trade Commission,

Underwood Tariff Reduction, Federal Reserve Act, and the new federal income tax.[14]

In a spirit of similar progressive beneficence, Wendell Willkie's "New Freedom" speech prescribed a new state constitution, a reformed supreme court, creation of state agencies to ensure fair banking and business practices, and not a few administrative improvements for the university. In the ensuing uproar resulting in Wendell's being passed over at commencement, various trustees, the president, and the law dean debated the "best all round student's" suitability to represent Indiana University. After several days of agonizing uncertainty, a chastened Wendell presented himself, apology in hand, to learn if his diploma was rescinded. It was not. "Of course they wouldn't do that," President Bryan insisted when interviewed a quarter century later.[15] Willkie's 1916 law school graduation controversy augured a lifelong susceptibility to principled pugnacity.

That summer and fall, 1916, the firm of Willkie and Willkie's new associate was a busy civic and social presence about town. It may not have been the first courtroom case he ever argued, but Elwood locals recalled that when Wendell replaced brother Robert, the county's deputy prosecutor, in the trial of an alleged arsonist, he delivered a long, impassioned argument based on the thinnest of circumstantial evidence. After three hours of acting prosecutor Wendell's lively elocution, the lawyer for the accused summed up the defense in a few minutes and in a devastating peroration: "I believe my son will be a great lawyer," opined Herman Willkie. "He can make so much out of so little."[16] Maybe so, but some of Elwood's leading citizens were impressed enough to elect Wendell president of the Young Democratic Club. In an almost forgotten chapter of Hoosier politics, Elwoodians elected a Debsian socialist as mayor in the November election. Eugene Debs himself was running again for public office, this time for the House of Representatives from Terre Haute. Herman, a Debsian, stumped for Mayor John Lewis, and Wendell, although he must have voted for Wilson, found more in common with Lewis than with the local Democrats.[17] More often than not, the unconventional attracted either Wendell's curiosity or his indulgence.

Wendell had met Edith Wilk in fall of 1915 when she was maid of honor in his boyhood and university chum George DeHority's wedding to his Rushville, Indiana, fiancée. Edith introduced herself as "Billie," and the brown curls and lapis lazuli eyes of the slender Rushvillian of prosperous German ancestry summarily abbreviated whatever remained of Wendell's pledge to Gwyneth Harry.[18] Edith Wilk was a welcome match for a strikingly promising, unconventional Elwood personality. She hadn't minded a bit, unlike Gwyneth, that this large, disheveled, cerebral male couldn't dance and was clever only at talking. "Wilk and Willkie—it ought to be a good firm," Wendell had winked when introduced. Come September 1916, thanks to Herman's position on its board, Wendell engineered Edith's transfer from the Rushville Public Library to chief librarian in Elwood. The nice arrangement soon came a cropper, however, when Edith found herself in the cross fire of Wendell's full-throttle attentions and Henrietta Willkie's unmistakable coldness. After three awkward months, she fled to the familiar calm of the Rushville library and Wendell began trolley-car trips to Rushville, any pretext permitting, until Elwood and Rushville heard news of their engagement the following year.[19]

After Congress voted affirmatively on April 6, 1917, for President Wilson's declaration of war request, the Willkie family signed on with alacrity, firmly convinced that the German Empire was the incarnation of evil. Wendell and Robert were among the earliest officer candidates commissioned lieutenants that August after a month of infantry training by French officers at Harvard University.[20] At Fort Benjamin Harrison where an induction clerk mistakenly registered the new recruit as Wendell Lewis Willkie, Wendell let the error stand. He was now officially what he had been unofficially for years. "I think Edith married him for his brains," said a knowledgeable Rushville relative who may have thought Edith could have chosen a more socially accomplished husband.[21] They married in Rushville in early January 1918, two days late because First Lieutenant Willkie's train from Kentucky halted in a snowstorm at Indianapolis. He managed a frantic phone call about trains not running yet, and a nervous Edith query—"but you aren't going to change your mind, are you?" Edith followed her lieutenant to his artillery posting back in Louisville, then to Fort Sill, Oklahoma, where Wendell parachuted from a balloon on a $50 wager, an impulse that could have transformed his bride into a widow. Edith was probably too upset to tell Wendell what she thought of his adolescent explanation: "If you're going into war you can't be a coward."[22]

Few would have doubted Lieutenant Willkie's courage. His judgment, like that of millions pressed to reconcile American ideals with Old Europe's Machiavellian order, was another matter, however. He had signed on for Woodrow Wilson's war without misgivings that it would "make the world safe for democracy," or that Wilson's inspiring vision of "peace without victory," announced to a surprised Senate Chamber on January 22, 1917, heralded a new era of international understanding.[23] Yet not three months earlier, Wendell's Woodrow Wilson had won a second presidential term with a razor-thin California majority and the winning slogan, "He Kept Us Out of War." Pacifists of the Jane Addams and Eugene Debs stripe, neutralists such as Andrew Carnegie and Henry Ford, and radical agrarian politicians such as Wisconsin Progressive Robert La Follette already believed their fears confirmed by the Willkie family's old crusader William Jennings Bryan, who, Cassandra-like, had warned that Wilson's neutrality professions were inauthentic.

When a German U-boat sank the *Lusitania* on May 7, 1915, with 128 US citizens aboard, Bryan correctly suspected that munitions were in the British passenger liner's hold, and he strongly dissented from Wilson's decision to deplore Germany's right to defend its vital interests. Wilson righteously insisted that any restrictions on American citizens' travel undermined "the whole fine fabric of international law."[24] He left unstated the primacy of the fabric of international trade—more than $3 billion worth of goods sold to the British and French. The Nebraska idealist resigned as secretary of state a month later. The US entry into the war, then, could only be a matter of another sunken ship or two with Americans on board—or, finally, German Foreign Minister Arthur Zimmermann's fateful February 1917 telegram to the

Mexican government promising German support for reclamation of territory lost to the United States.[25]

Looked at objectively and remembering George Washington's parting warning against "permanent alliances," what was there for most Americans to gain by taking sides in the Great War? One historian summed up their feelings accurately as wanting to be "sympathetic yet completely neutral."[26] Arguably, neutrality was a logical policy for a nation of immigrants whose ethnic roots traced to the belligerents and victims in the Great War that had raged nigh four years before the Willkie brothers sailed away singing, "Lafayette We Are Here."[27] Old Americans of the Eastern seaboard and South—Anglophone and Protestant—sympathized with the British Empire and French Republic as embodiments of individual liberties and parliamentary democracy, but their biases were not shared by all Americans nor even acceptable to some. The Irish of the large Eastern cities had come to the United States because of historic conditions largely due to Great Britain's long occupation of their homeland. The insurrection mounted by the Irish Republican Brotherhood on Easter Monday 1916 in Dublin spoke the sentiments of most Irish Americans.

Italians, Slavs, and Jews from the urban Northeast to the industrial Midwest had warily watched in growing unease the militarily indecisive and even politically ambiguous performances of their respective Italian, Hungarian, and Russian homelands. Black people of the Deep South, with the notable exception of their most distinguished public intellectual W. E. B. Du Bois, mostly looked askance at what seemed to them a bloody and clannish brawl among foreign whites that had nothing to do with them. More to the point, on July 28, 1917, ten thousand of them marched in silent protest down New York's Fifth Avenue beneath large banners demanding, "MR. WILSON WHY NOT MAKE AMERICA SAFE FOR DEMOCRACY!"[28] That the southern-born president had remained silent in the face of lynch law and the recent, bloody East St. Louis, Illinois, race riot seemed to make a mockery of his high-minded professions of international justice.

Many of the Willkies' fellow German Americans remained

deeply conflicted about their country's renunciation of neutrality, particularly those of Roman Catholic, Mennonite, and Amish faiths. Second among the immigrant groups in numbers and spread across the twelve states of the nation's heartland, the Germans cherished their rich religious, cultural, and institutional traditions while simultaneously affirming their genuine patriotism in a climate of rising xenophobia that soon drove pretzels from saloons, proscribed German language newspapers, renamed sauerkraut "liberty cabbage," and would lynch a hapless Illinois coal miner, Robert Prager, on grounds of suspiciousness. *Burning Beethoven* was the apt title of a study of the anti-German hysteria encouraged by the Wilson administration's 1917 and 1918 espionage and sedition acts.[29] German Americans would emerge from World War I as a still large, prosperous, vital ethnic group, but with their erstwhile cultural distinctiveness greatly diminished by a self-imposed display of homogenized loyalty.

Herman Willkie should have been troubled, but, like the sons who admired him, he was even more anxious that the Hohenzollern world threat be seen for what he believed it to be. He felt called on to speak for the Forty-Eighters, ancestral people he characterized as uniquely endowed by history to judge imperial Germany. "I know Germany. I was born there," Herman declared before a packed meeting of the local County Council of Defense at about the same time Wendell's artillery unit disembarked on French soil at Le Havre in 1918. Although peace loving by nature, Herman explained that the German people had lived so long under the power of "Prussianism" that their children were taught that "Germans must lead the world." Unlike the German soldiers who had violated neutral Belgium and destroyed Louvain—"the Belgian Oxford"—Herman full-throatedly extolled the Forty-Eighters' grandsons marching under the Stars and Stripes to bring the "fruits of a world democracy that knows no divine right of kings and that shall mean for all peace and happiness."[30]

The written record offers scant encouragement to suppose that, when the guns fell silent on the western front, Captain Wendell Willkie had been much troubled by the Wilson administration's national security excesses—not even when it indicted, convicted, and sentenced to ten years and a lifetime disfranchisement Eugene Debs, national labor leader, twice socialist candidate for the presidency, and pacifist. Twenty-three years later, with Americans even more determined to remain neutral in another war among Europeans, presidential aspirant Willkie would step into Herman's shoes to warn his countrymen and -women of Germany's historic militarism from the second biggest platform available. Yet, when he did so in 1940, it would be distinguished by an exceptional civil liberties maturity yet to be learned in 1919. He came home an even more confirmed Wilsonian, inspired by the righteousness of the Presbyterian president's Fourteen Points (four more than recommended by God, sneered France's Clemenceau), exhilarated by his visionary League of Nations, hopeful that his country's leaders would embrace the challenge of what promised to be a peace to end all wars.

His ship docked at Newport News, Virginia, at the end of February 1919. Edith—"Billie"—surprised him there and went with him to Camp Chillicothe, Ohio, for his speedy demobilization and return to civilian life. The added weight suited Wendell. He looked a good deal bigger than her lanky law school graduate of some twenty months earlier. They were already settled in Elwood and professionally preoccupied when the "Red Scare" of anarchist violence and industrial strikes engulfed the country beginning that May, followed by the coterminous "Red Summer" of rolling urban race riots south, north, and west. What concerns were aroused by news of the Red Scare were likely subordinated by domestic matters and readjustment to civilian routines. It's likely that if Wendell read of the Red Summer, he passed it off as a sad and disgraceful anomaly. There were no black people in Elwood. Indiana was home to the country's largest branch of the recently reconstituted Ku Klux Klan, a good number of whose hooded minions resided in Elwood where they learned to be wary of Herman Willkie's wrath. This new Klan focused its venom on Catholics and Jews, of which Elwood possessed a large number of the former if only several of the latter.[31]

Captain Willkie had fully expected to resume his place in Willkie and Willkie on Anderson Street as the family firm's third member. Herman took the partnership arrangement for granted, an assumption that would have greatly reduced biographical interest in a successful Elwood lawyer. Instead, Henrietta vetoed the trio plan as a recipe for mediocrity. Her advice was to seek a wider, more challenging forum where Wendell might grow intellectually and professionally. She went further, scotching an unrealistic scheme hatched by Anderson County's Democratic boss for Wendell to run for the seat of an unpopular Republican incumbent. Anderson County voters were congenital Republicans. Some who believed they knew of a more personal motive for Henrietta's stubborness claimed she generally disliked her sons' wives.[32] Although surprised and hurt by Henrietta's partnership embargo, Herman compromised the family standoff with the craftiness of the veteran courthouse lawyer he was. Word came by way of a well-connected Indianapolis political contact of a position in the legal department of Firestone Tire and Rubber Company in Akron, Ohio.

Akron, thriving among the cornfields and family farms of northeast Ohio, was one of the fastest growing cities in the Midwest, the population leaping in ten years from 67,000 to 208,000 in 1920, an appropriate place for Henrietta's ambitious son to start his career with Edith and their five-month-old son, Philip. Wendell's introductory letter to Harvey Firestone giving the reason for wanting to leave Elwood was vintage Henrietta: it said, "the future of a lawyer in a town of 10,000 is very much limited."[33] Wendell reported for duty at the Firestone company headquarters as head of the employee legal department on the first day of April 1920. Akron was to be home for him, Edith, and Philip during the next nine years. Those years were both formative and transformative for Wendell in ways that justified Henrietta Willkie's tough-minded mothering. Equally determinative, however, were Herman Willkie's progressive values at the core of his son's professional and political growth during those years. Akron challenged Wendell's principles from day one.

Observing the fights his employee picked his first year, Harvey Firestone would predict that Wendell would "never amount to much" because he was a Democrat, and told him so.[34] Wendell was not only a Democrat, he was a Woodrow Wilson League of Nations Democrat in a city in the heart of the isolationist belt two weeks after the US Senate's final, definitive rejection of the Treaty of Versailles ending World War I and the League of Nations designed to end international aggression. By then, Wendell's hero had lain some six months semiparalyzed and all but secluded in the White House from the furious exertions of his public-speaking tour across the country to save his vision. That July, James M. Cox, Ohio's able reform governor, and his dashing running mate with the "first-class temperament," young navy undersecretary Franklin Roosevelt, had emerged after 44 ballots in San Francisco as the last best hope of a Democratic Party at once compromised by Woodrow Wilson's spoiled legacy and handicapped by the sick man's refusal to declare himself out of the running.[35]

Wendell took heart as Cox and Roosevelt paid a votive call on the invalid in the White House, reaffirmed their party's commitment to the League of Nations, extolled the positive role for government in righting society's ills, and campaigned vigorously across the country. Cox's Republican opponent and fellow Buckeye, the outstandingly inconsequential Warren G. Harding, campaigned from his front porch in Marion, Ohio, unflustered by rumors of "Negro blood." For the first time women voted in a newly Dry America, and the electorate voted overwhelmingly for the winner's winning neologism, "normalcy." "Harding," editorialized the progressive *New Republic*, "stands for a kind of candid unpretentious reaction . . . that a great many people momentarily desire."[36] American expatriate poet T. S. Eliot memorably summed up his country's fateful recusal from international engagement as "This is the way the world ends/ Not with a bang but a whimper" in the fateful lines from "The Hollow Men."[37]

To Harvey Firestone's new lawyer, his country's permanent rejection of the League of Nations was a disgrace that he and likeminded men of promise must pledge themselves to reverse. Meantime, his record of smart professional efficiency made such an impression by the end of the year that a partnership offer came from Mather and Nesbitt, a coming city law firm, and a $5,000 counter from Harvey Firestone. Edith told Wendell the choice between his name added to Mather and Nesbitt or the money at Firestone was an easy decision. Mather, Nesbitt, and Willkie's junior partner emerged as a force in the Akron Democratic Club in no time, a key member along with Joseph Thomas, Cletus Roetzel, Aldrich Underwood, and several other activist lawyers committed to New Freedom politics and the League of Nations ideal. The Summit County American Legion elected Captain Willkie post commander, a fortuitous decision because Wendell smartly turned the post headquarters into an unemployment center after a nationwide recession striking the country later in the year. He was visible and voluble in the 1922 reelection campaign of the local Democratic representative.[38]

As Akron's Democrats geared up for the 1924 presidential election, Wendell was to be seen speaking from trucks, street corners, meeting halls, schoolhouses, indeed, anywhere he espied a half dozen citizens willing to hear his argument on behalf of the League.[39] His speaking style was athletic, arms akimbo, the voice a mix of the revivalist and defense attorney, the large, well-proportioned body looming over audiences, the blue eyes twinkling with perhaps a hint of Clarence Darrow. The revivalist and defense attorney composed a remarkable letter in April 1924 to Newton Baker, Wilson's former secretary of war and Cleveland's erstwhile reform mayor. The great Presbyterian crusader had been interred in Washington's National Cathedral the previous month, leaving the diminutive Baker presumptive heir to the Wilsonian legacy. Like Wilson, the prim, pince-nez-adorned Baker projected a Waspy Johns Hopkins intellectual superiority. Appointed war secretary in the administration's second term, Baker, a pacifist, confessed to the press of not knowing "anything about this job" as the United States edged into the Great War. Yet, he had proved politically astute enough to hire an astute man of color, Emmett Scott (confidant of the deceased Booker T. Washington), special assistant for Negro affairs when one of America's largest hyphenated groups protested the rank injustice of fighting to save democracy abroad in the absence of racial democracy at home.[40]

The task Baker now faced equaled the challenge of winning the war against the Central Powers. It was the war to win victory for a noble ideal at the Democratic National Convention in New York City that June. Wendell's letter volunteered his services to Baker to help reinvigorate Wilson's grand scheme of a binding contract among the nations in which American might and morality served as guarantor. Aside from his loyalty to favorite son James Cox, no cause moved him more than fighting for the League at the convention. His feeling about the United States' entrance into the League "almost reaches the point of religious conviction," Wendell proclaimed. Could Baker suggest "anything" he might do to help "toward getting the convention to adopt such a plank in its platform?" Impressed by Wendell's ardor, Newton Baker and James Cox arranged his appointment as delegate and floor lieutenant to the 1924 Convention, until the party chaos at Chicago forty-four years later the most fractious Democratic convention of record.[41]

A Tammany wag is supposed to have said that the Democratic convention, which lasted fourteen days and ran 103 roll calls from June 24 to July 9, and was the longest national political convention in American history, ran so long in order to force Governor Alfred E. Smith's opponents to leave town because they could no longer afford their hotel bills.[42] Then there was the grid-locking two-thirds majority the winner needed for a successful nomination. Some, it was true, must have feared that if geography truly foretold destiny, then the dissonant regional origins of the delegates guaranteed fireworks of an ethnopolitical intensity unexcelled among Americans, that those from the South, the Border States, and the West—Protestant, agrarian radical, antiurban, dry, and racist—would come as crusaders sworn to repel the new immigrants of the machine-ruled cities of the East and of the industrial forges of the Midwest, people the former stigmatized as religiously suspect, quasi-assimilated, unopposed to Negroes voting, and, even worse, opposed to Prohibition.[43] Surely, Democrats might hope, the rumors surrounding President Harding's sudden death in August of the previous year and the underhanded sale of the US Navy's fuel reserves at Teapot Dome would cost Harding's silent successor, Calvin Coolidge, the White House.

But the final, depressing outcome of those many sweltering days spent in Manhattan's old Madison Square Garden was to be worse than foreseen even by the most apprehensive delegates. Moreover, much of the proceedings were radio broadcast for the first time in national convention history. When a child asked one of those delegates afterward if he had fought in World War I, he was said to reply, "No, son, but I went through the New York convention."[44] Captain Willkie had been spared action under fire, but Willkie the Ohio delegate who positioned himself as far front and center as possible was to see combat on the convention floor that mimicked a battlefield. The action inside Stanford White's ornate Madison Square Garden was a distillation of the national immigration crisis outside. The land of proud immigrants was experiencing its greatest identity crisis since the Know-Nothing Party nativism of the 1850s. Then, the menace had been the hoards of Irish in thrall to the Roman pope. Now, postwar predictions that multiple millions of so-called unassimilables from the Russian Pale and southern Europe were poised to sail steerage for the land of opportunity sent hoards of earlier arrivals into klaverns of the Secret Empire and voting booths demanding major restrictions on immigration. As Wendell and twenty thousand delegates of all descriptions except a single person of color poured into the specially enlarged Manhattan meeting hall, old-stock Americans, cultured or unsophisticated, crossed their fingers that the new Johnson-Reed immigration restriction act, signed by President Coolidge but a month earlier, could safeguard the country's English-speaking, white, and Protestant majority.[45]

William Gibbs McAdoo, Woodrow Wilson's son-in-law and treasury secretary, and Alfred E. Smith, Tammany Hall's progressive governor, were the generals commanding the Democratic Party's two antipathetical factions. Catholic, rough-edged, rising above Tammany origins, "Al" Smith personified the multicultural, "wet," working-class, big-city America. Paladin of Henry Grady's New South and chief engineer of the Wilson administration's racial segregation policy, McAdoo led the alarmed hosts of nativism, of which the Ku Klux Klan comprised the hard core. When McAdoo's name came before the delegates, ethnic America hollered foul-mouthed disdain for a deafening ten minutes from the Tammany-packed galleries.[46] If memory is history cherry-picked, Wendell Willkie's experience of a notable historical moment on June 26 is a curious example of it. The nomination speech on behalf of New York's governor by the delegate from Dutchess County, New York, appears to have made no impression. Ramrod erect, shriveled legs locked in steel braces, Franklin Delano Roosevelt, felled three years earlier by polio, conjured a near miracle before the surprised, suddenly hushed convention as he "walked" six paces to the podium to endorse Al Smith in one of political oratory's memorable phrases as "the 'Happy warrior' of the political battlefield"—"the most perfect nominating speech . . . ever listened to," limned one veteran news reporter.[47]

Wendell appears not to have listened to Roosevelt or even to have commented later about the speech that jolted the convention. Possibly because he would leave New York convinced—erroneously as it happens—that Roosevelt betrayed those "religious convictions" that brought Wendell and Newton Baker to Manhattan to uphold.[48] For Wendell, the 1924 convention was memorable primarily for two reasons: the Hail Mary pass to embed the League of Nations as a political reality in the Democratic party platform and the defining fight against the Ku Klux Klan for the soul of the party. After a dogged clause-by-clause effort failed to modify the Committee on Resolutions' anodyne League statement, Baker, as Wendell recalled afterward to the Akron Kiwanis, caucused with his Wilsonian faithful to find strength for a final effort. Never would he forget those early-morning hours when this "slight man" derived "fresh stimulation from our naïve and infectious belief," Wendell still recalled in a Birmingham *Age-Herald* interview long years after. Baker's defense of the League ended with a bang that T. S. Eliot never heard, but that Wendell heard as a speech for the ages when the former war secretary regained the podium as the organist played "Onward Christian Soldier."

Sitting with the resolutions committee "for five days and nights," he had heard nothing, said Baker solemnly, but "talks about 'expediency' and votes" until he became sick. But he proposed now to talk about "life and death and love and duty," because there was "no logic for luck. There is no calculus for expediency. But we do know how to do that which is right, and that is the only rule we need to follow if we want to win and deserve to win in politics." The only rule of right was endorsement of the League of

Nations "without qualification or referendum." So much treasure expended, so many lives sacrificed, so reasonable a prescription for peace and justice, Baker reiterated with quiet forcefulness. Moved to his core, Wendell watched "hard, stern men, men of the Western plains, cry during the plea for the issue." The delegates paid their respects to Newton Baker with sustained applause, but they still voted the majority report of the Committee on Resolutions. Baker's plea against war—"a plea for thousands of mothers and fathers in the country"—would stay with Wendell Willkie the rest of his life. It was the twentieth century's unfinished business that drove much of the purpose of his last years. How many times after entering politics would he turn to Edith to insist, "Billie, at least I didn't compromise"?[49]

The all-white convention finally voted on the resolutions condemning the Ku Klux Klan the night of June 28. Reborn in the wake of D. W. Griffith's 1915 film *The Birth of a Nation*, the "invisible empire" was six million strong by then and claimed some 400,000 followers in Ohio. The twentieth-century reincarnation—fastidiously observant of middle-class proprieties and only somewhat less discriminating in recruitment than the Masons—shifted primary focus from African Americans to Catholics, Jews, the new immigrants from southern and eastern Europe—Italians, Slavs, more Jews—and all the "Wets" (consumers of alcohol).[50] Fiercely motivated, advancing north and west, the Klan was that familiar political phenomenon of a minority intimidating a majority. So it was that the opportunistic McAdoo, supported by the Willkies' old agrarian populist idol William Jennings Bryan, equivocated when the convention turned to debate the majority recommendation of the Committee on Resolutions.

Having finessed the League plank, the resolutions committee presented its majority text that denounced efforts "to arouse religious or racial dissension," which left the relevance of the unnamed Klan to be inferred by all who wished to do so. A moment of surpassing irony came when a Georgia Confederate officer's descendant dismayed McAdoo's legions with an eloquent appeal that the convention speak for the nation since the South had failed to take the lead in condemning the Klan. Chairman Thomas Walsh gaveled for order a futile fifteen minutes. When the Great Commoner Bryan rose to blame disunity on the minority advocates and cried out for the majority resolution, feelings in the hall were greatly exacerbated by his longwinded invocation of scriptural justification. The old man, a venerable relic from a fast-fading time, would die five days after his winning argument against Clarence Darrow in the Scopes monkey trial the next year.[51]

A single vote defeated the minority plank. Wendell's active part on the floor in support of the anti-Klan resolution even earned him a warning telegram from the Akron Klan. It asked when he'd sold himself to the pope, to which he preferred to be remembered retorting, fully in character, "When I ran out of money." For Wendell, the disgraceful irony in the situation was that Al Smith's relative newcomers were upholding American ideals of tolerance, inclusion, and opportunity while Woodrow Wilson's accomplished son-in-law and his settler legions clamored for restrictions based on religion, race, and origin. He would shortly give the *Beacon-Journal* a jaunty summing up, telling the interviewer that the defeat of the resolution "by only one vote means that the Klan was absolutely exposed." They didn't win anything just by keeping the "name of the Klan out of the plank," he insisted.[52]

But Wendell's was an upbeat version of reality belied by the Klan's outrageous demonstration in New Jersey five days before a dogged Thomas Walsh had gaveled the convention to its unhappy close. On July 4 the Invisible Empire materialized in force on a field in Long Branch, visible across the Hudson from Manhattan. Twenty thousand hooded Klansmen, joined by hundreds of convention delegates, held a picnic in the seedy old beach resort where they exulted raucously in their success at quashing the enemy plank. Baseballs were thrown at effigies of Smith while a speaker lampooned the "clownvention in Jew York" in the glow of a huge burning cross.[53] McAdoo peaked on that day at 550 votes, far short of the two-thirds needed to win, but Smith's delegates, promising to keep the convention going indefinitely, held fast to the governor whose three-hundred-plus votes guaranteed deadlock. During the previous day, Wendell and his Ohio delegation had held solidly for favorite son Cox through sixty-one ballots, then for Newton

Baker until the seventy-fourth ballot on July 4, when Wendell and twenty-seven others of the forty-eight-member Buckeye delegation declared for Smith. Back in Akron, the story of Wendell's pivotal role in the numbers game played by the Buckeye delegation was front-page news. The stalemate finally concluded on July 9 when all sides yielded to the sanity of a dark horse compromise on the 103rd ballot.[54]

The 1924 Democratic Convention, to be known in history as the "Klanbake," chose quiet, able West Virginian John W. Davis, Wall Street lawyer and Woodrow Wilson's ambassador to the Court of St. James's, as its standard bearer. Still, with Davis or even Coolidge as president, the election, Wendell believed, would turn on "able and dignified presentation" of truly important issues like tax reduction, the League of Nations, and corruption in office.[55] Presidential candidate John W. Davis disappeared from national public notice after his defeat by Calvin Coolidge until thirty years later when, as counsel for the state of South Carolina, he reappeared to face the NAACP's Thurgood Marshall before the US Supreme Court in the "separate but equal" *Briggs v. Elliott,* companion case to *Brown v. Board of Education,* another, and this time final, defeat for Davis.[56]

As Wendell must have seen it, the Akron KKK virtually dared him to keep out of the city's affairs after the local newspaper accounts of his somewhat inflated role in supporting the convention's minority plank. His friends mostly advised against any further public display of animus. This is not the advice Wendell would have heard from Herman, who was spending most of his time those days speaking out against what he called an intolerable Indiana infestation.[57] The power of the Akron Klan—some fifty thousand strong—was such that by summer 1925 three members of the public school board resigned to protest the biases of the four remaining members. It was all but certain that the election in November would deliver the school board and its young people into the hands of the not-so-secret society.

In retrospect, the situation was made for Wendell Willkie's intervention—inescapably, after news that the Klan Kleagle had thrown down the gauntlet to any and all opponents. "Let me take it up and fight it out," Wendell challenged in a tense public meeting that June, promising Akron's wary citizens that if they "organize and fight that the people who believe in the American form of government are in sufficient number" to recapture the school board. Which, under his leadership, they did in numbers and resources enough to elect three of the four anti-Klan candidates after the votes were counted in November.[58] The school board battle marked the beginning of the steep decline of KKK influence in Akron but also of the continually remarkable rise of Wendell's professional fortunes in the city. The political dividend of his Ku Klux Klan chapter would surprise him a decade later.

Harvey Firestone soon learned how wrong his prediction was when Mather, Nesbitt and Willkie's junior partner, ran rings around the tire mogul's legal team in a 1925 property rights case. It was probably in connection with his defense of the Akron businessman William Kroeger that Wendell boasted that "all a man needed to get up in the world was a powerful adversary."[59] Firestone sued to have Kroeger enjoined from selling fifty-seven shares of stock in the Akron *Times* after the city's major newspaper was sold to the Scripps-Howard newspaper chain. Plaintiff's attorneys claimed that Kroeger merely held the greatly appreciated shares in trust for Firestone. At the trial's highly publicized opening, it might have seemed that Harvey Firestone's distinguished, big-city Chicago attorney Amos G. Miller and his large retinue of nattily suited assistants would prevail by intimidating professional comportment alone, especially in a courtroom in a city riding on Firestone tires.

Wendell showed up alone, slightly unpressed, his client missing, a writ-quashing objection to be announced straightaway in open court. Kroeger, Wendell drawled, couldn't be cited for contempt and enjoined from selling stock given him in lieu of salary because the defendant had never been legally served by the plaintiff's attorneys. Wendell won the first round, followed by depositions, demurrals, and a plethora of motions until the Kroeger case was eventually favorably settled out of court and to the rising esteem of Mather, Nesbitt and Willkie. Out-lawyering one of the richest men in America was a superlative way for a man to "get up in the world." They elected him, age thirty-three, unanimously the youngest president in the history of the Akron Bar Association. A friend said he was "the hardest working, fastest thinking lawyer" of the bar. A juror who served in a potentially costly accident compensation case that Wendell won, despite the testimony of a dozen witnesses, explained, you "never saw a lawyer who could make a jury swallow so often." The Akron *Beacon Journal* carried his take-charge image front-page among a dozen "Citizens Prominent in Development of Akron" for July 21, 1925.

For an ambitious professional, however, Wendell showed only occasional if any interest in clubhouse bridge or the links. He preferred occasional gin rummy, solitaire, and fishing. He was much more likely to sit out a game of golf chain-smoking and keeping another player fastened on a particular concern of his. He was also just as prone to decline a clubhouse panjandrum's invitation to his socially exclusive soiree with a brusque egalitarian put-down that he'd come to the fellow's house anytime, "but I don't want to meet your rich friends." Nor, in a city whose principal manufacture was indispensable to Detroit's, did he ever find the convenience of an automobile necessary. Memory of a 1911 experience in younger brother Ed's Willis Overland almost certainly explained Wendell's aversion—the afternoon when Wendell had frantically scraped dirt and pebbles from Ed's mouth and nostrils after both landed under the upturned car. Wendell, talking nonstop, hands gesturing emphatically, had left the wheel to steer itself.[60]

Wendell was seldom home and passed off Edith's frequent suggestion that he moderate his fierce work tempo, like most of his peers, so they and their son might spend more time together. She began to feel that he was finding her less interesting. He told her rather impatiently, "I won't be a clock watcher." He was "going to make a place for [him]self." Had her health been better during the early Akron years, Wendell might have been more companionable. His obsession with work did compensate for the meager social life imposed by Edith's frailty. Philip's birth had been a trial from which 120-pound Edith recovered very slowly. She was unwell much of the early Akron years. Another pregnancy seems to have been deemed medically unwise, and although the record is silent on the matter, it may have especially disappointed some-one nurtured in a tribe. A doting mother, a prepossessing spouse who admired her large-dimension mate but had little craving for the limelight, Edith may have remembered Wendell's first words when they met—"Wilk and Willkie—it ought to be a good firm." Instead of a firm, Edith had wanted a nice home. By the time they left Akron, she may have begun to fear that their lives were on a course leading to a quietly endured alienation. The sad truth, she would confess years later, was that she never felt "as if Wendell and I had ever had time to play in our lives."[61]

For Wendell, recreation was directorships and multiple board memberships. He was president and director of the Acme Mort-gage Company, director, at age thirty-five, of Ohio State Bank and Trust, as well as the South Akron Savings & Loan Association (of which William Kroeger was president). The accumulated distinc-tions were propelling him to the pinnacle of prominence in Akron as a large fish in a moderate-sized pond when an appointment as the youngest board member of the powerful Northern Ohio Power and Light Company attracted the attention of utilities impresario Bernard Capen Cobb. Life for Edith and Wendell then took a sud-den, unanticipated turn. Wendell's first biographer, advantaged by a personal interview, described Bernard Capen Cobb as a "genius of finance," an encomium that may seem exaggerated today for an ectomorph businessman with a somewhat hangdog expression whose only extant monument was a recently decommissioned 500-megawatt coal-fired power plant in Muskegon, Michigan.[62]

Bernard Capen Cobb's Dorchester, Massachusetts, beginnings were propitious enough: Mayflower ancestry; Boston Public Latin School; Phillips Andover Academy. He bypassed Harvard Col-lege and headed west at eighteen for a job with the Pennsylvania Railroad in Grand Rapids, Michigan. A born technocrat, he rose quickly in the railroad's hierarchy, then hired on with the construc-tion department of Grand Rapids Gas Light Company in 1895 just as Thomas Edison's incandescent lightbulb had made candles, coal, kerosene, and coal gas all but obsolete. Three years earlier, Americans had been bedazzled by the greatest electric light show in history powered by the Edison Company and George Westinghouse's mammoth power plant at Chicago's Columbian Exposition of 1892. As city streets lit up from New York's Broadway to Wabash's Main Street, Cobb surveyed the unregulated landscape of electric power with a Yankee perspicacity that espied a commercial way out of the technical confusion and commercial profligacy of the "war of the currents"—the clash between Edison's Direct Current (DC) system and Westingthouse's Alternating Current (AC).[63] When the pragmatic Cobb arrived in New York City at the turn of the last century, his reputation as an astute entrepreneur was noted in some of the city's powerful financial circles.

Fifteen years later, after a phenomenal run of building, acquiring, financing, and consolidating some 165 businesses into eleven operating units covering much of the Deep South and parts of the Northeast, the "genius of finance" assembled one of the nation's mightiest utilities holding companies, Commonwealth & Southern. Cobb's financial genius was genuine, but its potential owed much to the seed millions from the powerful House of Morgan and the securities underwriting services of Landon Thorne's omni-competent Bonbright & Company. He possessed, too, an eye for the talent needed to help run Commonwealth & Southern soon after Delaware chartered his billion-dollar entity in May 1929.[64] Cobb heard that a new board member at Commonwealth & Southern's Northern Power and Light might fit the bill. Quickly informing himself about the Akron lawyer with the boundless work capacity and lawyering kudos, Cobb decided to reel him into New York City as a partner in Judge John Weadcock's white-shoe law firm with a threefold salary increase as counsel to Commonwealth & Southern Corporation.

Cobb's thunderbolt disoriented the Willkies. Life in Akron had worked well for them until now. They had become esteemed fixtures in the city's social and civic life. They would have preferred to take more time deciding. Later, Wendell revealed that he had wanted "to stay right there" in Akron.[65] "Billie, what do you want me to do?" she recalls his almost plaintive worry about the New York prospect. She told him the decisions was his, but secretly Billie liked the idea of New York City. Cobb's message to relevant Akron movers and shakers carried the force of a veiled *diktat*:

"Don't let that young man get away from us." His offer virtually prescribed acceptance—the prestigious New York partnership, the $36,000 salary, the prospect of exceptional influence in one of the nation's pivotal industries. To Henrietta, the call to New York must have been but one more validation of her refusal to let her son become the star of the Elwood family law firm. There were the obligatory tributes, fine and heartfelt farewells.

On the first day in October, Wendell, Edith, and young Philip moved into their seven-room apartment overlooking Fifth Avenue at number 1010. The new setting overlooking the Metropolitan Museum of Art would take some getting used to: leaving for the office without locking the door; shedding the habit of greeting people on the macadam streets. It struck him as odd that he recognized not a single face. Suddenly, on October 29, there was Herman, delivered at 1010 by ambulance from Lenox Hill Hospital terminally ill with cancer. "Quite insistent he was feeling well and wanted to go home, which is impossible," Wendell telegraphed Julia. She must come to New York and take their father home, he pleaded.[66] She would do so, and three years later the redoubtable Herman Willkie would die in Elwood. The day that followed Herman's upsetting appearance was Black Tuesday, October 30, the beginning of the Great Depression.[67] The Willkies' Akron portfolio nest egg mostly disappeared.

CHAPTER 4

WILLKIE v. FDR:
THE POLITICS OF BUSINESS,
THE BUSINESS OF POLITICS

Left: FDR, Eleanor Roosevelt, et al., Tupelo, Mississippi, first TVA electric power hookup, 1934. *AP Photo.* **Right:** Willkie leaves White House after tense conference with FDR on utilities, 1937. *AP Photo.*

Samuel Insull was a London-born autodidact whose organizational gifts as Thomas Edison's twenty-one-year-old bookkeeper carried him to a founding partnership in Edison General Electric and runner-up at thirty-three for the presidency of the new General Electric Company. He did not cause the Great Depression by himself, as Franklin Roosevelt found it convenient to claim, but Insull was, nevertheless, the ideal stand-in for the role of principal perpetrator. He could have been called the Midas of electricity, such was the power of Commonwealth Edison of Chicago, his holding company that sat atop four great utility systems with combined assets of approximately $2.5 billion. In 1930, these companies or their subsidiaries were reported to serve more customers electricity and gas in thirty-two states "than was consumed in any other country in the world"—"nearly one-eighth of the electric power produced in the whole country."[1]

When Commonwealth Edison imploded, the catastrophe was of epic proportions, a crash more scandalous than its Enron Corporation imitation seventy years later. Chicago shareholders discovered that $88 million worth of their special Commonwealth Edison gold debentures were backed by only $460,000 in cash remaining. The savings of 600,000 investors were wiped out. The city's public school teachers went without pay for months as a result. Meanwhile, the electric car or traction mogul's monumental Civic Opera House gift opened to a gala performance of *Aida* less than a week after Black Tuesday. Three local progressives whose People's Traction League had warned Chicagoans against Insull's matchless ingenuity of stock pyramiding and reckless system of interlocking holding companies needed only say, as economist Paul Douglas, and attorneys Donald Richberg and Harold Ickes forcefully and factually did, that Sam Insull bore full blame for destroying their world. Public fury directed at men like the Chicago utilities kingpin and the now forgotten Howard C. Hopson, a gas magnate whose rapacity stretched to the Canadian Maritimes and the Philippines, raised the alarming prospect of an entire industry being punished with federal sanctions.

Holding companies—a peculiarly American business invention originating in 1888 in New Jersey—were notorious for their control of multiple properties through dummy entities behind which capital investment was sometimes pitiful and profits of the controlled companies milked through inflated service charges. Will Rogers's memorable holding company description was "a thing where you hand an accomplice the goods while the policeman searches you." Usually, what the policeman found, said another observer, were "miracles of confusion in accountancy."[2] Not all utilities holding companies were precariously stacked pyramids, their capitalization un-auditable, their regional services unregulated and overpriced—as with Insull's Commonwealth Edison—but a notable number of them indeed deserved their castigation as the "spider-web of Wall Street." When the utilities barons met in New York City in the first winter of the great crash, a pall of unwonted unease and strategic hesitancy enveloped them—all except Insull, who called on his fellow clubmen to choose offense as the best defense against the tide of accusations and revelations from journalists, elected officials, and citizens' groups. But for the unexpected temerity of the newest member of their club, Insull's large, commanding presence might have gone unchallenged.

The young lawyer from Akron who left his Fifth Avenue apartment door unlocked as folks in Indiana did and was still warming his chair at Weadcock and Weadcock ventured a contrary opinion. Commonwealth & Southern's chief legal officer presumed to counsel the utilities barons against vindictive tactics to intimidate industry critics, and he wondered why the industry should fear scrutiny or opposition so long as its reasons were sound and its practices were proper. Wendell never forgot Insull's reaction. "Mr. Willkie," Insull growled, "when you are older, you will know more."[3] Still, Wendell believed he knew enough to be concerned about punitive regulatory policies the winner of the impending presidential election might be provoked into adopting. One contender in particular for the Democratic nomination was expected to dedicate significant campaign rhetoric to the cupidity of the captains of the utilities industry.

Of the leading candidates—Roosevelt, Al Smith, and John Nance Garner—at the 1932 Democratic National Convention in Chicago that June, Wendell knew that utilities interests were safest with Texas's "Cactus Jack" Garner, the affable, undistinguished speaker of the House of Representatives who, in reality, served at the bidding of publisher William Randolph Hearst. But Wendell was still tethered to the old favorite of the Wilsonians, Newton Baker, current member of the Permanent Court of Arbitration at the Hague, an undeclared but still quietly determined presidential candidate. The New York governor reconfirmed Wendell's mistrust by placating party isolationists with a public disavowal of the importance of League of Nations membership. In a replay of 1924, Wendell worked as one of Baker's assistant floor managers as three rounds of balloting left Roosevelt ahead of Smith but just short of the necessary two-thirds.

A turn to Baker as the least of evils seemed certain when Roosevelt, now at odds with "Happy Warrior" Al Smith, his former patron, momentarily offered the former secretary of war his support. The deadlock victory for Baker vanished, however, with an eleventh-hour vice presidential deal between the Roosevelt and Garner forces engineered by press mogul Hearst and Wilson's memorably sidelined son-in-law William Gibbs McAdoo. McAdoo hated Al Smith more than he did Roosevelt. Hearst's animus for Baker was greater than his aversion to Roosevelt. Commonwealth & Southern's lead attorney took a deep breath, switched to Roosevelt on the fourth ballot, and sent the party's standard-bearer a campaign contribution. Garner's opinion of his own vice presidential nomination—not "worth a bucket of warm piss"—went into the lexicon of famous quotables.[4]

What Wendell Willkie thought of Franklin Roosevelt's decision to fly to Chicago to deliver an unprecedented nomination acceptance speech before the convention is unrecorded, but the squire of Hyde Park's cathartic words promised a regenerative compact between the leader and his people that should have spoken to Herman's son's core of beliefs. "I pledge you, I pledge myself, to a new deal for the American people," intoned the voice that would spellbind most of the nation in the years ahead. "Let us all here assembled constitute ourselves prophets of a new order of competence and of courage. This is more than a political campaign. It is a call to arms."[5] Much of the business community either dismissed or, like Wendell, underestimated the policy significance of the campaign speech Roosevelt delivered in Portland, Oregon, that September. The object of government was "the welfare of the people," which meant, said he, that "when the interests of the many are concerned, the interests of the few must yield." Seven years earlier, the man in the White House had ordained that business was the "chief business of the American people." At Portland, a new message, shockingly delivered by a Brahmin but at variance with Calvin Coolidge's, privileged the business of the people at the expense of the business of business.[6]

Portland was of a piece with Roosevelt's indictment of "Ishmael or Insull whose hand is against everyman's during his West Coast campaign."[7] Although surely not forgotten by many was the New York governor's recent rebuff of General Electric, DuPont, and Alcoa's oligopolistic hydroelectric power plans for the Saint Lawrence River. He was all in favor of hydroelectric power on the river but said he wanted the public "to get the benefit of it when it is developed," and the Power Authority of the State of New York (PASNY), the country's first such authority, was a signature Roosevelt accomplishment. Cautious Democrats and nervous businessmen and -women may have asked themselves whether Franklin Roosevelt sounded more like a federalist student of the social critics Thorstein Veblen or Herbert Croly than a limited government disciple of Thomas Jefferson's. But most voters assumed that most campaign rhetoric was to be written off as rhetoric for a campaign. Assuring the American people that they had only "fear itself" to fear, Franklin Roosevelt took the oath of office on March 4, 1933, and the New Deal began in earnest.

Five months earlier, Wendell Willkie had become the youngest president of the third-largest utility corporation at a princely $75,000 salary when Bernard Cobb, seriously ill and uneasy about prospective Federal Trade Commission investigations, relinquished the position, although temporarily retaining the chairmanship of the board.[8] A Chamber of Commerce boast attributed to Wendell ran that, although he and FDR had taken office at about the same time, "my company was running at a profit while his company is running at a loss." All of which seemed true enough from appearances in his twenty-first-floor office on Pine Street. In a humming cockpit where a new ticker tape instrument clattered in the corner, where piled high ledgers buried a trio of desk telephones, and a suit jacket was invariably found slung over the back of an outsized swivel chair, the thirty-nine-year-old president managed and monitored a great national business enterprise in the heart of Wall Street.[9]

In reality, Commonwealth & Southern's common stock had fallen from 23¼ to less than two dollars a share since the 1929 Crash. From gross annual earnings of $150 million in 1929, the holding company's revenues had dropped a million dollars monthly when Wendell reported gross earnings of about $100 million to his board in late May 1933. Three months later, turning down a Coffeyville friend's appeal for a loan, Wendell wrote of being "compelled to let go close to 10,000 employees in four years"—hardly surprising with national unemployment peaking at 25 percent that summer.[10] Commonwealth & Southern's predicament would have been worse but for Cobb's prophylactic restructuring as the Great Depression took deep root.

As he edged into the shadows, Cobb handed his heir a streamlined corporate structure of unique supervisory and service design, a balance sheet relieved of more than a half billion dollars of watered stock, a directors board of industry professionals in lieu of colluding bankers, and the final consolidation of Commonwealth & Southern into six separate systems comprised of eleven operating companies almost evenly distributed into a northern and southern group stretching from Michigan to Florida. The southern power companies of Tennessee, Alabama, Georgia, Mississippi, and parts of South Carolina and Florida served the 4.9 million white and black people of the Mississippi Valley.[11] Their record of service when Franklin Roosevelt took office was uneven.

Cobb's holding company innovations might be the boast of utility reformers, but, as Wendell found when explaining them before congressional committees, they required patience because of Commonwealth & Southern's ingenious dual existence as both a Delaware chartered holding corporation and a New York chartered service and management corporation. The unique feature of this plan was that all C & S stock was owned by the operating companies. The New York service corporation rendered supervisory and management services under contract to the operating companies for less than 2 percent of gross revenues. The Delaware holding corporation collected no fees nor exercised any management or supervisory services for its eleven subsidiaries. Its income derived exclusively from interest and dividends on securities it held for the eleven power companies—an amount valued at $72 million (1.3 billion current dollars).[12]

The creation of the Tennessee Valley Authority (TVA) on May 18, 1933, was among the first executive actions of the New Deal's epic One Hundred Days. The 1916 National Defense Act had dammed a bend in the Tennessee River at Muscle Shoals, a place in Alabama either thought to resemble a flexed muscle or named after freshwater bivalves, where nitrates were produced for munitions. By 1924—its military raison d'être expired—Muscle Shoals and its finally completed Woodrow Wilson Dam were government surplus whose proper disposal bitterly divided Republicans and Democrats. Henry Ford had offered to buy Muscle Shoals cheap while several powerful western senators fought to convert it into a public corporation. The back-and-forth contest between business interests and government advocates stalemated final determination of the great facility throughout the Coolidge/Hoover decade. Essentially, by Roosevelt's signature on May 18, Muscle Shoals became the Tennessee Valley Authority.[13]

What this vast public works project portended in all its multiple constitutional, hydroelectric, flood control, navigation, phosphate production, soil reclamation, reforestation, social engineering iterations was not yet even fully defined by Roosevelt himself, as he airily confided to Nebraska's Senator George Norris shortly before signing the enabling legislation. Norris, a species of progressive, independent, pro-labor, isolationist Republican inconceivable today, having worked up the legislative nuts and bolts of TVA, asked how the president would explain it to the people. "I'll tell them it's neither fish nor fowl," FDR joshed, "but whatever it is, it will taste awfully good to the people of the Tennessee Valley."[14] The first of several such behemoth energy projects planned under the New Deal, its huge George W. Norris Dam immediately underway in October, TVA raised the specter of gradual death of Wendell's Commonwealth & Southern Tennessee, Mississippi, and Alabama operations from federally subsidized electricity rates.

Constructed on an Ozymandian scale, the authority's dams and hydroelectric power stations would irrigate and literally light up the impoverished, soil-eroded, monocrop southern United States, lifting the region from sharecropping, preindustrial socioeconomic stasis into rough parity with the rest of the nation. It was an economic, technological, and social experiment whose achievements at the price of an extraordinary intervention by government into the private utilities market of the nation would be largely judged as justified by their stupendous beneficence. TVA subordinated private ownership to public benefit. Between 1933 and 1959 when federal legislation made TVA self-financing, twenty billion tax dollars would have been expended on the people of the Tennessee Valley by a public entity supplying cheap electricity throughout seven southern states drained by the Tennessee River. By then, Wendell's sardonic verdict that the Tennessee River "waters five states and drains the nation" was a long-forgotten reproach unappreciated by the vast majority of voters.[15]

In another of history's major examples where the dominant narrative was written by those who prevailed, to question the cost-benefits of TVA more than a decade after it became fully operational invited academic censure and political disrepute. Historians, notes one acknowledged authority, have called TVA "probably the greatest peacetime achievement of twentieth-century America," a judgment enshrined in David E. Lilienthal's TVA: Democracy on the March, the title of a New Deal classic written by one of its proconsuls.[16] "And, even if TVA failed to create a new way of life in the Valley," wrote the New Deal's preeminent historian, "no one could deny how magnificent it had improved the old." In soaring prose, continued New Deal champion Arthur Schlesinger Jr.:

TVA built twenty-one dams; their combined mass was more than a dozen times that of the great pyramids of Egypt. Copper and aluminum wires, glistening from lofty steel transmission towers, carried new life from the foaming waters of the river to the farthest corners of the Valley. In December 1932 there had been in all the rural homes served by the Alabama Power Company a total of 85 electric sewing machines, 185 vacuum cleaners, 645 refrigerators, 700 radios. One out of every 100 farms in Mississippi had electricity, 1 out of 36 in Georgia, 1 out of 25 in Tennessee and Alabama. TVA introduced a new age. Where people for decades labored by hand and lived by kerosene lamp, there was now the magic of electricity.[17]

The orthodox verdict, thus, of history.

Yet Wendell Willkie argued with what seemed quixotic obduracy for nearly a decade that TVA's success should have been accomplished far more economically in partnership with private enterprise. He insisted that only Roosevelt's eventual surrender to his party's western progressive ideologues and the federal bureaucracy's junta of yesteryear's best and brightest finally nullified the practical government-business alternative advocated by experienced professionals, academic experts, reasonable politicians, and, above all, by the country's leading drainage engineer and founding TVA chairman, Arthur E. Morgan. When Morgan, Roosevelt's anointed master builder, met Wendell for dinner at the august University Club on New York's Fifth Avenue at the end of June 1933, neither man yet foresaw fully the Authority's ideological dimensions, to say nothing of its constitutional ramifications. The president's May 18 signature on the legislation was barely dry.

Two months before meeting Morgan, Wendell had appeared before the House Military Affairs Committee as it prepared to vote TVA Bill H.R.5081 into existence on April 14. He did his best to expose the catch-22 of the so-called TVA yardstick to the committee's unreceptive members.[18] How, he demanded to know, could C & S be expected to compete with a federal entity whose product was underwritten by the public treasury and whose unit price "yardstick" could be set by policy considerations instead of market forces? With a quarter of the national workforce unemployed, banks shuttered, and teeming Hoovervilles ubiquitous, Wendell must have realized that the vote of the Military Affairs Committee's bill, 306 to 92, was foreordained, and equally so in the Senate—easily 20,000 prospective construction jobs were involved. The forfeiture of C & S's $600 million capital investment in the Tennessee watershed where its six companies supplied 65 percent of the electrical power may have seemed only justice to millions of Wendell's fellow citizens. "The public had not been greatly stirred by the debate," noted his first biographer.[19]

Morgan, not quite three months on the job and still bedazzled, had abandoned professional wariness about the TVA only after a hypnotic ninety-minute Oval Office monologue, wherein, Morgan still recalled after forty years, "[the president] spent most of our time together talking not about dams or electric power or fertilizer but about the quality of life of the people in the Tennessee Valley." Pounding the table, Roosevelt startled the noted engineer with the forceful declamation, "There is to be no politics in this!" Arthur Ernest Morgan had set the standards of his profession for twenty of his fifty-five years, drafted drainage codes for state legislatures from Arkansas to Minnesota, completed scores of national water control projects through Morgan Engineering Company of Tennessee. His middle name befit a man remembered for saying, "Lack of something to feel important about is almost the greatest tragedy a man may have." Elected president in 1921 of Antioch, the Ohio college founded by the legendary educator Horace Mann, Morgan greatly enhanced the institution and his own renown by publishing the *Antioch Review*, to which the squire of Hyde Park made known he was an avid subscriber.[20] "Haven't I been reading *Antioch* all these years?" Roosevelt virtually back-slapped Morgan. "I like your vision."

The TVA legislation created a three-person directorate appointed to nine-year terms each, but with two original directors limited to terms of six and three years, thereby limiting the Authority's vacancies to one at a time. Morgan had quickly assembled a candidates' wish list exclusively based on professional criteria and the president's nonpolitical assurance. When bemused Postmaster General James Farley, the administration's formidable gatekeeper and campaign manager of Roosevelt's two gubernatorial wins and Oval Office occupancy, objected to Morgan's "unusual way of doing business," Morgan rebuked the astonished Irish kingmaker, then took his principles to the Oval Office for reaffirmation. Morgan had gotten "quite 'wrathy,'" Farley said.

The president found several of his own recommendations declined due to Morgan's perception of their antibusiness bias.[21]

The good fit of Harcourt A. Morgan as the first associate director must have impressed Arthur Morgan as self-evident. Mid-sixtyish John Harcourt Alexander Morgan was the Canadian-born and educated president of the University of Tennessee as well as of the all-white Association of Land Grant Colleges and Universities. He brought a wealth of entomological and agronomic expertise combined with regional celebrity for his concept of the "common mooring," a somewhat vaparous theory of the essential unity of organic life. Harcourt Morgan decided to switch from nitrate fertilizer to phosphates almost immediately at considerable cost to the small farmer. Only the big farmers could make the shift right away. Even so—and despite minimal regard for black farmers and his promotion of the interests of large agricultural establishments in the Tennessee Valley—Harcourt Morgan's TVA tenure would be praised as having promoted "grass roots democracy."[22]

Tall, good looking, thirty-four-year-old David Eli Lilienthal possessed a surplus of impressive attributes and accomplishments evidenced early on by a precocity twinned with pugnacity. At De Pauw University, he played football, boxed light heavyweight, won election as president of the student body, and graduated at twenty-one not only Phi Beta Kappa but regionally noticed as a pathbreaker. "The Mission of the Jew," a self-assured essay composed as a sophomore and orally delivered at the Western Interstate Competition, won second place just as the reborn Ku Klux Klan marched into Indiana.[23] Seven years his junior, David Lilienthal's Hoosier formation bore a passing resemblance to another precocious, pugnacious comer, Wendell Willkie. He finished Harvard Law an acolyte of progressive professor Felix Frankfurter and of Frankfurter's own intellectual mentor, Supreme Court Justice Brandeis.

The timing of a Lilienthal article, "The Regulation of Public Utility Holding Companies"—published just as Wall Street decomposed and authoritatively recognized as the "first piece of legal scholarship to address the issue"—positioned its author near the front rank of progressives populating Roosevelt's New Deal.[24]

It seems highly unlikely that Wendell would have missed reading Lilienthal's influential article. It confirmed the rightness of his criticism of Sam Insull's bluster. For crusty Harold Ickes, Roosevelt's interior secretary, and the administration's young Brains Trusters—Columbia University professors Adolph Berle, Raymond Moley, Rexford Tugwell, and Harvard law professor Felix Frankfurter's acolytes Thomas Corcoran and Benjamin Cohen— the call to arms was a summons to put Wendell Willkie and his fellow utilities chiefs at the top of the list of malefactors to be called to account.

When Arthur Morgan set about recruiting the best candidates for TVA leadership, then, it was almost a given that he found enthusiasm for Lilienthal to be almost unanimous. Justice Brandeis had recommended Lilienthal for his outstanding service on the Wisconsin Railroad Commission. Felix Frankfurter pressed his appointment as one of his sharpest former Harvard law students. George Norris's endorsement was seconded by his fellow senatorial progressive, Wisconsin's Robert La Follette Jr. Norris even boasted that it would be impossible "for any scheme, however well disguised, to be put over" on Lilienthal. Nevertheless, a dissenting minority warned Morgan of what it decried as Lilienthal's brash brilliance and experienced opportunism. As Morgan would have good reason to remember in his memoirs— years after David Lilienthal's renown as "Mr. TVA"—the particular warning of a Chicago University senior TVA staffer proved almost true. "He will steal the show![25] The shape of discords to come emerged during the grueling eight-hour inaugural meeting of Morgan, Harcourt Morgan, and Lilienthal in Washington's old Willard Hotel on June 16.

Chairman Morgan unsettled his colleagues from the start by disclosing a grand conception inflected by Edward Bellamy's utopianism of the Tennessee Valley as a "laboratory" for social, environmental, economic, and even race relations transformations. Aspiring to mitigate the iron rule of separate but equal, he enforced equal wages for blacks and whites and brought on board black Charles S. Johnson and white Will Alexander, two of the country's most known and respected race relations authorities, as senior advisors to the Authority.[26] Morgan imagined the inhabitants' lives transformed in small settlements supplied with abundant electricity where crafts abounded, irrigated crops flourished, land and water usage supported new occupations, and industry served people, not the other way. All this, Morgan not only proposed in a great hurry, but with a professorial authority that caused Harcourt Morgan to bridle. Both directors were disturbed when the chairman proposed to explore the feasibility of a working arrangement between the Authority and Wendell Willkie's Commonwealth & Southern interests.[27] Morgan expected to have preliminary results of his discussion in Manhattan with Wendell Willkie in time for the next directors' meeting.

The irony of their University Club dinner on the evening of June 28 was that when Willkie and Morgan tried to accommodate the oppositional goals of Commonwealth & Southern and the Tennessee Valley Authority, the utility president and the TVA chairman set in motion, instead, the very battle of egos, ideals, politics, and institutions that they believed avoidable and unnecessary. In the chairman of TVA, Wendell met an engineer who was a visionary, while Morgan met in the president of C & S a responsible capitalist who ran a holding company. Two major problems confronted both men: the government's vague terms for C & S's continued existence and the meaning of the TVA "yardstick." Roosevelt's vaunted "yardstick" concept was a dubious electrical power algorithm that the president and his "Brains Trusters" already seemed inclined to define more politically than metrically as (in the clearest explanation of the controversial concept found in the literature) the minimum level of rates at which any efficiently operated, privately owned, power company "could afford to sell energy at retail and still earn a fair return upon its capital investment."[28] But rates to be set by whom and calculated how?

Wendell had instantly gauged Morgan as a personality type who wanted tomorrow's objectives accomplished yesterday. Morgan faced the engineering-construction imperative of raising the new Norris Dam in short order to augment the power capacity of Wilson Dam, the wartime barrage built by the Army Corps of Engineers for nitrate and fertilizer production. Yet even optimistic projections put off the completion of Senator Norris's dam until the end of the decade—until which time, as Morgan hardly needed reminding, Wendell's Alabama Power Company at Muscle Shoals would be needed to transmit the electrical power generated by the underpowered Wilson Dam. The two men devised a working agreement, then, that essentially reflected the conditions on the ground at Muscle Shoals, Alabama, where the government's grandiose hydroelectric project confronted a Gordian knot of engineering and property rights problems. The TVA chairman and the C & S president took leave of the University Club with a satisfied handshake and an interim understanding. Morgan agreed that TVA would confine its operations temporarily to a limited area. Willkie offered to renegotiate a long-term Alabama Power Company transmission contract with TVA to handle the Wilson Dam output. The yardstick conundrum was punted to the near future.[29]

Two weeks later, at their second directors' meeting on August 12, Morgan found his associates decidedly ill disposed to his somewhat utopian vision, breakneck operational timetable, and "naivete" about Wendell Willkie's operation. Before taking up the chairman's conference with Willkie, then, the directors unanimously agreed that Harcourt Morgan would direct the agricultural program, fertilizer production, and rural life planning. Lilienthal assumed responsibility for the power program and the legal department. Chairman Morgan would preside over engineering and construction matters, direct social and economic planning, forestry, and assume responsibility for the "integration of the parts of the program into a unified whole."[30] Arthur Morgan's engineering and construction operations would consume three-fourths of the Authority's budget.

When the chairman proceeded to the business with Willkie, Harcourt Morgan was primed to support Lilienthal's forcefully expressed concerns. Arthur Morgan was certain that if the TVA area experienced a warfare of duplicated facilities with "hard feelings and bitterness and other unfavorable developments," TVA would be less effective. Lilienthal retorted that he was "most skeptical" of any hope for "genuine co-operation . . . if it involved voluntary relinquishment by [the utility companies] of part of territory they now serve exclusively."[31] The tenor of Lilienthal's criticism suggested that well-positioned allies already promised full support of his concerns. In fact, Felix Frankfurter's private communique to Lilienthal the day after Morgan and Willkie's University Club *modus vivendi* deplored such a prospect as "fraught with every kind of danger . . . and wholly unscientific in proposing commitments at this stage of development."[32] Frankfurter was free to put in writing to his former student what would have been improper of Justice Brandeis.

TVA, for Brandeisian progressives, represented an extraordinary investment in human capital, a sovereign instrument for the realization of genuine popular democracy.[33] Brandeisian progressives were shy of a majority among the New Deal's embedded progressives, but nearly all New Deal progressives had sworn a virtual oath to build the postdepression Jerusalem on the bones of Wall Street and its holding company spawn.[34] All the more disturbing to them, then, when, two days after their second directors' meeting, Arthur Morgan handed a flustered Lilienthal President Roosevelt's concurrence in the C & S working agreement. Pragmatism had prevailed, but the chasm dividing Roosevelt's and Morgan's vision predetermined a conciliation on the former's part that was only strategic and temporary. Morgan and Lilienthal were about to play a game of chess whose moves would be determined by Wendell Willkie and Franklin Roosevelt.[35]

The opening gambit took place at the Cosmos Club in Washington in late October. Lilienthal never forgot their first encounter: "Two exceedingly cagey fellows who met at lunch that noon." Wendell shambled in, persuaded that TVA was likely to prove a casualty of its own scale, its $30 million Public Works Administration (PWA) appropriation insufficient to keep it going through the midterm elections. Lilienthal found Willkie "a much better looking article" than he was before those "marks of battle" awaiting them both. Wendell claimed later that bluster suited the occasion. Commonwealth & Southern could handle TVA's rural electrification mandate for a fair price—"take all your power off your hands" for $500,000—Willkie boasted. Moreover, Morgan's construction teams had just begun the Norris Dam that October, which convinced Wendell that his Alabama Power contract at Wilson Dam would be indispensable for at least six years.

Lilienthal left the Cosmos not just "somewhat overwhelmed" by Willkie's "cocksuredness," but disappointed to find Roosevelt agreeing with Morgan that an immediate truce with C & S was imperative.[36] On January 4, 1934, then, three days beyond the expiration of the Wilson Dam contract with Alabama Power, a dutiful Lilienthal and a buoyant Willkie signed a five-year TVA– C & S truce stipulating that if the Norris Dam was completed at any time within the five-year period, the truce was to expire within 90 days. TVA had options to purchase some C & S subsidiary electric systems in northeast Mississippi, northern Alabama, and eastern Tennessee. C & S was to sell TVA a transmission line and properties near Norris Dam and renounced selling power in TVA's new distribution area. TVA agreed to forgo further incursions into the power market. TVA and C & S were to cooperate in promoting sales of electrical appliances, and one C & S company agreed to make a rate reduction totaling $415,000 annually.[37] Although he should have been as pleased as Lilienthal was not by the *New Republic*'s opinion that he had bested Lilienthal, Wendell took realistic measure of an opponent who proceeded to contest every book-value dollar of C & S subsidiaries, optioned Tupelo, Mississippi, and Knoxville, Tennessee, for demonstration of "yardstick" power service scaled 40 percent under prevailing rates, and who evangelized the gospel of the TVA across the Valley with the fervor of a Baptist divine.

Associate Director Lilienthal waved Roosevelt's yardstick as if it were a magic wand: a monthly rate of $1.50 for "small users," a scaled rate for large consumers decreasing with kilowatt-hour use to a monthly low of $4.50, both rates undercutting the C & S rates, with further TVA reduced rates a certainty.[38] He was, he proclaimed in one meeting hall, "honored to count among our leading enemies the whole Tory crowd concentrated in New York and Chicago that always fights every move toward giving the average man and women a better chance."[39] Lilienthal brought more than the gospel of concern for the "forgotten man." His

Electric Home and Farm Authority (EHFA) proffered the end of domestic drudgery—water pumps, refrigerators, electric stoves, washing machines—the beatitudes of modem living with electricity through purchase of home appliances at reduced prices and layaway.[40]

To show what efficient private enterprise could do, even faced with the infinite resources of a government Leviathan, Wendell devised his own "objective rate" for electricity consumption (lower rates tied to increased use) that reduced his corporation's rates 27 percent under the industry average. He owned boasting rights for having implemented business and sales policies at Commonwealth & Southern that anticipated Lilienthal's innovations by hiring five hundred salesmen to pitch electrical appliances—standardized with TVA's—purchasable on credit (prorated over monthly electrical bills) with a quadrupling of sales. C & S subsidiaries reeled transmission lines into remote counties and backwater locales whose surprised denizens signed up gratefully before learning of cheaper rates offered by the advancing TVA.[41] When TVA announced plans to locate Lilienthal's EHFA headquarters near Chattanooga, Tennessee, C & S withdrew advertising from the *Chattanooga News* and major businesses and boycotted local suppliers, a successful maneuver that indefinitely delayed the municipality from transferring its electrical power sources from Willkie's subsidiary to the federal power behemoth.[42]

Outwardly cordial relations between the two egos carried on well into the fall of 1934, with Wendell informing Lilienthal in early June of C & S arrangements in Georgia, Tennessee, and Alabama to accommodate EHFA "display and demonstration of electrical appliances." The truce continued. Lilienthal assured Willkie of his "very high estimate" of the utilities president's personal integrity. He was "thoroughly convinced that any contract you enter into . . . will be carried out completely and whole-heartedly."[43] Neither Wendell nor Arthur Morgan could have known that five days prior to lauding the holding company president's integrity, Lilienthal had received Roosevelt's definite assurances on July 9, 1934, that TVA would soon be able to disregard the interests of Commonwealth & Southern. FDR confided that a "national power policy committee" was to be established in yet another alphabet agency—the enormous Works Progress Administration (WPA)—to be headed by his favorite consigliere, the indefatigable but perennially ailing Harry Hopkins, an introverted, former New York child welfare executive described by his biographer as "faintly ominous" and as Franklin Roosevelt's "own creation in large measure." Because Congress, in its slapdash legislative rush, had not explicitly authorized TVA's direct transmission of its own power, nor the right to extend its power service by purchase of private utilities, Roosevelt left Lilienthal to draw the obvious inference that—until corrective legislation arrived—TVA's objectives would be carried out through the omnibus employment and construction activities of Harry Hopkins's WPA.

FDR's well-advertised inspection visit to Tupelo, Mississippi, was meant to reaffirm his Portland campaign speech that put private utility cartels on notice of a reckoning day.[44] Samuel Insull tried to evade his proper reckoning day, but FDR had ordered him fugitive-like tracked down across Europe by the full force of the US government. Extradited from Turkey, Insull stood trial for mail fraud and antitrust violations. To the consternation of the Justice Department, the accused epitome of financial chicanery was acquitted of all charges by twelve Chicago male jurors awed by the defendant's fabulous success story only two weeks prior to the president's radio broadcast from Tupelo. On a seasonably temperate November 18, the optics were classic New Deal in Tupelo, birthplace of Elvis Presley and the first community opting to buy its power from TVA. Head aloft, fedora waved, a seated Roosevelt spoke from the open Buick limousine as the smiling First Lady, and a curiously furrowed Arthur Morgan, followed by Senator Norris and David Lilienthal, acknowledged the come-from-miles-around crowd that would have been the envy of Dorothea Lange and Walker Evans. "What you are doing here is going to be copied in every state in the union before we get through," an elated president promised.[45]

The Tupelo project and the attending photo-op were tantamount to a federal declaration of war on private power. Whether or not the New Deal demanded Commonwealth & Southern's unconditional surrender was still unclear. The mood projected from the White House, however, did seem pretty menacing. Newton Baker's "old friend," hearing that Baker's law firm intended to defend the electric power interests, had suggested an Oval Office visit just ten days before the Tupelo set-piece so that Baker might use his influence, as FDR matter-of-factly warned, to "prevent bankers and businessmen from committing suicide."[46] In reality, Baker's White House mission was irreparably compromised even as it occurred. The week before Roosevelt's Tupelo visit, George Ashwander and several stockholders had sued to enjoin C & S from selling Alabama utility properties to the TVA, virtually nullifying the Willkie-Lilienthal truce and making Wendell a defendant against himself. "The mask is off," Lilienthal pounced in the *New York Times*. "We now have, in the open, the clear issue between the people who use electricity and those who have controlled it."

In a telegram verging on operatic, Wendell protested wounded innocence to Marvyn McIntyre, FDR's secretary: "I say to you that any such statement made to you by anybody is an absolute and unqualified falsehood and readily demonstrable as such." Although legally correct that he was an involuntary party to *Ashwander v. TVA*, it stretched credulity to believe that he was ignorant of the $50,000 funneled to Ashwander attorneys through the Edison Electric Institute, of which the C & S president was a director.[47] As one legal Machiavelli to another, Roosevelt affected haughty umbrage at the C & S president's legerdemain. Even so, the Oval Office meeting between FDR and Wendell Willkie twelve days before that bleakest Christmas of 1934 was marked by superficial jollity as the two outsized egos puffed up like roosters. "Mr. Willkie, I am one of your customers," the president bantered. "We give you good service, don't we?" Commonwealth & Southern's chief jousted (Georgia Power served Roosevelt's Warm Springs retreat where he would die eleven years later). After which, to Wendell's bemusement, FDR led them on a rambling discussion of "hunting and fishing" and membership in an Akron sportsmen's club.

Breezily thanked for his time by his host, Wendell departed

the White House with little more to say to the interested press corps than that "nothing" of great importance had been discussed during their pleasant meeting. Later that day, when several newsmen phoned for a reaction to the president's statement that he'd outdebated the C & S chief—"reduced him to stammered admissions"—Wendell should have been put on permanent notice of the famous guile of the occupant of the White House. A private note sent the following day urged Wendell "give as little credence to the many statements you hear about me as I do the many statements I hear about what you say and do." Wendell wrote Edith, FDR's "charm greatly exaggerated. I did not tell him what you think of him." Secretary of Labor Frances Perkins, the first woman to attain cabinet rank, always believed FDR relished this first of several such matches to come with this straightforward Hoosier. One of the few men he took a "special liking to," she insisted. "He hadn't expected to, "[but Willkie] had some of the same characteristics as himself."[48]

The Oval Office jousting occurred against an ominous backdrop for the utility industry as a whole. FDR had been annoyed by Wendell's Jesuitical disclaimer of involvement in funding *Ashwander* and understandably concerned about the federal district court's pending decision in the case. *Ashwander*, until finally decided in February 1936, "hung over the New Deal and the TVA like a sword of Damocles," opined the *Herald Tribune*'s intimately knowledgeable Joseph Barnes.[49] FDR's reaction was stark. On January 4, 1935, the president called for the "abolition of the evil of holding companies" in his second State of the Union address. Specifics of the legislation remained to be disclosed, but young policy maven Benjamin Cohen, another of Felix Frankfurter's "happy hotdogs," was busy in Harold Ickes's interior department refining legislation to housebreak the private power industry.[50] Specifics of the holding company legislation emerged after a fraught conference among the power ideologues at the Warm Springs White House in Georgia, followed by the more punitive determinations reached in the Oval Office on January 21. Announcement of the legislation hit the news almost simultaneously as a full dress debate between Wendell Willkie and David Lilienthal unfolded before a joint meeting of the New York Economic Club and the Harvard Business School Club at the Hotel Astor, James P. Warburg presiding.[51]

In light of such ominous pending regulatory legislation, few businessmen would have thrown down the gauntlet with such forcefulness, not to say bald hyperbole. Wendell declared that he had neither patience nor respect for the enemies of his industry who assumed "an attitude of superior virtue and patriotism." They sought to "paint us who represent private enterprise . . . as anti-social, unpatriotic and despoilers of men." He disliked personal references, but he wanted it understood "that no duty has ever come to me in my life, even that in service to my country, that has so appealed to my sense of social obligation, patriotism, and love of mankind . . . to say and do what I can for the preservation of public utilities privately owned." He was called by all that he knew "to stand firm and foolish against this foolish fad and fancy of the moment."[52] Faced with the rhetoric of Armageddon, Lilienthal's lucid critique of holding companies' inherent perniciousness won no acknowledged sympathizers in an audience roused to give Wendell a standing ovation. "The issue, as Willkie saw it, was simple justice," his second biographer decided. "His company had been honestly and efficiently managed; now the government was trying to destroy it."[53] But whatever practical gains Wendell may have hoped would come from his forensic victory vanished three days later when he and Lilienthal continued their dispute at the White House.

On January 24, a tight-lipped Willkie left his second Oval Office conference confronted with a virtual company death sentence rendered. Famous for making decisions on the advice of his last persuasive visitor, FDR—primed by Ickes's consolidating Brains Trusters, Norris's congressional populists, and Lilienthal—had decided to proceed with the immediate dissolution of utility holding companies as an earnest act of the administration's transformative zeal. Sensing the president's determined mood, Alabama Power & Light's suave Harvey Couch tried to lighten the mood of the meeting. Lilienthal noticed Wendell's flushed expression "getting hotter and hotter" as FDR moved circuitously through reasons for the enforced dissolution of holding companies. Finally, removing his pocketed spectacles and pointing them directly at Roosevelt, Wendell (according to Lilienthal) interrupted the president and barked, "Do I understand then that any further efforts to avoid the breakup of utility holding companies are futile?" Reiterating a reasonable solution twice proposed to congressional committees, Wendell argued for a federal incorporation bill "guaranteeing the obligations of [the C & S system]." Caught off guard, his chin "jutting out" (according to a not displeased Lilienthal), FDR reacted brusquely, but Wendell barreled on. He committed to reducing "every rate in our companies by one third" if such a bill were enacted. Couch, Federal Power Commissioner McNinch, another utility man, and Lilienthal "recoiled as if Willkie had produced a gun and started shooting." The silence in the room ended with an unambiguous declaration, "It is futile."[54] With those words, Franklin Roosevelt guaranteed four years of judicial and media combat.

On February 22, the federal district court in Alabama effectively nullified the tenuous TVA–C & S truce by enjoining the sale of Alabama power properties. By finding no statutory justification for its acquisition of private property, Federal Judge W. I. Grubb's decision questioned the constitutionality of the Authority itself. The administration pushed Congress to enact a preemptive fix to amend the TVA Act even as *Ashwander v. TVA* was on appeal to the Supreme Court. Wendell, in a replay of his solitary protest in 1933, spoke for the private power interests with sharply reasoned amendments in hand before the House Military Affairs Committee. The house committee was untroubled by FDR's blatant gambit to have federal statutes situationally parsed in order for TVA to make the very contracts challenged in the courts and to authorize the borrowing of $100 million at no more than 3½ percent interest on the credit of the United States. "The loaning of money to municipalities to build duplicated distribution systems does not distribute wealth; it destroys it," was Wendell's parting shot.[55]

Senate and House hearings on the president's holding company dissolution bill (based on Benjamin Cohen's meticulous drafts) and bearing the names of Independent Senator Burton K. Wheeler

(Montana) and anti-monopoly Representative Sam Rayburn (Texas) began in late February in a political climate soon to become toxic. Wheeler and Rayburn, who would become speaker of the House in 1940, had added FDR's draconic death sentence at the bidding of Frankfurter's precocious acolytes Cohen and Thomas "Tommy the Cork" Corcoran, the latter soon to sideline veteran Jim Farley (now ideologically more uncomfortable by the month) in New Deal insider politicking.[56] All existing public utility holding companies— except those controlling "a single integrated system" of power production and distribution—were given three years either to liquidate or restructure themselves. All were required to register with the Securities and Exchange Commission (SEC), which had the authority to decide what holding companies fell under the liquidation rule—"the death sentence" (Wendell's phrase).

Public opinion shaped by raw memories of Insull and holding company octopi with tentacles stretching beyond state lines to encircle power, gas, transportation, and 75 percent of the nation's electricity—all of it virtually unregulated—at first applauded the legislation. Public opinion and political dynamics began to change, however, when Wendell came to Washington at the head of a delegation of utility officials on the morning of February 26. "The fight was the most bitter that Washington observers had seen in years," a careful student of the period decided. It ran through the summer of 1935 on into the fall and represented the first effective challenge to the New Deal's congressional control.[57] The holding company president lived on Fifth Avenue and worked in Pine Street, a stone's throw from Wall Street, but his Hoosier ways, the flat vowels, the loping gait, the brown shock of hair over the right temple reminiscent of Will Rogers, and the self-effacing bonhomie made him studio-cast as an ingenuous opponent in an uneven combat, the David of his industry, a role none of his peers could have filled as resourcefully—and as attractively. "It was an asset to my business to look like an Indiana farmer," Wendell ribbed Big Business associates. Ickes, the Insull-slayer, claimed to see right through the pose and called Wendell "a simple, barefoot Wall Street lawyer."[58]

Wendell Willkie counted on the public being more gullible,

however, and it soon became clear that Main Street found some justice in his protest against unfair government competition and bureaucratic intransigence. Hadn't his industry made a good-faith offer of selective rural divestiture in exchange for retention of key urban markets? Hadn't it made a reasonable-sounding request for a partial moratorium on TVA development and final resolution of disputes by multiparty arbitration? Deftly upgrading the stakes, Wendell cast the dispute as more than a question of profits—as one of political philosophy. In "The New Fear," an address delivered before the US Chamber of Commerce that May and much heralded afterward, he evoked Roosevelt's famous inaugural address of 1933 that banished fear in the "darkest hour in our nation's history." Now—but two years later—the only thing to fear, said Wendell, was the justified fear inspired in American business and industry "by the hostile attitude of Government itself." He conceded that Big Business had been the problem before the New Deal. But now a new threat of domination had arisen. "Power is just as destructive on Pennsylvania Avenue as it is on Wall Street," he warned, and he carried this message in written speeches and country club talks.[59] Republican-owned newspapers and magazines spoke of executive highhandedness and carried well-crafted underdog ads from citizens groups and organizations financed by the utilities cartel. "Subsidized government competition established in one industry, threatens all industry" was a message crafted to stroke Americans' Jeffersonian heartstrings.

As Franklin Roosevelt and Wendell Willkie began a wary political dance taking full measure of each other's confidence and canniness, the New Deal's omnibus National Industrial Recovery Act of 1933 (NIRA) was summarily declared unconstitutional in a unanimous Supreme Court decision, with even Justice Brandeis participating, at the end of May. The ruling drove a stake through the heart of what Roosevelt had grandiloquently cast as "probably the most important and far-reaching legislation ever enacted by the American Congress." NIRA was, in any case, as one authoritative historian judged, "the mainspring of the early New Deal." Government codes regulating production and competition in business (the NRA "Blue Eagle") and Section 7a standardizing wages and hours and incentivizing unionism were, for the time being, abolished or imperiled by a "horse-and-buggy definition of interstate commerce," FDR snapped.[60] Donald Richberg, Ickes's former Chicago law partner and now multipurpose New Deal counselor, advised the president that the analogous 1933 Agricultural Adjustment Act (AAA) could well be next of the Court's chopping block. With *Ashwander v. TVA* undecided and Wendell's nimble bulwarking of the utility industry, the likelihood of adverse majority rulings on TVA from the nine justices now seemed alarmingly high to the administration.

Like George Norris of Nebraska, Senator Burton K. Wheeler of Montana, a colorful maverick who ran as vice president on the senior La Follette's 1924 Progressive Party ticket, consigned utility holding company officials near the bottom of Dante's Inferno. Peering down at Wendell from his perch as chair of the Interstate Commerce Committee, the labor-friendly, isolationist Wheeler reminded Wendell, "You started out that way, too, didn't you, as an idealist?" "And I hope I still am, Mr. Chairman," Herman's son insisted. "I still have my western views!"[61] In mid-June—but only after the White House called in IOUs—the Senate sounded the death sentence knell by a single vote, 45–44. Then three weeks later, the House defeated the president's entire holding company bill 216–146. Hardboiled Sam Rayburn, a few years away from his lifetime House speakership, told FDR that Willkie's was the "richest and most ruthless lobby Congress has ever known." And with good reason: Rayburn's own committee had balked, voting to remove the death sentence after 800,000 telegrams and letters called on the House of Representatives to vote down the public utilities holding bill. The parties were stalemated.

Advantage awarded FDR came with the lifting of the *Ashwander* injunction against TVA by the Fifth Circuit that July. Although Wendell's public-relations maneuvers moderated the death sentence, the finally reconciled 1935 Public Utility Holding Company Act (PUHCA) still forced holding companies to divest themselves of multiple businesses in order to operate as regionally integrated systems. "While a strait-jacket will keep a man out of trouble," Wendell wisecracked, the amended PUHCA was still tantamount to a life sentence in prison. It simply was not "a suitable garment in which to work." He declared somewhat later in words summing up bedrock belief, "The true liberal will not tolerate executive or legislative domination."[62] It followed, then—as his barrage of looping legalisms month after month to harried Ben Cohen argued—that although FDR could enact unfair laws, the PUHCA, absent Supreme Court review, was unenforceable. He simply refused in the interim to register Commonwealth & Southern with the Securities and Exchange Commission by December 31 as required under the act.[63] Moreover, Wendell had discovered two unlikely allies in Joseph Kennedy and Arthur Morgan.

Invoking his own business-friendly "conception of what is wisdom in government," Securities and Exchange Commissioner Joseph P. Kennedy, who had presided over a huge bootlegging empire, startled the White House by questioning his own authority to decide the proper operational structure of holding companies. FDR's picaresque rationale for putting the dashing, temperamental multimillionaire businessman in charge of the new SEC—"set a thief to catch a thief"—had proved to be a perversely unsatisfactory move, "a grotesque choice," as the New Republic had predicted. During Joe Kennedy's SEC tenure, although 2,300 cases of possible securities fraud were investigated during the first year, "not one major member of the New York Stock Exchange was prosecuted or the subject of a proceeding," according to the tally of a Kennedy biographer.[64] Kennedy's self-imposed abstention tested the political patience of his president and bought needed time for Commonwealth & Southern to make its case to the country. Five years later, Joe Kennedy would be in a position to render Wendell a momentous favor.

The Supreme Court decided 8–1 in Ashwander v. TVA for TVA in mid-February of 1936. But this good news for TVA had come on the heels of another major blow to New Deal regulatory authority when the high court had ruled in January that the Agricultural Adjustment Act (AAA) was unconstitutional. Moreover, Ashwander was merely a temporary reprieve from FDR's TVA troubles. In late November, Arthur Morgan had insisted on seeing the president at the Warm Springs White House where he surprised FDR by recommending that Lilienthal not be reappointed when his term expired the following year. Asked who might be a suitable replacement, Morgan urged his assistant Neil Bass, and departed Warm Springs with the treacherously expedient president's agreement.[65] What FDR actually intended to do about the dilemma of choosing between Arthur Morgan and David Lilienthal, probably even he did not yet know.

As lawyers litigated and politicians legislated, Arthur Morgan's construction teams raised the eponymous Norris Dam near completion while work on the eponymous Wheeler Dam and three others sped along. Rivers and tributaries were dredged, widened, rerouted to enhance the Delta's navigation and irrigation. The town of Norris, Morgan's Clinch River town for TVA construction workers, was nationally heralded as a new paradigm in modern habitation. To be sure, as with Eleanor Roosevelt's modem township experiment (Arthurdale) in West Virignia, local law and custom imposed a grievous racial corruption of Morgan's ideal of living space contoured to the landscape and centered on a common green perimetered by neat all-electric houses made of local materials. Blacks were summarily excluded, an egregious concession to white southern lawmakers that Morgan's Brains Truster ally Rex Tugwell famously deplored later as "an example of Democracy in Retreat."[66] Morgan grieved that such compromises were politically unavoidable, but he had come to the end of abiding further compromises that could be avoided.

His two associates still refused, Morgan believed, to comprehend the largeness of his conception of the Valley as a laboratory. They "stopped entirely all my work in land development for economic and recreational use," he would claim in a bitter memoir. He deplored the incursion of big agriculture and large industry as travesties that foreclosed the small-scale, interrelated social economy his work could have fostered. Lilienthal, on the other hand, waspishly told a local farmers cooperative that he was not only against the "second coming of Daniel Boone" but also "against 'basket weaving' and all it implies." His dynamic message, he preached and wrote, was that "we cannot return to a simpler standard of living, for that is to begin a retreat." Still, whatever the increasingly public controversies swirling about it, Morgan remained the face of TVA. "It was Arthur Morgan who built Norris Dam and the town of Norris—the two achievements which have most captured public imagination," opined the Memphis *Press Scimitar* in July 1936.[67] Five months earlier, FDR had with celebratory fanfare pushed a button releasing the first outflow from the finished fourth-largest dam in the world.

To Morgan, public versus private control of electrical power in the Valley and the noisy publicity engendered by the partisans were deplorable distractions. The righteous engineer had finally decided (deftly encouraged by Wendell) that Lilienthal's ideological animus for private power would finally destroy the obvious, ready-made convenience of collaboration with Commonwealth & Southern. That Norris and La Follette had persuaded FDR to welsh on replacing Lilienthal that May had driven Morgan to resign summarily, only to rescind his decision after placatory Oval Office pleas promising an equitable Lilienthal resolution *after* the November election. Morgan took an extended leave to ponder a careful response to what he saw as an unsustainable dilemma. Wendell was not altogether surprised to receive Morgan's two-page September memorandum secretly sharing his concerns. Although momentarily disconcerted, George Norris still saw the stern, driven TVA chairman who summoned into existence a mighty dam and a model township bearing Nebraska's senior senator's name as "perhaps as near perfect as a human being can become."[68]

That May, millions of theatergoers met a rumpled-suited, tousled-haired Wendell Willkie virtually in the flesh for the first time in a twenty-minute TVA feature: Henry Luce's new *March of Time* movie series. Simultaneously, Wendell's Alabama affiliate mounted an attack in *Alabama Power Co. v. Ickes* on the legality of Public Works Administration contracts with Alabama municipalities served by C & S. "One shot across the Administration's bow" was soon followed by another. *Tennessee Electric Power Co. et al. v. TVA* was mounted by the full force of Wendell's industry: nineteen utility companies challenging the constitutionality of the Authority's enactment. "NO QUARTER FOR TVA," blared *Business Week*. "From now on everything [TVA] does or attempts to do will be carried into court." Normally reticent Pierre du Pont acknowledged Wendell as the best hope of business. He hoped "that you and your associates will win out in this unwarranted attack . . . the great importance [of which] should be recognized and due respect paid thereto."[69] The Atlanta *Constitution* misinformed readers that TVA had abandoned further challenges to C & S territorial integrity. The *Herald Tribune*'s arbitral Walter Lippmann was inclined to accept Wendell's insistence that TVA's reduced rates and increased sales of appliances were "grossly exaggerated."[70]

Some students of the time cast Wendell as the cat's-paw of Wall Street. He sat on the board of Chase National Bank. Thomas Lamont of J. P. Morgan was, if such feelings possess intrinsic value, one of his closest business friends. But Wendell was more than the smiling face of a powerful consortium, no mere puppet ventriloquized by the utility superpower group controlled by the J.P. Morgan and Company interests that served as the financial backbone of C & S.[71] It was, after all, Wendell's deft exposure of New Deal regulatory overreach, combined with his well-funded mobilization of the press, real and bogus citizens' groups, and a Chamber of Commerce animated by his unbuttoned leadership, that emboldened the private power cartel to throw down the gauntlet. Even then, it was common knowledge among journalists that leading financiers, brokers, and corporation executives regularly "begged Willkie to 'pipe down for the sake of all of us.' " The utility president was still a Democrat, had been one all his life, as he wrote brother Robert. "All my life, as you know, I've been an ardent Democrat and here I find myself after one is elected with almost a phobia on the subject. However, if it weren't him it would be somebody just as bad or shall I say 'good'?"[72] He still saw himself as Herman's son, faithful to his Forty-Eighter family lineage of resistance to enveloping authority. He believed he was a true liberal who couldn't tolerate "executive or legislative domination."

Understandably, Harold Ickes, David Lilienthal, Thomas Corcoran, and Harry Hopkins suspected this "true liberal" of perpetrating sophisticated skullduggery with the untroubled conscience of one of Ida Tarbell's robber barons. FDR's already strained patience gave way to cold anger when a House committee investigation uncovered hard evidence that tens of thousands of the telegrams and letters sent to Congress against the holding company bill bore names copied from telephone books. No evidence directly implicated Wendell Willkie, but Norris urged the president to make Willkie and his confederates a capital 1936 reelection issue, a strategy applauded by Frankfurter and encouraged by Ickes and Lilienthal.[73] For the present, nevertheless, a reactionary high court was a complicating factor in the administration's dragging dealings with Wendell's obdurate, powerful lobby. The suit filed by the nineteen companies worried the government, and Wendell had hoped the president would welcome a friendly late May letter. The sale of all of Commonwealth & Southern to TVA was on offer for the fair market price of $90 million. He was of the opinion "that you, and you alone, are the one person who has the power to bring such a settlement about."[74]

Roosevelt and Willkie met once again in the White House in early September, one of their two or three meetings before the 1936 election. The two men agreed to a three-month extension of the Commonwealth–TVA truce—their differences to be settled after the election. FDR championed federal regulation and the benefits of TVA in the election run-up, but shied away from personalizing the utilities controversy. Then, six weeks before the November election, September 17, both were surprised by an unbeckoned possibility suggested by the National Recovery Administration's chief of the economic research division, Alexander Sachs. Another Brandeis protégé, Alexander Sachs, forty-three, Lithuanian-born, was a polymath whose long service to his adopted country as social scientist, jurist, investment banker, New Deal administrator, university professor, and bearer of the future Einstein-Szilard nuclear fission letter to FDR, was *sui generis*.[75]

Alexander Sachs's "power pool" concept—of British origin—was simplicity itself, a virtual deus ex machina: all suppliers of electricity in the Tennessee Valley would transmit their power to a neutral pool organization, which would then distribute electricity to municipal, private, and cooperative purchasers at a predetermined and uniform wholesale price set by FDR's yardstick for production and distribution. The pool organization would purchase bulk power from the least expensive source first, enabling TVA to demonstrate the superior efficiency it had been claiming all along. Direct competition between TVA and C & S would be greatly reduced.[76] Initially, FDR appeared to be captivated by Sachs's proposal. Morgan was enthusiastic. Wendell, fixated on the territorial limitations of TVA, reacted guardedly. The progressives, suspecting a C & S escape hatch, were panic-stricken.

The president's September 17 directive calling for a rudimentary "power pool" experiment immediately, to be followed at month's end by a "World Power Conference" of private sector notables (Owen Young of General Electric, Frederic Delano of National Park and Planning Commission, Russell Leffinger of J.P. Morgan) and alphabet agency directors (Federal Power Commission, Natural Resources, Rural Electrification Administration), the TVA directorate, together with Sachs and Wendell, stunned the progressives. George Fort Milton, preliminary power pool participant and *Chattanooga News* publisher, whose family newspaper had been bankrupted by C & S, reported almost hysterically to Senator Norris that Arthur Morgan's "treason . . . [was] even more ignominious" than Benedict Arnold's.[77] The appalled Milton had watched Wendell and Lilienthal come close to blows in the White House, then been shocked when Wendell and Arthur Morgan contradicted the president.

Before the World Power Conference commenced September 30, Lilienthal reassured George Norris that the utilities were unready "at this time to agree to any pooling." Counting on the power pool deliberations stringing on until the national election, Lilienthal thought chances were good that TVA would survive intact. That is, "if you and the President are reelected," he added with no great certainty. Surprisingly, on the likelihood of the administration's electoral defeat, Wendell and Lilienthal saw eye to eye. The Gallup polling organization was a year old, and much of the national press favored a Republican electoral rebound with Alf Landon as its presidential contender. The eminent *Literary Digest* confidently declared Roosevelt's defeat certain. It's doubtful that

Willkie and Lilienthal knew New York bookies and some Wall Street brokers gave FDR 9–5 odds.[78]

In the interim—high stakes awaiting the November results—Norris, his faith in Arthur Morgan destroyed ("Dr. Morgan has become sordid") and plainly exasperated by FDR's indulgence of a clever utilities legerdemain, lectured the president. "Personally, I think this conference never should have been called. I do not believe anything can be gained from conferring with men who have disregarded all professional conduct and ethics as the Commonwealth & Southern has done under the agreements you made in 1934." La Follette and Mississippi Representative John Rankin piled on, the latter a cosponsor of the TVA legislation and an insensate hater of blacks and Jews, the former a progressive icon. La Follette, dismayed that Wendell and his utilities peers seemed about to escape their legislative fetters, pleaded with FDR, "Don't let them out by making concessions at this conference." Norris followed up with an SOS: C & S "is an outfit that would destroy you in a moment if they had the power." La Follette should have felt reassured by FDR's personal note: "My policy, of course, remains exactly the same."[79]

In the fall of 1936, with the presidential race seemingly offering an attractive Republican alternative with Alf Landon, Wendell still considered himself a good Democrat. He was a member in good standing of Tammany, New York City's Democratic patronage trough, elected the previous year in the same class with Jim Farley and the ubiquitous multitmillionaire presidential advisor Bernard Baruch. New Deal policies had rescued the country from economic collapse and political crisis, but Wendell had come to the conclusion that cures could become worse than the maladies with four more years of Washington's alphabet ministrations. He kept rhetorical company with another alienated Democrat who had expressed similar fears at the beginning of the year. Al Smith skewered FDR's creeping socialism in an American Liberty League keynote in Washington. The *March of Time* appearance marked Wendell's debut as an attractive subject of the *Time, Life, Fortune* empire then in the fourteenth year of its enormous influence on shaping American popular opinion. Since then, his gravelly voice had become familiar on NBC and CBS radio networks and in country clubs and business fora as it reiterated in the months before the November election that "the abuses that corrupted the 1920's have been transferred from Wall Street to Washington."[80]

Wendell's admonitions have, by and large, a commonplace conservative reasonableness today. He was, nevertheless, one of the first attractive public figures during the troubled 1930s to assimilate traditional critiques of government power, streamline them, and package them in Hoosier homiletics that have become conservative boilerplate. Still, prescience about the dangers of big government served him poorly in the political reality of the moment. He voted as a Jeffersonian Democrat for Alf Landon, the governor of Kansas and as politically reasonable a Republican presidential candidate as imaginable. Nonetheless, Landon lost his own state and garnered the eight electoral votes of Maine and Vermont to FDR's 525 electoral votes in a debacle in which 71 percent of the black vote (despite Jesse Owens's endorsement of Landon) deserted the party of Lincoln to give the victor 60 percent of the popular total—the largest presidential win since 1820.[81] Norris saved his Senate seat. Ickes kept the Interior Department. Frankfurter, Lilienthal, and Corcoran rejoiced, and Harry Hopkins was ready to tax, spend, and plan for another election.

Faced with a virtual partisan massacre, it took Wendell an impressively brief time before he foresaw a different, paradoxical outcome from the New Deal electoral triumph. It surprisingly aligned with that of original Brains Truster Robert Moley who coined the phrase "New Deal" and whose New Deal loyalty had since frayed badly. Moley recoiled from the economic levelling influences exercised by Ickes, Hopkins, Corcoran, and others—FDR's fabrication of "economic royalists" uncloaked during the 1936 election run-up. His new magazine carried some of the most reasoned criticisms of what were seen as the administration's mistaken policies. Moley predicted that the size of the Democratic majority "in itself would produce that overweening confidence that would blind Roosevelt to the dangers of his situation."[82] How right both were was shown three months after his reelection when FDR stunned the country with a plan to enlarge the number of

Supreme Court justices to as many as fifteen. When Corcoran dropped by his office a few days after the election to gloat that TVA would take over C & S—"and all the rest of them too"— Moley believed his prediction solidly confirmed. After reading one of Moley's speeches a few months later, Wendell wrote that he agreed with him completely: "The moderate middle of the road course is what we need both on the part of government officials and business men." Moley's *After Seven Years* bemoaning the New Deal's swerve into class warfare would become a celebrated anti–New Deal classic after it was published in 1939.

Relations between the president and the C & S chieftain went from aggrieved to terminal when—in the midst of the resumed World Power Pool Conference—Federal Judge John J. Gore issued a sweeping temporary six-month injunction against all TVA operations on December 14, 1936, in unperturbed disregard of the national election results. FDR's initial umbrage over the district court's ruling—fueled by Lilienthal, Corcoran, and Hopkins— became a towering rage. Even Ickes was caught off guard by the Oval Office fiat of January 25. "President Roosevelt simply swept this whole group out of the door without so much as a 'What's your hurry?,'" an Ickes diary entry revealed. The obvious answer was that FDR decided that his historic reelection justified terminating TVA's further dalliance with Commonwealth & Southern. The Authority acquired a much-needed general manager. Lilienthal, quietly reappointed, again offered the same unacceptable $50 million C & S buyout.

Most corporation heads would hardly have hesitated after the November elections to accept David Lilienthal's settlement offer. Instead, the president of Commonwealth & Southern not only held to his $95 million counterproposal, he promised his stockholders he would fight big government until it either conceded the right of utility holding companies to compete in a fair market or it agreed to indemnify them satisfactorily.[83] C & S now operated at a profit. Net earnings rose from one cent in 1935 to 13 cents the next year, climbing to 18 cents a share in 1937. Six of Wendell's subsidiary companies were among the top ten in national sales of electrical appliances. His preferred stock sold at 30 to 40 points below par, however, and refund of bond issues and access to lower interest rates were adversely impacted because of the uncertainty caused by TVA competition.[84]

He would have to fight several years more against an encroaching TVA before he achieved an equitable settlement. Meantime, the realist in Wendell eventually prepared a memorandum for FDR's private consideration. On November 23, 1937, a year since the November election returns, the two combatants talked for almost two hours in the Oval Office. Mightn't he and "Franklin" work out a satisfactory relationship between the private utilities and the federal government? He was disposed to accept FDR's concern that their overcapitalization made the writing down of utility values hugely problematic. FDR admitted that TVA could serve at best no more than 10–20 percent of the US power needs. He implied moreover that his administration might not pursue its year-old gambit to build "Seven TVA's."[85]

Once again, though not quite a tête-à-tête, Wendell left the White House guardedly optimistic. The memorandum he left for careful consideration—a masterful four-page compression of previous proposals rejected by Lilienthal—stated that Wendell had always believed that a solution of the Tennessee Valley problems was achievable "without injury to legitimate investment and well within the broad framework of [FDR's] social objectives." In acknowledging Wendell's document, the president's secretary regretted that FDR would be too busy to study it properly for some time. When asked at a press conference soon afterward about the status of the TVA–C & S relationship, the president claimed not to know what the holding company chief had in mind to resolve the problem, a response—unsurprisingly—calculated to put Wendell on the defensive.[86]

Arthur Morgan, deeply troubled by the turn of negotiations over Lilienthal's replacement, decided no other principled course of action remained but public denunciation of sinister influences. FDR had promised, "Arthur, there is to be no politics in this!" But as Morgan told the *Birmingham News,* Lilienthal's "getting TVA involved in politics." During what turned out to be a heated Oval Office farewell, FDR pleaded with his master builder, "Arthur, you can't trust them [Willkie's crowd]," but his master builder had aired his concerns in September 1937 in a lengthy, critical *Atlantic Monthly* essay deploring men "ruled by a Napoleonic complex" and deaf to compromises. The TVA board had been presented with three alternatives, Morgan rehearsed: (1) open warfare with the utilities; (2) capitulation, by selling off TVA's power for distribution; (3) compromise with the power pool. The *New York Times* praised the essay as "a model of what a state paper should be."[87] Morgan's formal dismissal was to be delayed by a congressional hearing until late March 1938. "I think we feel equally badly about this whole thing," the White House told the press.[88]

Meanwhile, Wendell's apotheosis as the straight-shooting, cracker-barrel loner ready to face down FDR and his phalanx of Brains Trusters and technocrats truly began during the second year of the so-called second New Deal. A large, celebratory Willkie feature, replete with handsome color photos, appeared in the May 1937 issue of *Fortune* magazine. Wendell's dedication to private ownership merited praise for its uniqueness, said the magazine. "He knows all the arguments. They are persuasive . . . not because they are new, but because he frames them intelligently, and hence he makes them sound new." The June *Atlantic Monthly* carried the high-decibel "BRACE UP, AMERICA!," Willkie's evocation of the people's rugged individualist roots and a call for repeal of New Deal paternalism. In Washington, later in the week, he spoke emphatically of the "New Fear," no longer FDR's "fear itself," but the legitimate fear of government. In August, the *Atlantic Monthly* presented Willkie the self-taught political scientist and author of "Political Power: The TVA," a well-knit dissertation on the economic injustice of government ownership of electric power. The Luce empire served up Willkie again as the year ended, in the November 1937 issue of *Life*.[89]

On January 3, 1938, the guillotine descended on the legitimacy of *Alabama Power & Co. v. Ickes*, the action brought by the utility against the Department of Interior on grounds of harmful collusion with TVA. The suit was firmly rejected by the Supreme Court. A bitter though not unexpected blow to Wendell's cause, it appeared merely to stiffen his ideological disillusionment with the

Roosevelt administration. Three days later, on January 6, America's Town Meeting of the Air, the popular weekly radio-broadcast forum, hosted a debate between Wendell and one of the brightest stars of the administration, Robert H. Jackson, the new US solicitor general, whose role in prosecuting Insull, Andrew Mellon, and Alcoa as former head of the justice department's Antitrust Division was widely known. His speech vetted by Cohen and Corcoran for compelling content, Jackson matched himself against a consummate court house lawyer. Four million households heard Wendell trounce one of FDR's favorite officials in a bravura performance. Jackson's promising prospects for the New York governorship vanished. The source of their dispute was obvious, the private utility champion explained to the federal enforcer: "Government officials and business men fail to understand each other . . . because one thinks and speaks the language of politics and emotionalism, while the other thinks and speaks the language of economics and realism." One of Wendell's listeners, Frank Altschul, whose Lazard Freres's wealth quietly funded progressive Republican Party initiatives, made a note to inform himself of the thought and speech of this economic realist.[90]

Even though the Supreme Court followed its January *Alabama Power* decision with another negative utility ruling in *Electric Bond & Share Co. v. SEC* on March 28, Wendell salvaged their arguments insofar as an influential public-opinion sector was concerned.[91] The forensic drama at the Harvard Club that same month set much of the Eastern establishment buzzing. Felix Frankfurter, a formidable New Deal presence but a year away from unanimous confirmation as the second Jewish Supreme Court justice upon the retirement of Louis Brandeis, appeared as the invited speaker to address the club's influential bankers, brokers, and lawyers. A group of friends persuaded Wendell to join them, with explosive results. A rapt audience sat through three hours of freewheeling debate on business, government, and law between Wendell Willkie and Felix Frankfurter. At one point, Wendell charged that Frankfurter's students "were subverting the United States," an argumentum ad hominem that rightly induced a follow-up note to Frankfurter apologizing for his aggressiveness.[92] The president

of Commonwealth & Southern's impressive Harvard Club performance elicited fan-club admiration among bankers, brokers,
lawyers, but also, increasingly, among many middle-class citizens,
even as his industry went down in a 5–2 final defeat before FDR's
now housebroken Supreme Court.

On January 30, 1939, in a decisive ruling on federal regulatory
powers in *Tennessee Electric Power Co. et al. v. TVA*, the high
court determined that the utility complainants had no standing to
challenge the operations of TVA as they possessed no immunity
from lawful competition (even though, once again, the decision
ignored the central issue of the Authority's constitutionality—
which it would never address). It quashed the private utilities
industry's last argument.[93] Quashing Wendell Willkie was another
matter. Acclaimed in the February 1939 issue of the *Saturday
Evening Post* as "The Man Who Talked Back," the Hoosier
wonder continued speaking out to a rapidly widening audience
as writing and speaking invitations poured in. Little wonder that
General Hugh S. Johnson, FDR's alienated former NRA administrator, speculated in his syndicated column that the utility executive would make a formidable Republican presidential candidate.
Asked his reaction, Wendell served the reporter a thigh-slapping
quote. "If the government keeps on taking my business away," he
chortled, "I'll soon be out of work and looking for a job. Johnson's offer is the best I've had."[94]

Time placed a handsome, slightly jowlish Wendell Willkie on
its July 31, 1939, cover. "The New Deal is going to be on trial
again," the utility czar opined.[95] If Roosevelt decided to try a third
term, the two of them might have "a great discussion." His mother
had told him to seek his fortune beyond Elwood. Henrietta wrote
how proud she was of him "and our standing in this great nation."
Also, she had found a little pin that he lost nine or ten years ago.
She promised to keep it till they next saw one another. They never
would. Henrietta died the following spring.

CHAPTER 5

1940: POLITICAL SCIENCE
AND SERENDIPITY

John Cowles, Willkie, and Gardner "Mike" Cowles, American
Newspaper Publishers Association dinner, 1940.

he Republican party's regulars had needed help in catching
up with Wendell Willkie's meteoric rise. Until the candidate's
warp-speed materialization in May and early June 1940, most
of them expected the unlikely or dark horse names in play to be
Frank Gannett, the upstate New York newspaper owner; Charles
McNary, the Senate minority leader; Joseph Martin, the House
minority leader; or favorite son Arthur James, the Pennsylvania
governor. The reaction of one veteran party regular, Kenneth

Simpson, a New York national committeeman, spoke volumes. When asked to pitch Wendell Willkie by a Lazard Freres director and major fundraiser, a dismayed Simpson listed the difficulties:

> So I am supposed to go back to the clubhouse and tell the boys that we have to pull together now to get the nomination for Wendell Willkie. They'll ask me, "Willkie, who's Willkie?" And I'll tell them he's president of the Commonwealth and Southern. The next question will be, "Where does that railroad go to?" And I will explain that it isn't a railroad, it's a public utility holding company. Then they will look at me sadly and say, "Ken, we always have thought you were a little erratic, but now we know you are Just plain crazy." And that would be without my even getting to mention that he's a Democrat.[1]

This story is a good one. The truth about Wendell Willkie's unlikely run for the presidency of the United States makes an even better one. It begins in Roosevelt's second term soon after the humiliating 1936 defeat of the genial Republican Alf Landon in the largest Electoral College upset in US history, and second largest landslide to date. "As Maine goes, so goes Vermont," FDR's veteran campaign manager, Jim Farley, famously scoffed of Landon's only eight Electoral College votes.[2] By his guarded acceptance of New Deal reforms, the moderate Kansas governor, a self-described "oilman who never made a million," gave the voters insufficient reason to elect a Republican Roosevelt. Roosevelt's return consolidated the "masses and the minorities," as New York's caustic Justice Joseph Proskauer put it, and inaugurated the Second New Deal of unrestrained federal power, prodigal taxing and spending of Harry Hopkins, the allegiance of organized labor and the transferred loyalty of millions of African Americans, as well as a poisonous rhetoric of class reproach.[3] In the wake of Landon's rout, as they thought about their party's presidential prospects four years on (even if spared a third Roosevelt challenge), a hand full of likeminded northeastern national committeemen believed that the party of Lincoln, absent new leadership and a retooled platform, was destined for yet another rejection that might leave it on life support after 1940.

The challenge this group of party reformers faced was dauntingly twofold: for starters, they needed to script a new GOP victory scenario for the 1940 election; then they needed to find a surprise candidate unfettered by shopworn partisan dogma and politically ambidextrous enough to make the reforms of the left palatable to the right and the promised prosperity of the right credible to the left. Once they had a viable party platform, this group of anxious reformers decided that the winning candidate would emerge to fit the plan. Build a winning GOP agenda and the winning standard-bearer would come. This was precisely the prescient confidence circulated among the reformers from an influential insider: "If a Republican is elected in 1940," a New York financier believed, "it will be because . . . a leader has appeared and has been built up in such a way as to seize hold of the imagination of the people."[4] None of these ad hoc reformers imagined at the time, however, that the combative head of the third-largest utility holding company was the solution awaiting discovery. Meanwhile, just off stage were the party's next presidential prospects—a pool of predictable, unexciting possibles—none whom fit the reformers' bill: Robert Taft, brilliant son of a former president (politically hidebound and rigidly isolationist); Arthur Vandenberg, another fierce Midwestern isolationist and champion slayer of New Deal legislation; Thomas Dewey, a politically untested law and order *wunderkind* from New York; and Herbert Hoover, the economically unrepentant, dogged ex-president.

The men who set about planning what was to become not merely a remarkable recovery from the 1936 Roosevelt landslide, but a resurrection that came within an ace of a political revolution four years later, probably numbered less than two dozen. Natives of New York, Connecticut, and Massachusetts, they were Ivy League graduates almost without exception, internationalists of varying intensity, progressives in the spirit of Theodore Roosevelt, and, with one or two significant exceptions, country club WASPs most of whom wore their class privileges lightly. Three influential Connecticut public figures took the bit of party overhaul somewhat ahead of their fellow reformers. They began deliberating sometime early in 1937 at the old Beefsteak Club, a comfortable faux Edwardian eatery in Waterbury, a favored place to strategize and convenient to GOP former state representative Raymond Baldwin. Besides Baldwin and his two associates, other Beefsteak Club participants, varying from regular to occasional, probably numbered three or four.

Raymond Earl Baldwin, a tall, heavy-set forty-four, was the state legislature's erstwhile majority leader and present town chairman of Stratford and the Republican party's obvious choice for the 1938 gubernatorial contest. Baldwin's long, outstanding public service to Connecticut and the nation was to be exemplary enough to draw the infamous Senator Joe McCarthy's habitual character assassination during the Eisenhower presidency. Samuel F. Pryor Jr. of Greenwich, the trio's stellar achiever, was the short, trim, thirty-nine-year-old, pipe-smoking future vice president of Yale classmate Juan Trippe's global air carrier, Pan American World Airways. Born into upwardly mobile old wealth, Sam Pryor had the compensating pugnaciousness of a short, wiry man whose native intelligence, elite education, and world travel after college made him a leader in business and politics. He was at ease among South America's and Europe's rich and powerful, and such a close friend of Charles and Anne Morrow Lindbergh that he would share their resting place in Hawaii.[5]

Pryor took control of the state GOP after the recent suicide of the party's legendary kingpin John Henry Rorbeck. "Sam was a staunch Republican and a man of considerable means," Baldwin observed, "a man with some good wealthy connections." Baldwin's other collaborator, Westport's representative J. Kenneth Bradley, a rumpled, overweight thirty-nine, and with not so many "good wealthy connections," was a fount of encyclopedic knowledge based on careful observations of what was legislatively viable in the halls of Hartford. Ken's understanding of the Hartford ground game was an invaluable asset to Baldwin's noblesse oblige reformism and Pryor's *grand seigneur* politics.[6] Three years later Bradley served as Republican State Central Committee chairman. "The three of them tried to rejuvenate the

Connecticut GOP," Baldwin had hoped, recalling their mission fifty years afterward.

Raymond Earl Baldwin, a green-grocer's boy and future two-time Connecticut governor, went off to the more affordable Wesleyan while his teenage acquaintance Dean Acheson benefited from an expensive Yale education thanks to wealthy parents. "We had a very comfortable home," but New Haven meant finding "six or seven hundred dollars" beyond the family means.[7] Yale Law came later, after naval service in World War I, but Baldwin always proudly exemplified the melting-pot and race-relations values of liberal Republicanism. Reflecting on his changing nation many years later, the politician Wendell Willkie had wanted as his vice presidential running mate expressed satisfaction seeing "the third generation" of people he'd known as a boy—"Italian and Polish and Swedish and Irish extraction—whose families came here as immigrants, unable to speak the language, and yet made a way of life for themselves." In a line that could have come from E. L. Doctorow's *Ragtime*, then US senator Baldwin said "it strikes me as what America is really all about."[8] And really about a racially tolerant America, as when Governor Baldwin convened in 1943 the first meeting of Connecticut's first Interracial Commission to address jobs for Negroes at the Hartford Club. "No Jew had ever belonged to the club and no black man," but Baldwin broke racial and religious precedent. "They found jobs for black men." But the black man at the Hartford Club, Reverend Jackson, "came back" to remind Baldwin and the interfaith notables of jobs women also needed.[9]

Alice Roosevelt Longworth's memorably mordant remark—when she heard that cousin Franklin called Wendell Willkie's supporters "grass-roots stuff"—was that they "sprang from a thousand country clubs" instead.[10] Teddy Roosevelt's irreverent daughter was right at least about the country club origins of Willkie's future apostles. But Waterbury's Beefsteak Club and its several northeastern analogs were much less the bastions of myopic economics and rigidified snobbery that Alice Longworth had good reason to suspect, than they were venues engaged in the serious business of reforming the Republican Party to save their country

from the ongoing bureaucratic and economic excesses unleashed
by Franklin Roosevelt's Second New Deal.[11] Against the silver-
throated charmer in the Oval Office and his massive congressional
majorities, Republicans, unlike Archimedes, had found no ground
upon which to stand to move the nation since the great landslide.

Yet, throughout 1938, the Waterbury Beefsteakers felt the
winds of advantageous change also passing over a score of
club houses, party headquarters, and local meeting places as
the national economy barely staggered back from the so-called
Roosevelt recession—the administration's near-catastrophic
abandonment of Keynesian pump priming for the nostrum of
balanced budgets. Half the economic gains of the New Deal vanished in months amid claims of economic incompetence. Fifteen
million still remained unemployed in 1938. Public consternation
over the president's blatant early-1937 maneuver to intimidate the
Supreme Court persisted. Key legislation stumbled to passage or
even went down to defeat, as with the crucial bill to reorganize
executive functions. Fireside chats condemned the all-powerful
"Sixty Families" and "Chiseling Ten Percent." Obstructionists
in his own party ("Republocrats") provoked FDR to threaten a
purge in the next election.[12]

The administration had faltered badly during the summer of
1937. "Little Steel" (Republic Steel and Youngstown Sheet and
Tube Company) refused to negotiate with imperious John L.
Lewis's new Congress of Industrial Organizations (CIO) unions.
A Memorial Day march of steelworkers and sympathizers was
bloodily crushed by the Chicago police with only perfunctory
commiseration from the White House. Faced with an epidemic of
United Auto Workers sit-down strikes at General Motors plants
and management lockouts at Ford Motor Co., FDR retreated
behind a line from *Romeo and Juliet* at a memorable June press
conference: "A plague on both your houses." To which a furious
Lewis, dismayed that neither the Wagner Act nor hefty CIO campaign contributions availed his people, thundered, "Is labor to be
protected or is it to be butchered?" Black Americans—who all but
abandoned the party of Lincoln in the 1936 elections—expressed
growing disillusionment over their substantial exclusion from the

benefits of the new Social Security Act, the 1938 Federal Labor Standards Act, and the Federal Housing Assistance Act. NAACP and National Urban League lobbyists, together with publishers of several large-circulation black newspapers, found Eleanor Roosevelt's high-minded gestures poor substitutes for filibustered Costigan-Wagner anti-lynch legislation and failed amendments to Social Security and the Wagner Act.[13] GOP prospects in the off-year congressional elections began to feel almost too positive.

Astutely calculating that no percentages were gained from the usual GOP wholesale disparagement of New Deal alphabet-agency plethora, Baldwin, Pryor, Bradley risked fielding a philosophy of New Deal correction that would have been an anathema to the Connecticut party establishment dominated by its legendary overlord, John Rorbeck. Rorbeck—Baldwin's mentor and Pryor's predecessor—had liberated himself by a pistol head shot from a painful physical debility some months earlier.[14] Dropping "Pay as You Go" Rorbeck economics, Baldwin announced his gubernatorial candidacy and risked apostasy by proposing—in Jeffersonian voice—that New Deal alphabet agencies should be routed through the states and administered through "state, city, and town governmental organizations." In fact, they were really channeling a special reproach among even a growing number of influential Democrats that FDR had betrayed the 1932 Democratic Platform calling for decentralized government relief. "He threw that in the ashcan," lamented Al Smith's advisor and former speechwriter Joseph Proskauer, "so that everybody was feeding at the public till and Roosevelt was Santa Claus."[15]

On the morning of November 9, 1938, Baldwin and the GOP awoke to 81 new GOP House seats, 6 new senators, and 11 new governors, three of whom reflected the new progressivism that gained Baldwin the first GOP governorship since 1930: Ohio's John Bricker, Massachusetts' Leverett Saltonstall, and Minnesota's thirty-one-year-old Harold Stassen.[16] The electorate's rebuke of the Democrats, auspicious and unexpected as it was, nevertheless threatened to plunge the GOP national leadership into acrimonious confusion. "The swing back to Republicanism and Americanism has been so great" that he hadn't "yet been able to figure it out," Indiana congressman and a future House majority leader Charles Halleck wrote Frank Altschul, a partner of the puissant Lazard Freres investment bank.[17] Halleck's uncertainty bespoke the generalized GOP mindset of the moment. Sam Pryor's impatience with such hesitation stemmed not only from temperament but also from confidence that Baldwin's victory offered his party the operational template for the recapture of the presidency. Indeed, that a faithful rank and filer like Halleck confessed his unpreparedness to the cosmopolitan head of Lazard Freres was a clear sign that even in the heartland the party faithful sensed that new ideas backed by ample capital were about to change the way business was done at Republican national headquarters.

Fifty-one-year-old Frank Altschul, a remarkable citizen as thoughtful as James Madison and as rich as Croesus, was certainly an important source of those new ideas and, as vice chair of the RNC finance committee, a significant source of their financing. Sam Pryor had appealed to Altschul for the funds that helped propel Baldwin's winning campaign. Six months ahead, Pryor and Altschul would find themselves major backers of Wendell Willkie by force of logic and a bit of luck. For the present, the search for a winning presidential contender for 1940 remained an unknown imperative, whose discovery Pryor and Altschul intensely committed themselves to. The late November dinner Pryor arranged for governor-elect Baldwin to meet Herbert Hoover and Thomas Dewey at the home of the Lowell Thomases in Pawling, New York, was such a discovery scenario. Pryor and Thomas were in-laws, but Ray and Edith Baldwin mostly knew their host as one of America's most famous journalists and news broadcasters—the war correspondent by whom T. E. Lawrence snarkily claimed the misfortune of having been discovered in Thomas's 1924 book *With Lawrence in Arabia*. None of the evening's guests would have been surprised had Thomas mentioned that he was to anchor the first live television coverage of a political convention: the 1940 GOP National Convention.[18]

The Thomases' large house had "a sort of extra-large recreation or assembly room, and we went there to talk after dinner," Baldwin recalled. "That occasion was my first meeting with Tom

Dewey."[19] He never forgot it. Baldwin had just won his state's highest office and Dewey had just lost New York's to Democrat Herbert Lehman by a slim 64,000 votes. (Wendell had voted for Lehman.) But on this evening the natty, cocky thirty-six-year-old lawyer with the mellifluous voice and banderole mustache exuded the confidence of a man destined for rising Gallup poll percentages. "In the summer of 1938, Dewey was an authentic national hero," his diligent biographer reports. New Yorkers had followed their district attorney's Sunday radio broadcasts with the avidity of sports fans.[20] His dynamic, well-staged pursuits of malefactors drove alarmed mobsters to gun down Dutch Schultz and astonished the public by sending Schultz's rival, Lucky Luciano, to prison for running the largest prostitution ring in the northeast. His crime-busting capers spawned "Gang Busters," a popular national radio serial. Running for governor of New York, the politically labile Dewey had called himself a "New Deal Republican" (FDR, no stranger to being labile himself, denounced him as a fraud) but sprinkled anti-Semitic slights in his depiction of Governor Lehman—"mere bookkeeping is not my line."[21]

That evening Dewey made it clear that he considered himself the Republican Party's most promising presidential prospect. There was no mention that fall of 1938 of Wendell Willkie, although Pryor had had quiet discussions with Frank Altschul about the prospects of "the man who talked back." Hoover seems to have said little. As they took their leave, Thomas regretted, sotto voce, that Baldwin hadn't had "much chance to say anything." "I came over to hear Mr. Hoover talk," said, simply, Connecticut's new governor. On January 4, 1939, he was to be sworn in as Connecticut's seventy-second chief executive and the first Republican in a decade to occupy Hartford's historic executive mansion. Meantime, Baldwin's message to political insiders was that Hoover—"really a great man"—completely lacked "the warmth that you need in a political candidate." Dewey, on the other hand, abounded in glazed charm and fungible convictions. "What Dewey thought was what ought to be thought," Baldwin decided, and at age thirty-six.[22] Republican reformers needed a candidate capable of exploiting the intoxicating 1940 presidential promise.

In late September 1938, *United States News* had captioned a letter from Frank Altschul—"Business Leader Urges Liberal Platform for Republicans"—whose imperative summed up the cause to which the Lazard Freres senior partner pledged his considerable financial and organizational resources: "We must place the welfare of the United States above the welfare of the Republican Party." Altschul's previous service as RNC paymaster enabled him to gauge the GOP frontrunners' domestic and international strengths and limitations with especial insightfulness in a time of exacerbated global complexity. Because he was a political centrist and an internationalist in a party that was overwhelmingly isolationist, Altschul necessarily threaded the needle of leadership with almost surgical dexterity. A good look at "GOP Plan for 1940," prepared by Wisconsin University president Glenn Frank's program committee, depressed Frank Altschul. To his internationalist eye, the party front-runners Dewey, Taft, Vandenberg, Landon the titular party head, along with Pennsylvania's Arthur James and the unavoidable Hoover, presented the worst possible answer to the looming crisis at the end of a violent decade. As Arthur Schlesinger Jr., perhaps the decade's premier spectator, remembered, "the war was everywhere. It lay behind everything you said or did."[23] Germany annexed Austria without an invitation in March 1938. Hitler's diplomatic gambit succeeded at Munich that September. The Italo-German-Japanese Pact of Steel materialized in May 1939, followed three months later by the shocking Nazi-Soviet Non-Aggression Pact. The gallantry of their cavalry squadrons notwithstanding, the Poles succumbed in less than one month to the Nazi blitzkrieg struck on September 1, 1939. World War II began. History's clock was ticking, and Frank Altschul was among those Americans with especially keen hearing.

San Francisco–born to a wealthy Jewish family, Yale '08, Army captain in World War I, Legion d'Honneur recipient in 1920, one of five partners in the great family banking house of Lazard Freres (founded ninety years earlier by Alsatian émigrés in Louisiana), Altschul served as a governor of the New York Stock Exchange and a director of the Chase National Bank. Altschuls married Lehmans and vice versa. During the Landon presidential campaign, he was the vice-chairman of the GOP National Finance Committee. Yale was his principal philanthropy, the production of beautiful books on his Overbrook Press his avocation. The defense of liberal values—political, intellectual—was his passion. "One of the most successful financiers of his time," eulogized the *New York Times* May 1981 obituary with justice, "Mr. Altschul was, in many ways, a renaissance man. . . . He lived well, befitting a very rich man, but considered money most useful in a worthy cause."[24] The cause was liberal democracy served by money intelligently used, which Altschul believed had not been the case in 1936 with the Landon presidential campaign. For Altschul, any winning domestic platform for 1940 had to be twinned with a responsible internationalism.

Yet, except for those whose sophistication, education, or business or cultural ties distinguished them from their compatriots, the great majority of Americans wanted no part of Europe's troubles. The consensus was that one prodigious expenditure of blood and treasure to repay Lafayette and save Europe for democracy was enough—and definitely not worth repeating. So said authoritative historians such as Charles Beard, powerful publishers such as Colonel McCormick and William Randolph Hearst, automotive magnates such as Henry Ford, organized labor generals such as John L. Lewis, princes of the church such as Father Coughlin and Harry Emerson Fosdick of Riverside Church. Distinctions deep and subtle separated isolationists, noninterventionists, and pacifists, but all held fast to the legal doctrine of neutrality, strictly reenacted from 1935 to November 1939. The slayer of Wilson's League, aged Senator Borah of Idaho, and America's heartthrob Colonel Lindbergh, recently returned from residency abroad, swayed millions by deploring so-called misconceptions about Hitler's Germany, the horrors of *Kristallnacht* notwithstanding.[25] Yet, like Frank Altschul, whom he barely knew, Wendell Willkie foresaw the engagement of the United States in the foreign conflict as inescapable.

As Altschul pushed against the party's conservative borders, his uppermost calculation involved a presidential hypothetical that was better characterized as a unicorn rather than as even a dark horse in the fall of 1938. Wendell's two blockbuster articles "Idle

Money, Idle Men" and "Brace Up, America," appearing pell-mell in June 1937, had been revelations. "Idle Money, Idle Men" in the *Saturday Evening Post* went to the heart of New Deal economics, its dogma of the demonstrated incapacity of private enterprise to lift the lives of the masses of people, that government's imperative was the redistribution, not the production of wealth. Vice President Henry Wallace, a former Republican, was on record that "the free play of competitive forces is proving definitely destructive." He warned, "Opportunities of the past are gone, and it is a mistake to educate children as if such opportunities were still there." With $4 billion idle in banks, "the question is," Wendell urged, "can we cause our great reservoir of capital to flow into the channels of industry? If we can, our democratic system will be preserved."[26]

Frank Altschul decided, after hearing Wendell memorably trounce Solicitor General Robert Jackson over America's Town Meeting of the Air, that the holding company president subscribed to the desired international and business policies.[27] At his request, John Bricker, Ohio's attorney general and next governor, quietly sampled select Midwest grassroots reactions to the holding company paragon. Results were sufficiently favorable by February 1939 that Altschul told Bricker of "rather extended conversation with Wendell Willkie this morning." A widening network of "Beefsteak" Republicans learned of further discussions "in an atmosphere of complete and confidential exchange of ideas."[28]

Operating low key within the folds of Republicanism, Altschul suggested a series of articles to Dorothy Thompson to be called "Preview of 1940," a replication of the recently terminated "On the Record," Thompson's syndicated newspaper and radio broadcast series that made her as famous as Eleanor Roosevelt. Among this volcanic Syracuse University alumna's professional distinctions was the unique honor of being the first American journalist expelled from Germany after her dismissive biography of Hitler. Just some "random notes dictated in haste," Altschul described his March 1939 notes, which ran six typescript pages covering six GOP presidential likelies and a "number of minor lights," ending with a "Mr. X." So much for the candidates "considered politically available," Altschul profiled his "Mr. X" for Thompson's article:

He is not considered politically available. He has never run for elective office. He is identified with big business. He has no political machine. He has no coterie of political bosses . . . to corral delegates for him before the Convention. Yet, it is my considered opinion that if he could be nominated he would sweep the country by storm, and give to the United States of America the kind of government that the people . . . really want.[29]

The man the Lazard Freres partner had in mind and in whom "an aroused public opinion [would] place itself is WENDELL Willkie." Although Thompson didn't accept Altschul's "Preview of 1940" commission, she embraced his Willkie advocacy and incorporated his judgments of the GOP presidential aspirants in her hugely influential radio speeches and *Herald Tribune* articles from spring of 1939 on. Thompson's employers—Ogden and Helen Rogers Reid—fully concurred with Altschul because the *Herald Tribune* carried a letter endorsing Wendell Willkie's GOP nomination on its March 3, 1939, editorial page. Helen Rogers Reid's brother, the paper's former general manager, was the author.[30]

Ray Baldwin's opinion of himself as caretaker of his state had grown considerably since that evening at the Lowell Thomas home where he listened to Tom Dewey's opinion of himself. Sam Pryor, now the Republican National Committeeman of Connecticut, favored a Dewey presidential nomination and a Baldwin favorite son nomination. Still, as Lazard Freres beneficence had helped the Baldwin gubernatorial campaign, Pryor acceded to Altschul's suggestion, conveyed by Republican National Committee chairman John Hamilton, that Wendell be the bicentenary speaker at Greenwich's historic, high Anglican Christ Church that May. The gospel according to Wendell Willkie professed the indissolubleness of religion, freedom, and free enterprise. "You cannot have either one of them without free enterprise," he told the attentive Christians of Greenwich. And they would surely lose their free enterprise with too much regulation, the sin of these times. Wendell captivated the audience and made "a tremendous impression on me," recalled Baldwin. With a farewell handshake, Wendell told him, "Ray, I want you in my corner. Your record is the one that I admire." Even so, because the battle with FDR over Commonwealth & Southern remained unresolved, Baldwin thought Wendell hadn't "really seriously thought of running for the presidency."[31] The Beefsteakers had found their candidate, but without yet quite knowing so.

Wendell's favorable Greenwich reception prompted another early presidential speculation. *US News* publisher David Lawrence's syndicated column of May 22 discerned "an independent Democrat with a business ability and leadership capacity which would fit the pattern that nine out of ten Republicans really want but do not venture to ask for." Precisely Frank Altschul's belief as Lawrence's opinion came on the heels of the oracular Arthur Krock's suggestion printed on President's Day in the *Times*. "He'll go down as the darkest horse of the stable for 1940," Krock wagered. "I'd watch Willkie. He still has his hair cut country style." Within days of Krock's blessing, the February *Saturday Evening Post* offered an accurate description of Wendell as "attractive, articulate, and courageous."[32] That attractive, articulate, courageous person—"the only businessman in the US who is ever mentioned as a presidential possibility"—occupied the July cover of *Time*.

Pressed for his opinion of the accumulating accolades, Wendell offered what passed for earnest demurrals. "Really, from my standpoint," he insisted to an Atlanta acquaintance, "it cannot constitute more than a joke that the American people would even consider the election of a utility executive with an office in the precincts of Wall Street for constable, not alone president." Then had come the syndicated column speculation in November of the NRA's imperious ex-director General Hugh Johnson—"that if elected President, Willkie would make a terrific one."[33] To make a terrific Republican president, Wendell would have to change political parties, a fact mostly either forgotten by or somehow unrecognized among the swelling chorus of enthusiasts.

Not only was he still registered as a Democrat, Wendell was in good standing with Tammany, the New York County Democratic organization. After one of their occasional lunches, his Tammany brother Jim Farley stopped by the Oval Office to tell an amused FDR that—but for the TVA wrongheadedness—Wendell respected many of the president's achievements. "I am still a Democrat," said Wendell in 1938, "but not a socialist. Therefore I am entitled to my refund."[34] Wendell's presidential obligation to the stockholders and employees of Commonwealth & Southern was another impediment to a Republican Party nomination for president of the United States. The Supreme Court's verdict in *Tennessee Electric Power Co. et al. v. TVA* on January 30, 1939, had irrevocably terminated a long, doughty, meritorious legal combat. Wendell's public statement acknowledged the obvious. From all appearances, Franklin Roosevelt had won.

The president had had every confidence that when the time came for the recently altered Supreme Court to decide the merits of *Tennessee Electric Power Co. et al. v. TVA*—without neolithic Willis Van Devanter and with friendly additions Stanley Reed and Hugo Black—his government's argument would prevail, as, indeed, it had on January 30, 1939. All the while fighting the odds, the president of Commonwealth & Southern had had to assume the inevitable correctness of Roosevelt's calculation. TVA engineers had proceeded to map a greatly expanded operational scope for federal power. Federal and municipal officials had already inventoried the corpus of generating plants, transmission lines, and distributing systems to be divvyed up. Two Lilienthal surrogates studio-cast for their role—Swidler and Krug—were instructed to be ready in the aftermath of the Court's verdict to discuss with Wendell the endgame specifics of dismantlement of private power companies in the Tennessee Valley. With bad luck, David Lilienthal suffered a spell of serious milk poisoning, effectively removing him from the stage until the final act.

Two years earlier, Willkie had priced the asset value of Commonwealth & Southern at a stratospheric $95 million Depression-era value. The government insisted on half that amount, less depreciation of 10 to 15 percent. In all likelihood, the imminent *Tennessee Electric Power Co.* decision offered C & S a stark take-it-or-leave-it fait accompli. Or, conceivably, virtually nothing. But the political climate had become less favorable to the New Deal since the 1938 off-year elections. Avenging "Republocrats" and emboldened Republicans turned the Seventy-Sixth Congress into something of a legislative sandpit for FDR. After the Supreme Court's adverse *Alabama Power Co. v. Ickes* decision of January 3, 1938, Franklin Roosevelt reached an overdue decision himself to remove the chronic embarrassment of C & S from the 1940 presidential landscape. It was obvious that the Supreme Court's almost certain favorable legal resolution in *Tennessee Power & Light Co. v. TVA* would leave an unsatisfactory aftermath of unresolved property rights and vexatious personal antipathies. Wendell Willkie's biographers have speculated on the seemingly sudden denouement of the controversy. "And then, suddenly, at the beginning of February 1939—after the Supreme Court had ruled for TVA"—Ellsworth Barnard marveled, "something happened."

On the morning of October 13, three months before the final *Tennessee Power Co.* verdict, the much aggrieved George Fort Milton, publisher of the defunct *Chattanooga News,* telephoned Wendell Willkie on behalf of Franklin Roosevelt. Months earlier, Wendell had proposed off the record that the president appoint an ombudsman to facilitate a final, mutually satisfactory resolution of the war between federal and private power. Milton explained that since Wendell had agreed "to have any man whom the President would designate, fix a fair price" for his properties, the president had such a person in mind—the old Dutch trader, FDR himself. "The President asked me to ask you if you were willing to accept him as the individual to be the judge of a fair price." Wendell dodged a direct answer, saying he preferred to make his case in person together with Milton present as an observer in order to negotiate "with [FDR] for a definite sales price." Milton relayed the request to the president. White House secretary McIntyre phoned Milton FDR's immediate, annoyed response to Wendell's "definite evasion." To make the terms conveyed to Wendell crystal clear, Milton reiterated them in a follow-up phone call to the White House—"I related to Mr. Willkie that you were not willing to engage as a negotiator," he parroted, "but that your offer to act as judge still stood." It was take it or leave it on Roosevelt's terms, Milton said to Wendell Willkie. There was silence for a few moments, then a resigned acceptance: "Yes, I will do it"—if the buy-out was not less than $74 million. Milton then relayed the C & S chief's further understanding to McIntyre that the telephone agreement was "off the record, in the sense that it will not be a public act."[35]

The final act, on August 15, was staged over three and a half hours with flair before newsreel cameras in the offices of the First National Bank at 2 Wall Street. Lilienthal looked the dutiful, overworked federal official that he was as he handed the Commonwealth & Southern president a blowup of a check for $78.6 million, roughly equivalent in 2017 to $1.3 billion. Willkie hammered the scene with the practiced lack of sophistication of a lucky hayseed. "Thanks, Dave," he drawled. "That's a lot of money for a couple of old Indiana boys to be handling." This was an understatement heard round the world of the eastern establishment. His *Time* cover article that July all but announced his prospective candidacy for president, if—Wendell was quoted to say—Roosevelt dared to run again.[36] Whether engineered, as some speculated, by Harry Hopkins or the result of the second midterm election, the congressional bill FDR signed on July 26, 1939, acquired C & S for a sum that redeemed its preferred stock at par with $6.6 million available to common stock holders, retained the majority of the system's employees on the federal payroll, and required TVA to seek specific congressional authorization in order to expand its territorial footprint. The system's generating plants and transmission lines were transferred to TVA. Chattanooga along with other municipalities committed to buy the C & S distribution systems.[37]

The final, pragmatic settlement of TVA versus Commonwealth & Southern might well have been possible when Wendell Willkie and David Lilienthal met in Washington for the first time at the Cosmos Club in the winter of 1933. As his train carried him away from the drama to a much-needed family vacation, Lilienthal mused about the meaning of it all. He simply found himself unable to realize yet that it was "all over. That after all these years of battling and planning, after all these crises and worries and the uncertainties and the thin ice and the long, long chance—it is over, and beyond recall."[38] It was, after all was said and done, a settlement that could have arisen much sooner from a pragmatic appreciation of the realities on the ground, one eventually espoused by Arthur Morgan, one that two directors of the Federal Power Commission might have entertained until ideological fixity imposed unconditional surrender as the political desideratum. That the constitutionality of TVA to be its own judge and jury in the matter of its competition, compulsion, displacement, and appropriation of Commonwealth & Southern in the Tennessee Valley was left carefully unaddressed in every majority decision by the Supreme Court spoke volumes—as Wendell Willkie contended—for the primacy of a politics that sacrificed technology and economic efficiency to ideology. From the outset, Commonwealth & Southern was caught between the crosshairs of Tupelo: between the triumphant raison d'être of the New Deal and the generic culpability of the electric power holding companies.

Willkie was not quite ready to believe that life after Commonwealth & Southern could lead to Republican candidacy for the presidency of the United States. Yet he kept company these days with new admirers who encouraged him to believe that the Republican party and the nation urgently needed his leadership. One such admirer was the literary book editor of the *Herald Tribune,* Irita Bradford Van Doren, a brainy Alabama-born belle raised by her widowed mother in Florida, a 1908 English lit alumna of Florida State College for Women, who abandoned her Columbia PhD studies to marry fellow graduate student and literary paragon Carl Van Doren. They worked together on the *Nation,* produced three daughters, achieved remarkable early success, he as a leading Herman Melville scholar, Columbia University professor, and Pulitzer Prize biographer, she as literary book editor of the *Nation* and in 1926 Sunday book review editor of the *New York Herald Tribune.*

In 1935, however, the Van Dorens divorced. Two years later, Wendell Willkie happened. Women—especially sophisticated women—found Wendell immensely appealing, if bumptious and a poor dancer. "Actually, he has the well-organized balkiness of a healthy bear, and singularly brilliant eyes," was a typical Rebecca West assessment. "A personality to charm a bird from a tree— if he wanted to," said the popular novelist Marcia Davenport, "and he radiated a stunning combination of intellect and homely warmth."[39] As near as can be exact about these things, Wendell and Irita met at a cocktail party given by one of the most famous couples in America, Sinclair Lewis, this nation's first Nobel laureate in literature, and Dorothy Thompson, syndicated columnist and leftwing political scold.

She was a year older than Wendell, a lithe, vibrant woman whose intelligence and bearing evoked admiration from both sexes, and usually a degree of physical attraction from heterosexual men. "She was not pretty, but she was beautiful," was how William Shirer, historian of the Third Reich, described Irita to Wendell's biographer, Steve Neal. Her professional prominence was enhanced by a southern charm that had wonderfully accommodated itself to New York efficiency. Thanks to Irita's courteously demanding standards, the quality of the *Herald Tribune*'s *Sunday Book Review*, despite its smaller staff, was often considered the equal if not slightly superior competitor of its analog at the august *New York Times*. She had distinguished herself by writing gauzy short stories about Lost Cause bliss in her Florida college literary magazine and claimed a classic antebellum genealogy—an ancestral Alabama planation teeming with slaves and a Confederate general grandfather. Wendell later discovered but was too loyal to reveal to Irita that the putative Confederate general grandfather, William M. Brooks, had been a mere colonel in the Alabama reserves. However, it was the mutual Civil War interest, thinks another biographer, that prompted Wendell shortly before meeting her in person to invite her opinion of a bulky manuscript by the wife of an Atlanta employee of C & S. What Irita thought of Margaret Mitchell's Civil War saga is unrecorded, but she probably found it admirable.[40]

Almost instantly after the cocktail party meeting, Irita became Wendell's great passion and he hers. Almost from that moment, Edith Willkie's already diminished emotional importance was reduced to spousal formality as Irita filled the role of partner in thought and affection. It was an open secret among Manhattan's well connected and well-read that Wendell spent more time with Irita than with wife Edith. She was her lover's passport to a circle of sophisticated types who gave smart dinners and frequented the Algonquin Hotel. FDR, who made certain to learn about Willkie's personal affairs, can be heard on the earliest Oval Office taping system describing her as an "awful nice gal, [who] writes for the magazine and so forth and so on."[41] Through it all, Edith ("Billie," as Wendell called her) compensated with the derived prestige and significance of her husband's fame, her devotion to their son, Philip, of whom his father expected too much too quickly, and the ultimate satisfaction of knowing that Irita could never become Mrs. Willkie. "You couldn't help but admire her," their friend William Shirer said. "She was probably terribly hurt. But she wasn't going to ruin [Wendell's] career."

Irita exaggerated her influence on Wendell, Edith insisted many years later, but it was true, she conceded, "he liked her—admired her brilliance."[42] More than that, as Marcia Davenport described Irita's effect on Willkie: "Before they met, he was just a big businessman." From her he learned eastern pronunciation, new terms, literary style. "She brought him into a world where his intellect was stimulated." She fixed his "lousy" prose, Irita's daughters recalled. Unexpected evidence of her literary tutelage in 1939 was Wendell's gracefully insightful review in the August 27 *Herald Tribune* of Lord David Cecil's *The Young Melbourne,* an exquisite biography of young Queen Victoria's first prime minister and embodiment of the political decline of the Whigs. Applause from accomplished southern novelist Julia Peterkin—"not fair for the review . . . to be better written than the book"—brought such pleasure that early the following year wordsmith Wendell, accompanied by Irita, hosted an elegant dinner in Charleston for the literary elite—Balls, Ravenels, Pinckneys, the Du Bose Heywards—and several local professors.[43] Wendell's review deserved Julia Peterkin's compliment. Its felicity of expression was remarkable, nor does one doubt Lord Melbourne's Whigs' appeal for the reviewer: "rowdy, reckless and robust," who dined and danced, gambled and drank "and make love until breakfast—and still put in a hard day's work on their estates or in Parliament." Irita Van Doren's part in the reviewer's debut, such as it may have been, remained inadequately acknowledged by design.[44]

Those surprisingly polished, thoughtful contributions in *Atlantic Monthly* and *Saturday Evening Post* owed much to Van Doren. Irita helped him to write better and think out his ideas out of genuine admiration, but she was also responsive to political cues from the publishers of the *Herald Tribune*, *Fortune*, and *Atlantic Monthly* who were beginning to regard Willkie as a plausible dark horse for the presidency. Joseph Barnes, a foreign reporter of the *Herald Tribune*, who had reason to know him better than any professional observer, said that she was largely responsible for Wendell's "acceptance of himself as a political leader with original and important ideas." That his acceptance of her importance to him sometimes verged on unacceptable behavior in public—scheduling press conferences in her Greenwich Village apartment—Wendell defiantly ignored. "Everybody knows about us," his biographer Steve Neal reports him telling friends. "There is not a reporter in New York who doesn't know about her." She was his "Dear Irita, you whom I admire inordinately and love excessively." Indeed.[45]

Suddenly, Van Doren found herself sharing Willkie's mind with the managing editor of *Fortune Magazine*, Russell Davenport. Tall, superior Russell Wheeler Davenport. Son of a Bethlehem Steel vice president, Yale Skull and Bones, awarded the Croix de Guerre for service in 1918 with the AEF, and a major figure in Henry Luce's publications empire, Davenport was a man of vaulting intellectual pretensions, a published poet and prospective author of a large book on American politics. In July 1939, Wendell was a guest at the *Fortune* Round Table run by Davenport. He "took the whole group by storm," Davenport expostulated— "put into words that day the things I've been thinking for years." As of that day, he committed himself to Wendell's political future as he raced home to tell his wife he'd met the man "who ought to be the next President of the United States." Whose idea was it, asked Marcia—"his or yours?" "It's spontaneous. You see him and you know it." About four months had passed since Frank Altschul shared the same conclusion with Dorothy Thompson, Davenport's wife's good friend. When he and Marcia entertained Wendell and Edith later that month at their country place in Saugatuck Harbor, Connecticut, Marcia Davenport found her dinner plans and bridge-playing guests ignored; she herself was noticed "only to the extent of a smile and a nod." Russell had had his tennis court rolled and arranged guest privileges for the local golf course. He need not have bothered. As Edith could have told their hosts, Wendell's entertainment was conversation. Husband and guest discovered an "intellectual and temperamental affinity like the anvil and the hammer," sighed Marcia.[46]

The August 19, 1939, weekend at the Davenports' would become part of the conspiracy lore surrounding Wendell's extraordinary political career. The then highly respected historian Harry Elmer Barnes told a group of colleagues at the annual American Historical Association meeting the following year that Ogden Mills Reid, publisher of the *Herald Tribune*, and Thomas Lamont, head of J.P. Morgan, engineered Wendell's meteoric rise shortly after the Davenport weekend. "Invent is precisely the right word," insisted journalist David Halberstam thirty-five years later in *The Powers That Be,* adding that the Commonwealth & Southern president was "the rarest of things in those days, a Republican with sex appeal." The whorl of strategic dinner parties at the Davenports' fashionable East Side Manhattan apartment that summer and into early fall, the marshalling of writing talent and expert opinion behind his public statements, added credence to claims of a collaborative manufacture of Wendell Willkie. Moreover, after Wendell and Henry Luce, accompanied by a skeptical Clare Boothe, finally met face-to-face at the Davenports, the publisher decided that his initial confidence had been well placed. Watching Wendell and Davenport interact, Luce wrote afterward of thinking of the former "as a force of nature." He thought of Davenport as a "force of spirit." Henceforth, Wendell had the full resources behind him of *Time, Life,* and *Fortune* ("shameless and endless puffery," said one historian of the press).[47]

The grounds for incipient optimism among some of the eastern establishment seemed well founded as the 1940 national elections approached. FDR declined to say whether or not he intended to seek an unprecedented third term. Reading the politics of the day as especially propitious, Wendell's well-connected new sponsors helped him prepare a call to action, a penultimate brass ring declaration in the April 1940 issue of *Fortune*. Davenport's lead editorial summoned Americans to make a clean break with the stunted experience of the New Deal. Wendell's essay bore the portentous title, "We, the People: A Foundation for a Political Recovery." It spoke powerfully to liberal Republicans and disaffected Democrats, to economically sophisticated business interests, conservative midwestern farmers, and middle-class citizens unsettled by the recent economic implosion, as well as to a fair number of the putative "Sixty Families"—reviled by FDR as plutocratic parasites—who were ready to risk supporting an unknown against what they perceived as the confiscatory terrors of a third New Deal.

Indictments of FDR dropped like guillotines from Wendell's *Fortune* essay. "You have usurped our sovereign power by curtailing our Bill of Rights," it charged, thereby "placing into the hands of a few men in executive commissions all the powers requisite to tyranny." Promoter of class conflict, FDR has "separated 'business' from 'industry' from the ordinary lives of the people and [has] applied against them a philosophy of hate and mistrust." "Therefore, abandon this attitude of hate and set our enterprises free," the author demanded. "We, the People" promised a New Deal devoid of class animus and faithful to the Great Depression reforms—a new New Deal with its budgets balanced (gradually) and bureaucratic waste and duplication eliminated.[48] In truth, the people no longer wanted "a New Deal any more. We want a New World."[49]

Those Republicans who read "We, the People"—favorably or not—primarily as a program for a smarter, less regulated, more productive New Deal, missed its essential appeal to the internationalists who comprised the minority within the Republican Party. Although the latter ranged from dogmatic opponents to pragmatic critics of the New Deal, they were united in their extreme alarm over the outbreak of war after the German invasion of Poland in September. "It makes a great deal of difference to us—politically, economically, and emotionally"—Wendell wanted it understood, "what kind of world exists beyond our shores." Opposed to war as he and those who shared his concerns were, they did not "intend to relinquish our right to sell whatever we want to those defending themselves against aggression."[50]

Reader's Digest reprinted the full text and William Allen White's new Committee to Defend America by Aiding the Allies broadcast "We, the People" as self-evident gospel. White, owner the Kansas *Emporia Gazette* and famous for his "What's the Matter with Kansas?" editorial, was a Teddy Roosevelt internationalist.

Putting down his April *Fortune*, Gardner "Mike" Cowles, publisher of the new *Look* magazine, wrote Willkie that his statement was "the most sensible statement I have seen anywhere of the issues facing America and of the problems which must be solved." A short time later, Gardner Cowles and older brother John, publisher of the Des Moines *Register and Tribune* and the Minneapolis *Star Journal*, met Wendell at the Davenports for the first time at Sunday dinner in late April after their attendance at the American Newspaper Publishers Association meeting. Exeter and Harvard men, they were Republicans in the internationalist tradition of Theodore Roosevelt. Willkie, the inventive businessman and frank-speaking politician, captivated the brothers, an affinity that would last until Wendell's premature death.[51] Another midwestern newspaper publisher encouraged the author of "We, the People" to waste no more time before declaring his candidacy for the Republican presidential nomination: this was Alf Landon's vice-presidential running-mate, Frank Knox, Boston-born owner of the Chicago *Daily News* and erstwhile Bull Moose internationalist. Wendell's ideas made equally good sense to Roy Howard, owner of the sprawling Scripps-Howard newspaper syndicate.

These pillars of the fourth estate, together with the *Herald Tribune*'s aristocratic publisher Ogden Mills Reid and *Time*'s driven Henry Luce, provided more than enough favorable commentary and publicity to transform a quixotic Willkie phenomenon into a powerful natural dynamo. The near simultaneous publication of young John Fitzgerald Kennedy's *Why England Slept*, ornamented by Henry Luce's minatory foreword, served as a major reinforcement of Wendell's prudent pitch for armed preparedness. Astute readers took away from Luce's foreword the command that America needed a leader who resembled the president of Commonwealth & Southern—"the ablest industrialists in America for the most efficient arming of America."[52] Three weeks after his electrifying *For-*

tune essay, the undeclared candidate—still a Democrat—pitched himself to five hundred GOP regulars for the first time in Des Moines, Mike and John Cowles at his side. Mike Cowles bought a half hour on CBS for Willkie to repeat his message (introduced by Minnesota's eloquent boy governor, Harold Stassen).

Wendell's radio message fell flat, foretelling a problem on the campaign trail. He was distressingly given to an uneven reading rhythm and odd midwestern phonetics, but when he tossed the pages over his shoulder after the microphone was silenced, his extemporized speech brought the assembly whistling and shouting to its feet. He was all for FDR's budget for American military readiness. Wendell had the answer to give the man in the White House: "Every time Mr. Roosevelt damns Hitler and says we ought to help the democracies in every way we can short of war," Mr. Roosevelt should be told, "We double-damn Hitler," he thumped with jacket removed, "but what about the $60 billion you've spent and the ten million persons who are still unemployed?" *Time* and *Fortune* boosted on cue. *Life* featured an eleven-page Willkie profile on May 13. According to *Life* and its unnamed national political pundits, Willkie was "by far the ablest man the Republicans could nominate at Philadelphia next month." Until *Life*'s blessing, only the New York *Sun* had noted that Commonwealth & Southern's president had recently switched his party registration from Democrat to Republican.[53]

On April 9, 1940, little more than a month before the opulent *Life* magazine spread, Wendell appeared on America's most popular radio quiz show, "Information, Please," and scored a near perfect performance. Challenged by the show's master of ceremonies Clifton Fadiman and its erudite regulars, the erstwhile businessman and utilities mogul amazed the radio audience with a relaxed, talkative disquisition on the "pocket veto," meaning of "carpet-bagger," a fluent recitation of the Preamble to the Constitution (with one slip), and a display of literary culture that surely surprised most everyone listening but Irita Van Doren.[54] Earlier that day, Wendell and his fellow citizens heard that German military forces had invaded Denmark and Norway. The considerable satisfaction he took away from the quiz show performance must have seemed less meaningful. The end of the unreal lull of the *Sitzkrieg* ("the Phony War") meant that Americans would soon be forced to decide whether or not to leave Europe to Hitler.

"We, the People" more than hinted that its author harbored Wilsonian sentiments. On April 9, however, that there was a realistic place for a Newton Baker loyalist in the Republican Party remained highly doubtful. The Gallup poll still gave Dewey a decided lead for the Republican nomination, with Taft closing. They, Vandenberg, and the other contenders accurately read the opinions of the country as overwhelmingly against involvement in the war. On Wendell's desk in Pine Street that full day lay a troublingly curious, unsolicited document from one Oren Root Jr., a twenty-eight-year-old associate attorney—"unmarried, living at home with my mother and stepfather"—at the prestigious firm of Davis Polk & Wardwell. Root, Princeton '33, was the grandnephew of Elihu Root, successively secretary of war and of state under William McKinley and Theodore Roosevelt, and recipient of the 1912 Nobel Peace Prize. Without seeking the permission of John W. Davis, the firm's founder and defeated 1924 Democratic candidate for the presidency—or alerting Wendell beforehand—Root had mailed "a couple of thousand" copies of his "Declaration" to 1924 and 1925 graduates of Ivy League colleges requesting fifteen affirmative signatures each and return of the self-addressed document to his place of employment. "We, the People," Wendell's powerful *Fortune* article brought to Root's notice by his mother, was the spark.[55]

Root's text bespoke twenty-eight years of patrician self-assurance, its argument a model of succinct exegesis, its summons a generational imperative. "For the first time in American history we have heard serious talk about classes instead of individuals. Our national debt towers over us, and our capital lies idle in the banks. As a kind of explanation of this we are told that our country has reached the limits of its growth and that the future has less to offer than the past." Decrying this "philosophy of defeat" Root arraigned his party's presidential candidates:

[They] differ from each other only in varying degrees of unfitness. If in this crisis of civilization the Republican Party turns to some ponderous isolationist or to some crooning vote-getter I say it is morally bankrupt. . . . Because Wendell Willkie does not believe in this philosophy of defeat we welcome him . . . . Because he has a hatred of persecution inherited from his ancestors who fled to these shores to escape the persecution of their era . . . he will be the defender of our power and not of the power of any institution or favored group. What Wendell believes he has written and spoken without quibble. But the essence of his political philosophy is in his heart, as it is in the hearts of the People of the United States.[56]

Oren Root hoped Mr. Willkie—"a meteor of unusual brilliance"—would approve.

Before news came from his "meteor of unusual brilliance," the firm's senior partners, stunned by a Niagara of partisan mail, intervened. John W. Davis was much distressed. Nor was the "brilliant meteor" or his new political advisor Russell Davenport pleased to have this premature advertisement of candidacy. Thomas Lamont, good friend and J.P. Morgan senior partner, placed a quick phone call to Davis Polk. Root was summoned to the phone and advised to abandon his activities, but his persistence brought Wendell on the line. An inquisitive lunch with Wendell and Davenport earned Root their conditional approval, followed by a leave of absence from the firm and funds for space to organize a Willkie nomination petition drive among Ivy League graduates. Root's petition garnered 200,000 names in less than a month from the eastern elite, a decided minority of the electorate, but a pivotal one.[57]

Two weeks after Wendell spoke to the Iowa Republicans on May 11, the *Wehrmacht* surrounded retreating British and French forces at Dunkirk. Norwegian resistance continued, but Belgium, Holland, and Luxembourg quickly crumbled, with France's collapse imminent. Millions of Americans were stirred by the "blood, toil, tears, and sweat" speech of Winston Churchill, Britain's new prime minister, to the House of Commons, but many millions more stubbornly refused to feel inspired to offer Churchill's people material assistance in their hour of crisis. Most Jews and Poles saw the German war machine as an existential menace, but most other Americans were deeply divided. Ethnic fissures played their part as Irish Americans and (after Italy's war declaration against France) Italian Americans felt little inclination to send military equipment to the imperiled island. Southern culture was historically prone to favor military solutions to foreign problems, but German Americans and the insular farmers and ranchers of the heartland were staunchly isolationist/noninterventionist. Small but well-organized, the American Communist Party absorbed the shock of the Nazi-Soviet Non-Aggression Pact and imposed a noninterference policy on some of organized labor's largest affiliates. Bitter grievances from service under segregation in the Great War explained the widespread African American skepticism about the merits of another European civil war. "Until May 1940," recalls the author of *Those Angry Days*, "most Americans viewed the war in Europe as if it were a movie—a drama that, while interesting to watch, had nothing to do with their own lives."[58]

For people to whom the drama in Europe was real, few exemplified their concerns better than New York Republican National Committeeman Kenneth Simpson. Simpson's elite Hill School, Yale Phi Beta Kappa key, *Yale Daily News* editorship, and Skull and Bones initiation made him a classic Lost Generation type: Paris expatriation; professional friendships with Edmund Wilson; Picasso; Gertrude Stein; Alexandre Kerensky, a stylish Latin Quarter apartment and socialite American wife. He and she returned to New York to an art-filled Manhattan townhouse in the "Silk Stocking District" (the Seventeenth Congressional). It was Kenneth Simpson's contrivance of an hilarious introduction to Wendell Willkie that, perhaps more than anything else, fostered the beguiling impression of an ad hoc, seat-of the pants presidential nomination that swept aside the Republican Old Guard like a populist windstorm. As described by Ken Simpson, the moment occurred in September 1939 when fellow Yale man Frank Altschul pressed him to back Wendell. "So I am supposed to go back to the clubhouse and tell the boys that we have to pull together now to get the nomination for Wendell Willkie," objected Simpson in feigned puzzlement? "They'll ask me, 'Willkie, who's Willkie?' And I'll tell them he's president of the Commonwealth and Southern. And the next question will be, 'Where does that railroad go to . . . ?' "[59]

Kenneth Farrand Simpson emerged from Mr. Wilson's war a captain, earned a Harvard Law degree in 1922, and returned to assist the French government's recovery of art stolen by the Germans. Simpson's cultured articulateness could run to pure gift of gab that sometimes belied the acquired WASP persona girdling a mercurial Scots Irish core. Thirty-six-year-old Tom Dewey had entrusted management of his 1938 gubernatorial campaign to forty-three-year-old pipe-smoking Kenneth Simpson. But when Simpson boasted of his role in the candidate's rising career, Dewey was not only infuriated, but refused Simpson the quid pro quo endorsement for Manhattan district attorney if Dewey won the governorship. For the sake of the party, Dewey was pressed to mend fences with Simpson. "Can't make friends with a man whose word is no good," was Dewey's final word. With Herbert Hoover's backing, Dewey proceeded to oust Simpson from his chairmanship of the New York County Republican Party Committee just as Wendell's candidacy gained steam.[60] In the fall of 1939, Simpson would hardly need to tell publicly aware Republicans that C & S was not a railroad or introduce Wendell Willkie. He and Altschul had already met that September for the express purpose of plotting the schism in the New York delegation that would deny Dewey the nomination at the Republican National Convention.

Altschul's entente with Simpson occurred almost simultaneously with his alignment with another like-minded GOP strategist, Charlton MacVeagh, a thirty-eight-year-old Harvard alum, publishing executive, published poet, and former chief assistant to RNC chairman John Hamilton. MacVeagh had written Hamilton's notable address at the 1936 convention. He brought to Willkie supporters the prestige of his family's service to successive Republican administrations as secretary of state, attorney general, ambassador to Spain, and—more meaningful—his experience at running a political campaign together with his "bible" of names of a thousand delegates and equal number of alternates to the Philadelphia convention. After MacVeagh arrived to set up a telephone command center, Davenport's unofficial Willkie for President headquarters in the Murray Hill Hotel was transformed overnight into a professional campaign powerhouse. Until then, "nobody had the thinnest idea how you organized the votes of delegates or how you reached delegates in a political convention," said Marcia Davenport.[61] Meanwhile, with Oren Root on leave from Davis Polk to run his Willkie Clubs Center (staff and printing budget underwritten by the Edison Electric Institute), legions of crusading Ivy Leaguers prepared to descend on Philadelphia.

From those bewildered days after Alf Landon's electoral debacle when—counting Ray Baldwin and Sam Pryor's Beefeaters— they hardly numbered more than a dozen, the ranks of GOP revivalists now swelled under the focused activism of Davenport, Root, MacVeagh, Altschul, and a now conscripted RNC chairman, John D. M. Hamilton. In Altschul's eyes, especially, Hamilton was the sort of "Tory" to be blamed for the ultra-conservative bent taken by Landon's campaign. But now, Altscuhl's largesse and Hamilton's position made for the strange bed-fellowship of political collaboration. Not all revivalists were interventionists; some subscribed to a New Deal minimalism just shy of hostile. Winning was almost everything for most of them.[62]

The influential attorney Raoul Desvernine, a self-described Jeffersonian Democrat, hosted a series of dinner parties for seneschals of business, politics, and opinion such as Al Smith (bitterly alienated from his FDR protégé), General Motors CEO Alfred P. Sloan, and the lapsed New Deal propagandist Raymond Moley, who became Willkie enthusiasts. Harold Gallagher was an exception to the general Willkieite profile, an Iowa University corporate lawyer and future president of the American Bar Association. Gallagher and Willkie shared a Midwest propinquity that turned into a deep personal friendship. The month before the convention, Gallagher set himself the charge of phoning a hefty percentage of the names in MacVeagh's book of operatives. Wendell would join the firm of Owen, Otis, Farr & Gallagher after the election.[63]

Lest appearance be mistaken for reality as this impressive manifestation of upper-crust voluntarism gained ever more momentum, Oren Root and Russell Davenport grew concerned that Alice Roosevelt Longworth's well-known country club jibe might undermine Wendell's claim to independence from what Americans were more than a decade from learning to describe as the "power elite." "Somehow," Root warned Thomas Lamont, they had to "get rid of the Wall Street stigma" and the impression of a northeastern establishment monopoly. As they all shamefacedly recalled, RNC chairman John Hamilton, who ran the 1936 campaign, had famously gloated that Landon would win "because every Rolls-Royce I see has a Landon sticker."

A few days later, Oskaloosa, Iowa, population 7,000 and site on the annual Southern Iowa Fair, opened its first Willkie Club and began mailing Willkie pledges throughout the Northwest. Root, his identity unobserved, had come and gone accomplishing a job well done.[64] Nor did Wendell Willkie at all fit the mold of a toady to the great financial houses and newspaper syndicates—"the rich man's Roosevelt," another Ickes jibe. He was his own man, principled and controversial whenever he felt the calling, as in "Fair Trial," a potential red flag article to rock-ribbed Republican and Democratic patriots in *New Republic*. Published three months before the Philadelphia convention, "Fair Trial" was certainly a provocative civil liberties excursus for a presidential possible. Justice was not something to hand out "at one time because it is convenient and withhold another time for the same reason," Wendell lectured FDR's Justice Department on behalf of the imprisoned CPUSA head Earl Browder and German American Bund leader Fritz Kuhn. "It is well to remember," iterated the author, that any man who denies justice to someone he hates prepares the way for a denial of justice to someone he loves."[65]

Solid GOP noninterventionism notwithstanding, the turn of the war in France raised questions about front-runners Dewey and Taft among even some true-blue party influentials. With the greatest regret, Bruce Barton, cofounder of the nation's premier advertising agency, BBD&O, informed Tom Dewey that "three months ago a huge majority of our people felt that you were the answer to the country's need," but no longer. "The war situation has introduced a wholly new and overwhelming factor into the Republican picture." Even though Barton was isolationist to the core, he decided the times were too parlous to risk the country to a thirty-eight-year-old. As Harold Ickes was heard to say with that gift of his for political evisceration, Dewey had "thrown his diaper into the ring." Barton switched to Willkie after learning of Wendell's circuit-riding triumph that swooped up en masse Ray Baldwin's Connecticut GOP. Barton may even have been privy to the understanding Wendell reached with Sam Pryor that Favorite Son Baldwin would pledge Connecticut's sixteen delegate votes on the first ballot.[66]

When Bob and Martha Taft accepted Ogden and Helen Reid's significant dinner invitation, they stumbled, either from uncharacteristic temerity or miscalculation, into a hornets' nest of fired-up interventionists a month before the Philadelphia convention. The blatantly interventionist *Herald Tribune* owners and their guests Dorothy Thompson, British ambassador Lord Lothian, Thomas Lamont of the House of Morgan, FDR's former budget director Lewis Douglas, and Wendell Willkie were in no mood that particular evening to suffer indifference or short-sightedness about the gravity of the situation in Europe. His Majesty's Ambassador, the terminally ill 11th Marquess of Lothian—now finally disabused of Hitler's intentions—painted an existentially somber picture of his country's material needs, which provoked an all-out insistence of military aid to the Allies from Wendell. Yet Senator Taft failed to see how this faraway settling of old continental scores concerned the United States. The Atlantic Ocean still measured the distance between the old and new worlds, he protested. With Wendell's gravel-voiced disagreement that Taft was "a blind, foolish and silly man" overwhelmed by Dorothy Thompson's pro-British hysterics ricocheting off the Reids' dining room walls, and the famously cool Bob Taft and his wife vainly trying to hold their own against the rest, no one in politics should have been surprised when *Time* magazine all but replayed the Reid dinner in its June 10 issue: "While Tom Dewey, with bravado, was fumbling with the topic of foreign affairs, while Taft appeared to be running toward the wrong goal posts, Willkie seized the ball."[67]

Much more painful to Taft than being provoked to fury by Helen and Ogden Reid's dinner guests was the chorus of Willkie endorsements from opinion-makers like syndicated columnist Drew Pearson and radio pundit Walter Winchell. In the first of what would run for years as unvarnished admiration of the transplanted Hoosier, Pearson exclaimed that for "sheer force of personality and character I believe Willkie makes the greatest impact of any man I've ever talked to. He rings true." As Henry Luce's *Time* anticipated, by the middle of June Gallup placed Willkie up from a mere 3 percent in early May to 5 percent ahead of Taft's 12 percent. Dewey's 67 percent lead in May eroded 15 percent.[68] Finally, when Wendell Willkie came to Washington on June 12 to speak to the National Press Club, he decided to end the speculation about his intentions. Indiana representative Charles Halleck, serving his second congressional term, was there to listen and was decidedly undecided. Wendell spoke quickly to Halleck and gained his momentary agreement to regard him as a viable presidential aspirant before addressing the audience. "Gentlemen, this is on the record," Wendell announced from the podium. "I'm going to be a candidate for President of the United States. And my good friend Charlie Halleck from Indiana is going to place my name in nomination." There were twelve days to go before the opening gavel fell at the Republican National Convention meeting in Philadelphia.[69]

CHAPTER 6

THE PHILADELPHIA STORY

Joe Martin announces Willkie nomination, 1940. *Courtesy the Lilly Library, Indiana University, Bloomington, Indiana.*

A week before the Philadelphia convention, Usher L. Burdick of North Dakota, a Republican representative after Alice Longworth's heart, rose in the House to warn his colleagues what the nomination of Wendell Willkie would mean to the Republic. There was nothing to the Willkie boom, Burdick declaimed with considerable emotion, "except the artificial public opinion being created by the newspapers, magazines, and the radio." And the reason for the phenomenon, he explained, was simply "money." There was still time to find out whether the American people "are to be let alone in the selection of a Republican candidate for the presidency, or whether the special interests of this coun-

try are powerful enough to dictate to the American people."[1]
During Harding-Coolidge years, the Republican Party's western progressives became known as the "Sons of the Wild Jack-
ass" because they were against the disproportionate financial and
political power exercised by the so-called Eastern Establishment,
and equally so because they abhorred the East's internationalist
proclivities—in a word, opposition to Wall Street and its readiness to entangle the country in European affairs. Wisconsin's La
Follettes (Robert Sr. and Jr.), California's Hiram Johnson, Idaho's William Borah (Alice Longworth's lover, removed by cerebral
hemorrhage that January), Nebraska's George Norris—all were
suspicious of Wendell Willkie's emergence.

No doubt a sizable percentage of the electorate already
believed that special interests were synonymous with Republican
Party politics. But Congressman Burdick's warning derived from
fact and fiction that all but charged a diabolical takeover of the
party of Lincoln: a monstrous consortium of bankers and industrialists; a strategically embedded cabal of British secret agents
and Anglophile collaborators; a fourth estate suborned by the
plutocracy, with Thomas Lamont of the House of Morgan as
masterful coordinator. Tom Lamont's unwise mere presence in
Philadelphia (and advisable early departure) the weekend before
the convention gave GOP isolationist insiders and future conspiracy theorists such as David Halberstam and Theodore White
plausible grounds for claiming Wendell's nomination was rigged
by an interventionist eastern plutocracy. Echoes of the putative
high political calculus of the "ambassador from Wall Street"
resound seventy years later in The Golden Age, Gore Vidal's
novelistic simulacrum. "[Roosevelt] is our savior. Willkie is only
our insurance," Lamont is supposed to have reminded Davenport and Walter Lippmann as he slipped away, but not before the
press caught sight.[2]

The man whose sudden absence from the convention actually
mattered more than Lamont's presence was Ralph E. Williams, the
seventy-year-old chairman of the committee on arrangements and
credentials, who thought himself in good health. When Williams
stood to address his Committee on Arrangements in the Bellevue-

Stratford Hotel ballroom on May 16, the supporting chair slipped from his grip and he crashed to the floor, dead of a coronary at 5:30 p.m. Although formally neutral in the office he had occupied since 1932, Williams was a known Taft man. Connecticut's National Committeeman Sam Pryor—vice chair and soon to be a known Willkie man—assumed control of the arrangements committee. "Although no one outside the Willkie camp realized it at the time," Sam Pryor's son confessed long after the protagonists were dead, "the entire convention machinery belonged to the Willkie team" as fifteen thousand Republicans streamed into Philadelphia's impressive Thirtieth Street Station on a scalding hot June 23.

Ralph Williams's death had come three days after the British prime minister, Winston Churchill, flew to Tours, temporary headquarters of the French government. Churchill found his counterpart, Paul Reynaud, surrounded by defeatists urging him to demand that Great Britain release France from her commitment not to seek a separate peace, an eventuality that would place the French fleet at Hitler's disposal. A shaken Churchill departed, leaving Reynaud and his cabinet preparing to decamp for Bordeaux the next day, May 14, the day the *Wehrmacht* entered Paris. On the very morning of Williams's fatal coronary, the British Parliament approved the "indissoluble union" of Britain and France as one nation, the most extraordinary act in its history.[3] When the extraordinarily extended archives embargo on British covert intelligence activities in the United States during World War II is lifted in 2041, those documents may put the quietus to persistent rumors that Robert Taft's chairman of the Committee on Arrangements for the GOP Philadelphia convention was collateral damage in Great Britain's desperate imperative to shape the outcome of the American presidential election of 1940.[4]

Wendell Willkie was no longer a dark horse, then, when the convention opened on June 24. Three days before the Philadelphia convention opened, Gallup placed Taft and Vandenberg tied at 8 percent; Wendell at 29 percent surged to Dewey's diminished 47 percent lead. It was then that FDR's cousin and influential syndicated columnist Joseph Alsop marveled that Wendell's meteoric rise must spring from the people—from "the grass roots." As Oren

Root's barrage of Willkie telegrams flooded Republican National Headquarters, Sam Pryor echoed Alsop: "There is no possible way this great spark of enthusiasm can be manufactured."[5] John Hamilton, chairman of the National Committee, was now a Wendell Willkie convert. Joseph Martin, the GOP House minority leader and the convention's chairman—although an isolationist—abided the pro-Willkie consensus of his Massachusetts delegation led by Leverett Saltonstall, the state's interventionist Brahmin governor. The convention keynote speaker, the ebullient Harold Stassen, had been a Willkie partisan since their joint Des Moines radio address sponsored by the Cowles brothers. The galleries would be occupied 10–1 in favor of Oren Root's Willkie Clubbers. Finally, Ralph Williams's keys were in Sam Pryor's pocket.[6]

When asked to explain his phenomenal emergence, Wendell affected that Will Rogers naturalness the public found so disarming: He told the press that his rising support might mean that he was "a hell of a fellow . . . but I think it means . . . I represent a trend, or am ahead of a trend." He guessed it meant that he was a movement. Indiana's great populist sage, Booth Tarkington, twice awarded Pulitzers for his fiction, certified Wendell's authenticity as one "familiar to us, a man wholly natural in manner, a man with no pose, no 'swellness,' no condescension, no clever plausibleness. . . . A man as American as the courthouse yard. . ."[7] Still, Alice Roosevelt Longworth stuck to her opinion that all the hullaballoo came from "the grassroots of ten thousand country clubs." Wherever it came from, the Willkie surge greatly alarmed isolationists like Senator Henry Cabot Lodge Jr. and New York Representative Hamilton Stuyvesant Fish III. Fish, fiercely against "interventionists and warmongers," yet a highly decorated officer of the famous Harlem "Hell Fighters" of World War I, brought fifty likeminded members of congress to the convention whose expenses were provided by a German intelligence operative.[8] But the Willkie surge continued.

Wendell's Philadelphia advent on Saturday, June 22, was pure Jimmy Stewart in *Mr. Smith Goes to Washington*, the Frank Capra box-office success released the previous year about a heroic hayseed congressman. Leaving Thirtieth Street Station with Edith,

Davenport, Halleck, and several others for his egregiously modest five rooms at the Benjamin Franklin Hotel, a relaxed Willkie jawed with a congenial swarm of reporters. A much complimented Edith departed all smiles by cab for their rooms. "I'm going to walk there to see what this convention city looks like," Wendell told the reporters. "If you have any any questions, why don't you walk along with me?" Too much of the "City of Brotherly Love," like its Second Empire–style old City Hall, suffered in those days from a municipal ambition overtaken elsewhere: in particular, by New York City for finance and culture or Chicago for industry and architecture. W. C. Fields's 1925 epitaph quip, "All things considered, I'd rather be in Philadelphia," revealed a want of dynamism that belied this third-largest American city's historic reminders of having cradled the birth of the republic.

As though he had actually been there with the gabbing reporters, Charles Peters in *Five Days in Philadelphia* virtually walked alongside Wendell to the Willkie campaign headquarters at the Land Title Office Building on Broad Street, and from there to Oren Root's Willkie Clubs storefront on Market Street. "Ask me any damn thing in the world. Nothing is off the record," Wendell guaranteed. "So shoot, ask me anything you want." Damon Runyon, as famous and as unbuttoned as Wendell, did just that, following the candidate as he headed "right into the bar" at the Bellevue-Stratford, the convention's headquarters. "He had a handshake like a guy squeezing an orange," admired Runyon.[9] The easy, breezy access of a contender who admitted to "usually" sleeping on Sundays, smoking three packs a day, and drinking heavily, contrasted with Dewey buttoned up in seventy-eight rooms at the Walton or elusive Taft and Vandenberg with 150 hotel rooms between them at the Franklin and the Adelphi.

Wendell served up opinions like a sweepstakes celebrant at the bar—all six feet one and 210 pounds—awing the packed room, opining darkly of a possible third Roosevelt term and asking rhetorically, "Since he won't discuss the principles of a third term, what does [FDR] think about a fourth term?" Wendell said he would keep much of the New Deal legislation. The problem was FDR and his army of bureaucratic parasites. The other problem,

Willkie made clear, was the foreign policy choices incumbent upon the Republican party in the face of a Nazi-occupied Europe. Joeseph Newton Pew Jr., the Pennsylvania industrialist and political boss, was another problem Wendell didn't care for. He didn't like or respect his brand of politics and "would not allow myself to become part of this policy of returning to the days of Harding and Coolidge."[10] Wendell's cultivated "hayseed from Wall Street" act resulted in a major misreading of his political sophistication by two of journalism's most sophisticated, Arthur Krock and Turner Catledge of the *New York Times*. Leaving their hot hotel that same evening to stroll the city, Wendell and Edith encountered Krock and Catledge, who ventured to ask about selection of floor managers. Astounded when Wendell claimed never to have thought of a "floor manager," the two columnists suggested Governor Baldwin and promptly reported their scoop. Newton Baker's erstwhile floor manager had already lined up Davenport, Halleck, Stassen, Kenneth Simpson, Sinclair Weeks, and a couple of others as floor managers.[11]

While the press had ready access to Wendell, delegates pledged to Dewey, Taft, and Vandenberg were finding guest tickets in suspiciously short supply. A veteran delegate had never seen anything like it. "Delegates can't even get an extra ticket for a friend," he complained. Pryor's arrangements committee had given all but 10 percent of the free balcony passes to Root's young Willkie supporters. Monday's main event, Governor Stassen's keynote, punctuated the first day, the twenty-fourth, but Willkie supporters were by no means alone in wincing at the formal address of RNC Hamilton's earlier in the day. "Americanism and Patriotism" was vintage John Hamilton, the party chieftain whose hardline philosophy some believed had spoiled Alf Landon's chance of defeating Roosevelt in 1936. On the eve of this their twenty-second National Convention, two of the party's venerables, Henry Stimson, Hoover's secretary of state, and Frank Knox, Landon's vice presidential running-mate, accepted positions in FDR's cabinet as secretary of war and navy, respectively. Speaking ex cathedra, as it were, Hamilton blistered these distinguished Americans in almost violent language as traitors excommunicated from the party of Lincoln. Wendell, secluded at the Benjamin Franklin, kept his peace uncomfortably, but there were to be repercussions from "Americanism and Patriotism."[12]

The theatrics preceding the "Boy Governor" Harold Stassen hushed the delegates and guests. On Hamilton's command and Pryor's instructions, a blue spotlight enveloped the convention platform where Archbishop Dennis Dougherty invoked divine guidance and the Philadelphia Orchestra and the Lynn Murray Chorus from New York delivered the spellbinding "The Ballad for Americans," A Federal Writers Project cantata by John Latouche and Earl Robinson originally called "Ballad for Uncle Sam." The cantata had been renamed and repackaged after singer Paul Robeson's magical delivery over CBS Radio the previous November. Innocent or ignorant of its New Deal origins, fifteen thousand Republicans belted out the lyrics: "Who are you?" "Well, I'm everybody who's nobody. I'm just an Irish, Negro, Jewish, Italian, French and English, Spanish, Russian . . . Czech and double-check American." Stassen, precocious and even five years younger than thirty-eight-year-old Dewey, delivered a lengthy, memorized Monday night keynote address, the first televised convention speech in history, transmitted by NBC cameras with Lowell Thomas commentary. The Minnesota governor ended his keynote in the moment's special glow of comity, then joined Halleck and Davenport as a Willkie floor manager amid deafening decibels from the hall's Willkie-packed balconies.

Root's Ivy League legionnaires would pack the balconies each day, their stentorian chorus of "WE WANT Willkie!" crashing down upon the delegates. Fifteen-year-old Gore Vidal, hugely enjoying his first political convention in the company of his blind father, remembered the expressions on the faces of Alice Longworth (Taft), Archibald Roosevelt (Willkie), Gene Tunney (Willkie), Theodore Roosevelt Jr. (Dewey), along with Mrs. Robert Taft, Rudy Vallee, H. L. Mencken, and H. V. Kaltenborn, as necks craned upward. "For the first time in history a convention was to be stampeded by the gallery," Vidal recounted, "the audience, [merely] the extras." A wry W. E. B. Du Bois observed in the *Amsterdam News* that

"Dewey and Taft brought a few hundred delegates; Willkie, a few thousand gallery gods."[13]

With more than two-thirds of the thousand delegates non-pledged, the outcome of the first ballot on Thursday generated a level of excitement unusual for a Republican convention. Anticipated excitement Tuesday evening was palpable. The convention was set to hear Herbert Hoover. Bishop John Andrew Gregg's invocation had already set the portentous tone of the day. Gregg, an aristocratic brown-skinned prelate of the AME Church, spoke of these times' vexations, "when nation after nation is crumbling before the onmarch of the powers of lust and greed, and in ruthless disregard of human rights; yea . . ."[14] Hoover, stern, stiff, Buddha-like, still exerted a powerful tug on the loyalties of Republicans. He embodied the loathing of the class traitor in the White House that gave economic and political raison d'etre to millions of his unreconstructed admirers: Republicans who remembered president-elect Roosevelt's back-of-the-hand insouciance when his desperate predecessor begged advice and coordination to mitigate the ravages brought on by the collapse of everything. They were the party's Bourbons, people who had neither learned nor forgotten. To them, Herbert Hoover had spent a good number of days composing a convention appeal of unwonted eloquence and of principled nonintervention. Those who had read portions of it thought it probably the finest document of his career—a speech calculated to ignite a Hoover nomination stampede.

The ex-president's calculation was immediately evident when chairman Martin gaveled the delegates to respectful attention at 9 p.m. But rather than rising from the California delegation, Hoover, entering from a door at the Convention Hall's far end, strode like an emperor to the speaker's podium accompanied by Pennsylvania's Governor Arthur James, to a rolling thunder of applause and cheers. For all appearances, the moment recapitulated William Jennings Bryan conquering the 1896 Democratic Convention with his "Cross of Gold" speech. So it must have seemed to Sam Pryor, who had ensured optimal auditory quality the previous night for Harold Stassen's keynote. As Hoover delivered his rehearsed address, the momentarily expectant delegates gradually fidgeted, shifted, and resumed talking among themselves. It was obvious few could hear a word being said. Polite, dutiful applause began when the hall realized that the disconcerted former president had finished his speech and was leaving the podium. The faulty microphone remained a mystery until depositions obtained by Hoover's people revealed many months later that Pryor had arranged for the sabotage of the sound system.[15]

Wednesday's formal nominations for principal contenders Dewey, Taft, and Willkie came after the business of the party platform, a scrambled package of pledges, priorities, and prejudices: a constitutional amendment limiting the presidency to two terms; another amendment guaranteeing equal rights for women (ERA); a plank denouncing the rise of "Un-Americanism"; a constipated declaration on international conflicts. The party favored "aid to all people fighting for liberty or those whose liberty is threatened" so long as consistent "with the requirements of our national defense." The idealism of the Negro plank still reads strikingly, its pledge that all American citizens "of Negro descent shall be given a square deal in the economic and political life of the nation. Discrimination in the civil service, the Army, Navy, and all other branches of the government must cease." The disgrace of lynch law was not just denounced (in contrast to Democratic Party's evasion), federal legislation "to curb this evil should be enacted." The demand that "universal suffrage . . . be made effective for the Negro citizen" trumped the other party's voting rights commitment.[16]

Even though 71 percent of their votes had gone to FDR four years earlier, disillusionment with Rooseveltian civil rights had risen markedly among African Americans, especially among those represented by prosperous professionals influenced by the venerable W. E. B. Du Bois. The drumbeat of editorial complaint in major black newspapers such as the *Pittsburgh Courier*, Baltimore *Afro-American*, and New York's *Amsterdam News* was an encouraging augury that Wendell seized upon on Tuesday. His open house for Negro delegates in his hotel rooms captivated most of these skeptical men and women and made unusually good press for the candidate. He recounted his successful fight with the Akron, Ohio,

Klan and pledged that his White House would be responsive to their rights and interests.[17] With characteristic largesse he let it be known that his administration would put the implementation of the 1940 Party platform front and center. To be sure, the gesture was indicative of shrewd ethnic politics, yet also of Willkie's civil liberties sensibility that would evolve into a singular commitment to the advancement of full citizenship for people of color.

Wendell's ascension as the Republican Party's standard-bearer commenced that Wednesday night with his formal nomination before the convention. Dewey and Taft preceded him, each candidate's presentation speech followed by scripted prolonged applause, noisemakers, banners aloft, and marching round and round by loyal delegations ongoing for well over a quarter hour. Vandenberg's nomination was scheduled for Thursday. Wendell's Wednesday moment was momentarily heart stopping. No one came forward. The hostility exuded by the nominee's fellow Hoosiers was palpable. Old former Senator James Watson had set the tone of the delegation earlier. Wendell Willkie had been a life-long Democrat, he was heard to snarl. "I don't mind the church converting a whore, but I don't like her to lead the choir the first night."[18] Indiana's Charles Halleck, frozen by indecision, finally approached the speakers rostrum only after being summoned by Chairman Martin. Reassured by Martin's comradely hug, the new congressman met the silent hall's misgivings unabashedly: "Is the Republican Party a closed corporation? Do you have to be born in it?" Halleck's rhetorical question evoked a roar of reassuring denials. Bruce Barton, Madison Avenue's advertising maestro, followed Halleck with a guarantee that he could distinguish between a sentiment "that has been carefully let down from the top, and an instinctive liking that springs up from the bottom." Wendell Willkie, "though a newcomer among us," was the genuine article. "WE WANT Willkie!" exploded from the balcony, but nothing moved on the floor—not even the Indiana delegation—until the mayor of Syracuse, 220-pound Rolland Marvin, wrenched loose the New York State banner from the startled Dewey standard-bearer and led a posse of Willkieites onto the floor. Astonishing and almost comedic, the spectacle of the huge mayor and his trotting group spread a marching contagion to Connecticut and soon to one delegation followed by another.[19] The convention's third night, June 26, adjourned to the aural pyrotechnics of Oren Root's three thousand Ivy Leaguers: "WE WANT Willkie! WE WANT Willkie!"[20]

Forty thousand telegrams calling for Wendell's selection inundated convention headquarters on Thursday. Helen Reid's *Herald Tribune* endorsed Wendell on the entire front page that morning. Favorite sons and vanity candidates were formally nominated, although most—even Michigan's Arthur Vandenberg—without the tedium of presentation speeches. Vandenberg's campaign was something of a puzzle. A major isolationist and anti–New Deal force in the Senate, this indifferently educated but sharp-witted politician recently displayed both seeming indifference to the office of president and moderation of his socioeconomics. "Honestly," he could say he had never "been bitten by the presidential bug." His "The New Deal Must Be Salvaged" in the January 1940 *American Mercury* might have been written by Wendell. Washington insiders joked that Vandenberg strutted while remaining seated, and some called him suggestively the "Senator from Mitzigan" because they believed his vanity made Vandenberg putty in Mrs. Mitzi Sims's hands, a Canadian femme fatale, but also a skilled covert operative of British intelligence. After the senator's migration from isolationism to an interventionism resembling Wendell Willkie's, he and his biographers offered the epiphany of Pearl Harbor as the reason. Mitzi Sims's contribution to the survival of Great Britain remains a speculation to be resolved in a quarter century.[21]

Balloting commenced on Joe Martin's command at 4:41 Thursday afternoon, Alabama led with seven votes for Dewey, six for Taft. Arkansas, following Arizona, gave two votes for Willkie, his first, followed by the alphabetized delegation count from California to Wyoming: for the forgotten Hanford MacNider (34); Frank Gannett (33); Arthur James (74); the distinguished Oregonian Charles McNary (13); Styles Bridges (28); Joseph Martin (44); the obdurate Hoover (17). Main contenders were Dewey with 360, Taft with 189, Vandenberg with 76, and Willkie with a robust 105 that captured all of Connecticut's sixteen in the tally, as Ray Baldwin relished recalling.[22] "That sixteen votes . . . set the galleries on fire," and Baldwin saw people on the fence who figured that "now was the time to change." Stassen as floor manager acquitted himself brilliantly on this first balloting as he would throughout, holding back some 20 to 30 votes peeled off from various delegations to keep Wendell's math up on the second ballot that was called right away. "Start in small never to fall below what we had," co-floor manager Baldwin boasted. "Keep growing all the time." The momentum to Wendell continued, rising to 171 and more slippage for Dewey (338), while Taft rose to 208. Martin gaveled a dinner adjournment of proceedings until 8:30.[23] Five hundred and one votes were needed to win.

The principal contenders wasted no time at dinner. Taft's allies pressed Dewey to withdraw and Hoover to support the Ohio senator. Dewey and Hoover refused the favor. Willkie floor managers urged Alf Landon's Kansans to throw their votes to the businessman who defied FDR, but Landon held his delegation's votes in reserve for Dewey. A telephone call from Taft's men to Joseph Pew's estate came a cropper because the butler had orders not to disturb the imperious Pennsylvania oil man in his bathtub. The Pennsylvania delegation's votes remained pledged to the governor and favorite son Arthur James. The second-ballot loss of 22 votes from Dewey's merely respectable 360 votes was an unpromising augury for the nominee as the delegates returned for the third ballot.

A development that day had long-term significance. News reached America of the formal end of the mighty French army and partition of France into an occupied appendage of the Third Reich and a Fascist rump state. With the full might of the German war machine about to fall on Great Britain, the next president of the United States would face decisions of unprecedented historic magnitude. District Attorney Dewey's youth and national inexperience now troubled many more in the party. Harold Ickes's demeaning remark that Dewey had "thrown his diaper in the ring" was well known among the delegates, as was ultra-conservative columnist Westbrook Pegler's opinion that "as a presidential possibility, Dewey is preposterous." At the close of the third ballot after proceedings resumed, Dewey's drop to 315 votes compared to Wendell's spurt to 259 caused him to seek support from Vandenberg's delegation to press Martin for an adjournment. "Young Tom Dewey . . . is all washed up," Drew Pearson pronounced. "[He's] the victim of two blitzkriegs. One was Hitler's conquest of Europe; the other the purge of Ken Simpson."[24]

Martin decided to let Thursday's momentum build since Wendell was steaming ahead and Taft was buoyed by his rise to 212. Wendell's third ballot tally had been miraculously boosted when Dewey's nemesis Kenneth Simpson engineered a recount of the New York delegation vote. The revised math yielded fourteen more votes for a hefty total of twenty-seven, an announcement igniting stupendous detonations from Root's occupied balconies.[25] But Wendell's fourth ballot, announced from the chair well after 10 p.m. as 306 votes, unnerved him. Taft was now at 254 with Kansas, Michigan, and Pennsylvania considered solidly in his corner as the convention moved to an unprecedented fifth ballot. William Allen White, a strong Willkie backer and chair of the Committee to Defend America by Aiding the Allies, failed to persuade Alf Landon to throw the Kansas delegation behind the Hoosier phenomenon. Believing he was certain to lose to Taft, Wendell told Mike Cowles, "it has been a grand fight," and it was better not to win "by making any deal." Kansas, Michigan, and Pennsylvania were thought to be holding their votes for the Ohio senator. Dewey, trailing Willkie badly, telephoned Hoover urging him to throw his support to Taft, but the ex-president stubbornly held on to his handful of delegates. In fact, the crucial fifth ballot put Willkie 429 votes out front, with an advancing Taft receiving 377, and shouts from the balconies splintering the rafters. At a count of fifty-seven, Dewey was beyond rebirth. The despondent district attorney was rumored to be on his way to the convention to declare for Taft.

At 12:20 Friday morning, the twenty-eighth, as the sixth roll call proceeded, Vandenberg's campaign manager approached the podium with an urgent message. Convention chair Martin broadcast the Michigan poll to a momentarily silent hall. "The chairman of the delegation has asked me to announce the result as follows:

for Hoover, one; Taft, two; Willkie, thirty-five." On the sixth and final ballot, the dark horse utilities company candidate for the Republican nomination for president held 499 votes, two short of the necessary total. Throughout the yawing unpredictability of the proceedings, Pennsylvania's delegation held the majority of its seventy-two votes back for favorite son Arthur James. The state's political overlord, the Sun Oil President Joe Pew, supposedly taking a bath, had fobbed off a telephone plea from Taft after the crucial second ballot. Not to be upstaged by Michigan, however, Pew ordered Governor James to throw Pennsylvania's reserve votes at last to the candidate the delegates suddenly sensed was riding a winning wave. Pennsylvania put Wendell over 501 with many votes to spare. A motion to amend the roll call to make the sixth ballot unanimous passed immediately. Wendell's 988 votes ratified, the one-of-a-kind convention adjourned at 1:30 a.m.

But not the nominee. Wendell stayed up celebrating and talking until even his astonishing vitality shut down at half past four. While he slept, however, his handlers discussed the unfinished business of the vice presidential nomination. The man Helen Reid, the Cowleses, Roy Howard of the Scripps-Howard chain, Halleck, and even Davenport and Luce preferred had not only tried to organize a stop Willkie movement at the convention, he considered the vice presidency a demotion. Charles McNary, the sixty-six-year-old Senate minority leader from Oregon, was a pro-tariff, isolationist force on the Foreign Affairs Committee, effective opponent of FDR's controversial Supreme Court gambit, a major proponent of federal power projects in the West, and famous for advising colleagues that battles were seldom lost by saying less (an admonition Wendell never appreciated). By seven that morning, Oregon's National Committeeman and McNary's spokesperson, Ralph Cake, had obtained Wendell's reluctant sacrifice of Connecticut's Raymond Baldwin and acceptance of geographical balance and political opposition as a winning ticket designed to appeal to internationalists and isolationists. Baldwin, one of the original Willkieites, who would stand with Wendell in the years to come, stood aside.[26]

In keeping with the amazing developments of the week, the

nominee-elect broke precedent to come to the Convention Hall to address the delegates. As Wendell Willkie loped to the speakers' platform on the evening of June 28, with the exception of smiling wife Edith at his side and a handful of others, few of the delegates bellowing "Hi Ho Hi Ho It's Off to Work We Go" (Willkie's campaign song) knew that their forty-eight-year-old candidate's registration as a card-carrying member of the Grand Old Party was less than a year old. "I stand before you without a single pledge, promise, or understanding of any kind, except the advancement of your cause, the preservation of American democracy," he assured them. Many of the rank-and-file would remember a disquieting sensation only some time afterward that Willkie addressed them as "*you* Republicans."[27] In the euphoria of the moment, however, there was scant analysis, except among stunned strategists of some of the defeated contenders, that they had selected as standard-bearer a political neophyte who had been virtually unknown to party regulars twelve months earlier.

Harold Ickes sounded shaken. "Nothing so extraordinary has ever happened in American politics," he warned FDR. He insisted that there could no question about the necessity of FDR accepting a third term. Roosevelt differed from cousin Alice in his public praise of the GOP nominee's "grass-roots" sincerity. Democrats were "going to have a heck of a fight on our hands with him," he predicted to Walter Winchell. H. L. Mencken headed for Baltimore muttering, "[He was] thoroughly convinced that the nomination of Willkie was managed by the Holy Ghost in person," and by that he meant Sam Pryor in a white Panama hat and linen suit.[28] Rumors and not a few credible reports of convention delegates having been pressured by their banks and corporations to favor Wendell Willkie circulated for a while. Ralph Williams's untimely demise, Herbert Hoover's audio problems with his speech, Oren Root's balcony monopoly definitely did trouble the losers and even embarrassed some of the winners by their anomalousness. To the much debated question, "What Nominated Wendell Willkie?," the *Christian Science Monitor*'s Washington bureau chief offered a more reassuring answer than Mencken. "The self-evident fact is that an overwhelming tide of public opinion took the decision out of the hands of the delegates and the delegates took the decision out of the hands of the party leaders," explained veteran columnist Roscoe Drummond— "That is dynamic democracy at work."[29]

Had the Republicans elected a different leader in Philadelphia, it is virtually certain that the party would have fought the 1940 presidential election on a noninterventionist platform, as all but the victorious nominee believed that opposition to involvement in the war expressed the sentiments of mainstream America. Less certain is it that they could have defeated FDR, but it is more than likely that the results would have been close enough to undermine the imperative electoral mandate essential to a wartime president (until the second Bush presidency). Taft would have assailed FDR as a warmonger ready to waste American boys' lives in a European civil war. He and Vandenberg would have inveighed against a third FDR presidency as de facto unconstitutional. Dewey would have pandered to the isolationist sentiments of the majority of Americans. With Wendell Lewis Willkie as the GOP's charismatic leader, the eliding of noninterventionism, if not its entire abandonment, seemed hugely probable, as was the retention of the New Deal's fundamentals.

CHAPTER 7

SAVING THE GOP
TO SAVE FREEDOM

Edith with her champion, campaign trail, 1940. *Courtesy the Lilly
Library, Indiana University, Bloomington, Indiana.*

The new GOP leader resigned his $75,000 Commonwealth
& Southern presidency in Pine Street on July 1, affection-
ately reassuring anxious son Philip ("giving up such a good job")
that an adequate return for his talents was assured even if he lost
the election.[1] That same day he conferred amicably and profit-
ably with Tom Dewey, who would run for president in 1944.
Dewey was a partisan challenger for whom Wendell would bear

an increasing antipathy that was almost visceral, but both managed to present their best egos that morning. More than proffering campaign advice, New York County's natty chameleon district attorney offered the campaign services of his economics guru Elliott Bell and his able press agent Lamoyne "Lem" Jones, the latter to stick by Wendell permanently. The following morning Wendell traveled to Washington for a reciprocal introduction with Charles McNary, his reluctant vice presidential compromise who had notably disparaged Wendell at Philadelphia as a "Wall Street tool." McNary, as most critics did, discovered that dealing with Wendell Willkie in the flesh inspired confidence. The advice the urbane old Senate minority leader gave the new leader of his party was politically priceless: "In politics you'll never get into trouble by not saying too much"—a habit Wendell was congenitally incapable of acquiring.[2]

He now had a willing vice presidential candidate, but what he described now as his "crusade" barely had an organization behind it. Russell Davenport's plan called for him to accept the presidential nomination officially at Elwood, Indiana, in mid-August. The immediate challenge, though, was the personnel and structure of his campaign. Wendell's nomination pathway had been paved by internationalists of the Frank Altschul, Thomas Lamont, Henry Luce, Ogden Reid, and Oren Root variety. It was carried forward by pragmatists like Raymond Baldwin, Sam Pryor, Joseph Martin, and Charles Halleck. Final success had needed isolationists of the stripe of RNC chairman John Hamilton, advertising pioneer Bruce Barton, and Senate powerhouse Vandenberg. On its face, with RNC chairman Hamilton in the mix, it was an inherently unstable combination. Imperious John D. M. Hamilton, forty-eight, physically impressive, organizationally meticulous, yet blamed by Alf Landon's partisans for mismanaging the 1936 presidential bid, had never been liked by several of Wendell's key supporters. Davenport and Oren Root suspected Hamilton's heart was still with the GOP Old Guard. The internationalists—Helen and Ogden Reid of the *Herald Tribune* and William Allen White of the Committee to Defend America by Aiding the Allies—called for the RNC chairman's replacement. Altschul and Hamilton had exchanged fairly recent correspondence in which the latter's tolerance of veiled anti-Semitism within the party had been called to account. Then there was Hamilton's strident reaction to news at the convention of GOP senior statesmen Stimson's and Knox's defection to FDR's cabinet. Many delegates had been embarrassed by the extreme personal vilification of Knox and Stimson. The whisper of a recent personal indiscretion also seems to have hardened Hamilton's opponents.[3]

A professional politician would have hesitated before jettisoning the organizer largely responsible for the repair and reshaping of a party badly shattered after its 1936 electoral rejection. But Wendell was not only not a politician, the politician's *sine qua non* compromises made him impatient. "He looked upon the party as something unclean," his earliest major biographer believed, and his own putdown of it could be supremely dismissive. "Justin," Wendell had growled to a senior C & S officer, "the importance of my campaign is that it is a spontaneous reaction of the people." He wanted no organization "of politically trained people in my office."[4] A day or so after Wendell's discussions with Dewey and McNary, then, John Hamilton departed Pine Street after a two-hour meeting astonished and deprived of his title as Republican National Committee chairman. Martin and Halleck, quintessential party men, voiced their misgivings. Party regulars—the county chairs and city bosses—would have been more dismayed had not Pryor, Stassen, Landon himself, and even "Boss" Joe Pew, Pennsylvania's GOP overlord, intervened to dragoon a flustered Joe Martin into serving as RNC chair in addition to his demanding role as House minority leader. Hamilton's wounds were salved with the honorific title of executive director, responsibilities for the campaign's western operations, and a large salary emolument. There was the added balm of his senior partnership in Philadelphia's prestigious Pepper, Bodine, Stokes & Schoch law firm.[5]

Superficially resolved it seemed, yet Wendell's unceremonious dismissal of Hamilton registered in the groves of plutocracy like an insolent manifesto. Notwithstanding his palliative intercession, an appalled Pew was said to have privately bemoaned, "Willkie carved the heart out of John Hamilton."[6] The GOP's great paymasters held their tongues in public about the party's curious titular head, but Pierre du Pont was as clear in 1940 as he had been when his vast wealth underwrote the neolithic American Liberty League in 1934 that major party decisions were the prerogative of "the chosen ones to run this country and have the ability to do it in every particular."[7] Irenee, Lammot, and Pierre du Pont, the GOP's Delaware paymasters, Joseph Howard and Joseph Newton Pew, the GOP's Pennsylvania bankrollers, and Edgar Monsanto Queeny, the GOP's Missouri financial powerhouse, valued not merely John Hamilton's organizational gifts, they valued his political science IQ. Financed by Pierre du Pont, Hamilton had returned from England in 1937 determined to infuse the party of Lincoln with High Tory discipline after studying the rejuvenated Conservative Party's return to power.[8] Pending the outcome of the election, du Ponts, Pews, and Queenys decided to suffer mostly in private their considerable annoyance over Wendell's unexpected ouster of John Hamilton. Meantime, Hamilton, a bachelor until his marriage to a strikingly beautiful thirty-year-old recent divorcee, reported for duty as agent of Joe Pew. The former RNC chairman would become Wendell's nemesis after the election.

On July 9, his national popularity rising steadily, Wendell flew to Colorado with Edith to recharge his energies, refine his New Deal criticism, organize an efficient campaign, and—far more difficult than his novice party leadership allowed him to see—to harmonize the old and new organizational and philosophical elements in the crusade he now saw as moving beyond the tired shibboleths that had drained both national parties of vision and velocity. The Colorado Springs interval would run five weeks, right through the reconsecration of FDR until the formal nomination acceptance event scheduled symbolically in heartland America for mid-August. Davenport, constantly at Wendell's side and on his own dime as voluntary campaign manager, devoted himself to scripting the coming Elwood extravaganza. Martin, Pryor, Hamilton, and Gardner "Mike" Cowles came when problems demanded or as often as their professional obligations permitted. Herbert Hoover arrived, expecting a premium placed on his wisdom, but was discountenanced to find Wendell much more interested in talking with

Elliott Roosevelt about his vacation plans. Celebrities—journalistic, financial—appeared, frequently unannounced.

His opinion about a probable third term for Franklin Roosevelt had been asked before. Wendell's gravel-voiced retort was prescient: "Since he won't discuss the principles of a third term, what does he think about a fourth term?"[9] Finally, after many months of signaling his wish to retire to sylvan Hyde Park where, assisted by faithful Sam Rosenman and Harry Hopkins, he would pen thoughtful *Collier's* pieces and manage the first presidential library, the Sphinx of 1600 Pennsylvania Avenue spoke. Whatever his genuine reservations, FDR finally decided in the last suspenseful weeks before the Democratic National Convention, it seems, that the exigencies of war, the New Deal's unfinished business, and the uniqueness of his own leadership capacities imposed once again his place at the helm of the nation's destiny. With but one exception—Ulysses Grant (and that one broken by a four-year hiatus)—no president had ever formally declared for a third term of office.

By declining to declare his candidacy until the last minute, however, the masterful juggler had disingenuously encouraged a cluttered field of aspirants that included Vice President John Nance Garner, alienated by his boss's aborted scheme to enlarge the Supreme Court; Postmaster General James Farley, resentful that his boss no longer held his political skills indispensable; and Secretary of State Cordell Hull, a distinguished but uninspiring hopeful. There were others: Texas business wizard Jesse Jones; fellow upstate New Yorker and deeply principled Solicitor General Robert H. Jackson; even, conceivably, isolationist Montana Senator Burton K. Wheeler—all of whom did their utmost to engineer each other's elimination. But it was permanent White House occupant and presidential shadow Harry Hopkins who, but for his recent problematic Mayo Clinic cancer prognosis, had had the most reason to expect FDR's encouragement as a contender.[10]

Listening to the radio in Colorado Springs along with Davenport and several others as the Democrats convened in Chicago on July 18, Wendell slapped his thigh in pure satisfaction over the news and the certainty that the match with Roosevelt meant an exhilarating, cleansing face-off of ideas, policies, administrative know-how, and—above all—robust leadership. The president made known that he would not volunteer himself for another term, but Oval Office memories of so many sleights of hand by the wily patrician led Wendell to expect well-oiled convention maneuvers. FDR's opening-day message on July 18 that all the delegates were free "to vote for any candidate" was in reality a message to endorse himself. Even so, puzzled by the messenger's abnegatory claim of long having wished nothing more than to retire to family hearth and pastoral calm in the Hudson Valley, many of the delegates were dumbstruck about the alternatives. If much of the country saw Wendell's capture three weeks earlier of the Republican nomination as an exciting improbability ("managed by the Holy Ghost in person," according to H. L. Mencken), what Wendell and millions heard over the radio broadcast from the Chicago proceedings made a mockery of participatory politics. *Life* magazine called it "one of the shoddiest and most hypocritical spectacles in its history."[11] A mystery voice from the bowels of Chicago Stadium boomed over the loudspeakers three or more times, then loudly chorused by sanitation workers strategically stationed outside the stadium—"WE WANT ROOSEVELT!" Like Root's thundering balcony, the "voice from the sewer" (traced to a factotum of the Chicago machine) accomplished its purpose. The convention renominated FDR by acclamation, after which the displeased delegates were induced by a game Eleanor Roosevelt in person to accept her husband's controversial choice of commerce secretary and erstwhile Republican Henry Wallace as his vice president.[12]

Wallace was almost as much a surprise to Wendell as Roosevelt's decision not to seek a third term would have been. Without Franklin Roosevelt at the head of the Democratic ticket, the fight for the presidency would have been as devoid of excitement as a Republican victory would have been a certainty, he told Davenport and others as they assessed the decision's impact on their campaign strategizing. The president's people were inclined to pay Wendell's candidacy a similar tribute. Harold Ickes agreed with recent Supreme Court appointee William O. Douglas, who told FDR that he was the only Democrat "who could beat Willkie."[13] Syndicated columnist Walter Winchell reported a recent Oval Office interview quoting FDR's assessment that Willkie was "grass-roots stuff." "His sincerity comes through with terrific impact." This was the same utilities chieftain who talked back the better part of a decade, after all. In an off-the record cabinet meeting about the same time, he served notice that the "aura they are trying to build up around Willkie" had to be broken down soon. He wanted senators and congressmen "to start in on him Monday."[14]

Whether the candidate's time was put to optimal use at the sprawling Broadmore Hotel with Pike's Peak looming on the horizon was much debated during both the sojourn's last two weeks and long after Wendell's crusade had been battle tested. A Willkie loyalist decided some years afterward that they spent "too much time in Colorado. We let what was the hottest thing in the world get cold." The Willkie campaign style—shambling, sharp, engaging—coalesced at the Broadmoor. Next to being there, no description could have excelled Drew Pearson's "Covering Willkie": "Press conferences at Colorado Springs are held twice a day, once at 10 AM, the next at 2 PM; but the boys are subject to call at any time of the day or night. . . . Willkie awakens at 6:30 every morning and takes a walk around Broadmore Lake at a speed of approximately one mile an hour—his only form of exercise. The rest of the day he spends in his apartment. . . . He doesn't like to fish, swim, play tennis or golf. . . . At an informal poll taken among the thirteen correspondents who accompanied Willkie from Colorado Springs to Des Moines, ten of them believed Willkie will be elected. They all appeared to have fallen under the influence of his charm. . . ."[15] And the GOP nominee's stream of talk, Pearson could have added.

That he talked too much too openly about too many things was the general opinion. There was "virtually a point-for-point endorsement of the New Deal," fumed the Parmets, two indispensable conservative critics of these days: all those "statements about the need to regulate the 'force of free enterprise,' . . . collective bargaining for labor and wage and hour standards, federal regulation of interstate utilities, securities markets and banking as well as pensions. . . ." The genteel Socialist Party's perennial presidential candidate, Norman Thomas, scoffed brutally, "[Willkie] agreed with Mr. Roosevelt's entire program of social reform and said it was leading to disaster."[16] Even so, no less a GOP notable than Michigan's Arthur Vandenberg had dismayed the GOP Old Guard a few months earlier with his widely commented article, "The New Deal Must Be Salvaged." With the textbook lesson of Alf Landon's failed presidential bid virtually at his bedside, Wendell had to have realized that his New Deal accommodations were potentially self-defeating (viz., Ickes's "rich man's Roosevelt").

The political risk had to be run, nevertheless. His freewheeling press talks from the Broadmore's porch and carpeted lawn evidenced an astute strategy of ideological triangulation in progress: making peace with the best of the New Deal in order to personalize the superannuated style and substance of Franklin Roosevelt's leadership in a time of international crisis. Concerned that the political palaver reaching him in faraway Manhattan lacked substance, Walter Lippmann weighed in with a long, didactic letter that should have bolstered Wendell's two-track gamble of New Deal revisionism and FDR deprecation. For the brilliant Lippmann, whose foundational 1922 book *Public Opinion* depicted the public as a "bewildered herd," the demystification of Roosevelt in the public mind could be accomplished by projecting a superior image of authority. Wendell's opportunity, advised Lippmann, arose from the fact that "people feel insecure and want . . . a strong competent man. Roosevelt is not a strong, competent man," Lippmann was quite certain. "You have nothing to lose . . . by being Churchill rather than the Chamberlain of the crisis. You must not let him be the Churchill, for he is not a Churchill."[17] Lippmann's advice was valuable. Still, it was probably unfortunate that McNary's advice never had a chance.

Sam Pryor said all the world's "screwballs" showed up at Colorado Springs, and that by the time Wendell hit the campaign trail he was already fagged from too much talk about everything to everybody while organizational chaos reigned. Chaos at its worst was memorably described by a scrappy Irish Catholic attorney in a telegram to his anxious spouse distraught that her husband's earnings were bound to suffer while he worked as a Willkie volunteer. San Francisco attorney Bartley Cavanaugh Crum was forty that summer and in mid-career of a civil liberties trajectory heading, as Marcia Davenport admiringly recalled three decades later, "far out to the political left field" to defend Paul Robeson, Harry Bridges, and the "Hollywood Ten." Bart Crum brought a politically informed California outlook to Colorado Springs that helped balance the Willkieites' distinctly East Coast focus, a shared concern of Davenport and Root. He weighed in to assist the experienced *San Francisco Chronicle* editor Paul Smith, but found their efforts undone by Wendell's availability to the press and indifference to protocol.

The scene at the Broadmoor stunned him. "They plan to stay here five weeks to rest up for the rest of the campaign," Anna Bosworth Crum read. "Luce thinks too long. Mailbags piled up in their hotel suite. Only one secretary; they need at least three; Paul Smith has been called in to pull things together . . . Everybody complaining about lack of organization. . . ." "Bart says he *must* work for Willkie," spouse Anna Bosworth Crum's June 1940 diary entry recorded. "In politics, you can have what you have in religion," he promised her. "All the guys . . . have a sense of incarnation . . . We're all searching for a meaning in life."[18] A "sense of incarnation" was a grandiose characterization of philosophical Russell Davenport or partisan Drew Pearson, restless men in their forties like Crum. More likely, though, it did apply to many of the political knights-errant under thirty summoned to the Willkieite colors by their paladin Oren Root—thousands of exhilarated Associated Willkie Clubs of America members awaiting marching orders.

Meantime, what orders were given to regular Republicans? The crusader-in-chief paid scant regard for traditional Republican Party expectations—for the way things were done. All very well that a brace of recognized Democrat names had announced for Wendell: John Hanes, FDR's former treasury undersecretary; Lewis Douglas, FDR's first director of the Bureau of the Budget; ex-Michigan governor William Comstock; and at the top of the list, Al Smith, FDR's original patron now warped by his *parvenu* vindictiveness. Much was made of their presence at Colorado Springs, but their shelf life had run. They were not to be the vanguard of a sizable

Democrats-for-Willkie movement that Wendell buoyantly anticipated, but whose significant numbers never materialized.

Perceived indifference at Broadmoor to the care and feeding
of Republicans reached a crisis point. The plaint, "Whose party
is this anyway?" grumbled through the ranks. Majority Leader
Martin sent word in his dual capacity as RNC chairman that
Wendell's powers of coercion were urgently needed. The result was
a mixed blessing success. A group of important party men were
invited to Colorado Springs to vent their concerns. The presence
of Martin, Pryor, Hamilton, and Stassen at the reunion signaled
its historic importance. Wendell heard them out and responded
with winning bonhomie and a promise to listen better. However,
alert Oren Root, learning of the invitation, had arrived from New
York the day before with Wendell's ready assent. When the party
officials deplaned, they were greeted by the leader of the party
with the head of the Associated Willkie Clubs by his side. The
day's outcome was a compromise that not only advantaged the
upstart Ivy Leaguers but, more consequentially, propelled the
momentous decision to create three separate organizations to run
the presidential campaign. The National Party was placed under
Martin's direction; Democrats-for-Willkie were to follow John
Hanes, ex–New Deal treasury undersecretary. The Willkie Clubs,
now formally recognized, were the responsibility of Root. This
anomalous troika answered to Wendell Willkie, to whom, however, direct access rested with the visionary Russell Davenport.[19]
It might have been anticipated that a three-legged political campaign would prove difficult enough to keep on a straight course.

That Wendell's aggrandized conception of his crusade extended
to what kinds of campaign contributions could be solicited made
that course all the more complicated. No opportunity was missed
to boast that he had captured the nomination uncompromised. He
told *The New Yorker*'s Janet Flanner he believed himself "the only
candidate except George Washington who accepted the nomination with no commitments." (An eleventh-hour Convention concession to a Michigan delegate about federal judgeships was never
mentioned and, quite truthfully, not remembered.)[20] The word
went forth from Colorado Springs that huge donations from mil-

lionaires were unwelcome, the taint of Wall Street forbidden. It was public knowledge that Democrats feasted on the swollen gains of big city bosses—Hague of Jersey City, Kelly of Chicago, Flynn of New York, Pendergast of Kansas City. The leader of the GOP broadcast an antithetical policy of unprecedented uprightness. Ernest Weir, early Willkie contributor, National Steel Corporation president, now serving as party finance committee chairman found objections to his robust fund-raising nigh inexplicable. "This is the people's movement and I am going to keep it that way," Wendell ordained from the Broadmoor, committing his Republicans to strict adherence to the new Federal Hatch Act (optimistically described as "An Act to Prevent Pernicious Political Activities").

Corporate donations were banned, individual contributions limited to $5,000, and all cash donations in excess of $10 rejected. When General Counsel Henry Fletcher flew to Colorado Springs to present an artful dodge of the Hatch Act's $3 million restriction on political campaigns (a proposed $3 million ceiling for each of the party's three campaign units), Wendell administered a brusque dismissal. "This is a fine time to clear up the abuses which have for so long existed in our politics," he reprimanded Fletcher. The tamping down of money from Wall Street, General Motors, and US Steel proved unsuccessful, nevertheless, once the campaign got underway and substantial du Pont, Pew, Rockefeller contributions poured into GOP coffers for a final reported expenditure of $15 million compared to the Democrats' total of $6 million.[21] Wendell's crusader principles were to be tested and shredded, yet they temporarily were sincerely vouchsafed even as they undermined his crusade's financial integrity.

On the afternoon of the fifteenth, fifty-five thousand Hoosiers cheered Wendell and Edith as their automobile caravan sped from the Indianapolis airport southeast to neat little Rushville, the seat of Rush County, Edith Wilk's birthplace, and Wendell Willkie's campaign headquarters. Ten thousand Rushvillians, now accustomed to all the attention paid by the national press to themselves and the GOP nominee's sizable acreage devoted to pigs, cattle, and corn, were there to greet them. Russell Davenport's Elwood stage set was all but ready for Wendell's August 17 annunciation. The largest political assembly in American history of between 125,000 to more than 200,000 persons had started arriving by train, car, and bus. "Confident of Willkie Victory," a happy breathlessness possessed the *Chicago Tribune.* "As the first of the trains from Chicago and other cities reached town, downtown Elwood became jammed with the marching delegations of Republicans from many states," it reported. People were coming to Elwood in the hope that they could wipe out "the last eight years of uncertainty and regimentation and destruction of individual effort." So many had heard what Wendell said after Roosevelt trampled the hallowed tradition of two terms—"If one man is indispensable, then none of us is free."[22]

On a blazing hot Saturday afternoon almost one month to the day after the Democrats' Chicago acclamation of FDR, Wendell Lewis Willkie, forty-eight, lapsed Democrat and businessman without public office experience, formally accepted the presidential nomination of the Republican Party. He promised to lead a rejuvenating crusade across America that pared back the tendrils of dogma and regulation from the people and their resources. "Only the strong can be free," he exhorted the great crowd in Callaway Park, "and only the productive can be strong."[23] Standard-bearer of his party, he announced himself committed also to a conception of politics in which principles subordinated party allegiance. Jeffersonian Democrats and Independents, liberals and Progressives were welcome, as were isolationists and noninterventionists who formed the backbone of the GOP such as the Hamilton Fishes, Bruce Bartons, Arthur Vandenbergs. To all who would follow him he avowed candidly a duty to espouse compulsory military service so that the United States became so well prepared that no foe dare threaten her and that she should have no need to fight foreign wars.

When their nominee shouted that two New Deal terms had been more than enough, the crowd's response almost drowned out Wendell's well-reasoned caveat. He told them that Wall Street had been the problem before 1932. The problem now was at 1600 Pennsylvania Avenue. The creed of liberalism he embraced opposed equally unregulated wealth and unlimited government power, the great extremes of recent times. Something more he knew not to say on this supremely partisan occasion was that he cared almost nothing about party loyalty and everything about his country's obligation to its ideals (obligations as *he* saw them). The address was long, some of it flat of affect, and the delivery uneven, but its conclusion roused the crowd to a standing five-minute hurrah, thrilled by Wendell's "spectacular challenge to debate President Roosevelt," the *Chicago Tribune*'s excited Philip Kinsley reported. "[The candidate] offered to debate personally his Democratic opponent on public platforms throughout the nation as did Abraham Lincoln and Stephen A. Douglas 82 years ago." Gloves were off, man to man in the best tradition of American democracy, yet readers must have noticed Kinsley's observation that Commander-in-Chief FDR said he knew "nothing about the challenge, since he had spent five hours visiting 84,000 men and 7,000 officers."[24] The historic day ended with a hardy midwestern dinner enjoyed with some of Elwood's leading citizens, followed by brief contemplation at his parents' gravestones, where Herman's inscription rang true: "He Dedicated His Life to His Children," while Henrietta's said everything: "A Woman Driven By an Indomitable Will."[25]

Gallup found Wendell leading the incumbent at the end of August in twenty-four states totaling an Electoral College majority. Middle-income voters were said to prefer Wendell by 53 percent.[26] FDR, unfazed, let it be known that he would find no time for forensic sideshows what with the survival of Great Britain a close call and the United States committed to becoming the "Arsenal of Democracy," as proclaimed in his eloquent address at Charlottesville, Virginia, that June. Still, although he claimed to be too busy to debate his Republican opponent, FDR—reading the man's inner conviction—had encouraged a cadre of distinguished New York interventionists to try procuring Wendell's tacit approval of a risky executive arrangement with the hard-pressed British. Lewis Douglas and William Allen White, members, as was Wendell, of the Century, New York's most prestigious literary club, had succeeded in doing so just before Wendell departed Colorado Springs. Century Club membership mattered to him. Its roster of leading interventionists listed FDR's cousin Joseph Alsop, future Secretary of State Dean Acheson, CIA founding director Allen Dulles, presidential speechwriter Robert Sherwood, and a dozen more who formed "Century Group," a subset of the club's influentials powerful enough to channel public acceptance of controversial national policy initiatives.[27]

Hoping he held a winning Poker hand, FDR nevertheless confided to his secretary, "Congress is going to raise hell about this"— his unprecedented executive action. On August 16, the day before Wendell's Elwood acceptance speech (and with what one supposes was pure coincidence), the White House released news of a stealthily crafted deal to exchange fifty mothballed U.S. World War I destroyers for ninety-nine-year leases on eight British bases in Bermuda, Newfoundland, and the Caribbean. Alert readers could have divined that a major evasion of the 1939 Neutrality Act was in the works at 1600 Pennsylvania Avenue.[28] The deal was generally well-received by the public as a savvy bargain, but congressional Republicans were infuriated. The GOP leader's duty, as they clearly expected, should have been unambiguous: deny Franklin Roosevelt all leeway from his own 1940 Democratic Party noninterventionist platform—to wit, "not [to] participate in foreign wars, and we will not send our army, naval, or air forces to fight . . . outside of the Americas, except in case of attack." The Roper Survey calculated that 29.9 percent of Americans wanted nothing to do with any warring country, even to trade with them on a cash-and-carry basis. Fourteen percent favored food and material assistance, but strict neutrality unless Great Britain was invaded.

Yet, Wendell Willkie's unofficial agreement not to attack the destroyers-for-bases gambit before it was formally consummated— as it was on September 2—spoiled for his campaign a decisive opening move.[29] The inescapable noninterventionist hindsight was that in the wake of those fifty obsolescent destroyers would follow a lend-lease armada, an end to neutrality, and an inevitable *casus belli*. His passive collusion ignited a party firestorm demanding bald prestidigitation on his part. A properly alarmed Wendell— sounding like a proper politician—declared, "This executive decision [was] the most dictatorial action ever taken by any president.

It does us no good to solve the problems of democracy if we solve them with the methods of dictators or wave aside the processes of democracy."[30] The protective-cover statement (which Wendell privately regretted) came too late to derail FDR's designs—sophisticatedly channeled by the influential Century Group—yet it did draw much of the poison from stung GOP isolationists like Hamilton Fish, Bruce Barton, and Arthur Vandenberg. Curiously, and temporarily unbeknown even to Wendell, his isolationist vice presidential running mate, McNary, had also promised FDR tacit acceptance of the exchange. All politics being local, Oregon's senior senator was grateful to the New Deal for the recently completed Bonneville Dam on the Columbia River.[31]

Pressed by Minority Leader Martin to massage egos and recharge enthusiasm, Wendell summoned eighty party leaders from twenty-one states to a two-day confessional in Rushville on September 2. The powwow succeeded. The local ladies outdid themselves serving up vast amounts of fried chicken at the Masonic Lodge. Oren Root's resented upstarts were nowhere to be seen. The standard-bearer spoke just the right words from the front porch of the house to which he said he would one day retire to write his memoirs. He told them they must carry back to the clubhouses the message that, "just as the leader expects loyalty, . . . so is the rank and file of the party entitled to the support and loyalty of the candidate."[32] He renewed his pledge to assail the third-term juggler in the White House, dismantle the spent force of his New Deal central planning, and above all expose the Roosevelt administration's covert interventionism. Surely, every one of those reassured party regulars departed Rushville without suspecting even the possibility that their leader believed himself constrained by a Wilsonian imperative to which party loyalty must be subordinate.

Not long before, he had secretly assured Lord Lothian, England's mortally ill ambassador to the United States, that he would do all he could to help Great Britain survive. To the amateur who had cut his teeth at the 1924 Democratic National Convention that abandoned the challenge of the League of Nations, what his fellow citizens faced in late summer of 1940 was, he believed deeply, the imperative that they honor a historical obligation. On returning from London to his Washington post, Philip Henry Kerr, Eleventh Marquess of Lothian, had abandoned diplomatic starchiness and rocked the American press corps and surprised the administration with his plainspoken averral: "Boys, Britain's broke!" FDR would honor the terminally ill Lothian's service with an unprecedented, well-scripted Arlington Cemetery interment that December. Well before then, Winston Churchill's government would receive Lothian's report of his confidential conversation with Wendell Willkie that the leader of the Republican Party was "in favor of doing everything possible to see that Great Britain did not get beaten in the war. . . . [But because] of the overwhelming desire of the United States not to get involved in the war . . . [it] would be necessary to convince the American people about every particular step."[33]

A father's son who imbibed in infancy the Prussian antipathies of the Forty-Eighters, Wendell had not been so absorbed by his losing fight with TVA not to predict the worst from Edith's alarmed concerns after her visit to son Philip at Heidelberg University two years earlier. Signs of war were brewing. "It gave you the creeps . . . the marching, marching," she told him.[34] *Kristallnacht* befell Germany's Jews later that year and an appalled FDR withdrew his ambassador. By summer 1940, the grand design of Hitler's thousand-year Reich was almost completed. As the Willkie campaign team prepared to leave Rushville, enough was known about the aerial apocalypse in British skies the day after his Elwood speech—the "Hardest Day"—when the RAF and the Luftwaffe fought their greatest air battle, to fear a British capitulation. For Wendell, then, the short-term partisan gain of checkmating FDR's destroyers would have been internationally dishonorable in the long term. Equally so, he now decided, would be his opposition to national military service introduced immediately after France's capitulation at the end of June. He had justified compulsory military service in his Elwood address. He held Martin and McNary to finding enough Republican votes to save the Burke-Wadsworth Selective Service Bill after its final presentation in early August.

The issue soldered solid a furious opposition of the unalike, antithetical, and unforgiving. Divines, Catholic and Protestant (Father Coughlin, Harry Emerson Fosdick), professors and university presidents (Charles Beard and Robert Maynard Hutchins), labor and the left (John L. Lewis alongside socialist Norman Thomas and CPUSA head Earl Browder). Congressional Republicans balked in the Senate, twenty-three against selective service to McNary's eleven on August 28, joined by Taft and Vandenberg. Montana's Burton Wheeler, isolationist to the core, foretold Armageddon if the bill passed. "You slit the throat of the last democracy still living," he thundered from the Senate well, and was joined in his jeremiad by Kansas's Arthur Capper who cried the bill would "Prussianize the young in the name of democracy." House Republicans unsuccessfully followed suit eleven days later, 112 nays to Martin's 51 ayes and Wendell's endorsement.[35] Wendell, hand in glove with Martin, prevailed against an amendment by FDR's own Hudson County representative, Hamilton Fish III, limiting selective service to 400,000 men and delaying its start by sixty days. So it well should have been that FDR publicly acknowledged his opponent's help when he signed the Burke-Wadsworth Bill into law on September 16. For both leaders, however, the struggle to defeat the isolationists, noninterventionists, and pacifists had just begun.

The twelve-car Willkie Special that would extend en route to sixteen, with Edith, a brace of GOP notables (a Lodge, a Roosevelt, a Vanderbilt, Robert Taft's law partner John Hollister), forty reporters, and thirty staffers aboard, steamed out of Rushville on the evening of September 12. It would travel a thirty-thousand-mile circuit in seven weeks, breaking William Jennings Bryan's 1896 campaign record, and generate more popular passion than the Great Depression election of 1932 and no less enthusiasm than the Obama-McCain campaign sixty-eight years later.[36] Fedora aloft, Wendell announced from the caboose that he would "talk in simple, direct Indiana speech," and he kept his promise more often than not. His Hoosier *élan* and four or more campaign managers (Davenport, Martin, Hamilton, Pryor, and Root) and alternating speechwriters of two or more (Davenport, Root, Crum, Joseph Barnes, and sometimes Mike Cowles and Henry Luce) inevitably made for confusion—as when Wendell, told that he was in Cicero not Chicago, shouted to the crowd, "Then to hell with Chicago!" Marcia Davenport remembered "the whole thing was hell—the journey, the crowds, the blasting heat, the noise, the confusion, the gnats . . . the plans that went awry." Large athletic Edward protected his brother's ebullience. Marcia said Russell was "a fountain of anarchy."[37] Harold Gallagher, fellow midwesterner, American Bar Association notable, and future Willkie law partner, more often than not kept the train on its furious schedule.

But ten thousand African Americans in Chicago's Negro League American Giants Baseball Park cheered his promise of an antilynching statute, an end to segregation in government, and abolition of poll tax disabilities in voting. Major black newspapers—Baltimore *Afro-American, New York Age,* and *Pittsburgh Courier*—endorsed him. The *Chicago Defender,* the country's largest black newspaper, praised Wendell's superior ability to inspire the common man, in contrast to FDR. For the time being, Colonel Robert McCormick's fiercely isolationist *Chicago Tribune* warmed almost as much to the candidate as the *New York Times, Herald Tribune,* and the mega-circulation New York *Daily News.* He was hit in Chicago (a near miss for Edith) by working-class eggs, but the real test lay in working-class towns ahead, as when his manhood was challenged after Edith was badly splattered boarding the campaign limousine in Pontiac's town square. Before her fighting-mad husband could shed his jacket, Edith gracefully defused the tension by handing out roses from her bouquet to small boys nearby. Grand Rapids was riskier, a large rock crashed through the limousine's plate-glass window. New York's Boss Edward Flynn called for punishment of guilty persons and Congress passed a resolution condemning rowdyism.[38]

The campaign began to draw huge crowds whom the irrepressible candidate (regularly abandoning the microphone to speak directly) inspired, amused, and sometimes confused. An unimpressed Taft snorted that "wisecracking which keeps the nominee on the front page every day [may] really gets results, but I rather doubt it." Franklin Roosevelt left him no other choice than to create a straw man, a chief executive whose incompetence left the United States militarily unprepared after wasting millions in a belated, confused rush to rearm. Then there were the nation's banks holding hundreds of millions of dollars for which no productive resurgence yet existed to capitalize. "Production!" his shouted mantra. "Production creates jobs. I can get the factories back to their production!" A couple of times, he promised results no presidential candidate would make until the hyperbolic campaign of the unfortunate Donald Trump. He would make this country "so strong economically, . . . build a defense program so great, . . . will teach the doctrine of national unity so much, that no dictator will dare to strike or touch this great free land of ours."

For good measure, he lambasted FDR for imposing "state socialism" but reaffirmed his commitment to an efficient, budget-balanced New Deal. Roosevelt's third-term apostasy—"NO THIRD TERMER!"—continued to serve as a well-received charge, although more signs announced "BETTER A THIRD TERMER THAN A THIRD RATER" on the hustings. Wendell tried out his new Wall Street Marxism in Cleveland that ruffled solid GOP Halleck. "Labor is prior to and independent of capital," he shouted. "Capital is only the fruit of labor and could never have existed if labor had not first existed." Cheers in Pittsburgh greeted his promise to appoint a labor secretary from the ranks of labor, a worthy pledge he spoiled by adding his choice—unlike FDR's Frances Perkins—would not be a woman. A meeting arranged by Sam Pryor with the powerful labor chieftain John L. Lewis was in the offing.[39]

The Willkie Special streaked westward where the candidate served up mixed messages to good effect in California, where he was told he had to praise that state's venerable isolationist Senator Hiram Johnson, and attracted monster crowds of adoring Republicans in San Diego, Santa Anna, and Long Beach. In McNary's Northwest, where the erstwhile private utility champion pledged to complete the gargantuan electricity-generating Grand Coulee Dam, Wendell's appeal soared.[40] He proved adroit at sidestepping or publicly disclaiming embarrassing endorsements by the German American Bund, the Italian Fascist Organization, the American Communist Party, and Father Coughlin's powerful National Union for Social Justice. As for Coughlin's movement, Wendell announced he didn't have to be president, but he did have to keep his ideas clear "in order to live with myself."[41] On the other hand, the new America First Committee (AFC) of strange bedfellows such as A. J. Muste, the Christian Pacifist, and Bruce Barton, leading isolationist politician, posed a trickier problem.[42] The AFC sprang into life at Yale University literally just as the Willkie Special had steamed out of Rushville. Names that would induce head-scratching years later signed its call: Gerald Ford, Potter Stewart, Chester Bowles, Kingman Brewster, with a significant donation from young John Fitzgerald Kennedy, despite his influential *Why England Slept* that suggested decided interventionist inclinations. At its peak under General Leonard Wood, president of Sears Roebuck, the AFC's 800,000 dues-paying members in thrall to the magnetic Charles Lindbergh would soon demand forthright opposition.[43]

By late September, Gallup interjected a dull note. It found that Wendell's Electoral College strength had slipped to 78 and 45 percent or less of the popular vote. Friction abounded in the Willkie Special "Squirrel Cage" where speechwriters, journalists, and policy gurus cohabited competitively and a consensus built that Russell Davenport was a disaster.[44] Hoarse from stubbornly shouting without a microphone, frustrated by Roosevelt's invisible presence, Wendell became reckless on the hustings and even charged FDR with having agreed in 1938 to "sell Czechoslovakia down the river" in a phone conversation with Hitler and Mussolini. Backing down from outrageous falsehoods, he made a calculation in the vintage tradition of transactional politics that dismayed William Allen White, Walter Lippmann, Arthur Krock, Dorothy Thompson, and his many internationalist supporters. Wendell commenced a series of fierce attacks against FDR as a warmonger. If Roosevelt refused to accord him and the nation the respect of forthright, reasoned, instructive discussion of the burning issues of war and national recovery, he resolved to paint the man in the White House in bloody red hues. Wendell Willkie II offered a ready forgiveness: "Grandfather just decided he needed to win," was his guess to an interested biographer.[45] In any case, "He treated the American people to the best knock-em-down-and-drag-em-out campaign since Bryan," *They Also Ran* presidential chronicler Irving Stone judged. Wendell "lash[ed] out at nearly everything Roosevelt did on both the domestic and international scene."[46]

On October 8 in the Bronx, all but calling FDR a warmonger, Wendell belted out rhetorically, "Who really thinks that the President is sincerely trying to keep us out of war?" He demanded to know, "Are there any international understandings to put America into the war that we citizens *do not* know about?" Elect me, he shouted on stops across the Midwest, and "when I am President I shall send not one American boy into the shambles of a European war." In St. Louis, October 17, he told the crowds the choice was peace with Willkie or "your boys will be sent overseas" with Roosevelt. The warmongering results were dramatic. Wendell's polls climbed in the last two weeks of October, trimming FDR's lead in half and smartening the odds on Wall Street to 7–5 from 12–5.[47] Hamilton Fish and Independent Democrat Burton Wheeler orchestrated tributes to the candidate in the House and Senate, respectively. Taft, Dewey, and Landon spoke on his behalf, as did the embittered Al Smith and other well-knowns of the Democrats-for-Willkie variety. Lindbergh and 800,000 America Firsters were buoyed by the assumption that the candidate would enforce the Neutrality Act, as were Communists and fellow travelers obedient to the *Realpolitik* of the 1939 Molotov-Ribbentrop pact (Stalin's prophylactic response to Munich). Historian Charles Beard and Chicago University president Robert Maynard Hutchins publicly applauded. The *New York Times* editorialized euphorically, "MR. WILLKIE ON THE UPSWING." Lord Lothian, on his last legs, took notice and reassured Churchill—his campaign rhetoric notwithstanding—that the British Empire might do quite well with a Willkie victory.[48]

The narrowing polls instigated sharp attacks from the *Nation*, the *New Republic*, and other progressive publications. The *New Republic*'s Willkie Special edition called Willkie "a Wall Street insider as slick as they come" and blamed the Great Depression on his ilk. Courtly New York Governor Lehman and feisty Mayor LaGuardia abandoned restraint to imply that Hitler, Mussolini,

Stalin, and Hirohito were rooting for Roosevelt's opponent.[49] Dorothy Thompson, parting ways with her *Herald Tribune* employers, libeled Wendell the American Hitler. An African American Democratic operative warned that Willkie was raised in a "sundown town," where blacks were forbidden after dark. Unfazed by Nazi and racist characterizations, Wendell bore down even harder on "Mr. Third Term's" hidden designs until, finally—fingers on the pulse of the polls and virtually ordered by the First Lady to face Willkie—the president emerged from his White House cover as commander-in-chief. To counter his opponent's willful misinformation and reckless accusations, he announced on October 18 that he would deliver five public addresses. Saving the British remained a low priority for many Irish Americans. The president's "stab in the back" remark about Mussolini's invasion of France had alienated a good many Italian Americans. Irving Stone's *They Also Ran* declared it was the first time since the 1916 Hughes-Wilson election that a presidential standoff entered its final weeks "with no one able to tell who was going to win."[50]

The Oval Office voice-recording system (the first of its kind), fortuitously not transcribed until four decades after his presidency, reveals the assiduous strategist of the Oval Office calculating not only the perfect moment to confront Wendell Willkie, but a Franklin Roosevelt roguishly engaged in the minutiae of his opponent's private life. With him to discuss the campaign were Sam Rayburn, the House leader, and future speaker, John McCormick of Massachusetts, both well attuned to the president's loquacity. "Now you'd be amazed at how that story about that gal is spreading around the country," Roosevelt laughed, relishing the Wendell-Irita affair and Edith's awkward part in it. "Now Mrs. Willkie may not have been hired," granted the president, "but in effect she's been hired to return to Wendell and smile and make the campaign with him." Politics makes strange bedfellows, was the point. However, Ickes had cautioned that they were barred using Irita Van Doren against Wendell because Vice President Wallace had compromised himself by corresponding with a mystic or psychic. As for his promised public duel with Wendell, FDR claimed he had calculated almost to the day when the polls would demand that he leave his wheelchair and appear to walk. The polls would show Wendell in "pretty good shape the first part of August," he mused within the hearing of the recording system. "Then . . . a bad slump, bad slump, so that I'll be way ahead on the first of October." After that, he predicted the polls would "start Willkie pickin' up, pickin' up—from the first."[51] FDR's timing was uncanny.

The capacity crowd in Philadelphia's Shibe Park stadium on October 23 saw a Franklin Roosevelt in top battle form as he disdained his adversary's libels. As for the existence of secret war plans, there were none, he declared. "I give to you and the people of this country this most solemn assurance: There is no secret treaty, no secret obligation of any form." On this same Wednesday, however, Wendell spoke before the annual Forum on Current Problems sponsored by the *Herald Tribune* at the Waldorf-Astoria where, again, he challenged FDR to a debate. Simultaneously, Al Smith, speaking to a Brooklyn Academy of Music audience, shared "a general belief among people that the New Deal is trying to get us into war." The following morning, the *New York Times* ended its two-term support of Roosevelt and endorsed Wendell, declaring the president's fiscal policies "disastrous failures" and his executive powers alarming. A day later, October 25, John L. Lewis, the most powerful labor leader in America, endorsed the GOP presidential contender over the three national radio networks.

Not as bizarre as it seemed at the time, the unexpected Willkie-Lewis entente brought together an erstwhile progressive Democrat and a lapsed righteous Republican, each equally enraged by Franklin Roosevelt's serene unaccountability. The *Nation*'s I. F. Stone guessed Thomas Lamont of the House of Morgan had arranged the Faustian bargain. In fact, as Mencken might have suspected, Sam Pryor hosted the meeting of the Republican leader and the United Mine Workers chieftain. Seething over FDR's alleged ingratitude to labor and his third-term arrogance, but soothed by Wendell's umasking of FDR's war designs and promise of a labor leader as labor secretary in a Willkie cabinet, the CIO founder summoned his unionized legions in his distinctive Welsh baritone to forsake the Democrats for a better New Deal. Although the publicity value of Lewis's endorsement was considerable, it remained to be determined in a few days if organized labor's response would be more than lukewarm. That William Rhodes Davis, a shady Texas oil man with Nazi connections, had paid the networks the $80,000 Lewis broadcast fee was unknown until after the election results. John Hamilton had perversely refused Joe Martin's plea and Wendell's demand to raise money for the broadcasts. In the event, Lewis's endorsement was ignored by the AF of L and seconded only by the leftist unions obedient to Harry Gold, Mike Quill, and Harry Bridges.[52]

Two days after the Lewis bombshell, the Willkie camp awaited a bombshell it believed would be powerful enough to sink FDR's third-term possibility. That Sunday evening, two of Wendell's most influential supporters awaited the arrival of Ambassador Joseph Kennedy from London at La Guardia's Marine Terminal.[53] The ambassador was expected to declare publicly his decision to back the Republican presidential candidate. Obsessed that his country was blind to the hopelessness of the British struggle, Kennedy had made himself all but spurned at the Court of St. James's. Joe Alsop's syndicated column for December 19, 1939, breezily revealed that "our ambassador to England freely predicts the collapse of capitalism and the destruction of democracy and the onset of the dark ages." Joe Kennedy had an ingrained Irishman's resentment of the English, a bigoted Catholic's dislike of Jews, and (Treasury Secretary Morganthau suspected) a possible financial interest in a depressed international market. FDR regularly received British intelligence intercepts of the ambassador's correspondence and telephone exchanges deploring his government's folly. A Kennedy diary entry secretly communicated to FDR predicted that the war would show the world "what a great service Chamberlain did to the world and especially for Britain." His preference for a business-friendly Europe run by Germany was well documented.[54]

Almost as well documented, as far as Wendell believed, had been the confident assurances of Clare Boothe Luce, a brilliant woman of boundless ambition and enabling equipment, that Kennedy intended to break with Roosevelt. Although the Luces were one of the diadem couples of mid-century America—Henry's alpha persona and publishing empire, Clare's scintillating success as a playwright and essayist—they had lived together separately by the time Joe and Clare discovered one another's availability in the fall of 1938. During one of their trysts abroad, Joe had told Clare the previous spring at the London embassy that he would come back home, "get off the plane, and endorse the Republican candidate for president," a promise British counterintelligence duly communicated to the White House.[55] It was during their last assignation in May 1940 at the Ritz in Paris that Kennedy, almost *persona non grata* in London, ignored by FDR, anguished by his government's anti-German policy, repeated his decision to leave his post, fly home, and "get twenty-five million Catholics to throw Roosevelt out." British survival prospects had reached rock bottom, Kennedy was certain, despite Winston Churchill's defiant determination to continue fighting. He returned to London resolved to ignore his president's instructions to remain at his post. The Ritz concierge informed Clare she must pack and leave the hotel because the Germans were coming. When asked how he knew this, Clare was politely informed, "Because they have reservations, Madame."[56]

But there was no Kennedy bombshell on Sunday the twenty-seventh. Instead of a dramatic endorsement to give a final, decisive surge for a close victory, this example of great material success to millions of American Catholics waved aside the press to speak with FDR by telephone, then departed without making a statement for the city, where he remained a short time until he and Mrs. Kennedy flew to Washington for dinner at the White House. Attempts by the Luces to reach Kennedy in Manhattan failed. Years later, Lyndon Johnson, then a second-term congressman, recalled witnessing FDR draw a finger across his own throat at the conclusion of his telephone exchange with Kennedy. Speculation as to what precisely transpired in the Oval Office runs from disclosure of compromising British intelligence reports to promises of political support for Joseph Kennedy Jr. In any case, Kennedy praised the president on self-purchased radio time on CBS the night before the president was to speak in Boston. "I have a great stake in this country," Kennedy declared. "My wife and I have given nine hostages to fortune. . . . In the light of these considerations," he believed that Franklin Roosevelt should be "reelected President of the United States." The charge that the president would involve the nation in war, he insisted, "was false." Some sixteen years later, when Clare Boothe Luce asked Joseph Kennedy what had happened, he said, "I simply made a deal with Roosevelt"—himself for president, son Joe for Massachusetts governor.[57]

On October 28, a day after Joe and Rose Kennedy dined at the White House, the president, head cocked at signature angle, convulsed a great crowd at Madison Square Garden as it joined him in his hilarious repetition of "MARTIN, BARTON, AND FISH"—the obstructionist Republican trinity of Joseph Martin, Bruce Barton, and Hamilton Fish. Wendell was heard to say that when Roosevelt hanged Martin, Barton, and Fish on him, that he knew "[he] was licked." But Robert Sherwood, FDR's facile speechwriter, doubted Wendell was serious, "because Willkie never knew when he was licked," he said, and Sherwood's surmise was well grounded.[58] Even as news emerged of Kennedy's reversed course, Wendell absorbed the hard blow with a restrained observation that the distinguished ambassador had been deceived about the president's war aims. Then came Roosevelt's Boston Garden address on the thirtieth, which drove a stake through the heart of Wendell Willkie's war-scare appeal.

Until Boston, Roosevelt, with the full accord of his cabinet, accepted the necessity of qualifying any promise of noninvolvement in foreign wars with the caveat, "except in case of attack." But Wendell's hammer blows had been unnervingly effective— so much so, FDR decided, that the caveat had to be jettisoned, regardless of concerns among his advisors. He had said it before, an adamant FDR intoned before the eager crowd, but he would repeat it "again and again and again. Your boys are not going to be sent into any foreign wars." The president's absolute pledge of noninvolvement elicited Wendell's expletive about "that hypocritical son-of-a-bitch Roosevelt!" that informed his own equally unqualified statement later in the day at the Fifth Regiment Armory in Baltimore. Both presidential candidates thought the election-day results were a toss-up; their exaggerated appeals were the stuff of electoral life or death in its final days. Nevertheless, on October 30 at Baltimore, Wendell Willkie went too far. "On the basis of his past performances with pledges to the people," he shouted hoarsely, "if you re-elect "Mr. Third Term' you may expect war in April!"[59]

Wendell's election-eve denouement obviously benefited from the deep pockets of GOP donors, despite the $5,000 limitation on individual campaign contributions imposed by the Hatch Act. He spoke to the nation from New York City on the three national networks twice during the day and once that night. From other parts of the country, Taft, Stassen, and Al Smith for Democrats-for-Willkie made radio appeals for the Republican standard-bearer. Boxing phenomenon Joe Louis joined Clare Boothe Luce and John L. Lewis at Madison Square Garden to hear a hoarse Willkie shout that the reelection of Roosevelt would mean "the destruction of our democratic way of life. Help me, help me, help me save it!" The major newspapers and Gallup conceded an edge to FDR yet considered the results too close to predict confidently. "As the campaign entered its final week, business and social life were paralyzed," recorded novelist-biographer Irving Stone. "Nothing but the election was talked about. Partisans on both sides went about with a hysterical glint in their eye."[60]

Fifty million Americans voted on November 5, a record turnout in a population numbering 132 million. FDR's 449 Electoral college result swamped Willkie's eighty-two. Thirty-eight of the forty-eight states decided for the Democrats, but the Democratic victory margins were close in seven states—even closer in Illinois, New York, New Jersey, and Wisconsin. Indiana and Michigan went for Wendell, the latter probably thanks to John L. Lewis.[61] FDR's popular vote count of 27,308,000 was almost five million more than Willkie's 22,321,000, still an impressive GOP presidential record not significantly surpassed until Dwight Eisenhower's 1952 election. Joseph Martin, the postwar face of the GOP in the House, summed up the election in his memoir with the flat statement that no Republican could have won in 1940— "once France fell. That was the thing that beat Willkie."[62] Yet, it was the fear of involvement and deep isolationism of millions of Americans that gave the Willkie campaign its surprising eleventh-hour surge. Wendell Willkie had been an enormously appealing, credible presidential candidate who would probably have matched FDR in face-to-face debate. Still, he, like Alf Landon in 1936, was trapped by the paradoxical necessity of representing himself as an improved version of Roosevelt in order to defeat Roosevelt. A great many Americans, however, found the genuine specimen more satisfying in comparison.

The broad appeal of Wendell's Republicans was another matter entirely. Because a vote for the Abe Lincoln of Wall Street was a vote for Business America, it was almost as true, as one academic authority claimed, that it was a "class-conscious vote for the first time in American history," one that appeared to accomplish "what the socialists, the IWW, and the Communists could never approach."[63] Yet, such hyperbole discounts the class-conscious triumph of business in 1896. If more a political realignment than an ideological consecration of groups, the 1940 electoral victory did consolidate the New Deal coalition of big city machines, organized labor, southern whites, liberals, and minorities (Catholics, Jews, and blacks). That the New Deal triumph represented the defeat of a traditional party rather than of an innovating party leader became stunningly evident six days after the election when Wendell Willkie reconceived the meaning of political partisanship.

It remains one of those pivotal surprises in American politics whose explanation justifies a reasonable speculation from a significant participant's colorful memoir. The night after the election, Marcia Davenport "went to open the door—to Harry Hopkins[!]"—"the man on whom we had concentrated as much mental and verbal opprobrium as any personification of the New Deal." She had never before met FDR's shadow. "Hopkins was like a walking corpse, bone-pale, emaciated, bent and stooped with weakness," she wrote. "He shuffled into the drawing-room with me, saying to Russell, 'Tell me all about it. Tell me how you did it.'" The two of them—Wendell's campaign manager and FDR's consigliere—spoke privately in the study well into the night. Marcia appears not to have known what was said precisely. But she understood Hopkins's appearance as "corroboration of the great crisis beyond domestic politics, which was the real concern of Wendell Willkie and Franklin Roosevelt."[64]

With a fine sense of occasion, Wendell spoke from Manhattan's Hotel Commodore on Armistice Day, November 11, offering an eloquent statement of the obligatory role of the party out of power. His was a powerful party, Willkie stipulated. "Let us not, therefore, fall into the partisan error of opposing things just for the sake of opposition." His was a party ready to constitute "a vigorous, loyal and public spirited opposition." "Ours must not be an opposition . . . [falling] into the partisan error of opposing things just for the sake of opposition. . . . It must be an opposition for a strong America." For America to remain strong, he declared straightforwardly that Great Britain must be supported "to the limit of our ability—short of war." In so far as the New Deal meant "fight[ing] for the rights of labor, for assistance to the farmer and the unemployed, the aged and the physically handicapped," its program must be endorsed. But government cannot "dominate our lives," he emphasized, and business must enrich the life of the republic.

The defeated candidate finished with a quote from his idol Woodrow Wilson, that it was better to lose in a cause that he knew "someday will triumph than to triumph in a cause that . . . someday will fail." The "Loyal Opposition" speech sounded a note whose admonition sounds depressingly relevant to early twenty-first-century Republican politicians.[65] His paean to constructive bipartisanship occasioned the greatest tsunami of laudatory telegrams ever before received by a defeated candidate. With that speech, as an otherwise alienated Joe Martin appreciated twenty years afterward, Wendell "got off on the right foot with the whole country, Republicans included," especially Republican officials who breathed easier because their titular leader also asked that the Willkie Clubs either retire from the scene or choose to persevere as a force in public life under another name.[66]

At the time, though, few prominent Republicans—aside from Kenneth Simpson, who called it a "magnificent challenge to America"—commented publicly. Nor was there comment from Hopkins's boss. Ed Flynn, leader of the Bronx Democratic machine, revealed that FDR had not found time to listen to Wendell, which provoked Arthur Krock to rebuke the president in the *New York Times*. The following week, feeling spent but rather satisfied, Wendell flew with Edith as Sam Pryor's guests to Hobe Sound, Florida, for a five-week rest and recharge—to do nothing, the ex-candidate promised, but "read and fish," and not even "going to talk politics." Still, Pryor had given him something to think about just as they were leaving New York. It went to the heart of the organizational obligations many Republicans believed Wendell's anointment at Philadelphia had imposed. "I shall never say this again," Pryor told his friend, "but you could have been President if you had worked with the party organization." Whether or not Wendell would ever be willing to make such an unqualified choice remained yet to be seen. As for taking a holiday from politics while in Hobe Sound, a reasonable speculation holds that he applauded FDR's stirring fireside chat on the evening of December 29 calling on America to become the "arsenal of democracy."[67]

In reality, as the months ahead revealed, the success of FDR's wartime presidency and the design for the postwar world owed Wendell an incommensurable debt. Walter Lippmann, shortly reconciled with him, understood immediately the role Wendell envisaged for himself as a transformational leader rather than a mere politician possessing transactional skills. "Under any other leadership but his," the political commentator asserted, "the Republican party would have turned its back upon Great Britain, causing all who still resisted Hitler to feel that they were abandoned." The post-election Willkie-FDR *pas de deux* commenced immediately. James Roosevelt recalled hearing "great bursts of laughter" as Wendell and FDR met in the Oval Office the January evening before his father's third inauguration. The GOP titular head had announced his intention to fly to England on a personal fact-finding mission the previous week.

CHAPTER 8

PAS DE DEUX:
WILLKIE AND ROOSEVELT

Willkie and Winston Churchill in front of
No. 10 Downing Street, 1941. *AP Photo.*

ranklin Roosevelt's lend-lease legislation designed to shore
up hard-pressed British defenses with vast shipments of war
material plunged the Congress and the country into fierce debate.
Introduced on January 10, 1941, as H.R. 1776, of which no more
portentous number could have been chosen, the bill authorized
the president to sell, transfer, exchange, lease, lend, and other-

wise provide food, oil, information, and military materiel "to any country whose defense the President deems vital to the defense of the United States." Poor Joe Martin, regretting more by the day his dual role as House minority leader and RNC chairman, said that no single piece of legislation "generated such pressures . . . in [his] lifetime as the lend-lease bill." General Robert E. Wood, chairman of Sears & Roebuck and president of the new America First Committee (AFC), denounced the scheme as nothing less than "a blank check with the power to write away our manpower, our laws, and even our liberties." Even Luce's *Time* magazine marveled that "powers would go to Franklin Roosevelt [under lend-lease] such as no American has ever asked for."[1]

Three days after the bill's introduction came a bombshell that dumbfounded most Republican congressmen when their leader, days returned from a Florida vacation as guest of the Sam Pryors, endorsed the legislation. Wendell Willkie stated that when extraordinary crises arise, "democracy cannot hope to defend itself in any other way." Several days later, in an address to the Women's National Republican Club, he expressed himself more emphatically in support of the proposed lend-lease legislation. "Let me say to you," he pleaded, if the Republican party "allows itself to be presented as the isolationist party, it will never again gain control of the American government."[2] The Republican leadership of both houses reacted with incredulity and consternation. Taft, Landon, Hoover, and Vandenberg presumed to speak for the party rank-and-file as well as the great combination of pacifists, noninterventionists, and isolationists, to whom enactment of lend-lease would mean de facto nullification of the 1939 Neutrality Act and, as a certainty, war between the United States and Nazi Germany in response to inevitable U-boat retaliation.

If less than a third of the American population was adamantly noninterventionist at the beginning of 1941, its articulate spokespersons were the cream of the professions: university presidents and professors; scientists and publishers; industrialists and union leaders; clergy and artists. Two of its spokespersons, the matinee-idol Icarus, Charles Lindbergh, and the Savonarola of Detroit, Father Coughlin, could electrify tens of thousands and alarm the national government by their perfervid isolationist appeals. So much so, indeed, as to give pause to the legendary Kansas journalist and founder of the Committee to Defend America by Aiding the Allies, William Allen White. Attacks by the new America First Committee and the newer No Foreign War Committee, headed by scrappy Iowa conspirator theorist Verne Marshall, rattled White into saying that if his committee had a motto it should be "The Yanks Are Not Coming." The awkward offhand would result in White's eventual departure from his committee, a notable example of casualties to come from the great debate as noninterventionist ranks closed with Colonel McCormick's *Chicago Tribune*, Roy Howard's Scripps-Howard chain, the Hearst newspapers, and, above all, with the powerful AFC and its eloquent Colonel Lindbergh.[3]

Wendell had found the isolationist general managers (as he called them) waiting for him upon his return on January 5 from Hobe Sound's idyllic Jupiter Island. Much of the Willkies' vacation time Wendell had spent playing gin rummy, reading a small library's worth of books, and pondering his role as the titular head of a national political party in a time of international uncertainty. An engaging narrative at about this time was spun crediting Irita Van Doren and several close friends of hers for Wendell's decision to fly to England shortly after his return to New York. True enough, he had found his way back to a delighted Van Doren soon after losing to Roosevelt, now that the public display of marital propriety could be retired. Women friends knew of the deep distress their campaign-enforced separation had caused her. On the morning of Wendell's successful fifth-ballot nomination, she had been assisted sobbing bitterly from a ladies' powder room.[4] She readily welcomed Wendell's coy query as to whether he might review another book for her. Still, as to the trip abroad, as Wendell has left a brief description of his embarrassed need to be better informed about current British politics, he might be permitted the privilege of ownership of an inspiration.[5]

In any case, it seems pretty clear that Wendell left this wealthy WASP enclave—whose exclusion of Jews ended under his protest—with an inchoate plan to see Winston Churchill's beleaguered island firsthand. When the lend-lease legislation was introduced five days later, one Jeremiah Millbank, an enormously rich and incorrigibly isolationist Republican businessman, offered $2 million on deposit to be drawn upon "for radio and other expenses" if Wendell led the campaign against aid to Britain. Publisher Roy Howard, owner of the Scripps-Howard news syndicate and an early Willkie enthusiast, telephoned next morning to say that a finished, anti-lend-lease radio text was ready for Wendell to read.[6] The imperious publisher boasted that he had prepared statements and talking points for Landon and Hoover to denounce "Roosevelt the Dictator." Wendell sidestepped Howard's presumptuous offer with the excuse that he needed to think more carefully about how he should craft his own response.

That controversial response had come three days afterward, January 13, when the party's titular leader endorsed the administration's lend-lease bill and announced his foreign junket decision. William Allen White, still leading his committee, praised the statement as fine proof that "Mr. Willkie is not the leader of Congress, but he is the leader of 20,000,000 Republicans." White's editorial probably spoke for two-thirds of American public opinion, but the majority of registered Republicans found the propaganda of the AFC more persuasive at the time. GOP leadership, with the qualified exceptions of Tom Dewey and Joe Martin, reacted almost violently. Martin, who knew the GOP "would have been finished if it had expelled Willkie," barely managed to derail a formal expulsion vote in the House. Alf Landon charged that there was "no essential difference between Mr. Willkie's position and Mr. Roosevelt's position, which is to go to war if necessary to help England win." Had he been honest, Landon fumed, Willkie could "never have been nominated at Philadelphia." A last-ditch effort was undertaken to save their leader before he followed through on his mission to England—before he missed "the biggest chance of his life," as Howard pleaded.[7] Although pretty thick-skinned, Wendell was badly shaken by the experience.

In a rather remarkable unlimbering at a dinner party given by Irita seven days before his flight, Wendell shared candid misgivings about his Republicans with Viking publisher Harold

Guinzburg and spouse, *Herald Tribune* Washington columnist Robert Kintner and wife, Supreme Court Justice Felix Frankfurter, appointed less than a year, and a now-reconciled Dorothy Thompson. Since their memorable March 1938 Harvard University Club debate, Frankfurter and Willkie had not met face-to-face frequently. Frankfurter and Guinzburg credited themselves with having planted Wendell's foreign trip idea with Irita at a New Year's party. The justice's lengthy memorandum of the evening conveyed a sharp, sympathetic picture of an "unusually honest, attractive fellow," tough, "but hurt and worried." "He naturally was feeling pretty mad," Frankfurter recorded, "and as the evening went on, limbered up to a surprising degree." On the one hand, Wendell said, the Republicans opposed his fact-finding trip abroad as a gift to Roosevelt; on the other—like Joe Kennedy and the Pews—some urged him to see that "the war could be fixed" if he helped the United States exert "the right influence." Europe organized under Hitler meant that Republicans "could do more profitable business than ever before."

Especially distressing, Frankfurter recorded Wendell saying, was the cynical suggestion—why not "go also to Germany"—of several business friends. For others, the Millbanks, who underwrote Marshall's No Foreign War Committee, for example, wartime high taxes and government regulations were anathema. Roy Howard and Bruce Barton—the Hoover Camp's "field marshals," as Wendell called them—had argued with him for three hours over dinner. Finally, he had ended the dinner fighting mad after the "little pipsqueak" Howard—disgusted that "all the time and effort . . . spent on helping you has been wasted"—told Wendell his newspaper chain will "tear your reputation to shreds."[8] The trip to England was mandatory, feisty Dorothy Thompson exclaimed, a blow to the rising organized appeasement in the country. Neither the recently dead isolationist lion, Senator William Borah, nor the scholarly Senator McNary, both senior members of the Foreign Relations Committee, had ever left the United States. The trip was a means "of putting himself in a position to reply, on the basis of firsthand knowledge, to the Republican isolationists" ganging up on him, Frankfurter reiterated.

Secretary of State Hull's approval of his passport request also informed Wendell Willkie that the president would make time to see him when he came to Washington to collect the document. The White House press secretary followed up with a statement that FDR would be "glad to talk to [Willkie] if he wished." If so, it was suggested that Wendell might carry a note from the president to Prime Minister Churchill. Eleanor Roosevelt described the excitement attending the encounter in the second-floor Oval Study on January 19 "when Mr. Willkie came to see my husband . . . and the household was so anxious to get a glimpse of him." She would have gone too, but "Franklin told me of it later." Stage managing the early-evening meeting only hours before his inauguration, FDR had son James spread some papers on a desk so he would look busy. Pausing from an apparently unfinished inaugural address to hail by first name his game Republican challenger, Franklin Roosevelt sportingly wished that Wendell "were going to stand out on that cold inaugural platform tomorrow" instead of himself. To which his defeated rival offered "the President" the generous assurance that when he reached London, the president "would want to change places with me again."[9] After FDR put aside his address, their conversation resumed *in camera* for some time, but noisily enough to be heard by fascinated White House staffers.

Wendell was advised to make good use of special envoy Harry Hopkins, serving since the first week of the month with uncanny success in London as FDR's eyes and ears and Churchill conduit. The suggestion elicited a revealingly disparaging remark from Wendell, however. Why did Roosevelt keep the man so close to him, he wanted to know? For Wendell, physically robust and straight-dealing, it was oil and water with Harry Hopkins, but the paralyzed president's response was, as speechwriter Robert Sherwood perceived, psychologically spot-on about their co-dependency. It was cruel of Roosevelt to call his sickly, devoted servant a "half-man," but should Wendell someday find himself president of the United States, Roosevelt said he'd "learn what a lonely job this is, and you'll discover the need for somebody like Harry Hopkins who asks nothing except to serve you." As Sherwood wrote of both men: "they were living on borrowed time." No one would have guessed that Franklin Roosevelt would outlive Wendell Willkie as he departed the White House with a historic note "addressed to a certain Naval Person." The president's message was Longfellow's exquisitely right verse: "Sail on, O ship of state, Sail on, O Union strong and great! Humanity with all its fears, With all the hopes of future years, Is hanging breathless on thy fate!"[10]

The trip was his own idea, and Wendell intended to bear the full cost of travel and his own expenses, with his traveling companions John Cowles Sr., publisher of the *Des Moines Register* and *Minneapolis Tribune* (Gardner's older brother), and Langdon K. Thorne, outstanding yachtsman and American Superpower Corporation president, each bearing his own expenses. Wise in the ways of Washington, Joe Martin saw Oval Office machinations— "Roosevelt just trying to win you over." A small crowd of well-heeled supporters saw their Pan American *Dixie Clipper* flying boat lift off from the new art deco LaGuardia Marine Terminal at 8:30 a.m. on the morning of January 22. Standing far forward in the crowd to be photographed was a worried little Roy Howard hoping to assuage several major advertisers displeased by his newspapers' attacks on Wendell Willkie.[11] The big Boeing headed out to the Azores, Lisbon, to splashdown at Southampton four days later. Monday morning, the twenty-seventh, the first day of his whirlwind visit, Wendell established a reserved but cordial tone with the press. He had come "as Wendell Willkie." He was "representing no one." He came to listen, to observe, to learn.

At the Foreign Ministry, he spoke with tall, suave, precise Anthony Eden, a fine specimen of aristocratic in-breeding. They were a study in physical and cultural contrasts. Lunch at Number 10 Downing Street with the prime minister and Clementine Churchill ran a loquacious hour and forty minutes. The photo of Churchill and Willkie taken as the latter leaves (another contrast in size and culture) bespoke the curious pleasure each took away from this first meeting—for Churchill, the "long talk with this affable and forceful man." Wendell would spend the night as guest of the Churchills at their Checquers estate. Roosevelt's note to a "certain Naval Person" deeply touched the prime minister. It was only revealed later at Checquers, when Wendell told the stumped

British authorities that the unidentified stirring stanza was by the American poet Henry Wadsworth Longfellow. Monday continued with a brief exchange with Harry Hopkins, two press conferences, an important talk about resources with Minister of Labor Ernest Bevin, about whom Irita had imparted personal details Wendell found helpful. Wendell's day ended with a solemn tour of the bomb damage in central London.[12]

Early Tuesday, his presence now widely observed and cheered by Londoners, Wendell visited St. Paul's Cathedral, struck by bombs in September and October. He heard that Londoners were convinced that Wren's great Anglican structure was impervious to Hitler's blitz. The same was said of Roman Catholic Westminster Cathedral. The politician in him probably appreciated the value back home of photographs of the Republican leader standing reverently before each iconic house of worship. Essential time was scheduled with three living institutions: lunch with Labor's Clement Atlee (Churchill's prospective alternative); dinner with press lord and Minister of Aircraft Production Lord William Beaverbrook, *sine qua non* player in future lend-lease planning; and tutorial with the Governor of the Bank of England, Montagu Collet Norman, regarded as "the most eminent banker in the world," notwithstanding his great age and whispered mental frailty.[13] The day's highlight, though, was the debate in the House of Commons. The government was being fiercely attacked for suppressing the *Daily Worker*. It was a forensic spectacle made for Wendell Willkie.

The temper of the populace was stiff upper lip—better times on the way despite constant air raids, traumatized loved ones, leveled neighborhoods. Wendell appreciated Londoners' heroic resolve, yet he sensed also a surprising undertone of licentiousness, a pervasive carnality that made ordinarily correct women indiscreet. "Sex hung in the air like a fog," United Press correspondent Harrison Salisbury said. At her friend Irita's request, Dame Rebecca West, the libertine novelist and literary critic, threw a lively party of writers, intellectuals, and theater types for Wendell at the Dorchester Hotel. West found her guest of honor physically "greatly superior to the impression given by his photographs," as she reported approvingly to Van Doren. The evening relaxed Wendell so well that he allowed himself to share West's leftist critics' opinion that Churchill's stellar wartime leadership qualities would be much less suitable after the war. It was a view fully shared by FDR, and immediately reported to MI5. The *Herald Tribune*'s Joseph Barnes suspected his friend probably also committed indiscretions of a carpe diem character.[14]

He began to be ubiquitous: competing in a round of darts at a pub; standing a round of drinks at another; clambering through ruins without the required steel helmet; tea taken with a crowd of Cockneys in the heavily bombed South Side. This author, mentioning his name to a docent at the FDR Presidential Library, was rewarded by a vivid childhood recall of the Republican leader's sudden, smiling appearance in her packed underground air raid shelter. "People rose from their beds and applauded," said she, still moved by the memory. All of them really did believe they would, as he heartily urged, "Knock the Germans back to Berlin!"[15] By now, his ebullient approachability had warmed the hearts of ordinary Londoners. Sauntering into a pub to have "a look around," he got a memorable welcome from the alert proprietor who produced a rare bottle of champagne. "I was going to keep this for armistice day," said he, "but you are as good as an armistice day to us and we will have this together."[16] It was just as well that no invitation came to dine at Cliveden House, Nancy Astor's appeasement purlieu favored by Ambassador Kennedy. Two more days in London before traveling to Dover to inspect invasion defenses on Friday, and then on to Birmingham and Coventry on Sunday, Liverpool and Manchester on Monday. In Manchester, the crowds swept him off his feet, cheering, as he left Town Hall.

The pace and stamina at forty-nine—for a large man who smoked two packs of Camels daily and for whom physical exercise consisted of brisk walks near Wall Street—impressed his hosts. Nothing much but rubble remained of fourteenth-century Coventry Cathedral after the Luftwaffe's November 1940 raid. On the move, he was emotionally shaken and required to answer an appeal from progressive New York Republicans to accept a bid to replace his friend Kenneth Simpson, one of his original and

most capable supporters, suddenly removed at forty-six by a fatal heart attack from his only weeks' old congressional seat. In this first of several such elective options he would decline, Wendell already knew that for him the presidency was the only elective office from which fundamental changes could be accomplished.[17]
On February 4, a Tuesday, Wendell flew in a private plane from Manchester to Dublin on what Churchill and Eden had predicted was an utterly quixotic mission. Premier Eamon de Valera turned down politely, but absolutely, Wendell Willkie's plea that the Irish coastline allow the presence of British observation posts. Joseph Kennedy might have spared Wendell a trip.

The time available that Tuesday to overcome three centuries of justified Irish Anglophobia was short. Wendell was expected to take afternoon tea with the king and queen at Buckingham Palace. He arrived punctually, was cordially received by George VI and Elizabeth. The royals revealed their subtle displeasure with Joseph Kennedy's politics over high tea—and scotch. The queen interposed a genteel observation about the ambassador's mistaken defeatism. "Mr. Willkie, it wasn't because I didn't try on him." It was obvious that their government desired that the distinguished American opposition leader return home much impressed by the top-down solidarity of the British people, their cultural and political affinity with their American cousins, their determination to carry on everlastingly if supplied by their cousins with essential fighting materiel. At midnight, Wendell took the train to Bristol from London for an extensive inspection tour of the region's aviation industry. The Bleinheim and Beaufighter planes were the best light bombers in the British arsenal.

Secretary Hull's telegram cut short Wendell's self-assigned mission. Hull urged an immediate return in hopes of marshaling enough Republican votes to guarantee passage of the administration's life-line legislation. While he (assisted by Hopkins) conferred with Churchill and the British political class to enthusiastic press coverage, Colonel Lindbergh and outgoing Ambassador Kennedy were presenting worst-case lend-lease scenarios before the House Committee on Foreign Affairs. The "Lone Eagle's" January 23 testimony impressed the representatives and most of the specta-

tors with its articulate sincerity. Nothing, he insisted, could justify abetting a civil war among Europeans. Kennedy's five-hour
statement was also regarded as important, although less well reasoned.[18] The Senate's foreign affairs committee hearings on lend-
lease were imminent. Republicans were united in the House and
Senate to kill lend-lease. The party leader left immediately on
Wednesday, February 5, aboard the *Dixie Clipper.*

According to angry John Hamilton, the man ousted from the
post of national chairman, Wendell Willkie couldn't "dig up ten
friends if his life depended upon it"—Martin included. The full
House approved lend-lease on February 9 just as Wendell reached
New York. The vote—260 to 165—fell along party lines, with just
24 Republicans out of 135 joining the majority. As things stood on
his arrival in the capital, Wendell thought he could count at most
on ten votes in the Senate. Watching the Gallup poll, however, he
believed he might succeed in inducing the party he led to catch up
with him. Public opinion had edged ahead. His well-advertised
appearance before the Senate's last public lend-lease hearing on
the eleventh gave a good imitation of Frank Capra's hero Jefferson Smith in the current film box-office success, *Mr. Smith Goes
to Washington.* A procession of household names preceded him:
Lindbergh cogent and persuasive in defense of fortress America;
Norman Thomas the personification of genteel socialism; Rein-
hold Niebuhr the Protestant philosopher; John L. Lewis inimical
to all that Roosevelt espoused.[19]

With the hall packed beyond capacity and thousands form-
ing the longest line outside ever seen on Capitol Hill, Wendell's
well-advertised entrance was preceded by popping flashbulbs and
fourth-estate jabber as he strolled to the witness table and—as
with his forgotten Elwood speech—promptly brought the hearings to a captivating forty-five-minute extemporaneous pause
while his missing statement was fetched from the hotel. Once into
his compelling prepared statement that the British, based on his
eyewitness and consultation, would carry on if given the material
wherewithal, adversary senators found themselves disadvantaged.
Lend-lease, he reasoned, was America's best self-defense against
foreign aggression. "American democracy has a fateful decision

to make at this time," he began. He believed the American people had not yet "fully grasped the extent of the crisis, or their responsibility with regard to it." Two choices faced them: isolation or intervention. The consequence of isolation he described as mortal. "If we isolate ourselves, Britain may have great difficulty in surviving." Senators inclined forward to hear Wendell's conclusion, Michigan's Vandenberg cupping his ear.

Not a pin dropped in the chamber. The Senate's most thoughtful isolationist needed to know if Wendell favored going to war if it was necessary to save England. Replying that he'd never vote for war "until the American people wanted it," his answer elicited a guarded approval from Michigan's senior senator. Wendell continued. "No man can say at this time whether or not Britain can win this war without our assistance in supplies, ships, and armaments. But we know that if she is defeated, the totalitarian powers will control the world. They will control not only Europe, but probably also most of Africa. They may also control the Atlantic Ocean." The second choice before the senators, then, of intervention seemed inescapable. "No man can guarantee to you that the policy of aid to Britain will not involve the United States in war." Correct decisions entailed risks. "Hitler will make war on us, or on our friends and allies in this hemisphere, when, as, and if he chooses. That is his record. But he is far less apt to be aggressive while Britain stands, than if she were to fall."[20]

North Dakota's Gerald Nye, leading isolationist and famous for his World War I munitions industry investigations, joined by Missouri's Anglophobe Bennett Champ Clark, challenged Wendell to square his committee testimony with his campaign charge in Baltimore that the United States would be at war by April 1941 if FDR were reelected. Batting an apparent contradiction aside as "campaign oratory," Wendell capped his riposte with a compliment that delighted the hearing room. He was "very glad [Nye] read my speeches, because the President said he did not." Forensic facility temporarily trumped a bald admission of insincerity, although a taint of opportunism would come to dog Wendell. He closed his testimony by iterating the advisability of a sunset clause in the lend-lease legislation, an amendment the regretted Kenneth Simpson had introduced—in any case, a requirement that the executive seek congressional approval of any additional lend-lease beneficiaries beyond Great Britain and China. Notice in the press of a private meeting with FDR immediately after his Senate appearance only hardened many Congressional Republicans' misgivings.[21]

Nevertheless, according to the Gallup poll, the favorable press generated by the Senate committee appearance tipped public opinion (Thomas Dewey and GOP voters included) in favor of the bill's passage.[22] Forty-nine Democrats and ten of twenty-seven Senate Republicans finally voted for lend-lease—no more than expected—in early March, and when Roosevelt signed the bill on March 11, he had the Republican leader to thank for the bravura performance before the divided Senate Foreign Relations Committee. It was, in a sense, an odd bargain: Wendell would never corral a majority of GOP congressional votes; yet his titular position steadily enhanced the party's esteem in the public eye. Churchill hailed the passage of the bill as "the most unsordid act in the history of any nation." That its real significance would remain symbolic for many months the prime minister understood, as well as did his new American friend. It would take almost two years before more than one percent of Britain's arms and munitions came from the United States.

For Wendell, to help the British really meant that we helped ourselves. A single paragraph in his Senate testimony revealed a two-pronged interventionist rationale—to save Europe from Hitler and to surpass the stasis of the New Deal's distributive economics. "For about a decade this country has maintained its standard of living by federal deficit financing," it lectured. To "lock ourselves up within our own shores" would preclude the economic breakout fueled by lend-lease and the war that he knew, but dared not concede, would ensue. Once the Gordian knot of the Neutrality Act was politically spliced, the lend-lease roll-out would entail administrative, technical, industrial, geographical, and logistical challenges of such titanic proportions as finally to wrench America out of her long palliated economic depression. (Before its axis adversaries were reduced to unconditional surrender, the United States would produce $50.1 billion worth of arms, munitions, ships, planes, and construction equivalent in 2017 to $668 billion.)

The Churchill government invited the Canadian government to favor the Willkies with a ceremonial reception. His and Edith's welcome in Canada that March exceeded in size and enthusiasm that of any foreign dignitary in recent memory, the crowds in Toronto and Montreal rivaling those for the last visit of the king and queen of England. Their gratifying reception north of the border was followed a few days later in Manhattan by a formal-dress United China Relief speech in which Wendell delivered a soaring vision-in-progress that denied the senseless economics and politics of isolationism. "The isolationist believes that while international trade may be desirable, it is not necessary." He believes that we can build a wall around America and that democracy can live behind that wall, Wendell said that evening, obviously emotionally charged by the Calvary of the Chinese fighting on alone for five years against their Japanese invaders. The isolationist believes America "can be made self-sufficient and still retain the free way of life. But the internationalist denies this. The internationalist declares that, to remain free, men must trade with one another— must trade freely in goods, in ideas, in customs and traditions and values of all sorts."[23]

This was a vision of global unity and equality that, in a real sense, anticipated the Atlantic Charter declaration of Anglo-American unity and international solidarity the Roosevelt administration would release in mid-August 1941 to a surprised American public. Wendell Willkie was finding the role of leader of the loyal opposition satisfying, although his experience with Roosevelt cautioned him not to mistake the courtesy of collaboration with the powerful, devious president for the genuine article of mutual confidence. For the present, however, it was obvious to them both that they could advance the nation's best interests in tandem as sympathetic adversaries. Months before the Atlantic Charter promulgation, however, Wendell returned to the practice of law as senior partner in the New York firm of Miller, Owen, Otis, and Bailey, with himself replacing retiring ex-governor

Nathan L. Miller after the white-shoe firm was reorganized after April 1 as Willkie, Owen, Otis, Farr and Gallagher—the Harold Gallagher who kept the *Willkie Special* on schedule.

From his new law-firm perch, Wendell monitored FDR's stealthy zigzag course from lend-lease to revision of the 1939 Neutrality Act to its ultimate goal of nullification. Some success had finally greeted the president's attempt to modify the act after Germany's September invasion of Poland on September 1, 1939, after which Europe plunged into World War II. In November, Congress acceded to lifting the Neutrality Act's arms embargo. Henceforth, belligerents were permitted to obtain American arms on a "cash and carry" basis provided they were taken away only on their own vessels. It was a breakthrough modification but not sufficient to save the British after their Dunkirk military debacle in June 1940. The revised act barred foreign loans to belligerents and prohibited American ships from transporting goods to belligerents. Nullification in all but name was FDR's cloaked objective. Private citizen Wendell Willkie had the privilege of impatience and the latitude of confrontation as his part in the objective. His "Americans, Stop Being Afraid" in the May *Collier's* took on Lindbergh, mocking the Lone Eagle's superior geopolitics. The author conceded Lindbergh's prediction that "the capital of the world tomorrow will be either Berlin or Washington." Wendell offered solid reasons to "prefer Washington."[24]

But it was Hollywood, not Washington, that needed immediate defending, the new senior partner of Willkie, Owen, Otis, Farr and Gallagher discovered. In a last-ditch maneuver to derail neutrality nullification, senate isolationists noisily seized upon Hollywood as the capital of seductive interventionism. Montana's Burton Wheeler, maverick chair of the Senate Interstate Commerce Committee, had earned FDR's gratitude in the administration's war with Wendell's Commonwealth & Southern. But now that the president's stealthy all-out support of Great Britain meant war and "plough[ing] under every fourth American boy," the firebrand isolationist joined his Republican colleague Gerald Nye in a ploy to expose some of the supposedly most devious pro-war manipulators of public opinion: Jews who owned most of the Hollywood film studios. South Dakota's Nye, architect of the 1937 Neutrality Act, claimed to be concerned that "Hollywood" was trying to make the nation "punch drunk with propaganda to push her into war." Nye's vituperative radio address from St. Louis in early August, "Our Madness Increases as Our Emergency Shrinks," had been a virtual declaration of war on interventionists in general and Jews in particular.

Charles Lindbergh's remarkable anti-Semitic diatribe at Des Moines, Iowa, was to follow in a few weeks, but Nye's radio broadcast identified the sinister forces he saw behind the country's interventionist drift with almost as much venom. Nye's "sinister forces" comprised those Hollywood producers who made *Escape, Flight Command, I Married a Nazi, The Great Dictator,* and *Sergeant York*—"at least 20 pictures . . . produced in the last year, all designed to drug the reason of the American people." "Great Americans" like Colonel Lindbergh and the AFC's General Leonard Wood were "in many places denied the use of a hall to speak up for America," Nye raved, while these men, "with the motion-picture films in their hands, can address 80,000,000 people a week, cunningly and persistently inoculating them with the virus of war."[25] Ambassador Kennedy, former studio owner himself, convened a special Hollywood meeting of major Jewish executives to warn them of dire consequences "if they continued to abuse that power." What better evidence of Hollywood's narcotic power for the crusading senator than the night of July 1 when interventionism's vanguard—Eleanor Roosevelt, the Wendell Willkies, the Henry Luces, General John "Black Jack" Pershing, Selective Service General Lewis Hershey, and select others—had sanctified Warner Brothers' *Sergeant York* at Manhattan's Astor Theatre. Alvin York, the highest-decorated American infantryman of World War I (York captured 132 Germans and killed almost a third as many), was opposed to war on religious grounds but had agreed to let himself be portrayed by film star Gary Cooper in return for Warner Brothers' sizable monetary gift to his humble country church. Cooper won an Oscar and the Tennessee folk hero enjoyed a well-publicized Oval Office chat with the president after the Astor Theatre premiere. FDR praised the rustic hero, the movie, the message, and Hollywood. His wish for a wide viewership was widely reported.[26]

When a special subcommittee of Burton Wheeler's Senate Interstate Commerce Committee convened on September 9 to begin two weeks of rambling hearings into the Hollywood film industry, Wendell, generously retained as counsel of the motion-picture industry, appeared before it to raise questions about the committee's sinister motives. With Idaho's ineffective Democrat D. Worth Clark as chair, Missouri Democrat Bennett Champ Clark, two mediocre Republicans, and a fledgling Democrat senator who would surprise the chair by his informed questioning, the subcommittee commenced proceedings with privileged testimony from South Dakota's Nye, who repeated his claim that "Hollywood" was trying to make the nation "punch drunk with propaganda to push her into war." Wheeler's film subcommittee proceedings were every bit as devious as the alleged offenses of the Hollywood moguls. Wendell thought the transparency of the subcommittee's reprehensible script would disgust the public. The slippery slope from investigation to suppression was unmistakable. "From the motion picture and radio industries it is just a small step to newspapers, magazines, and other periodicals," he reprimanded Senator Clark in a letter published in the newspapers. "And from the freedom of the press it is just a small step to the freedom of the individual to say what he believes."[27]

The subcommittee wrote rules prohibiting the film industry's attorneys from questioning witnesses. Wendell was reduced to taking notes, eructations of disgust, and occasional dismayed facial expressions. Senator Clark clashed noisily once with Wendell about his "campaign oratory" hypocrisy and was forced to apologize the next day. New Hampshire's isolationist Charles Tobey harassed motion-picture executives Harry Warner and Nicholas Schenck about a nonexistent movie. Missouri's Bennett Clark produced another list of offending movies. Although the celebrity subject matter kept the newspapers interested, the subcommittee's rationale had been effectively demolished in much of the public's estimation by Wendell's public letter to Chairman Clark and Senator Nye at the outset. After parsing both the committee resolution and Nye's St. Louis speech, Wendell concluded that if it was the committee's intention "to inquire whether or not the motion picture industry, as a whole, and its leading executives . . . are opposed to the Nazi dictatorship in Germany," then he wished to put on record a simple truth: "There need be no investigation. We abhor everything which Hitler represents."[28] The Wheeler-Nye-inspired subcommittee—confounded by its own premise—sputtered into incoherence, but Lindbergh's September 11, 1941, speech in the Des Moines Coliseum heaped coals on simmering accusations of a Jewish pro-war conspiracy.

The celebrated aviator, his Army Air Corps commission resigned indignantly but days earlier, brought the huge crowd to fever pitch as he urged Americans not to allow "the natural passions and prejudices of other peoples to lead our country into war." There were three groups whose subterfuge had brought the country to the brink of war, "the British, the Roosevelt administration, the Jewish people," Lindbergh declared. Unlike those three groups, his own cause had never indulged in "just campaign oratory," he swore. Lindbergh advised American Jews to take no part in appeals to war, "for they will be among the first to feel its consequences." Although he did not fully grasp its impact at that moment, it was the Lone Eagle who would feel the consequences of his own performance. Delaying a grave, stunning fireside chat for broadcast over the Des Moines Coliseum loudspeakers immediately before Lindbergh was to address the crowd, FDR revealed to Americans the turning-point news that the US Navy was under orders, henceforth, to "shoot on sight" German and Italian ships—"the rattlesnakes of the Atlantic"—because of the U-boat torpedoing of the destroyer USS *Greer*.[29]

After FDR's well-timed fireside chat, Lindbergh's indictment of "the Jewish people" lost much of its relevance. A day later, newspapers quoted Wendell's "campaign oratory" deploring "the most un-American talk made in my time by any person of national reputation." Prominent Republicans found it increasingly advisable thereafter to distance themselves from Lindbergh, an imperative ultimately depriving the powerful America First Committee of a potent popular asset. The sour mix of antiwar high-mindedness and supreme bigotry began to register negatively in the country. Most Americans knew that they were not fighting for Charles Lindbergh's ideals: the preservation of the white race; eugenically guided evolution; and the neo-Spartan future for mankind Anne Morrow Lindbergh, his beautiful, exceptional wife, described in *The Wave of the Future*. Most reconciled themselves to the near eventuality of war—much as their parents had in 1917. But it was the peace won in the Great War that left so much to be desired that explained the hard-headed isolationism of decorated warriors like Hamilton Fish or even of warped geniuses like Charles Lindbergh.[30] What was the peace Americans should fight for this time?

As they colluded to prepare the United States for the inevitable, Wendell Willkie and Franklin Roosevelt were exceptional in their shared vision of a redemptive peace that each arrived at separately in pretty much the same timeframe. Wendell had spoken emotionally to his Toronto audience in late March, telling it, "civilization cannot afford such another mistake. We must begin now to shape in our minds the kind of world we want. We must not await the war's end to make these purposes clear. . . . We can, if we have the will, convert what seems to be the death rattle of our time into the birth pains of a new order."[31] Franklin Roosevelt was much preoccupied with the very thoughts his loyal opponent had shared with his Toronto audience. He had slipped off secretly from Washington on the heavy cruiser USS *Augusta* to Newfoundland to meet Winston Churchill and the prime of the British Naval establishment, aboard the HMS *Prince of Wales* in Placentia Bay. Roosevelt took the elegant, super-competent Under-Secretary of State Sumner Welles with him. Secretary of State Hull would read about the extraordinary four-day venture between the neutral United States and a belligerent power in the newspapers. On August 14, the two leaders promulgated the Atlantic Charter with the goals of the Allies for the postwar world: freedom from fear and want, freedom of the seas, renunciation of the use of force, respect for the self-determination of peoples, and (despite Churchill's initial misgivings) freedom of trade.[32] Wendell's own astonishing articulation of the postwar world order that must be fought and won would virtually write itself in little less than two years.

While Wendell Willkie and Franklin Roosevelt engaged in their two-step of evading and encouraging a de facto alliance with Great Britain, world affairs imposed themselves on Americans' opinions as never before in the last half of 1941. The sinking of prodigious tonnage in the North Atlantic by German submarines had all but cut off Great Britain's lend-lease lifeline. FDR aggressively defended the "freedom of the seas" doctrine in a late May Fireside Chat and, finally, in early July had gone so far as to send US forces to occupy friendly Iceland in order to extend the surveillance reach of the US Navy. After months of failure by Mussolini's invasion forces, Germany's occupation of the Balkans and the Greek peninsula brutally succeeded that July. General Erwin Rommel's Afrika Korps, reinforced and rebounding from a British success, struck across the North African littoral that very month, besieging the Libyan port of Tobruk and seemingly on an unstoppable course for the Suez Canal.[33] A steady drumbeat of torpedoed US vessels continued after the sunken destroyer USS *Greer*: the USS *Kearney* and *Reuben James*, the freighters *Steel Seafarer*, *Lehigh*, and *Bold Venture*.

Impatience rose among the interventionists that the president chose to be led by public opinion even as the Axis pincers squeezed the life from Europe's last bastion of resistance. A momentarily shaken Harold Ickes questioned his chief's political courage. As he and others in the president's inner circle well understood, there were fast-approaching limits as to how long British resilience could defy a paucity of reserves. "Remember, Mr. President," Winston Churchill had cabled almost plaintively on New Year's Eve, 1940, "we do not know what you have in mind, or exactly what the United States is going to do, and we are fighting for our lives."[34] To the prime minister's question, interventionists began to think the president was unwilling to risk a clear answer. Wendell made it clear to Franklin that his loyal opposition role was conditional. Invited to another frank White House lunch on July 9, 1941, he brought assurances that the Republican rank and file supported the Iceland naval base as well as US escort ships for lend-lease vessels.

But Wendell's CEO experience caused him great concern about

the leadership quality and poor coordination of national defense production. Moreover, a major new development had complicated the interventionist argument and bolstered the isolationist cause. Operation Barbarossa, Hitler's delayed invasion of Russia on July 22 (delayed by Italian incompetence in the Balkans), made for considerable confusion, uncertainty, and bald cynicism now that the two great dictatorships might devour each other. Missouri Senator Harry Truman was quoted as saying that if Americans saw Germany winning, "we ought to help Russia, and if Russia is winning . . . help Germany."[35] As his part of the two-step, then, Wendell commenced a series of speeches designed to inspire or shame the Roosevelt administration and the American people into action. Frenemies like Dorothy Thompson—"we are within ten minutes of losing this war"—supplied copious unsolicited encouragement. "You can help the President. . . . You can recall Wilson, and the tragedy of a lost peace through the recalcitrance of an ignorant congress." But Wilson had no radio, "and Roosevelt and you have," she persisted.[36]

The enormous welcoming crowd at the Los Angeles airport on July 22, 1941, cheered Wendell's denunciation of FDR for failing to summon "the ablest men in the country and giving them power to act." The times were exciting, he declared, continuing with what audiences would soon recognize as vintage Willkie: "For it is only in such times as these, when men are in doubt, and when they must struggle for the truth, that the great achievements of history are brought forth." Speaking in the Hollywood Bowl the following day, Wendell tutored the huge assembly, "It was the clear intention of the founders . . . that in emergencies the President should lead." As for Russia, he reminded it that the country had never been "a military menace to us," that "even the ideological threat was now negligible."[37]

By the beginning of October his impatience with FDR's "faltering administration" led Wendell to call for his party to recommend the outright repeal of the Neutrality Act at a special dinner in honor of the British ambassador.[38] Three days later, again with deft timing on October 9, FDR sent his revision message to Congress asking that part of the act be repealed and for authority

to arm merchant ships. While debate raged over the administration's request for significant revision versus a variety of other
partisan modifications, Wendell telegraphed a bold request on
October 20 beseeching select GOP senators, representatives, and
prominent elected officials to add their names to a resolution for
total repeal "so that no man here or abroad may doubt where our
party stands on the issue of survival of freedom."[39] More than
one hundred prominent Republicans responded positively, Wendell's release of their names to the press having a persuasive effect
upon public opinion.

Tom Dewey strategically broke ranks with Taft, Hoover,
Landon, and Vandenberg to commend his party's titular leader.
More debate ensued (the vitriol heaped on "No. 1 war-monger"
Willkie by congressional Republicans shocked the public). Three
Republican senators who answered their leader's appeal (Warren Austin of Vermont, Styles Bridges of New Hampshire, Chan
Gurney of South Dakota) promptly cooperated to offer an amendment to the armed ships resolution calling for outright repeal of
the Neutrality Act, even in the face of dismal GOP congressional
response. Under the administration's prodding, their amendment
was appropriated by Senate Democrats as a bill to repeal neutrality outright. Two additional Senate Republicans voted with Wendell's original three to join with the Democratic majority. More US
ships were torpedoed before the 1939 Neutrality Act was finally
signed out of existence by FDR on November 17. Still, twenty-one
Republican senators out of twenty-six had voted against repeal
ten days earlier. In the House, Republicans had voted 132–22
against repeal on November 13.[40] Wendell's inability to deliver
affirmative votes bespoke the hard reality of the GOP congressional mindset, but he had in fact indirectly rendered a crucial
service to the successful repeal. Allowing due credit to his partner
in interventionism shortly after retiring the Neutrality Act, the
president, speaking at a Democratic Party function, praised the
leader of the Republican Party himself—"Mr. Wendell Willkie"—
who demonstrated the American meaning of patriotism "by rising
above partisanship and rallying to the common cause."[41]

The question both men had begun asking themselves and

their close advisors was the extent to which "the common cause" impelled common government, whether, indeed, FDR's collaborative olive branch to the GOP as early as the previous spring and now Wendell's unprecedented loyal opposition postulate should permit a leadership alignment foreign to American national politics yet—in spirit if not structure—approximating coalition governance? Viewed cynically, FDR's mid-October invitation to Wendell to join his administration could have been a brilliant maneuver to decapitate the opposition. FDR's messenger (White House factotum David Niles) had been careful to stipulate that the unprecedented arrangement "didn't mean that [Wendell] was to give up any of his partisan ideology." Given the political synergy between the two leaders and the grave situation abroad, an arrangement tantamount to coalition government arguably advanced the finest conceptions of leadership worthy of a great republic.[42]

Discerning labor secretary Frances Perkins, the first of her sex in American politics to head a cabinet department, seems to have had much the same impression, as did private secretary Grace Tully, who was fond of saying that "for Wendell [FDR] came to have a generous affection." Perkins tells us that her boss respected Wendell Willkie more than any of his other rivals and liked him better—man to man—than most of his own cabinet. "You know, he's a very good fellow," Roosevelt told her. "He has lots of talent." He wanted to offer Wendell "an important post in the government. Can you think of one?" he asked her at the end of the year. While Perkins tried to think of something suitable, the president decided that in light of the mounting tensions with the Japanese in Southeast Asia, the Republican leader could render special service by a visit to Australia. In a joking aside, he noted that some might perceive the invitation as an ulterior maneuver to send Wendell "out of the country."[43] FDR's letter was dated December 5, 1941.

Two days later, four battleships, three cruisers, and three destroyers sank to the bottom of Pearl Harbor with 3,500 killed and wounded servicemen after the Sunday morning Japanese surprise attack on the US Pacific Fleet that recently retired admiral

James Richardson had twice requested the president's permission to relocate to the West Coast. When Wendell congratulated FDR's powerful "day which will live in infamy" speech before the joint session of Congress, his letter respectfully elided the subject of Australia. Instead, with an ingenuousness rare for a leader of an opposition party, he wrote of his urgent need to find a way to be of greatest service to his country's commander-in-chief in the face of the greatest disaster since the Civil War. He had resolved to be in Washington on the coming Monday. He asked that one of the White House secretaries let him know if the president's busy schedule would permit their meeting on that date. In case no meeting was possible that day, "there [was] something [he] needed to say to [FDR]." Lately, "a few people, friends of yours," had suggested various ways in which they thought you might make use of me in our national emergency."[44] From tone and detail, Wendell's December 10 letter had to have been written under an informed impression that FDR had signaled a wish for a meaningful collaboration, one significant in the war officially declared on the eighth and respectful of his collaborator's partisan obligations.

What mutual affection there was between the two egos remained wary, and, on Roosevelt's part accompanied by a congenial and congenital duplicitousness. Lamoyne "Lem" Jones, a veteran of the Colorado Springs summer and indispensable confidante, discerned early on FDR's manipulative gambit: "Roosevelt always liked to exploit Wendell's virtues," said Jones, "knowing that he was aiding the country while injuring Wendell politically."[45] Their Monday meeting on December 16—a long lunch between them—resulted in mutual expectations but no specifics. Because he had publicly deplored the inefficiency of the National War Labor Board, jointly headed by General Motors executive William Knudsen and CIO chief John L. Lewis's rival Sidney Hillman, Wendell might well have urged Franklin to create a war production board directed by a masterful businessman. Asked by the eager press corps upon leaving the White House if he planned to join the administration, Wendell offered, "In times like these there is not an American who would not be willing to give everything he had in the service of his country." Indeed, he meant it, but a month later when FDR finally made an abrupt decision to create the new Office of Price Administration and Civilian Supply (OPACS), the position unexpectedly went to Sears & Roebuck officer Donald Nelson at the last moment. That very day Harry Hopkins advised against the GOP leader's appointment when he brought FDR's attention to yet another public criticism Wendell was about to make of the lackluster War Labor Board.[46]

At the moment, Wendell's standing with the public was excellent. A Gallup poll found that many Americans expected him to succeed FDR in 1944. Although party opinions about the leader remained a mixture of admiration by a significant minority and of grudging respect to feral hostility by the regulars, the December 1941 issue of *Republican* carried a national party leadership survey showing him the overwhelming favorite for 1944. A week before the Pearl Harbor calamity, Drew Pearson, probably the country's most popular syndicated pundit, recorded a wide-ranging interview with Wendell in the company of Philip. The candidate Pearson found that day was the man who had told his wife that losing the presidency hadn't been the worst possible outcome. "Billie, at least I was true to my conscience. My conscience is clear," Wendell had insisted. "That was the important thing to him," Edith understood. Abruptly, Wendell stopped Pearson dead in their interview to pound that point home, "look[ing] straight in the eye, [shaking] his finger." He wanted Pearson to understand who Wendell Willkie was: "You may not agree with him . . . but you will *understand* him." Since his childhood he'd followed "one definite creed," he announced, one he'd tried to implant in "the boy . . . sitting there. That creed is, 'I do what Wendell thinks is right.'" Drew Pearson, a professional skeptic, allowed that Wendell made "the greatest impact of any man I've ever talked to."

The admirable profile vividly captured in Pearson's piece—however principled and charismatic—adumbrated a leader pledged to a transformational politics that would be both the bane and promise of the Republican Party. Nathan Miller, whose senior law partnership Wendell assumed, offered years afterward a nutshell summation of his successor's paradox. "Parties were to him," explained the former New York governor, "mere instru-

Dorothy Thompson, correspondent and Willkie "frenemy." *Library of Congress, Prints & Photographs Division, photograph by Harris & Ewing, [reproduction number, e.g., LC-USZ62-123456].*

TVA directors: Harcourt Morgan, Arthur Morgan, and David Lilienthal at first board meeting, 1933. *Granville Hunt / TVA.*

FDR, Churchill, and US and UK staffs aboard the HMS *Prince of Wales*, Placentia Bay, Atlantic Charter Proclamation, 1941. *Courtesy of the US Naval Historical Center.*

Doris "Dorrie" Miller, Navy cook hero, Pearl Harbor, 1941. *US Navy.*

Willkie comes to Elwood, August 1940. *Keystone / Hulton Archive / Getty Images.*

Joseph P. Kennedy, US ambassador, and Joachim von Ribbentrop, German ambassador to UK, 1938. *Bettmann / Getty Images.*

Willkie and General Montgomery study campaign map, North Africa, 1942. *Bettmann / Getty Images.*

Samuel Insull in captivity reading about himself, 1934. *Charles Hoff / NY Daily News Archive / Getty Images.*

Four du Pont brothers: Irenee, Lammot, Felix, and Pierre. *Imagno / Getty Images.*

Joe Louis and Gene Tunney for Willkie, 1940. *Bettmann / Getty Images.*

Russian general Lelyushenko and comrade, Moscow front, 1942. *Bettmann / Getty Images.*

Henry and Clare Boothe Luce voting, November 1944. *Paul Popper / Popperfoto / Getty Images.*

Irita Van Doren, Wendell
Willkies's inamorata.
*Irita Taylor Van Doren
Papers / Library of
Congress.*

Willkie memorial plaque
and sculptor Paul Fjeld,
New York City, 1957.
*Courtesy the Lilly
Library, Indiana University, Bloomington,
Indiana.*

Young Willkie at Culver
Military Academy. *Courtesy
the Lilly Library, Indiana
University, Bloomington,
Indiana.*

Charles Halleck and Willkie
on their way to 1940 GOP
convention. *Courtesy the
Lilly Library, Indiana
University, Bloomington,
Indiana.*

Wendell Willkie and Edith
with son, Naval ensign
Phillip, 1942. *Courtesy
the Lilly Library, Indiana
University, Bloomington,
Indiana.*

Robert Taft, Willkie, Arthur Vandenberg, 1940. *Courtesy the Lilly Library, Indiana University, Bloomington, Indiana.*

Wendell relaxes in Colorado Springs, 1940. *Courtesy the Lilly Library, Indiana University, Bloomington, Indiana.*

Willkie speaks to university students, Chengtu, China, 1942. *Courtesy the Lilly Library, Indiana University, Bloomington, Indiana.*

Willkie arrives in Minneapolis from Edmonton, Canada. Honor guard carrying Japanese souvenir sword, 1942. *Courtesy the Lilly Library, Indiana University, Bloomington, Indiana.*

Willkie charm on the campaign trail, 1943. *Courtesy the Lilly Library, Indiana University, Bloomington, Indiana.*

Joseph Barnes, Stalin, Willkie, Mike Cowles, and translator in rear, Kremlin, 1942.

Herman's boys, Wendell standing left.

Turkish prime minister meets Wendell Willkie at the Ankara Airport, 1942. *Courtesy the Lilly Library, Indiana University, Bloomington, Indiana.*

Wendell Willkie dines with the young shah of Iran, 1942. *Courtesy the Lilly Library, Indiana University, Bloomington, Indiana.*

Oren Root Jr.
and Wendell
Willkie on the
radio, 1940.

Wendell Willkie and
Walter F. White,
NAACP executive
director, 1943.

Boss Joseph
Newton Pew Jr.,
Willkie nemesis.
*Jerry Cooke /
The LIFE Images
Collection / Getty
Images.*

Henrietta Trisch Willkie. *Bettmann / Getty Images.*

Basketball coach Willkie, Coffeeville, Kansas, 1918. *Courtesy the Lilly Library, Indiana University, Bloomington, Indiana.*

Wendell Willkie with David Dubinsky (right) and ILGWU group, 1944.
Courtesy the Lilly Library, Indiana University, Bloomington, Indiana.

Russell Davenport speechwriting on campaign train, 1940. *Courtesy the
Lilly Library, Indiana University, Bloomington, Indiana.*

Wendell Willkie and King George VI, 1941. *Courtesy the Lilly Library, Indiana University, Bloomington, Indiana.*

Celebratory dinner for Sam Pryor, 1942. *Courtesy the Lilly Library, Indiana University, Bloomington, Indiana.*

Wendell Willkie exits U.S. Supreme Court Building after the *Schneiderman* case, 1943. *Courtesy the Lilly Library, Indiana University, Bloomington, Indiana.*

RNC chairman John D. M. Hamilton (left), Taft, Raymond Baldwin, Clyde Reed, and Joseph Martin, 1940. *Harris & Ewing / Library of Congress.*

ments, not for political advancement or power, but to serve human needs."[47] Read less aspirationally, Governor Miller described a politician willing and able to indulge in inconvenient truths, as had "Fair Trial," Wendell's *New Republic* article appearing but weeks before the Philadelphia convention, in which he deplored the imprisonment on a technicality of an American Nazi leader (Fritz Kuhn) and an American Communist head (Earl Browder). Herman might have wished that his son had also flatly denounced FDR's February 1942 Executive Order 9066 consigning some 120,000 resident Japanese to isolated, primitive relocation centers for the duration of the war. Wendell's expression at a dinner for Justice Brandeis of merely a general distaste for "extra-judicial proceedings under which any group will be deprived of their rights under the guise of war emergency" suffered by comparison with Socialist Party leader Norman Thomas's forthright denunciation of FDR's action.[48]

Wendell's restraint in the Japanese relocation case should be twinned, nevertheless, with a civil liberties decision he made the day after the attack on Pearl Harbor. On the morning of December 7, as Naval Commander Fuchida Mitsuo's dive bomber groups headed in line for "Battle Ship Row" at Pearl Harbor, William Schneiderman, a nervous thirty-seven-year-old naturalized American, kept an appointment at 15 Broad Street. "A more incongruous meeting would be hard to imagine," as his autobiography put it, "a Communist faced with deportation, and a Wall Street lawyer who only the year before had been the Republican candidate for president." Brought to the United States as a child by his Russian parents, Schneiderman had successfully applied for American citizenship at age eighteen. After many years as a CPUSA organizer in Minnesota, his citizenship was revoked in 1939 by the government, and he was ordered deported on grounds that his certificate of citizenship had been falsely procured. Schneiderman's appeals had been denied by a District Court and a Circuit Court of Appeals.

The desperate appellant's attorney, Carol Weiss King, general counsel for the Committee for the Protection of the Foreign Born, argued his denaturalization case to the docket of the Supreme

Court where the odds for success before Chief Justice Harlan Stone and seven associates appeared no better than Russian roulette. Her brief, which she had somehow persuaded Wendell to read, was, however, excellent. Although law colleagues and party notables warned against taking on Schneiderman, Wendell wrote Bart Crum, the Willkie Club knight-errant and crackerjack California civil liberties advocate, that he would argue Schneiderman before the court himself. He was sure he was right "in representing Schneiderman. Of all the times when civil liberties should be defended, it is now," he was certain.[49] *Schneiderman v. United States*, yet to be heard by the Supreme Court, was a long shot to become a lodestar civil liberties decision. The opening chapter in *Schneiderman v. US* would commence soon after his return from an epic global inspection tour.

William Schneiderman could have noticed the *Nation* for December 6 on Wendell's desk. "Can Willkie Save His Party?"—a richly referenced Marxisant article by a junior member of Harvard's history department—answered that the chances were not encouraging. The Republican Party had "failed to measure up to the obligations of the [international] crisis," decreed Arthur M. Schlesinger Jr. "Now in this moment of irresolution, Wendell Willkie comes on the stage in his gallant but lonely attempt" to save his party. Reaching for a fateful political analogy, Schlesinger likened Willkie to William Seward, leader of the Conscience Whigs on the eve of the Civil War, a leader who "realized that the power of despotism had so grown that any compromise with it . . . would be fatal to democracy." The provocative prescience of Schlesinger's conclusion—"if the Republican Party does not follow the course taken by Mr. Willkie, it is likely to follow the course taken by the Whigs of 1852"—had demanded the well-thought-out assessment (assisted by Irita) that appeared on December 13 in the *Nation*.

Like Schlesinger's, Willkie's article had been submitted before Pearl Harbor. Arguing that Schlesinger's "Conscience Republicans," rather than leaving the GOP, were now well on their way to controlling its agenda, Wendell conceded that "their international position [had] not been translated into many votes on the floor of Congress." He agreed that unless his party recognized that America must assume world leadership, not only now but after the war, "it will suffer the fate of the Whigs, and suffer it quickly." Wendell wrapped up with a defense of those "obsolete economic positions" of his that Schlesinger discounted by iterating that his quarrel with the New Deal was not that it "sought to correct the abuses of the free-enterprise system or to cause a wider distribution of its benefits, but that fanatical theorists under the guise of reform . . . [tried] to destroy the system itself."[50] Arthur Vandenberg, also a contributor to this issue of the *Nation*, abandoned noninterventionism after Pearl Harbor. Lindbergh and the AFC followed suit.

Asked where his party was heading at the end of 1942, Wendell would give the Detroit *News* reporter a piece of his mind. "Look," he said, speaking of the hardcore isolationists, "if we go back, it will be so far back that neither you nor I nor anyone in this room can be a party to it. It will be way back. We can never let that happen."[51] The party leader had in mind the surprising outcome at the historic Republican National Committee meeting eight months before on April 20. There had been caustic words with Robert Taft at the Chicago Conference, after which Wendell pushed to a vote the repudiation of the doctrine of isolationism. The new RNC document and accompanying internationalist language made Hoover, Landon, and Hamilton Fish rub their eyes. "We realize that after this war," Wendell's text read, "the responsibility of the nation will not be circumscribed within the territorial limits of the United States; that our nation has an obligation to assist in bringing about understanding, comity, and cooperation among the nations of the world."[52]

Senator Taft could only warn darkly that Wendell's success meant that Henry Luce and Dorothy Thompson, "together with the wealthy crowd in the east, . . . will run the GOP into the ground."[53] Although the apoplexy of isolationists spoke for the Old Guard and a broad band of GOP regulars, *Republican*, the national party magazine, featured Wendell's updated Wilsonianism as its June "Speech of the Month." There, Wendell served up a profession of faith wrapped in a history lesson. His country's isolationism after the Great War had been a direct cause of the present war and of the "present economic instability of the past 20 years," it declared. Were Americans to repeat the past—"a withdrawal from the problems and responsibilities of the world after the war"—disaster would follow. "Make sure that you choose leaders who have principles . . . vote for straight-out men—not wobblers." As he wrote a month after his RNC platform success, "the League of Nations was the religion of my young life."[54]

Joseph Martin judged this RNC platform victory to be "Wendell Willkie's monument." In tipping it off its solid isolationist base, Wendell started the Republican party down a curious evolutionary path into an internationalism he hoped would fulfill the Wilsonian mission.[55] The Chicago platform coup was the high point in a season of defining initiatives, a run of signature engagements during the spring of 1942 that promoted Wendell's stature as an Emersonian public personality in the opinion of many Americans. He was seen more and more as the politician as individualist or, rather, the politician whose actions went against the grain of political convention in the service of the commonweal's ideals. In *America as a Civilization*, an interpretive masterwork published little more than a decade after his death, the author extolled the global "glimpse" possessed by a Wendell Willkie—"that despite divergences of economic systems, of race and color and language and social structure, the world is compassable, interdependent, organic."[56] "Glimpse" may not have been a strong enough characterization of an almost dramatically heightened sensibility about race, faith, and diversity in the short span of years after Pearl Harbor. During that time, middle-class African Americans, impatient with separate equality status quo, and cosmopolitan Jews, disgusted with quota-ed professional access, found his electoral appeal—based on political calculus and empathic earnestness—increasingly convincing.

Positive coverage in the African American press—disappointed by Roosevelt's acceptance of segregation in the armed services and widespread exclusion from defense industries—had followed Wendell across the country.[57] True enough, there were deeds he could rightly proffer as evidence of high-mindedness to both groups of Americans beset by bigotry: the defeat of the KKK in the Akron, Ohio, public school board fight; his singlehanded termination of Jewish exclusion from Florida's ultra-exclusive WASP enclave of Hobe Sound; his service to the beleaguered film industry.[58] Increasingly, though, deeds came wrapped in genuine fellow-feeling. His politics proved captivating because they served his ideals more than in reverse. It was an amalgam no other Republican contemporary—neat little Dewey, rigid Taft, pompous Vandenberg, precocious Stassen, or reactionary Bricker—possessed. It was during these post–Pearl Harbor months that someone called him the Wall Street Abraham Lincoln, an indication of his rising stature as an American original, a natural democrat in lower case.[59]

CHAPTER 9

EXCEPTIONALISM AT WORK

1943 Detroit Riot reenacted, Willkie and team. *Courtesy the Lilly Library, Indiana University, Bloomington, Indiana.*

To a Forty-Eighter descendant, the dividend of immigration was obvious after some two hundred years of "new blood, new experiences, new ideas." His essay in the June 1942 *Saturday Evening Post*, "The Case for Minorities," like his "Fair Trial" two years earlier, was a puissant apology for the fact that it had even been necessary to write it. Three months earlier, the *Saturday Evening Post* had caused a firestorm of protest with "The Case Against the Jews," an article by a non-practicing Jew blaming German Jews for their own plight and widely deemed anti-Semitic. Scrambling to recover from its self-infliction, and claiming "many readers" suggested a rebuttal from Wendell Willkie, the editors published what Wendell decried as "only disease and death in the wailing distortion of Mr. Milton Mayer's recent flagellation of the Jews." Because the benefit of racial and religious diversity was self-evident, Wendell conceded that the only purpose served by his rebuttal was as a forewarning, lest the tensions brought on by war and competing ideologies reintroduce the ignominies of the Ku Klux Klan and "such calamities as the series of race riots in our cities which grew out of the emotionalism of the First World War" (finally mentioned after two decades of silence).

Twenty-three years earlier, Captain Willkie had returned from the Great War without recorded notice of the "Red Summer" of 1919 during which a streak of interracial carnage from May to October reddened the streets of Charleston, South Carolina; Washington, DC; Longview, Texas; Chicago; Knoxville; and Omaha, leaving some African Americans lynched, many killed, and thousands shaken, abused, impoverished, embittered. Even though brief and belated, Wendell's article's acknowledgment signaled his keener appreciation of an American perennial: racism. For good measure, four good-sized iconic photos illustrating the nation's diversity dominated "The Case for Minorities"—a Native American, African American, Chinese American, Slavic American. Its author closed his notable piece with a warning that "our way of living together in America is a strong but delicate fabric. . . . For God's sake, let us not tear it asunder. For no man knows, once it is destroyed, where or when man will find its protective warmth again." Pearl Harbor had quieted the Nyes, Lindberghs, Father Coughlins, and Bilbos for the time being, but the prejudices they espoused lay ready for new marching orders. Six months later, December 17, the distinguished board of the *American Hebrew* magazine, honorary member FDR voting affirmatively, bestowed its annual American Hebrew Medal on a deeply moved Wendell Willkie.[1]

The evolution of Wendell's civil rights pivot in the spring of 1942 followed a steady course few politicians in either major party—with the somewhat later example of Henry Wallace—would risk until well after the end of the war. Unquestionably instigated by the prospective balance of power calculus of African

American ballots as the Great Black Migration, interrupted by the Great Depression, resumed, Wendell's race relations outreach was the principled prescience of a politician ready to advance democracy through demography. Against the equal rights petitions and threatened protests of African American leaders and their left-wing white sympathizers, the Roosevelt administration—accommodating the white South, skilled labor, churches, the business community, and much of mainstream public opinion—steadfastly resisted meaningful racial integration of the economy, military, education, and housing on grounds that disruptive "social experimentation" must be subordinated during wartime. In striking opposition to the status quo paradigm, Wendell's RNC resolution on racial integration as adopted in Chicago that April affirmed that "such things we do not consider in the realm of social experiment. They are wrongs under the Constitution" . . . to be corrected now.[2]

In light of the positive response to Wendell from the upper tier of African American leadership, the disaggregation of significant numbers of black voters from their New Deal fidelity seemed promising. He praised as a self-evident imperative the *Pittsburgh Courier*'s Double V Campaign proclaimed that February ("Victory for Democracy—Abroad and at Home"). He applauded the new Federal Employment Practices Committee (FEPC) wrenched from an intimidated White House by A. Philip Randolph, president of the activist Brotherhood of Sleeping Car Porters. Finally persuaded after their Oval Office visit in mid-June 1941 that Asa Randolph and NAACP head Walter White might actually bring the national capital to a dead stop with tens of thousands of marching African Americans, Franklin Roosevelt had issued Executive Order 8802 banning discrimination in defense industries and creating the FEPC to oversee the order. A further earnest demonstration of Wendell's civil rights politics was his forceful statement, together with an outsized photo, endorsing the National Urban League's (NUL) "Campaign for Negro Workers." Wendell's smiling likeness offered Americans the first match packet of the hundreds of thousands of NUL match packets emblazoned with "TRAIN THEM—HIRE THEM—WORK WITH THEM,

1/10th of America's Citizens are Negroes." Executive NUL secretary Lester Granger could hardly express adequate appreciation for the Republican Party head's launching the League's national campaign—a fine gesture "indicative of the kind of leadership which truly outstanding Americans are rendering to national unity and victory."[3]

The National Urban League was the race-relations tortoise, stealthily locating openings in commerce, business, and industry for African Americans through "education and persuasion" that the NAACP, the Brotherhood of Sleeping Car Porters (BSCP), and the brand new Congress of Racial Equality (CORE) demanded more by right.[4] Walter Francis White of the NAACP manifestly was a much different civil rights leader. *The Fire in the Flint*, his well-crafted 1924 novel of southern taboos, had helped launch the New Negro Arts Movement popularly known as the Harlem Renaissance. Besides writing successful novels (*Flight* came next), his hazardous service impersonating a white man as an undercover investigator of southern horrors made him uniquely indispensable to the NAACP until his heart-stopping reports in *Nation* magazine and northern newspapers finally put the KKK and local constabularies on the lookout for a blond, blue-eyed African American interloper. He was the face of *Time*'s January 1938 cover, the game "Negro leader" whose congressional allies soon plunged the Senate into seven unprecedented weeks of fierce southern filibuster of the Wagner–Van Nuys federal anti-lynching bill. Franklin Roosevelt sent word through Eleanor that Walter White and his congressional supporters were on their own.[5]

When Wendell finally met Walter White in the fall of 1941 at a private dinner at the Waldorf-Astoria, the Atlanta-born, socially ubiquitous man of color had run a top-down, efficient association numbering some 400,000 members as executive secretary since the legendary James Weldon Johnson's retirement ten years earlier. Officially, the NAACP was scrupulously nonpartisan, yet it was known that Walter White had toyed seriously with a proposal to manage a separate campaign organization for Al Smith's run for the presidency thirteen years earlier in 1928.[6] The titular party chief had made several attempts to meet Walter White before and after the Philadelphia convention. "Mr. NAACP" was a New York celebrity, a regular at the venues of power and culture, on a first-name basis with FDR's cabinet, Franklin himself, and much of the financial and political elite. His first Willkie meeting, White said, began "one of the three or four closest and richest friendships" of his life. He recognized it on both a personal and political level as developing out of the "increasing political strength and independence of the Negro vote."[7] Their collaboration—fueled by complementary outsized egos—produced mutual rapid-fire results for both men's national standing and political ambitions.

Spring of 1942 presented each with unusual opportunities to use his special experience and influence to make a durable impact on race relations and peace. For Wendell, his election to the board of Twentieth Century-Fox Corporation as its chairman was an unusual accolade Wendell accepted not only as professionally merited; he regarded the recognition as a remarkable opportunity to advance strategically and imaginatively the twinned causes of international peace and domestic civil liberties. An annual compensation of an opulent (rumored) $200,000 invited a West Virginia senator's derision that the "barefoot boy from Wall Street" was now the "glamour boy of Hollywood," but the value of his Hollywood position was in its power to sway serious public opinion. The idea of an ambitious life-and-times of Woodrow Wilson film seems to have occurred to Wendell immediately. Improbably, then, when Twentieth Century-Fox released Wendell's pet technicolor film project to praise (positive and stilted) two years later, *Wilson* (directed by Daryl Zanuck) would garner ten nominations and win five Oscars. Race, it is true, was completely unaddressed in the film. International peace and solidarity were its premises.[8]

To Walter White, for whom the so-called Harlem Renaissance had been a cultural production machine to transform the demeaning images of African Americans in the consciousness of hostile or ignorant white Americans, the friendship with Twentieth Century-Fox's new chairman held the promise of civil rights providence. At a lubricated lunch together where Wendell rehearsed the cultural and political stakes behind an invitation to address the Academy of Motion Picture Arts and Sciences, White

was quick to say that he saw no evidence that the film industry was willing to use its great power to advance the vaunted
democratic ideals advocated by the government's new Office of
War Information (OWI). "The most widely circulated medium
yet devised to reach the minds and emotions of all people all
over America and the world was perpetuating . . . harmful ste-
reotypes of the Negro," he said, adding that his own repeated
attempts to elicit meaningful responses from the studios had gone
unanswered—a case in point being David O. Selznick's disregard
of NAACP concerns regarding *Gone With the Wind*.[9]

Wendell's straightforward reaction, in White's recollection,
was wholly unexpected. "I ought to have a tiny bit of influence
right now," at least for the time being, Wendell thought he could
say. The new distinction required an address that February before
the Academy of Motion Picture Arts and Sciences at the 1942
Oscar presentations. He proposed that he and Walter go to Hollywood "[and] talk to the more intelligent people in the industry
to see what can be done to change the situation." They agreed
on the spot to meet at the end of February, when Wendell, at the
invitation of colorful Twentieth Century-Fox president Spyrous
Skouras, was to speak. In the interim, Wendell put the NAACP
secretary in touch with two film producers of known liberal
racial inclinations: Daryl Zanuck and Walter Wanger.[10] Zanuck,
the youngish Fox vice president, was moderately well disposed to
Walter White's improved images agenda. Wanger, a Dartmouth
sophisticate with German university exposure and an unabashed
Willkieite, was a member of the influential Century Group and
already well known to White. Wanger had produced the instant
Western classic *Stagecoach*.[11]

Arriving several days in advance of Wendell's Oscars speech on
the night of February 26, Walter White traversed the unfamiliar
professional landscape with limited success. Even with "a swell
letter from Mrs. Roosevelt" and introductions from Zanuck and
Wanger, the cachet of heading the country's oldest civil rights association opened few doors to the industry's other studio power brokers. Greatly to his surprise than decades of negotiated successes
inclined him to expect, Wendell also discovered that the studio

heads—the moguls whose Washington persecutors he had reduced to impotence—obeyed a collective code of profitable survival sinuous enough to stymie TVA's erstwhile nemesis and prospective president of the United States.[12] The seeming unassailability of the white South's veto power over movie content and distribution below the Mason-Dixon line raised an iron bar to positive representations of black life in film. Insofar as hopes of a meaningful audience for their concerns, White and Willkie realized that their cultural policy agenda demanded more time and background work for a successful outcome. Walter was left to the curious evening's experience of master of ceremony Bob Hope's comedy routine and Wendell's praise of the film industry's refusal to be silenced by small-minded officials. It must channel the ideals of liberty, freedom, and tolerance that America and her allies were fighting and dying to preserve, he exhorted. "Let's begin to strike. Let's begin to win, for the victories of totalitarianism have taught us that those who win strike first."[13] Broadcast over CBS to the nation, the well-received call-to-arms speech was an additional reason for Twentieth Century-Fox's president and board to pride themselves on Wendell Willkie's formal installation two months later as chairman of the corporation.

As his *Wilson* moved from conception to large budget, Wendell's race relations commitment had a corollary debut at the Freedom House dinner at Hotel Commodore on Thursday evening, March 19, 1942. Founded in January 1940 by Eleanor Roosevelt, Wendell Willkie, David Dubinsky, several Century Group activists, prominent clergy, leading academics, notable public affairs women and men, Freedom House still professes seventy-five years later to be the "clear voice for democracy and freedom around the world," although its annual subsidy from the US Treasury has caused its many recent critics to question its willingness to speak truth to power. Wendell used Freedom House's gala dinner as a platform for a speech soldering international justice to domestic race relations. Distinguished stars of stage and screen were in attendance. The Radio City Music Hall Glee Club serenaded. Even though founding board member Eleanor Roosevelt was unavoidably absent, Dorothy Thompson, whom some thought was the other first lady because of her journalistic celebrity, sat proud and adamantine with the principal speaker of the evening, Archibald MacLeish, the polymath librarian of Congress, and Herbert Agar, the Louisville *Courier-Journal*'s Pulitzer Prize–winning editor and the organization's first president.[14]

Dispensing with obligatory boilerplate straightaway, Wendell presented his race relations subject with an informed urgency that reflected a sharpened political and personal recalibration, embellished by details provided by the NAACP. "Freedom House, a house, as it name indicates, symbolizing freedom," was pledged to the "advancement of the cause of freedom throughout the world," he declared in his corn belt twang. But were these sincere, distinguished men and women "always as alert to practice it here at home? Do we accord freedom to all of our citizens?" Not if a citizen is a Negro who wanted to serve in the United States Navy, and, driving home the point, Wendell dramatically revealed the identity of the "unnamed Negro mess man" whose shipboard valor on the morning of December 7 had fascinated the national press and much of the public for weeks.

The anonymous "mess boy" hero, although untrained in ordnance, had manned a pair of machine guns on the signal bridge and blazed away at swooping enemy Zeros while his battleship keeled over, the captain lay dying, and flames finally forced him and a junior officer to abandon ship with the captain's body. Finally, continued Wendell, pressured by the NAACP and the *Pittsburgh Courier*, the Navy secretary Frank Knox acknowledged the serviceman's record that the head of the NAACP had just shared. He identified twenty-two-year-old Doris Miller of Waco, Texas. "The dispatches give us no further news . . . except that single fine act of judgment and self-sacrificing courage" (and that the Navy declined to honor with a citation). But one known fact was that Miller was barred "from enlisting in the United States Navy and only for the reason that he was born with a black skin." Holding on to his point, Wendell recalled the irony of recently watching world heavyweight champion Joe Louis risk his title to raise $100,000 for the Naval Relief Society. Yet Louis, preparing to fight for his country in an Army uniform, also would have been barred from any rank above mess boy in the US Navy. "Now you lovers of freedom," Wendell groused, "won't you, while you're proclaiming the necessity for freedom throughout the world, devote some time to bringing about a correction of this injustice at home?"[15] His distinguished liberal audience heartily applauded the indignation of his unanticipated remarks. Wendell's Freedom House elocution troubled the president, but Navy Secretary Knox's opposition to integration proved iron cast.

The Warner Bros. release in May 1942 of *In This Our Life*, directed by John Huston, starring Bette Davis and Olivia de Havilland, took Wendell and Walter White by surprise. The film adaptation of Ellen Glascow's Pulitzer Prize novel featuring a well-spoken young colored man aspiring to study law, but wrongly accused of vehicular homicide, was precisely what they had had in mind—a "magnificent treatment of the Negro," as Walter White wrote Harry Warner. "It was delightful to know that this progress has been made." Yet the titular leader of the GOP and the executive secretary of the association were understandably concerned that instead of representing an enlightened trend, *In This Our Life* was essentially a momentary accommodation by Warner Bros. of the inconvenience of the inclusivity pressure of the new federal Office of War Information (OWI). Their fears were justified. *Tennessee Johnson*, MGM's outrageous veneration of Abraham Lincoln's impeached successor, was scheduled for release during the Christmas holidays.[16]

All the more reason, then, that Wendell made the unprecedented decision—two months after being invested that April with the Twentieth Century-Fox chairmanship—to address the national conference of the NAACP in Los Angeles. He disregarded the risks of accepting Walter White's double-barreled proposal that they return to Los Angeles together the third week in July: the leader of the Republican party to address the NAACP; the head of the NAACP to appeal to the better selves of the studio chieftains. Elmo Roper, a record of consistent polling accuracy to his credit, warned Wendell's supporters that many white voters were increasingly troubled by their man's well-publicized association with African American causes. No similar warning appears to have caught his attention, unfortunately, that the perceived color-conscious elitism of Walter White's Hollywood agenda created heated debate in several black newspapers.[17]

The return to Hollywood was better planned and advertised. CBS granted thirty minutes of coast-to-coast air time to the NAACP for Wendell Willkie's address on Sunday evening, July 19. Walter Wanger telegraphed that a strategy meeting for Wendell with Bartley Crum, the liberal activist attorney, and several other California political insiders was set for Saturday and that he was preparing "everything for Walter White" on Sunday. He and Zanuck succeeded in drawing one of the largest bodies of actors, writers, producers, directors, and technicians in Hollywood memory from most of the six major studios to the luncheon planning session in the swank Café de Paris on the Fox lot.[18] Wendell opened with forceful remarks that went to the heart of the race relations matter. As a group, many of those present had recently experienced the organized force of religious bigotry. As it had been his professional privilege to expose the politics of prejudice against them, he presumed to call upon them to help another group of Americans whose similar hardships were caused by race prejudice as deep as the prejudice against their faith. Then he introduced his friend.[19]

Walter White's rehearsed, reasoned appeal that the world war all people of goodwill were pledged to win engaged all races, religions, and classes—but that the film industry had too long trafficked in shibboleths that perpetuated African American backwardness—was received with spirited applause. Moguls, directors, actors, writers, technicians—the lot—departed the Café de Paris with the understanding that the presence of an advisory or consultative NAACP bureau was a proposal worthy of serious discussion. Two studio heads offered to underwrite such a script bureau, a proposal astutely declined by the NAACP board as a probable infringement of independent judgment. The alternative, an NAACP-financed Hollywood presence analogous to the Legion of Decency, ultimately failed because of competing budgetary priorities in education and litigation. Walter White would try to take encouragement from several films produced during 1943 such as *Sahara*, *The Ox-Bow Incident*, and *Casablanca*—films in which a solitary black person displayed either a professional talent or a moral integrity the white movie-going public was willing to applaud. Ever the pragmatic optimist in the race relations business, he would write wistfully some years afterward, "As long as Willkie lived, the trend set by the 1942 luncheon continued." For some years thereafter, the studios risked conceding the NAACP a ratio of one black to twelve whites in movie street scenes.[20]

When Harry Truman addressed the NAACP's ten thousand members and spectators from the Lincoln Memorial in Washington, DC, on June 29, 1947, he was the first president in US history to do so, with Eleanor Roosevelt and Walter White standing by. Five years minus one month almost to the day had passed since Walter White presented Wendell Willkie to a capacity audience attending the thirty-third annual conference of the NAACP in Los Angeles's historic Second Baptist Church on the Sunday following their Café de Paris luncheon. As one Truman biographer claims, "none had ever spoken so unequivocally for the rights of Negroes (the preferred term in those days)" as the little man from Missouri. The unprecedentedness of the occasion and the expectation of legislative action seemed to augur a new era in domestic race relations. His words broadcast across the land, Truman reiterated that he meant "rights for *all* Americans."[21] Wendell, the first leader of a major political party to come before the premier organization for the advancement of the nation's largest minority racial group, read from a text suggesting Walter's concurrence and probably Irita's input, but the ideas were unmistakably his—that no distinction should now be possible between what was global and what was local in the fight for human dignity.

In the half hour CBS vouchsafed him, Wendell cast the titanic struggle for liberty as one brought on by the bane of imperialism, a fight to free peoples from its omnipresent arrogance. "We of the democratic nations are fighting an anti-imperialistic war. . . . We seek to liberate, not to enslave," yet there must be no truck with hypocrisy. But the truth was, Wendell said, that Americans practiced within our own boundaries "something that amounts to race imperialism. The attitude of white citizens toward the Negroes has undeniably had some of the unlovely and tragic characteristics of an alien imperialism—a smug racial superiority, a willingness to exploit an unprotected people." His audience comprised the leaders of a people insulted and wounded "and sore tried with many practices of our democracy," Wendell averred. Still, he believed that they would be sustained by their faith in the cause of freedom and liberty, that "those who contribute the most will have the most to do with fashioning the future."

He closed with the hallowed trope of American exceptionalism that "for all its defects—and they are many—American democracy is the only sure foundation we know upon which a world of justice and freedom can be built."[22] The old world was "breaking into pieces," and as it did would come "opportunity to fashion a newer and better life." Like so much else in his meteoric passage, Wendell's avoidable early death diminished the public remembrance of the unprecedented NAACP appearance. It represented, even so, a fecund race relations venture to be reenacted by a politically savvy president and a well-rehearsed civil rights leader some five years in the future.

For better and worse, Wendell reaffirmed his decision not to seek the New York governorship after his Los Angeles commitment. Columnist Drew Pearson spoke for a fusion of powerful New York interests (Fiorello LaGuardia's fusionists, David Dubinsky's ILGWU, Frank Altschul of the original Willkieites, Robert Moses, New York's Baron Haussmann, and FDR quietly) urging a Willkie run against Dewey. After the fatal cardiac removing newly elected congressman Kenneth Simpson from the scene in February 1941, the levers of the GOP state convention were all but securely controlled by Dewey's allies. The gubernatorial contest would have been fierce, but Wendell's public popularity polled strongly, firmly bulwarked by the resources of Henry Luce, Thomas Lamont, and party liberals had an even chance of prevailing. The sideshow of Albany with its quid pro quo of unremitting byzantine compromises revolted him. Nevertheless, Dewey supporters were prepared to wink at an exchange deal: their man's withdrawal from a presidential bid in 1944 in exchange for Willkie's endorsement of Dewey for governor. Dewey, it was widely rumored, had offered Wendell just such a deal: Willkie's tacit support in November 1942 for Dewey as governor; Dewey's pledge to leave the presidency to Wendell in 1944.

"The facts are these," a furious Wendell wrote Pearson. Months before, several Dewey representatives proposed that if he agreed to support Tom Dewey for governor, "they would assure to me the New York delegation at the Republican National Convention in 1944. I rejected their suggestion, saying to them that the proposal offended both my moral and my common sense."[23] Later, when Dewey approached him at a large political function, Dewey pledged to serve out his four-year term as governor. Wendell distrusted Dewey. As Herman's son, he regarded the governorship as an unworthy swerve from a historic opportunity to guide his country from the Oval Office in a time of world turbulence. Increasingly, a sense of superordinate destiny ruled serious considerations of conventional politics. Instead, on August 26, 1942, the head of the Republican Party flew off on a trip around the world. Joe Martin advised against it, as Willkie would be absent during the midterm elections campaign.

CHAPTER 10

ONE WORLD OR NOTHING

General Claire Chennault, Mme. Chiang, and the generalissimo with Willkie's hat, 1942. *Courtesy the Lilly Library, Indiana University, Bloomington, Indiana.*

Wendell Willkie's trip around the world was an extraordinary goodwill odyssey. The 1942 *Gulliver*, an upscale model of the massive Consolidated B-24 (on loan from the US Army Air Corps with a six-man military crew), lifted off from Long Island's Mitchell Field on August 26, 1942. It would carry him to Egypt, Turkey, Lebanon, Syria, Palestine, Iraq, Iran, and ten days in the USSR, with seven days in China, before returning along the edge of the Arctic Circle to the United States, touching down finally in Minneapolis on October 14. Actual mileage covered in seven weeks was 28,400, as officially logged by Major

Richard T. Knight, US Army Air Corps. The rounded figure generally reported by the press was 31,000 miles. No American airplane had ever undertaken such a flight. Joe Martin, house minority leader, dreading having to counter the belief among GOP regulars that their titular leader was AWOL in the service of FDR, had strongly advised against a trip that virtually removed Wendell from the midterm election campaign. Indeed, President Roosevelt had embraced the plan immediately and proposed the title, which Wendell graciously declined, of ambassador-at-large.[1]

Aside from the diminished part to be played in his party's 1942 congressional midterm success, Wendell's self-appointed mission to North Africa, the Middle East, Russia, and China also ended further consideration of his running for the New York governorship. By early summer he had pretty firmly decided that the New York governorship meant a detour to the White House through the quicksand of compromise, a way station from which he would emerge with flattened ideals and corrupted means. His eloquence on the subject was fierce and frequent. As he made clear to the loyal Lamoyne "Lem" Jones, his 1940 campaign factotum, in normal times he might have sought the governorship, given New York's "economic importance to the country." He recognized, however, that the times were abnormal, and he believed his voice was more needed on the national and international scene "than in a state office." Wendell's new civil rights advisor and sounding board Walter White recalled a Broad Street visit when, shoes on the desk, his friend interrupted talk of the governorship and pointed to an outbound troop ship, its deck crowded with enlisted men. "Look at those kids out there . . . I believe I can do more in fighting for what they believe and for what they deserve by staying out of public office," he mused, "even including the presidency" if he could do more as an individual free to speak his own mind.

On the other hand, he also had to know that opposition of Tom Dewey loyalists to a possible gubernatorial candidacy was fierce. Crusty Edwin Jaeckle, New York state chairman in the mold of Connecticut's deceased boss John Henry Rorbeck, tightened the party reins to make sure no Willkie stampede like Philadelphia's upended Dewey's candidacy at the Saratoga convention that August. Still, until he instructed his supporters to abandon their considerable efforts for governor in early July, Wendell's popularity, buoyed by the *Herald Tribune*, *Time*, liberal Republicans, and a conspiring FDR, might have posed a formidable challenge.[2] In the final analysis, Wendell, his high-mindedness conceded, probably made a virtue out of a political impasse.

During the fraught summer of 1942 there was so much going wrong with the world beyond Albany, New York, as to make a state governorship and even hands-on engagement in GOP electioneering seem to the loyal opposition leader inextricably interconnected with Japanese military victories in China and the Southeast Asia and German advances in North Africa and Russia. Because his part in the lend-lease debate had been indispensable and widely reported, Wendell found the message contained in a telegram sent on June 24 by three newsmen posted to besieged Moscow deeply troubling both to his patriotism and his businessman's know-how. Eddy Gilmore at Associated Press, Ben Robertson of *PM*, and Maurice Hinds of the *Herald Tribune*—men whose confidence he had earned on the campaign train—wired Wendell to come and see the situation for himself. "Already it is too late to help Russia as we should have helped," Robertson believed. "Russia will fight and fight but every day that country loses its offensive strength." Where was the promised Allied Second Front to relieve the USSR? FDR responded positively—gratefully even—to Wendell's letter five days later requesting permission to ascertain the success of the Allied project in three theaters: Africa, Europe, and Asia. Unlike his mission to England allegedly engineered from the Oval Office and Century Club, White House memoranda reveal the initiative for Wendell's global roundtrip to have been Wendell's.[3]

FDR's summons to "a good talk in regard to [the trip]" took place the first week in August at the White House. After an elaborate luncheon for Queen Wilhelmina of the Netherlands, dispossessed by German occupiers, FDR and Wendell spoke privately until other vital business brought their detailed, animated parley to a close at 4:30 p.m. When they met again at the White House six days before the *Gulliver* lifted off, FDR shared quite human concerns about perils that faced his Republican collaborator. Even though they'd differed politically in the past, he told Wendell, "I've got a very great regard for you. . . . I know you've got guts, but remember, you may get to Cairo just as Cairo is falling and you may get to Russia just at the time of a Russian collapse." The global situation continued to be dire indeed. Tobruk had fallen to General Rommel's Afrika Korps. Burma, Singapore, and the Dutch East Indies had surrendered to the Japanese. The *Wehrmacht*'s Sixth Army launched its massive Stalingrad assault on August 23.

Yet such was the possible value of Wendell's presence in the theaters and the capitals of the great Allied struggle that FDR believed it could help make a crucial difference to the war's outcome. As an earnest of the mission's importance, he handed the GOP leader his personal introduction to Generalissimo Chiang Kai-shek. The telegram already dispatched to Marshal Stalin stressed that his opponent in the last election was "heart and soul with my administration in our foreign policy of opposition to Nazism and real friendship with your government, and he is greatly helping in the war work."[4] The uniqueness of what must have appeared to the Russian dictator and the Chinese autocrat as an anomalous American form of coalition government was for many card-carrying Republicans almost as odd and suspect. The desertion of Frank Knox and Henry Stimson to service in Roosevelt's cabinet—Knox, Landon's running mate, as navy secretary, and Stimson, Hoover's secretary of state, as defense secretary—had dismayed Republicans. To have now their leader parachuting into far-flung capitals where the party of Lincoln would be memorably implicated in the opposition party's postwar commitments was, at the very least, irresponsible.

Taking leave from the president to confer with Secretary of State Hull and Soviet ambassador Maxim Litvinov, Wendell believed it clearly understood that he was free to express himself publicly on matters of mutual concern. Hull's revelation that India was excluded from the Atlantic Charter and off-limits for a symbolic visit or even open to public discussion of its future Wendell found truly surprising. Even more surprising, as he would discover weeks later to his considerable distress, was that the president failed to share the decision that "Operation Sledgehammer" had been deferred, allowing Wendell to think that the Anglo-American second front—as promised Stalin—was to happen before the end of the year.[5] Edith Willkie's awkward message from Clare Boothe Luce was another surprise. Told that Wendell was not at home to receive her telephone call, Luce ordered a stunned Edith to relay her demand to join Joseph Barnes, Gardner "Mike" Cowles, Army Major Grant Mason, and Navy Captain Paul Pihl aboard the *Gulliver*.[6] Barnes's credentials as a former *Herald Tribune* foreign news correspondent, Cowles's as publisher of *Look* and new OWI official, and Pilh's as a Willkie brother-in-law were regarded as more appropriate to the mission than Boothe's literary accomplishments. "That would make a great headline," Edith recalled Wendell chuckling when she told him of the phone call, "Wendell Willkie on Round the World Trip with Clare Boothe Luce." Helpfully, FDR insisted that women be excluded from the *Gulliver*.

The Saturday before their late August lift-off, Wendell and Mike Cowles arrived at FDR's country estate at Hyde Park in a driving rainstorm for an unanticipated luncheon invitation. The historic Hudson Valley setting was meant to impress upon them that their significance as global emissaries derived from Franklin Roosevelt's paramount authority as grand master of the embryonic United Nations. The manor house buzzed with the activities of Queen Wilhelmina and her entourage of ladies-in-waiting. Harry Hopkins's sinister presence appears not to have detracted from Wendell's relish of the afternoon. "First, we've all got to have one of my famous old-fashioneds," Cowles recorded the squire of the manor announcing as he wheeled himself into the room and to the bar. The talk over lunch skipped the alarming world events and ran to the 1940 campaign with both politicians reliving details of the not-so-secret matching contributions from the business community to the Democrats. FDR recalled once again the amounts each du Pont family member had given openly to Wendell, matched by each donating secretly to his own campaign treasury. Following the president to his study, they made them-

230   THE IMPROBABLE WENDELL WILLKIE

selves comfortable while he prepared a "personal letter to Stalin," which he took a half hour to finish, promptly sealed, and handed to the GOP leader, and grandly instructed that the letter "is to be handed by you to Stalin personally, and not to any aide no matter how important in the hierarchy." With that, Cowles remembered, "Roosevelt wished us great good luck and we left." The New York Republican committee sent what read like a relieved farewell to the national leader just before he and the twelve-man party rose above the clouds from Mitchell Field.

Major Knight, who would prove almost as politically sophisticated as his aeronautics was stellar, headed his silver four-engine behemoth south to West Palm Beach, stopped to see Naval ensign Philip in Puerto Rico, then to Belem on the Amazon, Natal at the tip of Brazil, and out over the Atlantic to the secret US airbase on Ascension Island, direct from there to Accra, Kano, and Khartoum on the Nile north to Cairo, touching down on Tuesday, September 1.[7] "Mr. Willkie, who looked genial as usual," announced the *Egyptian Mail*, "but showing signs of the strain of a long journey, said he had had a good trip." Though somewhat strained and rumpled, Wendell made the raison d'être of his trip crystal clear to the crowd of newsmen and welcoming party of military and civilian dignitaries. "As a member of the party in opposition to the President," he wanted it clear there was no division in the United States as to the question of both "winning the war and establishing a just peace." Recovered and temporarily unrumpled the next morning, he was received for a lively forty-minute parley by Nahas Pasha, Egypt's pro-Allied prime minister, followed by a baseball update with US servicemen, tour of the city, visit to the Sphynx and pyramids, and a more measured assessment of the local military and political mindset, given the palpable fear of the sudden evacuation of Cairo should Rommel regain the initiative against the British Eighth Army.[8]

Collier's Frank Gervasi cabled an over-the-top "Willkie at the Front," describing a "blitzvisit" crammed with statements, interviews, receptions, cocktail parties, "appearances before still and movie cameras, radio talks, calls on diplomats and kings, conferences with politicians, soldiers, more diplomats." Wendell "sass[ed] the censors," Gervasi wrote, "[made] formal diplomatic calls in a lounge suit instead of the sacred striped pants and tailcoat tradition." King Farouk seemed unconcerned by attire when he received his special visitor on holy Friday. Instead, the playboy monarch complained of luxury car import difficulties and his popularity drop in the American press. Nor did Farouk evince any readiness to commit Egypt formally to the Allied cause, the real object of Wendell's otherwise waste of time with the indulgent paper sovereign. The Axis armies were still within artillery range, and Wendell knew that a good percentage of the Arab population regarded the Germans as potential liberators. Young officers like Gamal Abdul Nasser, Egypt's future Pan African pharaoh, listened to the *Voice of Free Arabism*, proclaiming that the British "were, and still are, the cause of our material and spiritual weakness." Outside Alexandria lay France's barnacled Mediterranean fleet commanded by Vichy officers obedient to Marshal Petain and more antipathetic to the British than to the Germans. Nevertheless, after speaking with Admiral Rene Godfroy, Wendell was inclined to minimize the threat posed to any prospective Allied beachhead.[9]

A front-page group photo in Friday's *Egyptian Mail* was meant to banish fears of British contingency plans for a withdrawal to Palestine. Headlined "Willkie IN THE MIDDLE EAST," a pith-helmeted, khaki-suited Wendell, accompanied by US Major General Russell Maxwell, was shown with British commanders intensely studying engagement maps. His authoritative verdict was featured in bold type: "Recession of Nazi Tide Has Begun." Wendell offered incontestable facts and figures that showed that victory was preordained. The United States now produced more than 5,000 planes monthly. Against the 500,000 tons of ships sunk monthly, she built a monthly replacement tonnage of 600,000. "Our tank production is ahead of schedule," he boasted.[10] He had wanted to be even more categorical after a day and night he, Barnes, and Cowles spent at the field headquarters of the new Eighth Army commander, General Bernard Montgomery, soon to be acclaimed as the victor of El Alamein. In contrast to some of Egypt's British overlords imperturbably on display at Cairo's rambling Shepheard Hotel or on Alexandria's corniche—"Rudyard Kipling[s], untainted even with the liberalism of Cecil Rhodes"—Wendell found Montgomery's un-aristocratic background appealing, his almost priestly dedication a gift.

They discussed military tactics. Montgomery guaranteed that with three hundred US Sherman tanks (already on the docks at Alexandria and Port Said) he could finish the Germans and Italians. "It is now mathematically certain that I shall destroy Rommel," the diminutive general declared, and proposed that if such a statement were released under Wendell's name, an impressed Churchill might put him in command of the entire North African theater. A press conference was held on the spot with Montgomery showing considerable public relations canniness. "Egypt is saved. Rommel is stopped and a beginning has been made on the task of throwing the Nazis out of Africa," the jointly prepared text read. The "future world spirit," continued Wendell, was symbolized by the cooperation of different nationalities in the struggle led by a "fighting field general" like Montgomery. The refusal of the military censor to release their statement enraged Wendell Willkie, of course. "God damn it, boys," he erupted, "nobody's got the right to censor anything I say." Soon enough, though, he accommodated the advice of Barnes and Cowles that the British authorities were right to urge that he simply repeat his victory message as he continued his mission. Later, Churchill told Wendell that as news of his confidence in Montgomery spread, it had meant a great deal to the morale of the troops and the population at large.[11]

Turkey presented a delicate challenge sophisticated readers of the authoritative *La Syrie et L'Orient* readily inferred. "Mr. Wendell Willkie Brought a Message of Thoughtful Optimism to Turkey," it said in translation. Nervously neutral, the Turks refused airspace to the *Gulliver*, which necessitated Wendell and his team's arrival at Ankara aboard a small Pan Am flight from the British base at Lydda, no uniforms permitted to Major Knight and crew. "The Turkish leaders were watching events in Europe with great anxiety," Cowles understood. They had painful memories of their bad choice in World War I. President

Ismet Inonu, the country's cagey strong man, would remain unavailable. In the event, Turkey's prime minster, Sukru Saracoglu, hurried to confer with his visitor at the airport, and arranged for a broadcast of the news of Rommel's new difficulties with General Montgomery, as well as of the arsenal-of-democracy productivity numbers that augured the Third Reich's inevitable defeat. The numbers—delivered in Wendell's best courtroom brio—visibly impressed the foreign minister, who was recorded to have spent an unprecedented 130 minutes with the GOP leader.

"Mr. Willkie's forthright manner of speech made an excellent impression," the *Eastern Times* noted, no doubt thinking of Wendell's much-repeated debunking of German propaganda broadcasts mocking the credibility of his mission: "Invite Hitler to send to Turkey, as a representative of Germany, his opposition candidate." His free and frank exchange with the press corps—"ask me anything"—was vintage Willkie. The United States would stay engaged in world affairs after the war, he proclaimed. It had pledged itself to self-determination for all peoples. The Japanese Empire had already lost most of its navy at Midway. He praised his hosts' values when they made a point of showing local public schools and institutions that served common folk. "Yet nowhere . . . in the whole Middle East . . . except in Turkey," Wendell underscored, "did anyone suggest showing me a native school."

The thought of Turkey's forty-five well-trained infantry divisions fighting alongside the *Wehrmacht* kept Roosevelt and Churchill up nights. Washington's policy, however, called for continuation of Turkish neutrality rather than risk a German response thrusting *Wehrmacht* divisions into the Middle East. Cowles always believed Wendell "played a masterful role in convincing the Turks to stay neutral." The *New York Times* correspondent on the scene reached the same conclusion.[12] Turkey's decision to settle disputes with Russia soon after Wendell's departure—a decision that opened a southern corridor through Turkey of Harry Hopkins's vital lend-lease supplies to the Soviet Union—was also credited to the positive impact of the visit.[13] On Wednesday, September 9, Wendell laid a wreath on Ataturk's tomb. He left for

Beirut on September 10, Thursday morning. Churchill would hold an unsuccessful unofficial conference with President Inonu soon after Wendell's departure that was obviously influenced by reports of the mission's success. In August of the following year, Inonu, ever the opportunist, would declare his country at war with the Axis Powers. Among carefully prepared briefing papers aboard the *Gulliver* was a document about Kurdish national aspirations. Obviously, neither opportunity nor Allied priorities permitted Wendell to broach the topic of Kurdish autonomy with his Turkish hosts.[14]

The leader of the American opposition party deplaned in the temporary capital of Free France on a brilliant Mediterranean morning. Five-star General Albert Catroux, the most senior officer to rally to Brigadier General Charles de Gaulle's breakaway government, together with Brigadier General Sir Edward Spears, chief of the British Military Mission, welcomed Wendell Willkie at Beirut Airport in grand style as commander-in-chief of the Free French forces at the head of an impressive Anglo-American and Levantine diplomatic delegation. The "Star Spangled Banner" performed correctly, followed by a stirring "Marseillaise," and the obligatory spit-and-polish troop review, Wendell declared himself ready for business with a signature *elan vital* that marked him, according to the Francophone press, "as one of the world's most appealing personalities." "I'm here for two reasons primarily," said he: "to tell the Lebanese and Syrian people about the Lebanese in America, and to gather information about the countries in the region to take back to the President of the United States." With that, he bounded into the waiting limousine for a round of events starting with a cordial meeting and handshake photographed with Lebanon's president Alfred Naqqache and, after a lavish luncheon filled with ceremonial toasts, ending the day at General Catroux's palatial residence where, both of them stiffly erect and unsmiling, Wendell and General de Gaulle met and were photographed.[15]

The American consul, William Gwynn, felt he had almost sweated blood persuading Wendell not to create a diplomatic boner by insisting on hotel accommodations instead of lodging at General Catroux's magnificent Palais des Pins as the invited guest of the august de Gaulle. Of more consequence in Wendell's eyes, however, was a Hoosier concern for the humiliating subordination of Lebanese officials in the French-mandated territory ruled by Catroux and de Gaulle. Finally installed at the Palais des Pins, he and de Gaulle discussed the war situation and the role of France for several hours in a tapestried room dominated by a bust of the Emperor Napoleon and a statue of Joan of Arc. De Gaulle's conception of himself as head of state of legitimate France, although conceded by the British, was rather equivocally observed by an FDR still entangled in negotiations with Vichy satellites. Although he kept silent publicly, Wendell was fully supportive of the Free French Movement.

After listening several hours to de Gaulle's history lesson about the grandeur of France and wounded protests about treatment by the Allies, however, Wendell came to appreciate Churchill's observation that the greatest cross he bore was the "Cross of Lorraine"—the Free French emblem. When Wendell ventured to remind de Gaulle, a preordained instrument of history, that Syria was not part of the French empire but a mandated territory under international protection, the stern response was that France alone must decide the fate of her dependencies. Furthermore, Wendell, Barnes, and Cowles were informed that the characterization of the Free French "Movement" was intolerable. What they mistook for a "movement," said the general, majestically rising from his chair, was not a movement but France itself *en marche*. Placing his palm on Joan of Arc's head, de Gaulle, as Cowles remembered, said curtly, "She saved France. I will save France. Good day gentlemen." General de Gaulle's tutorial subsequently inspired Wendell to imagine the experience as a dramatic production for radio or film.[16] Taking leave of his annoyed host in the morning, he learned from Cowles, as they headed for Palestine, that a cancerous rivalry infected the Free French Movement. Cowles's account of the nefarious scheme proposed by General Catroux's wife during a glittering dinner in de Gaulle's honor belonged in a Twentieth Century-Fox script.

A handwritten note in French handed by a servant bade Mike Cowles meet the five-star general's attractive spouse in the garden

afterward. His bonafides confirmed to her as an important official with access to Roosevelt and known to Churchill, statuesque
Hélène Catroux confided that her husband and many other senior
officers found it almost unbearable "to cope with de Gaulle's monumental arrogance. Wasn't it true," she stated matter-of-factly,
"that even Roosevelt and Churchill were having problems with
him?" Quite simply, she proposed an arranged accident in Beirut to remove the "obstruction." In return for their service to the
Allied cause, her husband would lead French troops into liberated
Paris, and afterward General Catroux would be assured of playing a major role, "if not *the* major role, in the new French government." Required to repeat verbatim several times her proposal in
French and English, Madame Catroux extracted Cowles's pledge
to deliver it. Flying to Jerusalem on September 11 aboard the *Gulliver* after their extraordinary stop in Palestine, Wendell heard the
details of Catroux's proposal in the classic manner of a statesman
acknowledging an extraordinary revelation too extraordinary to
acknowledge. "Mike," he said after a long silence, "you never told
me that story. If it ever gets out, I'll say I never heard it. . . . If
you want to tell it to Roosevelt, you're on your own." FDR's reaction was similar when he heard the story from Cowles. He asked
that the Catroux scheme never be repeated until the war was over.
"After that," said the president, "I don't care."[17]

What awaited FDR's wandering legate in the city of the three
faiths would test his diplomatic stamina and reveal the limits of
reason to mollify ancient passions. A widespread fear was instilled
among Arabs of the region by Nazi propaganda that the Palestine
mandate would be opened to unrestricted Jewish immigration
after the war. Descending from the *Gulliver* in a reasonably neat
dark blue suit at the Jerusalem airport on September 11, Wendell was escorted immediately on a morning tour of the city and
of the holy shrines in the walled area. He filled the obligatory
press conference at noon with the arsenal-of-democracy statistics
of ever-increasing production of planes, tanks, ships, and men in
uniform—all of it greater than the production rate of "all the Axis
countries combined." He witnessed everywhere among the peoples of the Middle East a great commitment to the war effort,

grateful news he would carry back to the United States. The news he brought was equally significant, that all who struggled to bring victory to the cause of the future United Nations had America's assurance of self-determination and material assistance.[18]

Though consummate global cheerleader for the Atlantic Charter's uplifting four freedoms, he had begun to see enough of disease, appalling poverty, and dark-skinned subjugation at the hands of his fellow white men to dread the reckoning to come if fraud followed victory. Even as he prophesied a postwar Middle East of mutuality and progress, then, Wendell's Palestine dossier on the *Gulliver* overflowed with a bewildering crush of appeals, claims, demands, many of them desperately urgent but few of them capable of implementation in the prevailing power politics of the region. The Balfour Declaration's 1917 promise of a Jewish National Home in Palestine had all but vanished after the Arab uprisings of the late 1930s. By their Palestine fiat—the 1939 White Paper—the British favored the Arabs by imposing a five-year immigration freeze at 75,000 Jews. When Wendell flew into Jerusalem in the fall of 1942, Palestine was a pressure cooker. By then, the British immigration embargo had been defied by several thousands brought to safety from Occupied Europe during the *Aliya Bet* (clandestine delivery).[19] The exiled Grand Mufti of Jerusalem, Mohammed Amin al-Husayni, head of the Arab Higher Committee and partial to the Third Reich, enforced a fierce anti-Zionism among much of the Muslim leadership. Briefing books Wendell could see were of little use in the flesh-and-blood reality of his Arab-Jewish encounter. Two separate delegations, one of Jews, the other of Muslims, pressed their cases with him for the better part of a day.

Nothing symbolized the problem so depressingly as the venue offered by the American consul general for Wendell's announced reception of the parties' representatives. Consul Lowell Pinkerton's Jerusalem residence had a front and back staircase. Much of the afternoon and early evening the Jews and Arabs entered and left separately after pressing their grievances and demands to Wendell, Barnes, and Cowles. The reasonable advocate of increased immigration to Palestine, Moshe Sharett, the future state of Israel's second prime minister, called for another two million Jews; the fiery head of Palestine's Revisionist Zionist Movement, Aryeh Altman, demanded another ten million. The Arabs—moderate or obdurate—wanted all Jewish immigration ended and rejected all territorial claims, historic or trucial. From Henrietta Szold, Wendell profited a sophisticated American Zionist's discussion of the British overlord's practiced divide-and-rule policy in Palestine. Britain's high commissioner, Sir Harold McMichael, considered Wendell's recommendation that Arabs and Jews be given a role in the mandate's government presumptuous and unrealistic. A classified British document included in Wendell's Palestine briefs stated that, while Jews were admitted to the Palestine Regiment of the British Army, an independent "Jewish Army" would create "an internal security problem." When Wendell got around to recording his inchoate opinions on the Palestine Mandate, he expressed sentiments—wholly innocent of the eliminationist Nazi relocation camps—that would become commonplace decades later: that it was probably "unrealistic to believe that such a complex problem as the Arab-Jewish one, founded in ancient history and religion, and involved as it is with high international policy and politics, can be solved by good will and simple honesty."[20]

The *Iraq Times* described Wendell, his navy-blue suit still reasonably pressed, as looking "extremely well, and . . . all smiles when he shook hands with [Prime Minster] Sayid Nuri al-Said" in Baghdad on the morning of the twelfth, a Saturday, where he had just arrived. The *Gulliver* positioned itself directly in front of the terminal where the Royal Bodyguard presented arms while the King's Guard Band played "The Star-Spangled Banner." The prime minister's welcoming remarks were worthy of an American big-city mayor, flowery and extended. Wendell's advent on the first day of Ramadan, he announced, augured victory for the forces pledged to the ideals promulgated by the Atlantic Charter. He then segued to acknowledge the great debt owed Great Britain "for the creation of our state, for guarding it and guiding it during its early years." Altogether appropriate remarks from the leader of a country whose modern borders the remarkable Arabist Gertrude Bell had sketched on a napkin at dinner with Lawrence of Arabia.[21]

Left unsaid, as Wendell's briefing material umderscored, was the hard-fought victory of British air and infantry that removed the pro-Axis Sunni regime the previous June. Iraq's oil reserves were secure. Wendell's well-practiced arsenal-of-democracy presentation was well received. His hosts whisked him to the luxury suite in the Royal Court Hotel prior to dinner with Iraq's regent Prince Abd al-Ilah, the young king's pro-British uncle.

When told that the prime minister tendered a ceremonial dinner on Sunday, Wendell's boundless energy reserves appear to have finally faltered in Baghdad at least this once. Cowles and Barnes were told to arrange some sort of diversion. "I'm too tired, Mike, I'm going to bed. You've got to take over."[22] Major Knight's flight crew's surprising knowledge of the "famous dancing girls of Baghdad" seemed to save the day just in time to propose this cultural entertainment to the prime minister's emissary in Wendell's name. As Cowles's memoir reveals, "a strangely quizzical [facial] expression" accompanied Nuri al-Said's deputy's immediate assent: "It will be arranged." Meanwhile, the *Gulliver* delegation delectated over the regent's Saturday durbar held under a full moon on a vast lawn—"among the best we had in the Middle East." Prince al-Ilah received guests seated on a sumptuous thirty-foot-long carpet. To Mike Cowles, "the scene seemed right out of the Arabian Nights."

The Muslim prime minister's enormous Sunday dinner—serviced by a large screened liquor bar behind which Iraqis elbowed aside the Christians—proved one of the spectaculars of the mission. When Nuri al-Said ended speeches to announce the "Famous Dancing Girls of Baghdad," a recovered Wendell together with the full *Gulliver* component struggled to remain composed. To Cowles goes the explanatory last word: "I was almost as bewildered as Wendell, who was hearing about my request for the first time," his memoir relates. "Soon we understood the audience's reaction. As I suspected, the *Gulliver*'s crew member who came up with the idea already knew that the dancing girls of Baghdad were the city's whores. At least eight of the best whorehouses in town were represented. The madam of each whorehouse introduced her girls one by one, who did a little dance, waved to the customers they recognized, and trotted off." The British ambassador's wife, seated next to Cowles, was understandably discountenanced, as was her husband and the professional American chargé d'affaires, W. S. Farrell.[23] What should well have been regarded as a gross diplomatic and cultural faux pas was embarrassed away next morning as Wendell offered his parting demotic impressions, gratefully reproduced front-page in the *Iraq Times*.

Wendell said he wished to return to Iraq "and really enjoy without concern these delightful Arabian nights" once the war ended. He relished his two coffee-shop visits with ordinary people, witnessed backgammon playing that would have fleeced him, spoke with officials high and low committed to the great struggle of the region and beyond. The impromptu stop at an ordinary coffee shop for a coffee with the astonished patrons was widely broadcast. As he "said last night," he had "never said anything truer," enthused Wendell, than when he praised the prime minister as a man who would find himself elected to a high office were he an American citizen. Indeed, as would be publicly revealed only near the end of the war, the two extroverts, Wendell and Nuri, had hit it off so well that Nuri al-Said asked his distinguished visitor's assistance in drafting a formal declaration of war against the Axis (a decision the British ambassador successfully advised be delayed as premature). On balance, Chargé d'Affaires Farrell's report to the State Department judged that Wendell's unbuttoned diplomacy had been cathartic, that his intoxicating vision of a prosperous, democratic world at peace had resonated among Iraq's upper classes as well as its common people.[24] We know, too, from what he would soon write about it in *One World*, that Wendell anticipated the problem that Iraq's vast untapped oil reserves portended.[25]

Today, a fine Persian carpet given to Wendell by the Shah of Iran covers part of the room on a second floor in Indiana University's Lilly Library. The young Shah of Iran (placed on the Peacock Throne by the British and Russians after his father revealed Axis sympathies) was overjoyed to have his first plane ride in the *Gulliver*. The twenty-three-year-old sovereign's country was in a bad way when the Willkie mission arrived. British military forces had occupied its southern portion two years earlier, Russians the northern part. Russian planes had bombed Teheran. The well-equipped army that was his father's pride and joy melted away in the Anglo-Russian invasion that engendered a strong undercurrent of pro-German sentiment among Iranians. The national rail service was dysfunctional in the wake of the German managers' dismissal. Iran's economy was wrecked. Agricultural and petroleum output were strangled by war conditions. These were stressful conditions serving to make Wendell's official midday welcome at Teheran's Mehrabad/ghaleh Airport on September 14 exceptionally effusive.

The effect of Wendell Willkie's visit in Teheran was electric. A wide-eyed editorial in the *Journal de Teheran*, "Great Men," exulted, "When you see this man you can guess what a big people the Americans are even if you have not seen America, a people that has the highest degree of culture and civilization, the greatest part of the wealth of the world, without boasting." From the instant he stepped from the B-24, jacket unbuttoned, necktie garish, white fedora askew, the crush of dignitaries—government, diplomatic, military, press—responded to "the special representative of President Roosevelt" with geniality uncharacteristic of the region. Minister Dreyfus, the United States representative, welcomed him shoulder to shoulder with the Russian, British, and Chinese ambassadors. The masterful campaigner set forthwith the easy-breezy tone of his three-day sojourn, conveying straightaway the mantra of his mission. "My country seeks no advantage," he announced. "It wants no territory, no additional power and no control over others. But it does want to know who are those who fight with us."[26] To be sure, Iranians understood that their country was important to the Allies because its geography made it indispensable to the southern route to Russia for lend-lease shipments.

Wendell dined with Reza Pahlevi in his formal garden where the novice *Shahansha* confessed that an American military mission to train his army would greatly improve his regime's long-term stability.[27] The American military mission would fulfill its role as protector of the Pahlevi regime almost until the Shah's final overthrow in February 1979. He worried too that Iran's survival could benefit from a mutual security pact with neighboring Turkey. Later, Prime Minister Ahmad Qavam and Foreign Minister

Muhammad Said expressed glowing appreciation of Wendell's understanding of their country's needs, his "understanding of the difficulties of the world today and the world after the war," as Minister Said was pleased to underscore. Washington's verdict on the Iranian phase of Wendell's global mission was also positive. Less than a month after the *Gulliver* lifted off from Teheran on September 17 with a Russian navigator and a radio operator aboard, three thousand American tanks were underway to the hard-pressed Soviet Union over the Persian Railway system now fully under British management, with an additional thousand under Atlantic convoy. The insecure Shah's appeal to have an alliance facilitated with Turkey was being negotiated at Wendell's recommendation by the US Department of State.[28]

Perhaps an equally significant gauge of the impact left in the train of Wendell's progress was that of the *Christian Science Monitor*'s discerning foreign correspondent. That transformative impact amounted to "the Four Freedoms taken out of the realm of the abstract and clothed in a rumpled blue suit," declared Edmund Stevens. The correspondent's admiration led him to request, unsuccessfully, reassignment and passage aboard the *Gulliver*. His employers kept him in Teheran, but his confessional letter should have meant a good deal to Wendell. "What you said, especially as to your faith in human nature and a better world is etched in my memory," wrote Stevens. "Please take my word for it that never before had I been in contact with anyone who combined all the attributes of greatness with so much plain humanity."[29]

In contrast to the future of the Middle East, Russia clearly inspired a much greater awareness in Wendell, as well in Barnes and Cowles, of fateful historical stakes in play. A voracious reader like Wendell may well have ruminated on the celebrated muckraking journalist Lincoln Steffens's prophetic statement about the USSR—that he had been "over into the future and it works." Proletarian Russia, the seeming success of whose socioeconomic experiment had rivaled the New Deal, now stood as the big second leg of the Allied cause. The telegram from the working future arrived in Teheran on Wednesday, September 16. Transmitted by the American ambassador in Kuibyshev to Wendell Willkie on behalf of the Russian Foreign Ministry, it ordained the mission's ten-day schedule in the USSR: afternoon ETA, September 16, Kuibyshev, the wartime capital; September 17, day-long inspection of wartime factories in the Kuibyshev area, evening reception and dinner; September 18, river trip to hydroelectric station under construction, visit to collective farm, special evening ballet performance by the Bolshoi.

Eleven months earlier when the *Wehrmacht*'s Seventh Panzer Division halted 22 miles from the Kremlin, Premier Stalin ordered the government and cultural institutions removed to Kuibyshev, 500 miles southeast of Moscow. US Ambassador William Standley emphasized that Soviet officials were "quite anxious that [Mr. Willkie] should remain in this city . . . in order that he may be shown Soviet accomplishments which the military situation around Moscow would bar him from seeing there." Moreover, instead of the ambassador's original accommodation plan, Soviet officials preferred to offer a house to Wendell and the entire mission. A flicker of annoyance on its way to acute displeasure, the more he dealt with his distinguished visitor, was discernible in Admiral Standley's telegram. His predecessor had been bypassed by special presidential emissaries Harry Hopkins and Averell Harriman, who gained exclusive access to Stalin. Stonily disinclined to suffer marginalization, Standley intended to chaperone Wendell Willkie. Unfortunately for Standley, both from personality and friendly advice, the head of the Republican Party was incorrigibly independent and urged by Joe Barnes to fend off State Department eminences.[30]

The *Gulliver* reached Kuibyshev the morning of September 17, flying north from Teheran across the Caspian Sea to the temporary capital on the Volga. Wendell's mission arrived only days after much of the Russian leadership, confident of having foiled Hitler's massive Operation Typhoon, resumed business in the official capital. Still, the prescribed pace of the two days in Kuibyshev was an education: a massive airplane factory filled with gleaming rows of half-assembled attack fighters (the "now famous Shturmovik"); the hydroelectric construction site reminiscent of his own C & S power stations; a performance of *Swan Lake* at the temporary

Bolshoi. To Ambassador Standley's dismay, Wendell leapt from their box to the stage with a bouquet and planted a kiss on the prima ballerina's cheek to cheers from the audience.[31] But dark thoughts were evoked of families destroyed to make way for the huge collective farm they visited.

The Russian people were under strict orders to make themselves available to a distinguished visitor who good-naturedly debated the virtues of communism and capitalism at the drop of a hat. Barnes, fluent in Russian, often diplomatically interposed that the big American extrovert didn't mean to proselytize. Language permitting, they responded to Wendell's queries, even entering into bantering about mundane concerns or desires for the future, but, as Major Knight and his flight crew discovered, they invariably asked *ad scriptum*, "When will the second front come?" To the insistent second front question, he replied responsibly—at first—that "all fronts belong to all the allies, and no nation can afford to be individually self-protective." Dinner on their first evening was hosted by the owlish Andrei Vishinsky, currently deputy foreign affairs minister and the soul of engaging candor, but a man described by a Western authority on Stalin's monster bloodlettings as "educated, intelligent, cowardly, and servile."[32] As the procurator general in the treason trials of the late 1930s, Vishinsky had the blood of thousands on his hands. Cowles found it difficult to believe their scholarly looking host "was the same person responsible for the purge of some of the most beloved and honored heroes of the Russian Revolution." "I caught myself," Wendell recalled later, "studying his white hair, his professor's face . . . and wondering if this could possibly be the same man who had purged some of the oldest heroes of the Russian Revolution."

Wendell left for Moscow on a cold, wet Sunday thinking, as he wrote soon afterward, that an "entire generation of men and women had been destroyed, the families had been shattered, the loyalties had been broken . . . in the name of revolution." Yet upon reflection, he tried to understand the ordinary Russian's understanding of his brutal, bloody past as a story of "heroic achievement."[33] A young engineer in Kuibyshev had abruptly halted Wendell's paean to personal liberty: "Mr. Willkie, you don't understand. I've had more freedom than my father and grandfather ever had. They were peasants. They were never allowed to read or write."[34] Good lawyer that he was, it occurred to Wendell that his free market brief could use more discovery. Informed that he would be summoned to the Kremlin at the earliest by Premier Stalin, Wendell filled the Moscow days roaming and talking, escorted by several bodyguards. Lenin's Tomb was closed. Ilya Ehrenberg and Alexander Werth, Russian-born journalists culturally at home in Paris, London, or New York, sought him out, and they joined a group of reporters for a gab fest. "We ate smoked sturgeon and drank hot tea and talked most of the night," something Wendell liked to do all night.[35]

But what Wendell learned from Foreign Minister Vyacheslav Molotov the next evening shook his faith in the purpose of his mission. News of what seemed unaccountable bad faith on the part of Wendell's own country came from the foreign minister who had negotiated one of the blackest betrayals of the century: the Molotov-Ribbentrop Pact or the German-Soviet Non-aggression Pact of 1939. There was to be no European second front before 1944—no Sledgehammer, Molotov revealed. Instead, "Operation Torch," the invasion of North Africa led by Dwight Eisenhower, preempted the much awaited, US-led cross-channel beachhead. Winston Churchill had brought this news in person to Stalin a month ago, Molotov stated. For better and worse, FDR, out-argued and out-maneuvered by Churchill and the Imperial General Staff, had overruled his own military advisors' plan for a cross-channel invasion of France no later than spring 1943. Army Chief of Staff George Marshall was quietly enraged. General Eisenhower considered the decision the "blackest day in history.[36] Wendell knew nothing of these recent Anglo-American strategy scrimmages, but he had certainly assumed until then that FDR's second-front commitment given to Stalin in 1942 was still binding.

Now blindsided in Molotov's presence, he found himself in what presidential speechwriter Robert Sherwood described as a circumstance "incomprehensible to the Russians and the Chinese, and even to the British: that a statesman of the finesse of Roosevelt could authorize a globe-circling jaunt by any compatriot of Will-

kie's eminence without 'briefing' him thoroughly in advance . . .
[on] which points to emphasize and which to soft-pedal in all his
statements, public and private."[37] Molotov's revelation about the
second front was depressing. The situation at Stalingrad, Wendell
learned, could also well change the war's outcome for the worse
before the end of the year. On the day the *Gulliver* left Mitchell
Field, Stalingrad had proclaimed itself under siege. Preceded by
a Luftwaffe reign of fire, General Friedrich Paulus's Sixth Army
commenced the encirclement of the city with more than 225,000
battle-hardened German, Italian, and Romanian troops.[38] Understandably, Wendell felt a burning need to visit the Moscow front,
stabilized some 130 miles to the west. He contained himself when
news came that Stalin would send for him the night of the twenty-
third, Wednesday, and that arrangements immediately afterward
to inspect the front were in place. Cowles's recollection of the first
Kremlin evening is dramatic, Wendell's almost casual.

The absolute leader of the Soviet Socialist Republics Wendell
met that night invariably disconcerted foreign emissaries by his
physical appearance, his diminutive stature—a bow-legged unim-
pressiveness belying what stood before them as the essence of
incommensurable power, malevolence, peasant malice, and revolu-
tionizing genius—a lapsed divinity student now clothed in a marshal's uniform. A car fetched the titular head of the GOP from the
luxurious guest house around 8 p.m. A desperate, frantic search
for Roosevelt's sealed letter to Stalin—remembered and found in
the nick of time—was uncrumpled and inserted in Wendell's breast
pocket. Barnes and Cowles exacted Wendell's promise to ask Premier Stalin's permission to allow them to be photographed with
the Soviet leader after his private meeting with Wendell, which
was granted. Surprised by his short stature, Wendell recognized
immediately that the second most powerful ruler on the planet
possessed exceptional powers of concentration—"a hard, tena-
cious, driving mind" that fired questions "like a loaded revolver."
Yet, as grim as was the evening's business, Stalin appeared to be
affected by Wendell's forthrightness. Telling the general secretary
of the USSR that "the first thing you know, you might educate
yourself out of a job," because of his impressive public schools and

libraries, brought a roar of laughter. Mr. Willkie, Wendell recalled
Stalin's riposte, he did not make pretty speeches, "but I like you
very much." When *Pravda* announced the next morning Wendell's
exclusive discussion with Stalin and Molotov, Ambassador Standley rubbed his eyes in apoplectic disbelief.[39]

The crux of their three-hour meeting was that the Russians
knew about the Anglo-American deferral of the second front in
advance of Churchill's awkward visit, that Stalin believed that the
British government was determined to let Russia exhaust herself
while promised lend-lease materiel was diverted to Montgomery
and Eisenhower's North African campaign even as an Italian
sideshow under General Mark Clark was being planned. Dogged
by memories of his own mistakes in World War I, Churchill had
pledged not to "lose the flower of British manhood on the fields
of Normandy," a secret vow that was known among Allied commanders.[40] In cold anger, Stalin wanted to know from Wendell
why FDR "let Churchill run the war?" He fumed over 152 US
attack aircraft the British had diverted from Murmansk to North
Africa. It was plain to see that Russia would fight on and win
without the second front, if need be. With Wendell writing down
his demands on a pad, the premier clipped off imperative requirements he expected Wendell's friend Roosevelt to meet.

The USSR was ready to forgo temporarily delivery of certain
American war materiel, Wendell wrote: "all of the deliveries of
tanks, artillery, munitions, pistols, etc." What his country must
have, however, were the following "monthly supplies: 500 pursuit planes; from 8,000 to 10,000 trucks; 5000 tons of aluminum, from 4000 to 5000 tons of explosives." Additionally, Russia
wanted millions of tons of grain, "concentrated food and canned
meat." Stalin dictated a sobering wrap-up observation. "The
region of Stalingrad has worsened due to the fact that we are
short of planes, first of all pursuit planes."[41] In the time remaining,
Wendell introduced the contentious postwar status of an independent Poland without, however, any more assurance of an equitable
Atlantic Charter solution than de Gaulle had given about Syria.
Barnes and Cowles were announced. The photograph of Willkie,
Barnes, and Cowles with Stalin, Molotov, and the Kremlin inter-

preter was taken. The group left the Kremlin at 11:30 p.m. for its prearranged travel to the front at Rzhev. Wendell, however, forgot to give Stalin FDR's special letter.

Their Rzhev trip lasted all of Thursday and Friday, September 24 and 25. Besides his *Gulliver* traveling companions, Wendell's party included the US embassy's lend-lease officer, General Philippe Feymonville, Major General Follet Bradley, and the military attache, Colonel Joseph Michela, together with several Russian guides. Wendell had wanted to see actual combat, and the reality of the experience challenged his endurance and almost surpassed his imagination. From Moscow up the Leningrad highway past Kalinin to little Staritza at dawn, the party left the comfortable, heated rail cars for lend-lease Jeeps, carrying on, Wendell groaned, "for endless hours over what seemed endless miles." Fourteen hours, actually, Cowles never forgot, "in a steady rain through marshlands and forests," and for the first time Wendell appreciated those stories Herman told his sons of "conditions in pioneer Indiana." Several good miles north of the actual fighting front at Rzhev, the party shambled into army corps headquarters. Cowles was startled by human remains lying about, but more startled to see several of the soldiers were women.

The corps commander of Rzhev's sixteen infantry divisions, "a man so colorful and engaging" that Wendell found him the "most vivid among all the persons [he] met," was Lieutenant General Dmitri Lelyushenko, thirty-eight, photogenic, bow-legged, and the spitting image of Yul Brenner. Wendell probably had no knowledge of the fact that this was the officer whose airborne brigades and T-34 tanks had stopped Hans Guderian's unstoppable Forty-Seventh Panzer Division a year ago. Lelyushenko, a short, bull-chested Cossack, whose charismatic sense of himself leaps from the photograph page, imposed classroom attention in his underground quarters to explanations of battle maps, placement of troops, forthcoming plan of attack, the stakes involved in the battle then raging. From a wooded rise above the general's headquarters after dinner, the group saw and heard German artillery about eight miles distant.[42] Ever as inquisitive as opinionated, twice Wendell unintentionally provoked corrective explana-

tions from Lelyushenko that soon prompted Wendell to diverge
from Washington's war policy. After his escorts led them almost
to the limits of reconquered desolate, obliterated terrain, Wendell
asked an interpreter to ask the general just how large a section
of Russia's two-thousand-mile front he was defending. His stern,
offended response was to tell Wendell, "Sir, I am not defending.
I am attacking." Granted permission to speak to freshly captured
German prisoners, Wendell was astonished upon closer inspection to find these "thinly dressed, emaciated consumptive-looking
men" the same supposedly "terrifying, unbeatable Huns." He
shared the thought with Lelyushenko, who warned him not to
be misled. "Even with such men . . . the German Army is still the
greatest fighting military organization in the world," he told Wendell, but added that if the United States sent Russia the necessary
equipment, the Russian Army would defeat Germany "on every
front from the Caucasus to the North Pole."[43]

Although General Lelyushenko could have asked where Russia's missing American partner was, Wendell decided the question
finally had to be addressed. He did so on Saturday afternoon at
the conference of American and British correspondents held before
the farewell Kremlin banquet that evening. There were facts that
Americans needed to know, he told them, adhering fairly closely
to his distributed text. Five million Russians were dead, wounded,
or missing. Sixty million of them, "or nearly a third of the population," were slaves in territory occupied by Hitler. "Fuel will be little known this winter in millions of Russian homes." Millions of
women, side by side, with their children are running the machines
in war factories and the farms. "Yet no Russian talks of quitting.
The Russian people have chosen victory or death. They only talk
of victory."

Then he spoke frankly. "Personally, I am now convinced that
we can best help by establishing a real second front in Western Europe at the earliest possible moment our military leaders
will approve. And perhaps some of them will need some public
prodding. Next summer might be too late." Wendell's Moscow
press conference landed like a grenade in Washington, London,
and Ottawa. Republican opinion regretted his implication that

American generals needed "prodding." Many Democrats took offense that their president's emissary had seemed to impugn the commander-in-chief's straight dealing with a hard-pressed ally. FDR breezily downplayed the value of the mission in his first press conference, describing what Wendell was reported to have said as an example of "mere typewriter strategy."[44] Then, characteristically, he amended his press remarks later with the statement that "Mr. Willkie was carrying out extremely well just what he had asked him to do."

What was most memorable about the forty-five-course Kremlin banquet in Wendell Willkie's honor was Josef Stalin's insult to Archibald Clarke Kerr, the British ambassador. Present were most of the politburo, a plethora of generals, Admiral Standley and the diplomatic corps, the full *Gulliver* complement, an interpreter behind each foreign guest's chair. When Wendell suddenly slipped under the table after his sixth vodka, William Standley helped him to his seat with an avuncular assurance that he had merely experienced a visitor's rite of passage. Cowles, on the other hand, handled his liquor well enough to best both generals seated beside him. The whirligig of toasting reached Joe Barnes who offered the thirtieth in flawless Russian, followed by Cowles whose thirty-first toast proposal plunged the great hall into uneasy silence—"to the greatest man living in the world today." Was Coles thinking of Stalin, Churchill, FDR, or Willkie? With the Russians looking petrified and the foreigners eyeing the exits, the owner of *Look* magazine, grinning like a frat boy, chose "the unknown Russian soldier who is winning the war."

Stalin signaled his satisfaction, then directed a challenging gaze at his thirty-second guest, the *Gulliver*'s Major Grant Mason, a Pan Am director in civilian life. He toasted the Russian and Allied pilots "who dare in the sky they share." The mention of flying brought an aroused general secretary to his feet to deliver a blunt denunciation of the British and their prime minister—people who kept American lend-lease supplies for themselves and sent planes to Soviet flyers they "did not want." A shaken Ambassador Clarke Kerr defended his country's delivery record, specifically the sensitive matter of the missing Lightning attack planes. If any planes had been diverted from Russia, it was only "to further the cause of all three [allies]." Seeing that Stalin was plainly not mollified, Wendell rose, approached Stalin, who had murdered millions, and delivered a moving appeal for mutual understanding and unity. Stick together now, said he, and after the war there would be peace and prosperity "such as the world has never known." Wendell then offered a toast to the Great Alliance, to which a smiling Stalin riposted, "You are a plain-speaking man, I see. I like plain-spokenness, but you wouldn't have stolen 152 planes from me."[45]

In a rather bleary chat next morning, Wendell shared his unease with Cowles and Barnes over Stalin's lack of plain-spokenness about Russia's designs on Poland. There would be little postwar value to the Poles of his mission without the determination of the United States to build a robust United Nations. The more immediate result of his time in Russia was that Stalin's pragmatically reduced wish list of vital supplies that Wendell sent on to Washington got the imperative attention it deserved. A much grander significance that appeared achievable from the *Gulliver* mission was a postwar international order based on peaceful USA-USSR coexistence that he and Roosevelt believed possible and that his geopolitical best-seller, *One World*, showcasing the Soviet Union, he believed might do a great deal to bring about. But can a man who was in an alliance of expediency two years before with Nazi Germany "mean what he says?" Wendell tried to convince himself. Political expediency was anathema. "Every drop of blood saved through expediency will be paid for by twenty drawn by the sword," was his credo. Yet he was born long enough ago to know that political expediency was an equal opportunity transgression. "A Russian, feeling that by the German alliance his country was buying time, might well remind the democracies of Munich," Wendell conceded, "and the seven million tons of best grade scrap iron . . . shipped to Japan between 1937 and 1940."[46]

To reach China, the *Gulliver* flew from Moscow on September 27 to Tashkent, Uzbekistan, to Yakutsk in Siberia—across ten times zones—where bad weather delayed the mission two days. Yakutsk was an unexpected fascination. The *oblast* was twice the size of Alaska with a population of some 400,000, not counting

252 THE IMPROBABLE WENDELL WILLKIE

the reindeer, and looked "big and cold and empty" from the air.
But the tall man standing on the runway with a dozen others Wendell found unforgettable. "Muratov," saluted the crew: "President
of the Council of People's Commissars of the Yakutsk Autono-
mous Soviet Socialist Republic." Muratov carried himself, Wendell recalled, "with the air of a man flanked by brass bands and
guards of honor to welcome a foreign visitor." As they drove into
Yakutsk, Wendell found that Muratov's "enthusiasm knew no
subtleties" as he pitched his republic's assets. Challenged whether
or not Yakutsk had a library, Muratov sped to a large wooden
structure containing 550,000 volumes for a town of 50,000 people. Yakutsk also had a theater and cinema. And think of it, Mr.
Willkie, Muratov enthused, "160 combines at the Arctic Circle."
When the Liberator resumed flight, Wendell told Muratov he'd
like to come back in a decade to gauge his republic's progress.[47]

What Wendell, Mike, and Joe called their "backdoor" access
to China took them out of Siberia along the Ili River passage
between some of the planet's highest mountains, the Gobi desert,
and breathtakingly green landscape. China opened to us "like
a slowly opening fan," Cowles limned. China's "front door"
ports (Shanghai, Nanking) were occupied by the Japanese. Since
the 1937 incident at the Marco Polo Bridge that detonated the
Sino-Japanese War, the southwest and center of this huge country was ruled from Chungking by Chiang Kai-shek's Nationalists. The north was controlled from Yenan by Mao Tse-tung's
Communists. China's historic east (Beijing, Nanking, Shanghai)
was under the so-called co-prosperity heel of the Japanese. An
uneasy truce between the Nationalists and the Communists was
expected to endure until the Japanese invader was expelled.[48] The
Gulliver reached Tihwa, the capital of Russo-Chinese Sinkiang
Province (Urumchi to the Russians), on the morning of September 29. On the way, Wendell re-studied Russell Davenport's
engagingly written ("highly indiscreet") profiles of virtually all
the significant players in Generalissimo Chiang Kai-shek's government, especially focusing on the paramount Soong dynasty.
Minister of Foreign Affairs T. V. Soong expected the Republican
Party leader to succeed Roosevelt in 1944. Nationalist China's

reception of Wendell, therefore, was lavish and loving. Davenport's memorandum praised the generalissimo: "Of him it would
be too hard to speak too highly," even if Russell conceded that
Chiang Kai-shek "always shot the wrong people" instead of one
or two of his ministers.

The three Soong sisters—Ai-ling (finance minister's wife),
Ch'ing-ling (Sun Yat-sen's widow), Mai-ling (Chiang Kai-shek's
wife)—were the regime's vivacious nodes. Of Wellesley College
alumna Mai-ling or voluptuous Madame Chiang Kai-shek, Davenport advised Wendell, "she will reveal herself to you at once and
there is little that I need to say about her brilliance, intelligence,
sprightliness of mind and manner, charm and so on." Wendell
was also alerted to a person he'd "almost certainly meet" bearing
"the uncommon name of Hollington Tong," Missouri journalism school, minister of publicity, and "one of the Generalissimo's
keenest instruments." Don't be misled by "Holly's" "flashiness,"
Russell added. If he felt sure of his ground, what Holly says about
China "is worth listening to." On the other hand, Dr. H. H. Kung,
minister of finance and Ai-ling Soong's husband, whom Wendell
would have "the speedy misfortune of meeting," was the very
personification of "defeatism, folly, shallowness, crookedness."
A longtime European resident, who said later that "no one ever
saw a fat Chinese below the rank of Minister of Finance," blamed
China's backwardness on well-fed officials like H. H. Kung. Pre-
dicting that his welcome would be fast and furious, young and
soon famous China hand Theodore White offered to arrange a
press conference of foreign journalists. It appears he did so.[49]

Hollington Tong and General Chu Shao-liang, commander-in-
chief of the northwest war zone, accompanied by the American
military attache, Lieutenant Colonel James M. McHugh, fluent in
Chinese, met Wendell's party at the Tihwa airport. Tihwa "had
little to boast of," Wendell found. It was "sleepy looking and
incredibly muddy," but the land around the town was remark-
ably rich and the spirit of the Chinese officials was high. Respects
were paid to the governor of Sinkiang, followed by an impressive
military parade ground demonstration next morning.[50] The Gulliver carried Minister Tong and General Chu away from Tihwa

over stunningly beautiful landscape to Lanchow, Kansu Province, on the Yellow River. More official calls and receptions were endured. The embassy's able second secretary, John Service, represented US Ambassador Gauss. Wendell and Service would several times more find themselves in close contact in China, which invites the counterfactual regret that the foreign service agent's controversial opinions of Chiang Kai-shek's government appear not to have been shared nor invited.[51] Wendell's party winged south from Lanchow into agriculturally opulent Szechuan Province, touching down at Chengtu on October 1. The officials there were more important, receptions larger, dinners grander. An invitation to address four thousand teachers and students from nine war-relocated universities on the campus of West China Union University elicited translated remarks that were exceptional for ingenuousness and historical pertinence. An especially thoughtful letter from an anonymous Chinese student proposing a postwar annual "Peace, Freedom, Pleasure Day" along with the worldwide construction of peace monuments may well have been on Wendell's mind at the time.[52]

To the audience's amusement, Wendell began by saying that when he was a student, college presidents wouldn't have found much to say about him. To have a college president for a translator was a first, he confessed. Speaking seriously, he recalled graduating college twenty-six years before when his country began to fight and win a war that cost millions of lives and millions of dollars of lost property. Afterward, however, his country, together with others, "turned inward instead of outward. They abandoned the effort to make the world safe for democracy." Yet, even had Woodrow Wilson's dream of peace been realized, Wendell now realized, it would have contained too many "old shibboleths of imperialism, colonies, mandates and such by which one nation tries to rule another." China has been the first to resist the Axis onslaught, and after five years of war she had paid the full price for victory. Now the rest of the world must take up her burden and help her "to the limit of the resources of the [United States]." But unless her victory served the objective that every man—Chinese, Hindu, or American—is free, she would fail to be a leader "in the new world order." In light of the prickly interaction ahead between Wendell and the American ambassador, the embassy's glowing report to the State Department about the address at Chengtu's West China Union University was certainly notable.[53]

Finally, Wendell's eventful six October days in China's wartime capital began on Friday in the late afternoon of October 2 with an official welcome to Chungking by Clarence E. Gauss, another US ambassador Wendell quickly infuriated. Chungking, the defiant, high-altitude capital of "Free China," leapt in less than five years from hardscrabble western backwater to a million souls squeezed within a ring of mountains creased by the Yangtze. Its people were spared frequent Japanese bombing raids during the winters thanks to the enveloping mountain mists. Summers turned Chungking into a cauldron and a target range for Mitsubishis whose bombs would have killed many more bureaucrats, businesspeople, and Kuomintang officials but for their privileged access to deep air raid caves. The distinguished reception delegation met the Willkie party some miles beyond the city. Chungking's sand bar of a runway in the middle of the Yangtze presented a challenge to the B-24 greater than the skilled Major Knight had cared to risk.

The chiefs of diplomatic missions, ranking officers of the Kuomintang Party, and Russell Davenport's sinister Dr. Kung welcomed Wendell on behalf of Generalissimo Chiang Kai-shek. He made brief remarks to the press. He said he had come "to find out some facts," adding, however, that one falls so much in love with the Chinese people that "it is difficult to form a critical and fact-finding judgement." Standing tall and skeptical among the dignitaries was Lieutenant General Joseph Stilwell (dyspeptic "Vinegar Joe"), commander-in-chief of US army forces in China, Burma, and India, and a favorite of Chief of Staff General George Marshall. Stilwell's relations with the generalissimo and Madame Chiang were poisoned beyond an antidote. The latter's effort to persuade FDR to recall Stilwell had almost succeeded. The former's attempt to persuade Chiang Kai-shek to attack the Japanese in Burma a second time had no prospect of succeeding.[54] Wendell would find himself entangled in this stalemate. Observing the gorgeous tumult engulfing the great American emissary, Stilwell already anticipated that he would be easily manipulated by the Soong machine.

To Wendell and his posse, as Cowles would never forget of the ride into Chungking, "the show of friendship was a deeply moving experience for us. Even if they didn't know who Wendell was," thousands and thousands of men, women, and children "all waving little paper Chinese and American flags" up and down the hills of the city was marvelous. There had been nothing of this Chungking scale even on his presidential campaign trail, Wendell realized. No matter the hardboiled appraisal of one of the European newsmen, who derided the enthusiasm as manufactured and mostly ignorant. Behind the dragooned schoolchildren with their little flags "were the very poor . . . hired as substitutes for annoying . . . duties . . . the useless non-working people sent out by their own families." At intervals behind them, he claimed, "police were posted to see that they did not escape until all the cars had passed." Wendell also had doubts about its genuineness, but "in spite of all my efforts to discount it," he confessed, "this scene moved me profoundly." The day closed at the magnificent, modern home of Foreign Affairs Minister Soong placed at their disposal and thereby placing Wendell and his party in the calculating care of the Soongs.[55]

October in China was remarkable for the interaction of Wendell Willkie and Madame Chiang Kai-Shek. The word from the Luces and other well-placed friends in the United States was that Wendell Willkie was almost certain to win the presidency in 1944. The verbally fluent, Wellesley-educated member of the Soong family dynasty extended herself to cultivate her influential American visitor. "So essentially human," she purred on their second meeting, "that anything written down would not express the welcome felt in our hearts for him." General Stilwell and foreign service officer John Paton Davies noted that "Little Sister," Madame Chiang, "accomplished one of her easiest conquests." Foreign males regularly swooned in her presence like lonely GIs entertained by Hollywood stars—hard-bitten General Claire Chennault, astute Owen Lattimore, mystical Henry Wallace. When FDR finally met her at the White House he told daughter Anna he had steeled himself against being "vamped."[56] John Paton Davies passed a quick judgment on Wendell's judgment: "So what chance did the impressionable Willkie have when Madame Chiang upped her projection of charm a notch to include coquetry?"

Stilwell and Davies observed the tried routine: "The Chiangs plied the gullible Willkie with food, wine, flattery, and propaganda." Their objectives were clear, said Davies: as big a loan from the US Congress as possible (FDR had approved $500 million in February); as much lend-lease as Harry Hopkins could send over the "Hump" of Japanese-occupied Burma; the recall of General Stilwell and enough fighters and bombers to enable General Chennault of the Flying Tigers to bring Japan to her knees. Like fellow "China Hand" John Service, Davies had all but concluded that Kuomintang corruption and alienation of the peasantry seriously reduced the postwar survival prospects of what they called off the record the "Cash My Check" regime.[57] The absence of evidence does seem to be evidence of the absence of corrective evidence that China Hands could have imparted to Wendell Willkie. Nor does the Theodore White of *Thunder Out of China*, his forthcoming autopsy of the decline of Nationalist China, seem to have found time or opportunity to deflate Wendell's too sanguine image of a fighting "Free China."

Wendell met Mai-ling in the flesh when he accompanied Ambassador Gauss and Counselor John Carter Vincent to pay an official call on the generalissimo on Saturday morning. The meeting consisted of ceremonial boiler plate prior to the lunch offered by China's figurehead president Lin Sen. He and she appear to have sensed a mutual attraction. Later in the day, Wendell gave a forceful speech to twelve hundred public functionaries at the Central Training Corps that was well received by his hosts.[58] Afterward, the special reception in Wendell's honor afforded the Soongs a much surer sense of their distinguished guest's sympathies. It was a sumptuous affair staged at the National Military Council, where seventy of the regime's political military, business, and educational leaders, joined by the foreign elite, endured after-dinner translated remarks of Generalissimo Chiang Kai-shek and the honorable guest. Wendell scored the affair "the most appealing dinner [he] attended around the world," enhanced by various entertainments, music and folk singing. The presence together of General Stilwell and his professional nemesis, Brigadier General Chennault, advocate of air power as a panacea, was a notable happening. Chiang spoke after dinner of humanity's deliverance "from barbarism and decadence" by peace-loving survivors of "hardship and tribulations." Wendell praised the hardy people of western China in whom aggressive self-confidence had been instilled much as in the people of Wendell's Midwest.

Mike Cowles's report of Wendell and Mai-ling's quiet departure from the busy reception scene survives as one of the most surprising narratives of the mission's 31,000-mile global circumnavigation. A whispered request from Wendell that the guest of honor and hostess of the evening wished to spend time alone sent Cowles to occupy the generalissimo with a barrage of interesting questions. Their animated Q&A continued for some time until the evening ended with a polite clap of the hand by Chiang Kai-shek. Cowles was awakened when Wendell sauntered into the guest house at four in the morning, exhilarated and preposterous, claiming he was in love for the first time. Cowles not only got a "play by play account," he almost gagged to hear Wendell "blithely" say that he had invited Madame Chiang "to return to Washington with us." He called his friend "just a goddamn fool!" Wendell's prospects for winning the presidency in 1944 would vanish. Think of the scene when Edith and Philip met the *Gulliver*. Arguments that sent Wendell huffing to bed had registered by breakfast. Cowles dutifully went off to give Madame Chiang news of her flight cancelation. He found her in a secret hideaway apartment in the Women's and Children's Hospital. When he returned, he bore fingernail marks down his cheeks that lasted almost a week.[59]

The mission continued in full swing Sunday morning, October 4. Fully refreshed, the distinguished visitor saw industrial areas in the company of the minister of economic affairs and attended the minister's luncheon. As honorary chair of the China Chapter of United China Relief, Mai-ling hosted an elegant tea at which she welcomed Wendell with remarks that were unmistakably coquettish, as Ambassador Gauss noted in his State Department dispatch. She found Mr. Willkie a "very disturbing personality," she admitted. She decided to discard her prepared speech because he was not the "sort of person" for whom a speech was made. She found that she must speak "from [her] heart because he is so spontaneous, so warm-hearted, so essentially human that anything written down would not express the welcome felt in our hearts for him," to which a be-smitten Wendell Willkie replied that his "heart has been taken away."

From what Ambassador Gauss reported to the State Department, it seems likely either that Mai-ling intended to keep her reserved seat aboard *Gulliver* or that Wendell allowed a subterfuge to continue. He devoted the time at the tea to "pressing an invitation . . . to visit the United States, traveling in the Willkie plane," reported Gauss, adding that Wendell reassured Madame Chiang that her visit "would get all the planes [she] might desire." Moreover, Gauss noted that the generalissimo "smiled throughout this conversation, but made no comment" except to say that his wife always desired to revisit the United States. That evening, the Chiangs carried their guest to their country house above the city for an extended, relaxed getting-acquainted opportunity. Holly Tong and Mai-ling translated as Chiang Kai-shek, in addition to polite distress over lend-lease shortages, explained thoughtfully his fear that the best of China's ancient traditions and her small-scale manufactures would be seriously impaired by the social and economic upheaval brought on by Western industrial manufacturing.

Interestingly, although the former holding company president and GOP standard-bearer commended the advantages of peasant and craft productivity, Wendell suggested that there was another economic model well worth the generalissimo's consideration, "an experiment going on much closer to him than any in the Western world, the Communist one in Russia." The two of them had talked of automobiles produced in China, but without Russia's large-scale industrial progress essential to unit price efficiency he said he feared Chiang's dream of a Chinese car might never come to pass.[60] Disposed as he was to see the best in his hard-pressed hosts and to make their case to the outside world, Wendell would not have disagreed (off the record) with Theodore White's judgment that Chiang Kai-shek was woefully ignorant of economics.[61]

Like Chiang, Nationalist China somehow operated without paying much attention to its economy, a reality Wendell must have swallowed hard to play down at his Monday morning AP and UP press appearance on October 5. Asked his opinion of Minister of Finance H. H. Kung's plan to combat China's rampant inflation (retail prices were sixty times prewar prices), he mitigated the inconvenient and extolled the positive, a presentation that led many to believe Wendell had been suborned by Madame Chiang Kai-shek to soft-pedal the corruption and inefficiency of her husband's regime.[62] But the controlling rationale for his China mission, as with all the others, was to keep or win allies for the war against the Axis and a victorious peace pledged to the ideals of the Atlantic Charter and the United Nations. This was the expediency Wendell Willkie permitted himself when he urged wide public confidence in Minister Kung's program. In fact, however, he would leave Nationalist China "baffled by its present economic and inflationary problems," as he later admitted in print, and frankly predicted that China's inflationary problems should have "long since been disastrous in terms of a money economy." They would be.

When he was asked his opinion of an editorial appealing to the United States to call for the abrogation of the "unequal treaties" imposed by Europe on China, Wendell's forceful support of the Chinese daily's demand influenced Under Secretary of State Sumner Welles to declare the formal advocacy of the United States for repeal of "extra-territoriality," the odious jurisprudence shielding foreigners from criminal or civil prosecution in Chinese courts. He was equally supportive of the hope expressed by the decidedly independent editor of *Ta Kung Pao* that the US and United Nations members accelerate the reoccupation of Burma.[63] In fact, he may have suggested the Burma question as a diplomatic way of spotlighting Stilwell's apparently forlorn plan to oust the Japanese from Burma with American troops based in India in coordination with the generalissimo's well-equipped Fifth Army. That Chiang Kai-shek regarded military offense as almost always folly—which Wendell never quite grasped—had reduced Stilwell to brutally frank, frustrated demands that went nowhere for an aggressive Chinese military posture.

To his credit, seeing a disastrous problem needing urgent solution, he flew from the Monday press conference to see what could be done. Wendell found the legendary General Chennault, "tall, swarthy, lean and rangy," standing by one of his P-40 attack planes. A few hours at his airbase, a palaver with his pilots and maintenance crews about the National League pennant and their wish for women volunteers ("thought you came out here to fight?"), persuaded Wendell that Chennault was "a hard man to forget once you've talked with him." The talk was about Chennault's "amazing" plan, which he dictated to Wendell, to fly lend-lease over the Burma "Hump" and to defeat the Japanese Empire with 105 modern fighters, 30 medium bombers, 12 heavy bombers—all "within six months." Wendell left Chennault an enthusiastic convert, as his subsequent meeting with Stilwell made evident. "Didn't ask a question," Stilwell recorded in his diary.[64] "Completely sold on Chiang Kai-shek and Madame Chiang." Wendell's endorsement of Chennault's "amazing" plan persuaded FDR to recommend it to a skeptical General Marshall.

Tuesday, their penultimate day in Chungking, brought the crux of the mission's business to a head in several elaborate venues. An immense reception at the Chinese-American Institute of Cultural Relations given by eighteen Chungking cultural organizations was followed by a further invitation of the Chinese-American Institute of Cultural Relations to make a radio broadcast to the Chinese People that evening—and probably not at all to Gauss's liking.[65] Thus far, he had been the soul of discretion in China as to the priority to be given military fronts, whether European or Asian. What he had to say, however, about the third rail subject of colonial possessions set alarm bells ringing in Allied *inner sancta*. Wendell explained that he came to China "to find out facts." His own country—"great free America"—was pouring out its treasures "to help all who fight with it." But much more than armaments, ammunition, and planes was owed "so that China can be completely free," so that other peoples under domination will be completely free. Shifting into neo-Wilsonian voice, Wendell declared, "Mankind is on the march. . . . The colonial days are past. if they are not past, then mankind will degenerate into a wheel of war." He expected to devote the balance of his life, he pledged, "to seeing, speaking, working" so that the postwar world was reconstructed "on a basis where all men can be free and live under governments of their own choosing with economic rights and basic commodities." He ended with a wish that when next he saw or met any of his listeners, "we shall be both citizens of a free country in a world of peace and prosperity."[66]

This busy Tuesday ended with another Soong family dinner given by the economically dodgy Dr. H. H. Kung, Mai-ling's brother-in-law, and spread over a plush lawn under tables seating the Kuomintang elite. Gauss attended with politically ill-fated Counselor John Carter Vincent, embassy Navy and Army attachés, and General Stilwell. Mai-ling's plan for the evening called for a discreet retreat together to introduce Wendell to sister Ai-ling, Dr. Kung's absent ailing wife. The introduction pretext allowed for a scripted drama that brought a curious Dr. Kung to join them and hear Wendell's reported reasons for wanting his sister-in-law to come to America. "Mr. Willkie, do you mean that, and if so, why?" Kung needed to know. China urgently needed "someone from the section" to help educate us about China and India and their peoples," Wendell elaborated. "Madame would be the perfect ambassador with brains and persuasiveness, and moral force. . . . We would listen to her as no one else," he sailed on. "With wit and charm, a generous and understanding heart, a gracious and beautiful manner and appearance, and a burning conviction, she is just what we need as a visitor." His pitch worked perfectly.[67]

Two of Dr. Kung's unusual guests that Tuesday evening were present as result of Wendell Willkie's intercession, no doubt to the surprise of China Hand John Carter Vincent. Mr. and Mrs. Chou En-lai had rarely been received publicly among the Kuomintang (KMT), despite the KMT-Chinese Communist Party (CCP) truce. Chou En-lai, fluent in European languages, had met Wendell the day before to discuss politics. "This excellent, sober, and sincere man won my respect as a man of obvious ability," Wendell had decided. Nor was Wendell alarmed by Chou's

unwillingness to predict the postwar future of KMT-CCP cooperation. However, Chou did confess reservations about some of
Chiang Kai-shek's associates. Wendell felt that if Chou was representative of the communist leadership, then their movement was
"more a national and agrarian awakening than an international
or proletarian conspiracy." It was a seriously naïve assessment
of the ideological movement and autocratic personality of General Chou En-lai's master, Mao Tse-tung. But neither Wendell
nor the foreign service officers dutifully accompanying him (Vincent, Service, Davies) realized how faithfully Mao's China took
Stalin's Russia as its model, nor did he and they know that its
people had lived, since the beginning of the year, under a new
experiment of thought control and leadership infallibility called
"Rectification"—in every sense a prefiguration of Mao Tse-tung's
Cultural Revolution of the 1960s.[68] The nine-man fact-finding
"Dixie Mission" to Mao's Yenan, authorized by FDR, led by
John Service, and a future *causus belli* of the Cold War, was eighteen months in the future. Wendell's early death would deprive
his country of personal and ideological insights about postwar
China that possibly might have mitigated the professional dis-
grace of the "China Hands" sacrificed in the McCarthyite hysteria because they "lost China."[69]

The *Gulliver* left Chungking early Wednesday afternoon,
October 7, heading back to Chengtu in order to achieve Wendell's
indispensable need to assess China's war front near Sian on a bend
in the Yellow River. Nine thousand troops put on a clockwork display of obstacle-course derring-do at a famous military academy
near Chengtu. He traveled by luxurious sleeping car almost to
the Great Wall, descended after Japanese artillery fired near their
tracks, and reached the river by handcar. Under the chaperonage
of a studio-cast young Captain Chiang Wei-kao—the generalissimo's son by a previous marriage—he walked close enough to
the front to be able to look down the muzzles of Japanese guns
pointed at us "and see the Japanese soldiers in their own encamp-
ments." Cowles was impressed, but he still found the scene suspiciously artificial. They were told the front had been quiet for
some time. Mai-ling's warts-and-all biographer, Hanna Pakula,

believed that Wendell's impression of the Chinese army "was ludicrously off the mark." Still, without Chiang Kai-shek's armies, regardless of quality and equipment, and to a lesser degree Mao Tse-tung's, the Empire of Japan would have had, at a minimum, 600,000 more troops to deploy elsewhere as needed.[70] That fact alone, Wendell appreciated, justified almost as much praise as Rzhev's sixteen infantry divisions.

The real fireworks display had occurred on Wednesday as Wendell prepared to leave Chungking. His prepared statement to the press—an even more uncompromising anticolonial declaration than the previous one—was a no-holds-barred farewell to an odious geopolitical paradigm. "Even the name of the Atlantic Charter disturbed thoughtful men and women," it started. They asked if all the signatories agree that it applies to Asia? "We must believe this war must mean an end to the empire of nations over other nations. No foot of Chinese soil, for example, should be or can be ruled from now on except by the people who live on it. And we must say so now, not after the war. We believe it is the world's job to find some system for helping colonial peoples who join the United Nations' cause to become free and independent nations. We must set up firm tables under which they can work out and train governments of their own choosing."[71]

Other Chungking business that Wednesday was the poignant leave-taking of Madame Chiang Kai-shek. Mai-ling had arrived just as Wendell prepared to fly to Chengtu. They kissed in a long embrace. He promised they would see much of each other if she came to the United States.[72] That desire was to be realized six weeks later. She had yet to answer recent letters from Clare Boothe Luce and Eleanor Roosevelt urging that she come to America for medical attention and rest. Madame Chiang Kai-shek's return to the United States would reduce the movers and shakers—female as well as male—of the nation's capital and New York to fawning partisanship. She came to win arms, money, and hegemony for the Kuomintang. Her coverage in *Time* and *Life* furthered an image of Asian modernity, anticommunism, and business opportunity. When she addressed separately both congressional chambers, the overwhelmingly male solons were overwhelmed. Her impact on

Wendell Willkie remained undiminished. Even more surprising, so would his on her.[73]

Major Knight took *Gulliver* out of China on Friday, October 9, pointing her back through the Gobi and the Mongolian Republic of Siberia, across the Bering Sea, down the full length of Alaska and along the full width of Canada. He put the big plane down on the ground on October 13 with the gain of a day by crossing the international date line. Winston Churchill's haughty response was given in the Commons just shy of a month after the *Gulliver* alighted in Minneapolis. "Let me make this clear," sneered the prime minister. "We mean to hold our own." He had not become the king's first minister "in order to preside over the liquidation of the British Empire." Some of Wendell's compatriots anticipated Churchill's indignation almost as disdainfully. His old frenemy Dorothy Thompson deplored his disrespect for the historic ally in a time of war. The exceedingly well-bred Joseph Alsop and the pseudo-patrician Walter Lippmann spoke not only for the country's influential Anglophile demographic but also for large numbers of Americans unsettled by his statements' perceived lack of patriotism. The congeniality marking their Hyde Park meeting shortly before Willkie's world trip was conspicuously absent when FDR received Willkie in the White House on October 14.

CHAPTER 11

1944—NOT THIS TIME

Wendell Lewis Willkie. *Courtesy the Lilly Library, Indiana University, Bloomington, Indiana.*

When the *Gulliver* landed at Edmonton, Alberta, on October 12, it was the last time before delivering Wendell Willkie home that the big Liberator bomber would touch down outside the continental limits of the United States. What made an otherwise unremarkable Edmonton stop notable was the release of a prickly public statement by the plainly annoyed global emissary. Asked his reaction to statements credited to Wendell in Russia and China, FDR had twice seemed to discount their importance and even to ridicule the speaker. The tone of Wendell's press release suggests a slow burning fuse lit while in China and all but ready to explode by the time Major Knight cut off the plane's engines in front of the Edmonton air terminal. "As to flippant statements made by certain public officials" about his overdue second front opinion, Wendell sniffed that he had deemed it inappropriate to reply while in foreign lands "to such personalities and flippancies." But all restraints were off now. He was going to speak "to the people at home about such remarks," and—with an unmistakable forewarning meant for FDR—"in words which no one can misunderstand."[1] One of the great diplomatic and technological feats of World War II appeared to be headed for an inauspicious climax.

Indeed, Franklin Roosevelt's message awaiting Wendell's arrival in Minneapolis was a virtual summons to the White House before the press was spoken to. Wendell's impulse was not to comply until after a day's rest, but Sam Pryor's conciliatory phone call and his own proud need to elucidate his accomplishments prevailed. Of the two versions of their Oval Office deliberation on October 14—respectful and productive or tense and productive— the second is more likely, based on accounts from close associates and on the egotism characterizing their fraught relationship. Pryor's before and after recollection was of Wendell's determination both to register indignation about the "flippancies" and to insist that FDR (notorious for talking over his advisors) hear the full report. "Willkie raised hell," Sam Pryor claimed. Others revealed that Roosevelt took umbrage with Wendell's policy presumptuousness and that he told Dean Acheson he had been ready to offer Wendell the post of secretary of state. In any case, the president and the GOP leader concurred with the official version for public consumption.

Beyond its geopolitical conciseness that covered North Africa, the Middle East, Russia, and China, three supererogatory observations distinguished Wendell's five-page draft notes "For conversation with President Roosevelt": (1) Stalin's itemized lend-lease requests; (2) the need for "an independent American foreign policy" confirming the United States "was not committed to the perpetuation of British imperialism"; (3) the warning that Nationalist

China's inflation problem was "of equal gravity with Japan's invasion of the country." To these, he added a plea for a "modest force" of planes for General Chennault and the suggestion that ambassadors Dreyfuss, Standley, and Gauss be replaced on grounds of ignorance of Persian, Russian, and Chinese.[2] More was surely said about the great fund of goodwill America enjoyed worldwide— hers to lose by not honoring the principles of the Atlantic Charter.

Leaving the White House and heading straightaway to National Airport for New York City, Wendell commended the president's consideration but told the press little more than that he needed a few days of rest before he went to work on "the most important thing he could do"—bring home to the American people the great responsibilities imposed upon them equally by the war and the peace to come. Tanned and ten pounds lighter, he exuded the muscular ordination that might have reminded his father of William Jennings Bryan in his prime. "A lot of us are going to have to stretch our muscles and our minds before we win," he said challengingly, and with that he was off to do what he could by "reporting to [his] fellow citizens to help in this new job . . . of reeducating ourselves to win this war and to win this peace."[3] Immediately sizing up the political consequences of Wendell's promised report to the public on his globe-circling mission, FDR found that they made him decidedly uneasy with less than three weeks remaining before the midterm November elections.

Thirty-six-million-plus Americans listened to "Report to the People" on the four national networks on October 26, a radio audience half the size of FDR's Pearl Harbor address of December 8, 1941. Wendell Willkie's radio voice lacked the cosmopolitan sonority generally thought suited to grand topics, although it was certainly far closer in accent and diction to the way many millions of his listeners spoke than to the grandiloquence of their patrician president. The voice heard by millions that Sunday evening was the voice of the common man. Although it was indeed served by two or three striking turns of phrase, "Report to the People" was the triumph of its very title—a deeply thought, plainspoken, neighborly message about the still largely unexpected next chapter in the American adventure. If Roosevelt's Pearl Harbor threnody was believed to have closed the book on isolationism, Willkie's address was a word picture of the strange new international world awaiting his compatriots, like it or not.

Seventy-six years since the *Gulliver* circumnavigated the globe, it requires imagination to appreciate how unfamiliar yet fascinating to a 1942 radio audience were the novel images stimulated by Wendell's narration. The yesterday geographical palimpsest covered by an airborne Mark Twain carried millions along as he explained his need to know the people in distant lands who had a "stake" in the war. He had asked his president for permission to go in wartime "as a private citizen." FDR agreed and asked that he perform "certain specific tasks for him." Wendell readily did so, but he stressed that it was clearly understood that he was "at liberty to express my opinion while abroad and equally so when I returned home." Finally, he had paid all his personal expenses. Tonight he was reporting to the citizens of his democracy "as an American, interested only in the welfare of my country and proud that I am accountable only to my fellow-citizens."

His fellow citizens listened enrapt to a tour de force of grassroots opinion and Wilsonian prophecy. He had traveled 31,000 miles, "which sounds very far." But the crux of the lesson was not one of "distance from other peoples, but of closeness to them." At this point, his text's typescript shifted into italics. "*I say to you: there are no distant points in the world any longer. The myriad millions of human beings of the Far East are as close to us as Los Angeles is to New York by the fastest railroad trains.*" The world was changing: "*Our thinking and planning in the future must be global.*" In all the different varieties of places, people, workers, and leaders—from a "veiled woman" in Baghdad, Iranian "carpet weaver," Nigerian "water carrier," to "a Chinese soldier at the front"—"they, each and every one, turn to the United States," he preached with exceptionalist ardor. This was a reality affirmed in his personal talks with Marshal Stalin or Generalissimo Chiang Kai-shek or his wife, or the Shah of Iran and the King of Egypt: "I bring back to you this clear and significant fact: that there exists in the world today a gigantic reservoir of good will toward you, the American people."

But the reservoir was already being drained by insufficient mobilization and collusion with imperialisms, overt or disguised. The world awaited the promised second front: Russia and China had already lost more men in the war than the United States and the British Commonwealth together have soldiers under arms. A wise Chinese official warned Wendell, "and through me, you, that by our silence on India, we have drawn down heavily on our reservoir of goodwill in the East." Wendell closed by presuming to tell Americans what the world's yellow and brown and black people desired. "I am only passing on their invitation: *They want us to join them in creating a new society, global in scope, free alike of the economic injustices of the West and the political malpractices of the East. But as a partner in that great new combination they want us neither hesitant, incompetent nor afraid.*"

Clare Boothe Luce touted it as the message "of a global Abraham Lincoln." William Allen White concurred, and the *Christian Science Monitor* hailed the new Marco Polo of international relations. Wendell probably thought the *New York Post* captured "Report to the People" as it was meant to be understood best. "Everybody has been talking about the common man since the war began," it said. "Last night, in the person of Wendell Willkie, the common man talked back." It was noticed that the president had had to be nudged to say much to the press about the radio address.[4] A second press conference elicited a rather flippant cigarette commercial compliment that "not a controversy in a car load" existed between himself and Mr. Willkie—he would "sing it if necessary." FDR followed up by imitating a Hoosier pronunciation of "reservahr."

Republican party members decided to join the nearly unanimous applause chorus. Like FDR, they also needed nudging, though for different reasons. Wendell's absence from the fall electioneering had raised sharp criticisms among party regulars, but the net GOP gain of forty-four House seats and eight in the Senate on November 3 must have had some positive connection with his heralded return and extraordinary popularity in the three weeks until the election. Dewey, Willkie's potential rival (whom Wendell surprisingly, finally, endorsed), was elected governor of New York,

Clare Boothe Luce a congressional seat with Wendell's blessing, and Earl Warren, a presumed Willkie sympathizer, captured the Sacramento state house. Taft and Vandenberg publicly withdrew from candidacy for the 1944 presidential nomination.

Hamilton Fish, FDR's and Wendell's *bête noire*—the New York representative both had plotted together to defeat—kept his upstate New York seat despite their joint efforts to mount an effective Dutchess County opposition. Their occasional cross-party collaboration is revealed in a rare mid-April personal note. "I did enjoy that little party the other night," FDR wrote Wendell. "We did not get far on the Ham Fish matter." Wendell replied appreciatively a few days later, but he badly miscalculated the situation, writing, "I am quite confident Fish is going to be eliminated. As a matter of fact, I doubt if he even runs." Another miscalculation—understandable, given the midterm results—was his positive outlook that with Martin's help congressional Republicans would come round to broad acceptance of his leadership. He was not to be forgiven his global excursion, though. "Willkie became allergic to Republicans," one said. "He didn't consult them, work with them, or for them. After the campaign of '42, not five members in the House were willing to follow his leadership."[5]

Wendell went from his radio broadcast almost directly to the US Supreme Court on November 9 to argue the case of *Schneiderman v. US*. He met William Schneiderman in his office the day after the Japanese bombed the US Pacific fleet at Pearl Harbor. Having studied Schneiderman's attorney's excellent brief, he sized up the nervous thirty-eight-year-old secretary of the California Communist Party and agreed to represent him. Most Republicans seconded John Cowles's objections to an ill-advised expenditure of their party leader's time and talents. From their perspective, the Cowleses and the Martins should have breathed a sigh of relief that Wendell's reported reaction to FDR's forced relocation of Japanese citizens went no further than a distate for "extra-judicial proceedings" expressed at a dinner for Justice Brandeis.[6]

The Justice Department had ordered Wendell's new client deported to Russia in 1939 on grounds that his 1927 naturalization papers had been improperly obtained. His parents had brought

Schneiderman to the United States from Russia as a three- or four-year-old. From 1922 at age sixteen his professional life was spent in the service of Communist organizations. He was not merely a card-carrying Communist, Schneiderman had been the party's 1932 candidate for governor of California. But he had pledged "not to overthrow the United States by force and violence" upon signing his 1927 naturalization petition. Moreover, the Nationality Act of 1940, Section 338, required Wendell's client to have behaved five years preceding naturalization as "a person attached to the principles of the Constitution."

Schneiderman's appeal before the US Supreme Court was the first such case calendared for argument, but some forty-two denaturalization prosecutions had been successful under the revised Nationality Act of 1940, three hundred cases were pending, and more than two thousand were under active investigation—the great majority involved German and Italian subjects.[7] Two federal courts found the government's claim justified that Schneiderman's citizenship was fraudulently and illegally procured. Wendell's argument in the case was of a piece with "Fair Trial," his contentious March 1940 article in the *New Republic* remonstrating the imprisonment on a technicality of an American Nazi (Fritz Kuhn) and an American Communist (Earl Browder). To Wendell, the First Amendment values in play in the case were self-evident: Schneiderman, a registered member of the CPUSA, had a protected right to espouse his ideas.

But little was as it seemed in this case. The Justice Department had prosecuted Wendell's client seven weeks before the Soviet Union and Nazi Germany signed their August 1939 nonaggression pact. What seven justices of the Supreme Court found on their hands in November 1942 was—since Germany's invasion of Russia on June 22, 1941—an unacknowledgeable dilemma. Taking proper care to observe the formality of impartiality, Justice Frank Murphy, a 1940 appointee, who was to write the majority opinion, agreed with Felix Frankfurter, appointed the year before and who remained obstreperously opposed to Schneiderman, "that our relations with Russia, as well as our views regarding the government and the merits of Communism are immaterial to a decision in this case."[8] However, Frankfurter suspected Murphy's disclaimer to be little more than boilerplate, and with the added good reason that the elegant Sumner Welles (FDR's de facto secretary of state) had privately suggested that the justices might defer consideration. Solicitor General Charles Fahy proceeded, nevertheless, with no intimation from the White House that the case merited special considerations, he said afterward.

The appearance of judicial normality notwithstanding, all the actors in *Schneiderman v. US* could not have been more aware of the news from Russia. The outcome of the most significant battle of the war hung in the balance that November. Even had they not been so, Wendell Willkie's opening statement brought what was unacknowledged front and center. Recalling his remarkable recasting of her original brief, Carol King, Schneiderman's associate attorney, admitted later being unable to answer Wendell's question the day before the proceedings—"Where was Romanoff (Schneiderman's birthplace)?" The next day, however, the appellant's attorney opened the argument by saying, "Mr. Schneiderman was born near Stalingrad, in 1905."[9] Ten days later, on November 19, Russian armies would encircle Hitler's Sixth Army at Stalingrad, marking the beginning of the end of the mighty *Wehrmacht*.

As a dismayed Justice Frankfurter noted in his diary, the Justice Department had had ample opportunity not to persevere with this case.[10] To deny Wendell's client's appeal, affirm the nationality revocation of a senior CPUSA official, then to send William Schneiderman to the Russian ally at the moment when Nazism's defeat was being purchased with Russian bodies still unassisted by the promised second front might be correct jurisprudence, but it was a dismal augury for allied coexistence. Although no document has surfaced to confirm their discussion of the Schneiderman case, New Deal historian Warren Moscow insists there were clandestine White House meetings of Roosevelt and Willkie during this period.[11] In any case, Wendell argued the case as the important First Amendment question it was—indeed, almost as if his own presence at the bar legitimated his client's appeal.

In the spirit of Herman, he channeled the current of beneficent protest from the old world to the new: The *Communist Manifesto* of 1848; the repression sweeping Europe afterward; the exodus from Europe of the fine strains making "the melting pot that is America." "He ignored technicalities or left them to his brief," an admiring Carol King said. The violence advocated by Marx's *Manifesto* was a theme sounded in the second inaugural address of "the founder of my party," Lincoln, he quoted verbatim: "This country, with its institutions, belongs to the people who inhabit it. . . . [T]hey can exercise their constitutional right of amending it, or their revolutionary right to dismember or overthrow it." Carol King watched the members of the Supreme Court Bar "who packed the courtroom" and who "looked surprised at such directness." The following morning's *Herald Tribune* judged that "Willkie concluded with an argument as forceful as any he ever made on a campaign platform."[12]

Justice Murphy's unusual forty-three-page majority opinion would essentially incorporate the spirit of Wendell's demotic hyperbole when he rendered the court's final 5–3 decision of June 21, 1943, after the case was reargued before an eight-member court due to the resignation of former South Carolina governor James Byrnes. Wendell's presentation this time was said to have been less flamboyant and technically tighter. His original First Amendment premise prevailed unchanged, however, in the majority decision. In America, "beliefs are personal and not a matter of mere association," Murphy stated. "Am I to be held responsible for everything Ham[ilton] Fish says?" Wendell Willkie had asked. Murphy agreed. Guilt by association was unconstitutional. Justice Wiley Routledge offered the compelling concurrent majority opinion (of extraordinary twenty-first-century prescience) that to allow the government to examine the merits "of the very facts of the established judgment" seventeen years after the fact would mean "no naturalized person's citizenship is or can be secure." Chief Justice Harlan Fiske Stone dissented. Justices Frankfurter and Owen Roberts concurred, an angry Frankfurter insisting that he recognized Schneiderman as representative of a type.[13] The unfortunate unanimous decision approving the executive order relocating Japanese Americans in *Hirabayashi v. United States* was also ironically announced on the same day.[14]

Wendell's early November 1942 argument on behalf of William Schneiderman would prevail in June of 1943. On November 8, the day before his original Supreme Court address, the controversial American-British invasion of French North Africa—Operation Torch—commanded by General Dwight Eisenhower and organized into three amphibious task forces of more than 100,000 troops and 350 warships, converged on Casablanca, Oran, and Algiers. Based on his September onsite inspection of their manpower and materiel and a confidential talk with Admiral Rene-Emile Godefroy, Wendell had expected the 125,000 Vichy forces in North Africa to do no more than go through the motions of resistance to an Allied landing. Instead, miscalculation and confusion in the Vichy chain of command resulted in two days of considerable casualties on both sides at Algiers and Oran, and especially at Casablanca, followed on November 10 by a truce and problematic recognition of Vichy's François Darlan as supreme French authority in North Africa. This compromise, forced on General Eisenhower by tactical emergency and ratified as a political convenience by FDR and Churchill, enraged Wendell Willkie and distressed a considerable portion of American and foreign opinion.

The short, bantam-rooster naval officer of solid republican ancestry was credited with modernizing the fleet and was respected by the Allies for having pledged to safeguard France's great naval force from the Germans when the Third Republic collapsed. But Darlan had lost his republican principles in Vichy's shifting fascist sands by the time Churchill's success in persuading Roosevelt to drop the second European front sent an armada to invade instead French North Africa. As Marshal Pétain's prospective successor and an active-passive participant in the puppet regime's civil liberties restrictions and anti-Semitic legislation, François Darlan as proconsul of North Africa reeked to Wendell of all the vintage Machiavellian means that were yet again to be justified by noble ends.[15]

Details of the Darlan deal involved the pure coincidence of the Fleet Admiral's brief visit to Algiers to arrange the care of his polio-stricken son just as the Allied task force attacked the city. His presence upended American consul at Algiers Robert Murphy's careful cloak-and-dagger success in slipping six-foot-two General Henri Giraud (a heroic *Stalag* escapee) from Vichy by submarine to Algiers to take command of French coastal forces. Discovering that he was not to replace Eisenhower as commander-in-chief of Operation Torch, however, five-star General Giraud grandly assumed the role of "spectator," thereby sowing confusion among subordinate generals in Morocco, Tunisia, and Algeria. Moreover, making matters much worse, Charles de Gaulle, the messianic leader of Free France and Wendell's preferred candidate for Washington's best postwar French asset, had been excluded from Operation Torch—in large part thanks to FDR's de Gaulle animus. Determined to draw out public ire on what he saw as his government's deplorable evasion of Atlantic Charter values, Wendell prepared a hard-hitting presentation for the *Herald Tribune* Forum on Current Problems, to be read and broadcast on the evening of November 16. As Wendell would say some weeks later to Drew Pearson, "I really believe the things I say about freedom." He could not "watch the deviation from principle without saying so."[16]

"One of the high points of expediency in the whole war," according to foreign correspondent Joseph Barnes (presumably no pun intended), the administration's disturbing Darlan flirtation caused Secretary of War Stimson to assemble a group of Washington notables at his home on the November 16 to assuage their concerns. Shocked to learn from the group that Wendell Willkie would criticize the Darlan controversy that very evening, Stimson reached the GOP leader at home after a quick exchange with the president. Stimson's telephone call was a categorical imperative. He told Wendell flatly "that if he criticized the Darlan Agreement at this juncture, he would run the risk" of jeopardizing the success of the US Army in North Africa. Furthermore, Stimson warned, his speech "might cost sixty thousand American lives."

Wendell, fair to say, would hardly have credited the secretary's projected casualty figures after his own firsthand witness of the morale and readiness of France's North African military establishment. Nevertheless, the stakes as Stimson formulated them hardly admitted of any decision on Wendell's part other than deletion and revision of his speech in the forty-five minutes available before broadcast time. When he read the White House's carefully balanced Darlan Agreement press release the next morning, in which critics' concerns were acknowledged, Wendell's well-justified suspicions of his president were aroused, especially after learning that the overseas transmission of his own revised address was delayed by the censor for twelve hours. Nor was his suspicion alleviated that Stimson's eleventh-hour telephone intervention was motivated more by politics than military security when FDR, also speaking next day to the *Herald Tribune* Forum, deplored the second-front clamor of "ignorant outsiders" and the criticism "of those who, as we know in our hearts, are actuated by political motives." Wendell returned to the charge before the end of the month in Toronto, but FDR had spoiled the moment and the saliency of his message. Fleet Admiral Darlan presided over a Gaullist-free French North Africa with Washington's permission until an antifascist monarchist shot him dead on December 24, 1942. Even after that providential event, however, the US military continued to enable the anti-Gaullist officer class, a scandal that would last until the eve of the Casablanca Conference with FDR and Churchill in mid-January.[17]

The Darlan dispute was yet another example of the deviousness Wendell had come to expect from FDR, the president's "reputation for cunning and indirectness," as Roosevelt biographer James MacGreggor Burns long ago acknowledged. It sometimes imposed a high toll on the Loyal Opposition concept. By the winter of 1942, however, both these egocentric visionaries recognized in each other a commonality of ideals that made periodic dissembling the politics of necessity, but rarely one of principle. It was, as Eleanor Roosevelt judged, true that her husband "liked Wendell Willkie very much; he never felt the bitterness toward him he felt toward some of his other opponents."[18] As the year ended, however, it was the signs of determined, carefully planned, and well-funded recapture of the Republican Party machinery by the Old Guard that should have worried the titular party head. Compared with them, Franklin Roosevelt might have been said to be Wendell Willkie's best supporter. Riding a surf of national popularity after his global odyssey few politicians ever enjoyed, the head of the GOP was widely believed to be the inevitable presidential choice for 1944.[19] Until late June 1943, Gallup would rank him month by month as the clear majority preference of rank-and-file Republicans.

If Gallup and Roper polls, the *Herald Tribune*, the organs of the Luces and the Cowleses, and Thomas Lamont's Chase Bank spoke for the politics of much of the Eastern Republican establishment and the general run of GOP voters, to the du Ponts, Pews, Tafts, and other Old Guard Republicans invested in economic protectionism these were siren sounds seducing the faithful from the old-time religion.[20] But there was still time enough, they believed, to mount a regenerative movement. Presbyterian Joseph Newton Pew Jr., chairman of Sun Oil Company and Sun Shipbuilding Company and Pennsylvania's kingmaker, had already circulated the previous March an elaborate scheme to quash Wendell's control of the Republican National Committee by getting Joe Martin "off the embarrassing spot he now occupies." Robert Taft, like Pew, hoped for a sophisticated re-embrace of the gospel of isolationism. Republicans, he scolded, would never succeed by trying to "outdeal the New Deal."[21] He, too, set out to recapture the RNC from the Willkieites.

The election of Joe Martin's RNC replacement was scheduled for the National Committee meeting in St. Louis on a historic December 7. Martin's good-soldier unhappiness as House minority leader and RNC chairman had reached its breaking point in the weeks following the party's midterm electoral surge. His personal dealings with Wendell might have been described as a mixture of congenial professionalism and institutional anxiety—a relationship of good advice untaken. Martin, moreover, bore the unique responsibility as 1940 convention chairperson of having enabled Wendell Willkie to survive the fifth day in Philadelphia as his party's leader. In St. Louis, he would play the same role in reverse. Nominated by Willkie deputy Ralph Cake, Frederick E. Baker, thirty-five, a public relations executive from Seattle remindful of Oren Root's legionaires, was something of a surprise to himself: "Hard to believe that the National Committee would see fit to select me for any office." But it nearly did so.

Baker and the leading Old Guard candidate, an unreconstructed Taft isolationist from Illinois, bearing the Teutonic handle Werner Schroeder, tied on the first ballot 40–40, followed by
Harrison Spangler, a conservative Iowan, with fifteen; and the
irrepressible Frank Gannett from New York, and someone from
Missouri. The second ballot put Baker ahead forty-three to Schroeder's thirty-eight, not yet enough to win but, several observers
expected, victorious on the next round. The stakes were truly
high. The youthful energy and progressive politics of Baker as the
GOP's chief executive could have assured Wendell a leverage over
party platform and state organizations sufficient to meet the coming primary challenges. With it also came potent intra-party bargaining power, something Wendell Willkie too often disdained.
Taft was present to lobby his cause. Dutiful Ralph Cake stood in
for Wendell. Perhaps Wendell should have been there when Cake's
anti-recess motion lost 58–38, after which Martin recommended
that the parties recess before the third round. The conservatives
settled for Harrison Spangler during the hour break. Baker and
Schroeder combined to make the pedestrian Iowan the National
Committee's unanimous choice. Wendell professed to be quite satisfied with the outcome that spared the GOP the ministry of a
Werner Schroeder.

It was another question whether or not Wendell actually knew
enough about Harrison Spangler's heartland myopia to worry
that his surname sounded ominously like "spanner." Senator
Taft's gentlemanly motion to retain intact Wendell's breakthrough
April 1942 National Committee resolution on international cooperation temporarily obscured the political reality of St. Louis as
well. Taft and Willkie had gone to the mat over the resolution nine
months before. Now it passed overwhelmingly at St. Louis on
the former's recommendation. For public consumption, Wendell
framed St. Louis as a considerable victory. "My fight was to prevent the masthead of the *Chicago Tribune* from being imprinted
on the Republican party," he insisted, and added that Harrison
Spangler had a "great opportunity for progressive public service."
It soon proved a forlorn hope. RNC chairman Spangler made it
unambiguously clear that his job was to "build up an army of

voters in the United States to defeat the New Deal," and Spangler didn't think there were "any votes in China or Mongolia or Russia that I can get for the Republicans."[22]

In February 1943, Homer Capehart was still proud of the big part he had played in his fellow Hoosier's political career. As a friend and solid Republican who found Wendell's evolving unvarnished internationalism less to his liking, Capehart felt free to offer some good advice early in the year. "The public is with you," he wrote. "The professional politician is against you." Capehart's insight had been anticipated by ex–New Deal Brain Truster Raymond Moley in a November *Newsweek* opinion that Wendell Willkie "will be a public figure, not a political figure." Similar caveats came from John Cowles, always more orthodox in his liberal Republicanism than his brother, and from John Hanes, Sinclair Weeks, Raymond Baldwin, and even Henry Luce.[23] The sum and substance of these cautions seldom risked the wrath of advising compromised beliefs; rather, they suggested more care, feeding, and socializing of the regulars, less disdain for transactional arrangements, more patience with Old Guard paladins, a possible truce with Tom Dewey, and less New Deal castor oil and less temperament.

On the heels of Capehart, Cowles, Hanes, and others came the penetrating public assessment of the *New York Times* national correspondent Turner Catledge, worthy of framing in the titular leader's Willkie, Farr, Gallagher inner office. "Mr. Willkie has been anathema to the Republican Old Guard ever since he humiliated them by grabbing the nomination . . . in 1940. He will never be forgiven by the oldliners for that," Catledge reminded readers. "But he has added to that humiliation lately by constantly confronting them with the challenge to come on out and take a stand on the international front." It could only have depressed the lapsed Democrat and erstwhile president of the demobilized American Liberty League Jouette Shouse, and the Delaware du Ponts, to whom he submitted his careful March 1943 political finding that, "although many of the influential politicians of the party are behind [Ohio Governor] Bricker," the only American politician, other than FDR, "with any personal following of consequence is Willkie."[24] Wendell Willkie was a fait accompli that defied Old Guard solution.

Up the highway from Wilmington, the Philadelphia Pews vowed to stick with Bricker, a prospective presidential candidate they considered the anti-Willkie. Bricker's anti–New Deal politics played well enough among the Old Guard, but his bland personality encouraged some to imagine a more dynamic 1944 answer to Willkie and Roosevelt. Douglas MacArthur was mentioned or Hanford MacNider, also a decorated general officer and head of the American Legion. Dewey's promise to serve out his governorship supposedly removed him from active speculation. Harold Stassen's precocity and progressivism rendered him altogether suspect. Meanwhile, the titular leader's intention to declare his candidacy was reported on February 28 in the *Indianapolis Star*. Turner Catledge's op-ed presented Wendell Willkie as "at one and the same time one of the most important and one of the most troublesome elements in the Republican Party."[25] The momentous reality of that judgment enveloped GOP isolationists cum nationalists like a forest fire that April.

On April 8, a bright Manhattan Thursday morning, the most influential book published in the United States during World War II reached the bookstores. Wendell Willkie's young Simon & Schuster editor, Tom Torre Bevans, persuaded his author to accept a shorter title. "One War, One Peace, One World" appeared as *One World*. It was the third nonfiction book since 1900 that would sell more than one million copies. Although H. G. Wells's *Outline of History* and Dale Carnegie's *How to Win Friends and Influence People* matched Willkie's record, *One World* was unique in surpassing a million copies sold in seven weeks. Its prepublication history was also unique because the author's subject matter had been well served by four national radio broadcast systems. Sales of the two-dollar cloth edition rivaled the dollar paperback. It was an unprecedentedly great day for publisher's row. Simon & Schuster's rhapsodic July press release boasted that "no book in the history of book publishing has been bought by so many people, so quickly."[26] Wendell's 206-page phenomenon emerged from six weeks of writing sessions every morning from 9:00 a.m. until noon in Irita Van Doren's Chelsea apartment.

Because Irita had assisted, suggested, and polished Wendell's speeches and articles over the seven years of their extramarital union, male friends were careful to insist that *One World* was the author's creation. "She helped in assembling and organizing the material," Joe Barnes and Mike Cowles made clear, as did they also with their own notes from the *Gulliver* and from a score of guest accommodations around the world. Major Richard Knight, to whom he dedicated the book, provided the indispensable technical flight details. "But nobody ghostwrote *One World*," Barnes certified. Wendell sat "sucking the end of his pencil," walking up and down, and, said he, talking and rehearsing ideas, reviewing notes penned while the B-24 lumbered from Baghdad to Teheran, as he refined the ground rules for building a prosperous, interdependent, humane world order. The book's page-and-a-half introduction recalled the first words spoken from "Report to the People": "Today, because of military and other censorships, America is like a beleaguered city that lives within high walls through which there passes only an occasional courier to tell us what is happening outside. I have been outside those walls."[27]

The author led with a message about the rapidly shrinking planet, the universal familiarity of the different, the maxim that what is local is global and vice versa, and the plea that Americans' "thinking in the future must be world-wide." Walter Lippmann praised the book in *Foreign Affairs* magazine as "one of the hardest blows ever struck against the intellectual and moral isolationism of the American people." But what made the book truly distinctive was Wendell's prescient twinning of America's inescapable involvement in the future affairs of the world with the just and necessary death of colonialism and race prejudice. He cast the issue in vibrant terms that read like a sophisticated present-day NGO position paper on the West and the rest. But formal empires were passing arrangements, Wendell assured his readers. The problem was to understand what the complexities would be when they were no more, and the Republican leader understood that the United States would be called on to provide answers. Again and again, he was asked: "Does America intend to support a system by which our politics are controlled by foreigners, however indirectly, because we happen to be strategic points on the military roads and trade routes of the world?"

On the Middle East, *One World* stipulated, "the facts are simple enough":

> [T]hese newly awakened people will be followers of some extremist leader in this generation if their new hunger for education and opportunity [goes unanswered]. . . . If we had left the olive groves and the cotton fields and the oil wells on this region alone, we might not have to worry. . . . But we have *not* left them alone. We have sent them our ideas and our ideals, . . . our engineers and our businessmen, and our pilots and our soldiers to the Middle East; and we cannot escape the result. . . . If we fail to help reform, the result will be of necessity either the complete withdrawal of outside powers and a complete loss of democratic influence or complete military occupation and control of their countries by those outside powers.[28]

Wendell Willkie foresaw the postwar promise and peril for the United States as a beacon of democracy in a world of decaying empires, rising expectations, vast oil deposits, and flammable Islam.

One World was high-minded war propaganda in the service of ideals upon which a liberated world democracy would rise. The idiomatic people, picturesque places, and one-of-a-kind leaders its readers sighted in Iraq, Russia, Yakutsk, China, and elsewhere—from 30,00 feet, it sometimes seemed—comprised a tessellated travelogue whose interpretive acuity was sometimes sacrificed to what best served Allied solidarity or was simply obscured because antithetical to an American exceptionalist understanding. Stalin's Russia deserved a far better world press, Wendell decided. His country was "neither going to eat us nor seduce us. That is . . . unless our democratic institutions and our free economy become so frail through abuse and failure . . . as to make us soft and vulnerable." "The Generalissimo [Chiang Kai-shek], both as a man and a leader, is bigger even than his legendary reputation," was a geopolitical hyperbole, certainly, whatever its benefit for the visiting Mai-ling with whom the author's personal diary reveals he found time to spend in Waldorf-Astoria suite 42C.[29]

Harold Stassen's somewhat condescending *New York Times Sunday Book Review*, running one month after publication, offered just such deficits of intellectual robustness, absence of concrete suggestions, "understatement of the evils of Communism," added to what the outgoing Minnesota governor deplored as unjustified hostility to British colonial administration—criticisms Wendell found unfair and politically motivated, as they were. A surprised *Times* publisher Arthur Hayes Sulzberger offered the GOP leader a page to respond, a courtesy Wendell declined.[30] Plaudits in *Atlantic Monthly, Commonweal*, and from William Allen White, William Shirer, Clifton Fadiman, and John Gunther more than made up for the sour sounds from a competing GOP progressive. Gunther, the renowned global investigator, praised Wendell Willkie as "one of the most forward looking Americans of this—or any—time." Wendell's extraordinary opus beckoned the end of its readers' long idyll of innocence. In the short undisclosed time left to his visionary ambition, Wendell was to see his book materially nurture the United Nations movement underway to reification at San Francisco in June 1945.

Its remarkable contemporaneousness destined *One World* to an inevitable time-bound fixity that would have gratified the author. He wrote it in the confidence that Burma and China would be liberated, that the British, despite Churchill's defiance, would leave India, that coexistence with Russia was mutually beneficial— history's QEDs. The special concerns of African Americans and Jewish Americans *One World* addressed with laudable optimism. Wendell had received the American Hebrew Medal in New York City at the end of the last year, an annual award from *American Hebrew* magazine. Bestowal of the medal acknowledged the recipient's notable civic and business accomplishments, and especially honored him for the *Saturday Evening Post* essay, "The Case for Minorities," and for his successful disruption of a lethal assault on the Hollywood film industry by an anti-Semitic senatorial subcommittee. His book zeroed in on the "developments, industrial, agricultural, and cultural" made under the supervision of the world Zionist movement" that encouraged a sympathetic appreciation for a Jewish homeland in Palestine.[31] By macabre coincidence the Warsaw Ghetto uprising began eleven days after *One World* went on sale.

As for the "polite but skeptical" attitudes of colored people in a colored world dominated by Europeans, their Atlantic Charter misgivings—Wendell repeatedly emphasized—arose from what they knew of "maladjustments of races in America." The book's final chapter, "Our Imperialisms at Home," represented, for its day, therefore, an even more notable domestic race relations venture than had Wendell's July 1942 radio broadcast from the NAACP Convention meeting in Los Angeles. As America's second-most-powerful public figure—even its most admired of the season—the titular leader of the Republican Party believed it must be said again: "The attitude of the white citizens of this country toward the Negroes has undeniably had some of the unlovely characteristics of an alien imperialism at home—a smug racial superiority, a willingness to exploit an unprotected people." The book's larger point—whether it was Jews, Negroes, new immigrants, or cultural outliers—and with it the book's all but last word: "To suppress minority thinking and minority expression would freeze society and prevent progress. For the majority itself is stimulated by the existence of minority groups. The human mind requires contrary expressions against which to test itself." As a wide reader, Wendell Willkie may well have had in mind the two original sins of the American people described by de Tocqueville: majoritarian tyranny and antipathy to black people.[32]

The Old Guard and most of the GOP congressional leadership had had enough of their leader's "globaloney" by the fall of 1943. The Old Guard paladins—Pennsylvania's Joseph Pew, the Missouri chemical millionaire Edgar Monsanto Queeny, Colonel McCormick's *Tribune*, Roy Howard's Scripps-Howard chain, the new Republican National Committee chairman, Harrison Spangler, and the old RNC chairman John Hamilton—all had become alienated from a leader who no longer thought or spoke in their language. Even Luce had been made nervous by Willkie's excessive liberalism. "Greatly, as the old guard lords . . . hated Roosevelt," a sympathetic Democrat wrote, "they had come to hate Willkie even more." "And to his eternal credit," Robert Sherwood added, "Willkie went out of his way to court their hatred."[33] In a sense, he need not have cared to try. Events enhanced his already enormous celebrity that summer in an especially spectacular way.

With Margaret Bourke-White, Clare Boothe Luce, and Owen Lattimore, he gave generously of his time and influence on behalf of United China Relief. Since her arrival by special Boeing Stratoliner as Eleanor Roosevelt's guest in late November 1942, Madame Chiang Kai-shek had become one of the most appealing political apparitions ever to conquer Washington. The First Lady championed Mai-ling's appeal for planes and guns. The president, wary of being "vamped," said he, made sure to see his White House guest only on a few occasions. On one such meeting, however, FDR was plainly delighted by Mai-ling's response to his question about Wendell Willkie. "Well, Mr. President, he is an adolescent, after all." And even more delighted, certainly, by her opinion of himself. "Ah, Mr. President," she answered, "you are sophisticated." Mai-ling's unprecedented address to both the House and Senate had left the members dazed.

Wendell's Madison Square Garden presentation of Madame Chiang Kai-shek on the evening of March 2, 1943, would live on in the city's famously inattentive memory. Governor Dewey, General H. H. "Hap" Arnold, chief of the US Army Air Force, General Clair Chennault of the Flying Tigers, and the governors of all the New England states heard a revenue-raising address that yielded $300,000 for guns and planes. Later, Mike Cowles would learn again how curiously affected Mai-ling continued to be by Wendell Willkie. Obeying her command to a private dinner alone in her Waldorf-Astoria suite as she prepared to return home, he absorbed Madame Chiang's grandiose confidence that Wendell's presidential bid would have the wealth of China behind it; after which, she assured Cowles that she and Wendell would divide the world between them.[34]

In that same March week, Franklin Roosevelt took Wendell by surprise by sending a personally typed page and half apology. A fair amount of public comment had come from a Marquis Childs article in *Collier's* featuring examples of "flippancies" the Republican leader deemed insulting. "In regard to the press conference, I did not make a crack at your pronunciation of 'reservahr,'" explained Franklin. "I used the word in my own way which happens to be very close to your own way." FDR guessed that Childs "was trying to make trouble between us because I honestly think you are doing your best to help all of us, from top to bottom, win the war."[35] Bartley Crum thought he recalled Wendell passing off the matter with a shrug: "How the hell can you stay mad to a guy like that?" In fact, though, after quite enough experience with the wiles of the Oval Office, Wendell decided FDR wrote the letter for history rather than from genuine remorse.[36]

When the body count, property damage, and lost productivity caused by the worst race riot in American history to that date was estimated—two late June days and nights in Detroit in 1943—Joseph D. Keenan, vice chairman of the War Production Board, announced that the damage "cost the nation a worse setback in the production of planes, tanks, material, and other equipment than it had suffered from all the labor disputes in the entire nation in the first two months of this year." Detroit's indigestion of 400,000 white and black workers from the Southeast in under two years created the classic pressure cooker explosion of labor, management, housing, and race that also simultaneously detonated in Beaumont, Texas; Mobile, Alabama; and Los Angeles. The city's law enforcement collapsed after racist mismanagement that turned citizens into vigilantes. Finally, FDR dispatched 6,000 federal troops to restore order. Detroit's irruption was the worst by far. Axis newspapers gleefully reported the mayhem in occupied Europe. Japanese newsprint was distributed throughout China and the Pacific.[37]

The governor and mayor and their appointed committees of distinguished majority-white citizens held the advantage of the best narrative to cast blame on criminal black elements and lawless teenagers. The quick response of Wendell Willkie to Walter

White's appeal yielded an imaginative presentation of the riot that materially altered the public's understanding of its causes. With a promised half hour of CBS free time, the Republican leader and NAACP executive secretary formed an Emergency Committee of the Entertainment Industry that drew "so many top-flight artists"—from Tallulah Bankhead to Lillian Hellman to Paul Robeson and Orson Welles—there would only be time for a listing of names, White regretted. The solution was to reenact episodes of the riot, using stereotypical voices imitating rioters, soldiers, unionists, responsible citizens, women and children, climaxed "with a brief speech by an outstanding American."

William Paley, the network head, read the dramatic script to be read in Willkie's *One World* voice and immediately decided that CBS would sponsor the program in its name. The GOP's improbable standard-bearer, in collaboration with the creative Walter White, engineered a unique, Peabody Award–winning media response over the CBS radio network that seized the appalled, guilt-ridden, embarrassed attention of much of the nation for thirty sober Thursday evening minutes on June 24. "All the forces of fascism are not with our enemies," the gravelly voice preached. "Fascism is an attitude of mind which causes men to seek to rule others by economic, military, political force or through prejudice." Wendell's and Walter's Emergency Committee of the Entertainment Industry was the archetypal model for the organized Hollywood support of civil rights activism twenty years later.[38]

Frank Altschul, the original Willkieite, had become less sure of Wendell Willkie's political common sense, but he subscribed fully to the leader's internationalism. Fearing that the people around the RNC were planning to sell a platform that dodged the party's acceptance of postwar international institutions, Altschul warned Wendell's confidant Drew Pearson that this would be a great mistake. Wendell knew that nothing had been settled at the December 1942 election of Martin's replacement. The Republican Old Guard was determined to revert to isolationism—or *nationalism*, the preferred synonym. Harrison Spangler, the new RNC chairman, had come to Washington in January for a hotel breakfast meeting to propose that he and Wendell compose a united foreign policy statement for the postwar world. Neither man had trusted the other, though, with the messy result that a Spangler postwar policy group of conservatives eventually emerged as the Republican Post-War Advisory Council (RPAC), while a Willkie-friendly Republican Postwar Policy Association (RPPA) was formed immediately after the unsuccessful Washington breakfast with a liberal Chicago attorney, Deneen Watson, as president. Wall Street money and a higher policy IQ distinguished the increasingly resented Republican Postwar Policy Association (RPPA).[39] Wendell, however, made a point of his formal nonaffiliation.

The Willkieite Republican Postwar Policy Association's release at its conference that July of a detailed five-point program rejecting isolationism was seen by Spangler's Post-War Advisory Council as a virtual war declaration—a hostile declaration answered by the nationalists cum isolationists two months later on Michigan's Upper Peninsula. No one now doubted that Wendell Willkie was about to declare his candidacy. As requested, Lieutenant Commander Oren Root, serving under the commander of the Atlantic fleet, sent the names of former Willkie Club chairmen and a renewed vote of confidence. Meanwhile, finally persuaded by John Cowles, Henry Luce, and Sinclair Weeks, Wendell plunged into cross-country speech-making, glad-handing, meeting party regulars, and somewhat successfully abiding the advice of party veterans and dignitaries, saying little or nothing about Dewey—and perhaps just in time. "I am going to become the man who knows more of them than anybody else," he boasted to Luce "with boyish gusto."

Even so, at the end of June he slipped from first place among rank-and-file Republicans for the first time in the Gallup Poll. Dewey, MacArthur, and Bricker the anti-Willkie were gaining. Another survey of GOP legislators in thirty-eight states placed him beneath Dewey and Bricker. Joe Pew decided the signs of the "Republican Roosevelt's" weakness signaled a decisive turning point. "Regarding the Willkie situation," Pew gloated in a letter to South Dakota's Neolithic isolationist senator Harlan Bushfield, "I can see no need for caution." A man "who is completely honest and one who can unite the party" was bound to emerge soon.[40]

A curious July 4 letter in jerky, barely legible script on Beekman Tower Hotel stationery to Drew Pearson suggests that Wendell's famous brio may have sagged badly during this time. He was "determined not to make any compromises," it read. "If I don't get the nomination I am in a beautiful position to influence either party afterwards." Winning by losing, though, was altogether out of character.[41]

In early September, Chairman Spangler's Republican Post-War Advisory Council, stacked with forty-nine pre–Pearl Harbor non-interventionists, met on picturesque Mackinac Island, without extending an invitation to the party leader. For the sake of appearances, Hoover, Landon, and Stassen were also excluded, but the atmosphere within the big white lakeside hotel and meeting hall was one of convivial atavism. A journalist among the hundred-plus correspondents, reporters, and columnists remembered the panic on the faces of the delegates when a mischievous voice announced the arrival of WENDELL Willkie! As finally drafted, however, the so-called unity foreign policy resolution turned out to be a more post–Pearl Harbor document than Wendell had expected. Arthur Vandenberg's evolving ideas on engagement were present in the document. Earl Warren struck a relatively enlightened position. Dewey actually proposed the preposterous postwar alliance with Great Britain, Russia, and China for reasons that mystified a disgusted Bob Taft, likely prompted by Churchill's recent Harvard address. Outright rejection of internationalism had proved a bridge too far. Republicans at Mackinac pledged themselves to "participation . . . in post-war cooperative organization among sovereign nations to prevent military aggression and to attain permanent peace with organized justice in a free world." For the sake of unity and his presidential prospects, Wendell announced that Mackinac was "a move in the right direction." Only it was not the direction for his presidency.[42]

The leader and his party maintained a short truce until the October 5 special issue of Look carried "How the Republican Party Can Win in 1944," a candid response to Mackinac that was a virtual One World manifesto, capped off with a splendid cover likeness by John Falter. He promised "complete and undeviating service" to his party if it intended "to drive heart and soul for liberal objectives." In answer to five questions posed by the magazine's editorial board, Wendell presented again five indispensable liberal objectives: minority rights, efficiency in administration, a rebirth of *"real enterprise,"* guaranteed employment, a new foreign policy. His characterization of the free enterprise system was something of a red flag to the Old Guard. The system did not "belong to a few at the top. That is a vested system," Wendell spelled out. "A free enterprise system belongs to everybody in it."[43]

A once dismissively skeptical *New Republic* conceded that it found Wendell Willkie's political evolution impressive. *New York Times* columnist Arthur Krock wrote that he was impressed, that Wendell would be "a formidable contender for the 1944 Republican nomination" and knows where "his fences are weak, and [is] setting out to repair them." Yet, even as he began to do so, the Old Guard heavyweights struck with pent-up malice. Sizing up his party's improved options that September, Pew lectured fellow hardliner Frank Gannett, "the only great hurdle we have to overcome in bringing home to Mr. Willkie [is] . . . that he can be of great help to the Republican party as long as he does not try to rule it or become our candidate."[44]

Pew expected that message to be conveyed to Wendell in a strikingly awkward form with the composition in mid-September of nine litmus-test questions by some forty Missouri Republicans. The questions challenged Wendell's opinion on the desirability of flooding the country "with alien individuals with alien ideas," on whether the United States should become a member of a "world supranational state," on the "political and economic organization of the world," and so on. The Missouri group's organizer was industrialist Edgar Monsanto Queeny, the combative fifty-seven-year-old chairman of Monsanto Chemicals, a leading economic protectionist and significant contributor to Wendell's 1940 campaign. Newspapers gave play to the questionnaire and the challenge. On October 15, forty 1940 Missouri delegates and Edgar Queeny faced a game Wendell Willkie in St. Louis ready for questions. The RNC advertised $50 box seats to the event to pay off a $100,000 deficit, but Wendell volunteered the rental charge for the hall.

Before his speech, he was given a luncheon by a former president of the National Association of Manufacturers (reporters excluded). As planned without his knowledge, Wendell was introduced by Queeny as "America's leading ingrate," for whom he had raised $200,000 "and never got a thank you." After the surprisingly unpleasant luncheon, Wendell delivered a powerful attack on the failings of the Roosevelt administration but largely ignored the internationalist entrapments of the controversial Missouri questionnaire. At lunch on the next day before leaving, Wendell found Queeny's Chase Bank innuendos intolerable. His memorable explosion was captured by the St. Louis newspapers and reported across the country. Apparently, the Missouri Republicans had expected him to qualify his internationalist platform. Instead, they were given the back of their guest's hand. He didn't know "whether you're going to support me or not," and he didn't "give a damn," Wendell shouted. "You're a bunch of political liabilities anyway." Fired up, he barreled on. "The days are gone, which some of you want to bring back, when you could go to your plants and cause employees to tremble in fear of losing their jobs. Those days are gone forever and good riddance."[45]

The St. Louis donnybrook Wendell Willkie took in stride. The California disappointment was to be unexpected, even almost crippling. His time there was split between informal campaigning and the Hollywood Writers' Congress in late September, an effulgent assembly of intellectuals, actors, writers, and organization heads, consecrated to epoch-changing social proposals. Wendell and Walter spoke the same day, Thursday September 30, to the War Chest Appeal for Los Angeles, Wendell on the necessity to defeat the enemies' ideas as well as their armies. The Writers' Congress afforded Walter (served with the complimentary title of "Dr." White) the opportunity to encourage the people who control the "media of expression" to use their considerable powers to advance ideals of peace and equality.[46] A sour note in his Writers Congress distinction was that Walter's Hollywood friend Marc

Connelly of *Green Pastures* renown had shamefacedly insisted that Walter and Gladys accept his hospitality after discovering that the hotel reservations for the NAACP head were canceled because the management "has gone in for Southern Democracy.[47]

There was nothing embarrassed about Wendell's California campaigning that winter. An October poll among the state's GOP leaders placed him comfortably ahead of Warren and Dewey. Speaking open-necked and without jacket to a large group of party regulars, many of them delegates at the 1940 convention, he insisted that the party would win if it had the good sense to realize that the basics of the New Deal were settled, that the augmented role of the United States in international affairs and institutions was irreversible. His talks with West Coast labor leaders of the AFL and CIO assured them he subscribed fully to the Wagner Act. His hour-long talk with Earl Warren in Sacramento, however, did not go as well as both pretended for public consumption. The tall, Romanesque, silver-haired governor had cultivated an image of moderate progressivism, his indebtedness to Randolph Hearst and role as state attorney general in the relocation of Japanese Americans notwithstanding. At the Mackinac conference, he had been something of a conciliator among the opposed factions.[48]

Wendell had expected to like the person and the politics. Bartley Crum, Wendell's conscientious northern California consigliere, believed an opportunity had been missed either through unwillingness to bargain with the governor or, failing that, not to have foreclosed the governor's favorite-son inclinations by entering himself in the state primary.[49] Bargains, though, were verboten, and the likely discussion of a cabinet position in a Willkie administration would have disappointed the presumptive candidate, as Walter White, who saw Wendell immediately after his return from Sacramento, recalled in his autobiography. " 'What did you tell him?' 'Go to hell,' Wendell growled, 'I have never made a deal yet, and I'll be God-damned if I'll make one now, even to be president of the United States.' "[50] The forfeiture of California was costly, if not fatal, to Wendell Willkie's second attempt at the presidency. The forces at play were an assertive local party organization and the powerful machinations of the RNC. Speaking for fifty fellow delegates, National Committeeman William Reichel told the *Oakland Tribune* that Californians expected their National Convention votes to buy "a Western Cabinet member, a Western Supreme Court Judge, and a Western man on every high policy-making body in the government . . . or they won't get our votes."

The California machinations of the RNC emerged with ominous suddenness in the November 29 *New Republic*. Little more than a month before, the magazine touted his winning unofficial cross-country campaigning that Gallup saw drawing labor, Jews, African Americans, and independents to the GOP. Now its leading article—"Has Wendell Willkie Lost?"—revealed that Republican regulars were now confident that "any nominee can beat FDR." What this stunning turnaround meant, the November *New Republic* decided, was that "Joe Pew and Lammot du Pont still pack more wallop in the Republican Party than George Gallup." The *Pittsburgh Courier* smartly anticipated the *New Republic*'s diagnosis with the November 7 headline: "Hamilton Tries to Hide Willkie Bid Behind Smokescreen of Favorite Sons." The *Courier*'s Willkieite columnist Milton Akers rehearsed for its middle-class African American subscribers the mischief caused by lordly John D. M. Hamilton in the 1936 presidential contest. That experience ought to have taught Hamilton that "you cannot stop somebody with nobody." But it was also "a political axiom," syllogized Akers, "that you can stop somebody with everybody." Pew, writing overjoyed to Queeny after a meeting in Chicago with "people who supported Willkie in 1940," predicted that the tide of everybodies had welled "tremendously in the last couple of weeks." And there was more good news. "From Stassen's own lips," Pew claimed that Harold Stassen merely feigned support for Wendell.[51] During the year's final trimester, the Philadelphia Hamiltons, John and Jane, ranged from the Midwest to California and the Northwest in Joe Pew's salaried service and with the hearty commendations of Old Guard paladins Lammot du Pont, Edgar Queeny, Herbert Hoover, Colonel Robert McCormick, Robert Taft, Frank Gannett, Hamilton Fish, and more.

Served by his universal rolodex of national, state, and local committeemen and -women, *laisser-passes* to GOP statehouses, influential introductions to elected locals, Hamilton sent long, detailed accounts of successful annulments of Willkie strength state by state and capital by capital, filling several folders in the manuscripts and archives department at the du Ponts' Hagley Museum and Library. A brace of November letters written from San Francisco's Hotel St. Francis traced Earl Warren's sinuous recruitment from polite, wary, to eager—but, with a caveat from newspaper publisher and future senator William Knowland, "that if pushed it might be disastrous." On November 10, Hamilton conveyed the governor's appreciation for all that Pew had done for the party and assurances that "[Warren] has definitely made up his mind that Willkie shall not have the California delegation." On January 9, 1944, Governor Warren announced his entry in the California primary.[52] Bart Crum renewed his counsel that Wendell force Warren to share the honor.

There was to some degree a curious disconnect from the domestic politics his admirers and much of the public believed were his to command. Geoffrey Parsons, editor of the *Herald Tribune*, could only wish that his friend might pay more attention to one of his reporter's warnings that December, that "Spangler and the Republican headquarters forces are continuing to work night and day against Willkie and are doing him a lot of harm." Wendell's paramount concern, however, was with his country's postwar intellectual and international readiness. A major *New York Times Magazine* piece on January 2 titled "Don't Stir Distrust of Russia" was meant to encourage domestic understanding of Russia's proprietary touchiness over Poland, Finland, and the Baltic states, but also the obligation of the United States to press upon the parties mutually guaranteed arrangements. *Pravda*'s rejoinder on behalf of his friend Stalin was furious in the extreme, lumping Wendell with the Vatican, the British foreign office, and fascist sympathizers—an early augury of coming One World complications.[53] The views of Yale Law School professor Fred Rodell were somewhat less savage in the March *Harper's*, but Rodell's portrayal of an insincere opportunist and unethical utility magnate consigned Wendell to history as "Wall Street's William Jennings Bryan."

John Chamberlain's generous profile of Wendell in *Life* placed him at the head of a rival New Deal coalition of "the Negroes, the Jews, the liberal intellectuals, the Thurman Arnold anti-monopoly New Dealers, the foreign correspondents, the labor movement and the civil libertarians"—but if true, these potential voters held little appeal for du Ponts and Pews.[54] Wendell still had allies within the party. John Hamilton got nowhere with the old Connecticut Beefeater Kenneth Bradley. Ray Baldwin was determined to lead his state delegation to the National Convention pledged to Wendell Willkie. Likewise, William Henry Wills, Vermont's tall, self-made sixty-fifth governor, a laconic progressive Republican, was willing to take on the Old Guard and fight for a Willkie presidential nomination. Speaking over national radio from Montpellier on January 8, 1944, Wills heaped scorn on Hamilton, Landon, Nye, Pew, and the noxious Gerald L. K. Smith of the America First Party. In "Will the Republican Party Commit Suicide in 1944?," Wills called them "Four Locusts," united by nothing more than hatred of Wendell Willkie. Hamilton and his spawn were "the voice of negation."

The governor's broadcast exposed the American people to what was denounced as a shocking, well-funded reactionary conspiracy to steal the Republican Party. "The last ballot in Kentucky was hardly counted nine weeks ago," sneered Wills, "when the four-year locusts . . . blackened the horizon to blight the victory crops." Professional politicians claimed the GOP could win "with anybody." This, Wills asserted, could not be true. The ensuing commotion propelled Hamilton to a CBS microphone a week later to read an eight-page, carefully framed rebuttal. "Shocked" by Governor Wills's assassination of his character, Hamilton denied knowing Smith or of seeing Nye in decades, and proudly admitted friendship with two upstanding public figures, Landon and Pew. The facts as he deployed them were that, motivated by love of party and at his own expense, he decided to visit Republican leaders "of all shades of political thought in more than twenty states." Hamilton discovered that neither the state leaderships nor recent polls of regular members supported a Willkie nomination. Indeed, not a single pledged Willkie delegate had he met, despite Willkie's repeated boast of having "bagged 300–500."[55] Hamilton's unlikely explanation of personal initiative and finances nonetheless proved persuasive public relations.

Still official leader of his party, Wendell announced his presidential campaign on February 2, 1944. He made the notable pledge to appoint a person of color to his cabinet or to the Supreme Court and to use the full power of his office to end institutionalized racism. He called for his party to become again "the great American liberal party," the engine of economic and military strength. "Some of the talk we hear about 'free enterprise' or 'private enterprise' is just the propaganda . . . of powerful groups who have not practiced real enterprise in a generation"—a clear swipe at the Pews and Queenys. He followed the feisty campaign announcement with the bombshell release of a taxation plan calling for a drastic tax increase that added eight billion dollars above the revenues captured by FDR's budget request.

Once the war ended, Wendell asserted, the pain endured by high taxes to pay-as-you-go in wartime would be followed in a debt-free peacetime by major income tax reductions for the lower- and middle-income populations. John Hanes, Wendell's able campaign fundraiser, advised against releasing the plan. FDR was delighted to praise his opponents' "courage." Several major newspaper editorials commended its rigor, as did the doyen of American historians, Henry Steele Commager. Still, Wendell's tax plan was economically as sound as it was politically mistaken. Appalled Republicans and alienated labor unions roundly condemned the Republican presumptive leader.[56] Insisting that "the people" would soon approve his plan's long-term rationale, Wendell began a three-week speaking tour across much of the country.

A limited number of states at the time held presidential primaries, and of those available, his realistic options were New Hampshire's, in mid-March, Wisconsin's on April 4, followed by Nebraska's, Maryland's, and Oregon's. He won the New Hampshire primary on March 14 by a respectable six out of eleven delegates. He believed he retained the loyalty of the party machines in Vermont, Massachusetts, Indiana, Connecticut, and Kentucky. The ironic reality was that he was now even more a man without a party than he had been before those heady five days in Philadelphia in 1940. His gallows humor stayed with him, though. "Ham Fish is against me," Wendell said. "Gerald L. K. Smith is against me and I understand Landon is against me. If this keeps up I may be nominated in spite of myself." Henry Luce hadn't turned against his friend, but the publisher had told John Cowles weeks before that he rejected the party liberals' presidential alternative of Willkie or Roosevelt for president. *Time* and *Life* "would try to give Wendell all the breaks," but Luce thought Dewey's message might be more salable to the party than Wendell's extreme internationalism and New Deal revisionism. Luce had begged off membership in the Cowleses' informal Willkie presidential committee. Congressperson Clare Boothe Luce had expressed a clear preference for Douglas McArthur's anticommunism and concern for Wendell's alleged drinking problem.[57]

A face-saving telephone arrangement with Governor Warren supposedly had assuaged Wendell—50 percent of the California delegation promised at the national convention. Wisconsin, then, was the primary where a strong performance was essential if he were to succeed in garnering a significant delegate count from California, New York, Pennsylvania, Stassen's Minnesota, and a scattering from the South—states with more than 300 of the 1,057 delegate total. He went into it knowing, despite its La Follette progressivism, that Wisconsin's isolationism and pro-German sentiments made success a gamble for the country's leading internationalist politician. Two years later, Wisconsinites would turn out Robert La Follette Jr. and send Cold Warrior Joseph McCarthy to the US Senate. He campaigned almost maniacally, Edith by his side, delivering some forty hoarse speeches in thirteen days, the one at historic Ripon, "The Functions of a Political Party," evoking Marquis Childs's praise as a political classic. The duty of his party was to shape history, not to be held back by history, he warned.[58] The assembly speaker endorsed Wendell. Otherwise, there was virtually no local organization behind him. Lem Jones, Mike Cowles, and Edith traveled with him. Harold Stassen's shadow candidacy and Douglas MacArthur's nominal presence (both were in uniform in the Pacific) diminished what strength Wendell hoped to rally in a population of considerable German origins. Even though Dewey insisted that his name be withdrawn, several of his pledged delegates refused to honor the request.

Wendell Willkie crashed in the Wisconsin primary, far behind Dewey, Stassen, and MacArthur. Jones and Cowles were with him when news of the debacle reached him in Omaha, Nebraska. He delivered a strong denunciation of FDR's foreign policy, then calmly addressed about three thousand listeners without a text. Wendell said he wanted to speak from his heart. Yet, he couldn't. "If I spoke of what's on my mind, I would make too great a castigation of American politics." Continuing with emotion, Wendell said he had been "encouraged to believe that the Republican Party could live up to the standards of its founders, but I am discouraged to believe that it may be the party of negation."[59] It was obvious now that he could not be nominated again for the presidency. He terminated his presidential campaign, asked his friends to "desist from any activity toward that end," and went home to Fifth Avenue and Edith, Irita in the Village, and an uncertain political future.

An avalanche of fine condolences and well wishes came from the famous and the humble, many from African Americans whose young sons bore his first name. It seems no exaggeration, nonetheless, to find that virtually all those expressions of concern achieved near perfection in the consolatory letter from Walter Lippmann. "The part that you still have to play in American life will be greater, not less, than that which you have already played," Lippmann foresaw. "It often happens that those who cannot exercise power come thereby to exercise greater influence." Still, the erstwhile titular head of the Republican Party was frank about his bitterness. It always hurt him deeply to lose, Edith told an early biographer.[60]

Had the venue for the June National Convention been cosmopolitan New York City instead of heartland Chicago, his much-diminished party standing might have been reparable. But not even John Hanes's Midas touch of a munificent New York convention package had overcome Old Guard determination not to risk another Philadelphia. The Arrangements Committee invited Herbert Hoover to address the National Convention in Chicago, but it offered Willkie merely a seat among "honored guests." He spared himself the personal indignity and what he had no doubt was witnessing the political casualty of Thomas Dewey's nomination at Chicago on June 28. He wired the governor correct congratulations. Dewey had, it said, "one of the great opportunities of history." The early-July telephone call from Harold Ickes, however, entailed a wholly unexpected offer—a startlingly unusual political hypothetical.

Old adversary Harold Ickes joined Wendell and Mike Cowles for dinner the following evening at Manhattan's Ambassador Hotel. FDR wants to know, Ickes confided, "if you would accept if he nominated you for vice president on the Democratic ticket." That FDR really supposed he could convince the big-city bosses to accept an unpredictable Wendell Willkie for the progressive vagaries of Henry Wallace was certainly a stretch of political logic. Wallace, back that very week from an investigative mission to Siberia and China imitative of Wendell's global odyssey, heard from a confidant that "some of the people around the White House wanted a new face." The aloof vice president was a lapsed Republican as ideologically unpalatable to party power-brokers as the lapsed Democrat Wendell was to the GOP's Tories—mirror image casualties of their One World and "Century of the Common Man" faiths.

It was known in innermost Democratic circles that FDR had all but written off Wallace after his clangorous jurisdictional scrap with the powerful head of the New Deal's Reconstruction Finance Corporation, Jesse Holman Jones. Equally known was FDR's grudging respect—liking even—for Willkie. And because those inner circles were now silently appalled by the president's visible physical deterioration (MacArthur would give FDR six months), the sobering thought of Henry Wallace in the Oval Office many found more alarming than a Wendell Willkie replacement.[61] "Everybody who came into the White House could tell us that it would be dangerous to [re]nominate Wallace," Samuel Rosenman revealed well after the fact. Ickes left the Ambassador lunch persuaded that Wendell would give the proposal serious consideration. For the alarmed Cowles, the vice presidency temptation was another personal crisis reminiscent of the Mia-ling moment. To turn on all those friends "who'd supported the hell out of him since 1940" would be monstrously faithless, Mike challenged. "It wouldn't sit well with the country."

The matter died in secret of its own deviousness only to be succeeded by an even more unrealistic proposition, of which the precise genesis remains unclear. Sam Rosenman, the standby speech writer, remembers being surprised by Roosevelt's sudden enthusiasm for a scheme to form a third party. Something said, perhaps, by Pennsylvania's former progressive governor Gifford Pinchot, that Wendell Willkie was exploring a run for mayor of New York with the support of David Dubinsky's garment workers' union. "A new political liberation formation!" FDR exclaimed. The time had come for the Democratic party "to get rid of its reactionary elements in the South and to attract . . . liberals in the Republican party." On the evening of July 5, Wendell met Rosenman at Manhattan's St. Regis Hotel to hear details of FDR's unsolicited, astonishing invitation to plan together a new liberal third party. In the reasonable surmise of Dewey's definitive biographer, Richard Norton Smith, the meeting "undoubtedly had another purpose, to neutralize Willkie in the current campaign or perhaps even win his endorsement of the President."[62]

Wendell's response to Rosenman's mission delighted FDR. Dewey and his allies were said to be bearing down for his endorsement, but the rejected Republican had reached no final decision. "Both parties are hybrids"—the best of the worst, as it were. "You tell the President that I'm ready to devote almost full time to this," Wendell pledged. The two of them compared prospective lists then and there of liberals in both parties. A sound liberal government was essential. But it was also essential that he and Franklin proceed with utmost secrecy until after the election. As Rosenman recalled, FDR's reaction was enthusiastic. "From the liberals of both parties, Willkie and I together can form a new, really liberal party in America," the president salivated. Rosenman believed that his boss fully concurred with Wendell's insistence on the strictest secrecy. Instead, seemingly unable to contain his enthusiasm as he left Washington for Hawaii and Alaska, FDR sent a July 13 "Dear Wendell" letter that, if disclosed to others, risked sinking their visionary scheme. Explaining that his imminent departure precluded a signature, Roosevelt confided that he "want[ed] to see you when I come back, but not on anything in relationship to the present campaign. I want to talk to you about the future, even the somewhat distant future, and in regard to the foreign relations problems of the immediate future. When you see in the papers that I am back, will you get in touch with General Watson. We can arrange a meeting either here in Washington or, if you prefer, at Hyde Park—wholly off the record. . . . Always sincerely, Franklin D. Roosevelt."

While there is no evidence that he did so, it might have occurred to Wendell that FDR had invited himself to play a controlling (probably co-opting) part in what was Wendell's ambitious pact with Dubinsky's ILGWU to run for mayor to launch a new party. In any case, their secret appeared to hold through the fractious July 19–21 Democratic Convention at Chicago where, duplicitously assured of the president's support, a game Henry Wallace unexpectedly beckoned a tide of support that unnerved DNC Chairman Robert Emmet Hannagan and the party bosses—until all was saved for Harry Truman by temporary adjournment of the proceedings.[63] Drew Pearson kept real-time notes on the desperate eleventh-hour maneuvers to hoist a Willkie boom for vice president at the convention. Pearson, a Willkie source as indispensable as self-serving, put his subject at the center of a palpitating Chicago story that he insisted had all but actually unfolded. "You had a large number of friends there," Pearson revealed: Tammany chieftain Edward Loughlin; Foreign Economic Administration head Leo Crowley; New York's powerful senator Robert Wagner— influential Willkie supporters Pearson said he had devoted weeks cultivating. FDR had signaled approval of a spontaneous Willkie draft from the floor. After failing to gain the podium to nominate Wendell, Senator Wagner phoned Grace Tully in a desperate, unsuccessful gamble to reach FDR.[64]

Drew Pearson must have been unaware of the secret FDR letter or that the recipient had written a thoughtful, warm response to be mailed at the right time. Reaffirming intense interest in their prospective collaboration, Wendell respectfully reiterated, nevertheless, the *sine qua non* of secrecy. "However much you or I might wish or plan otherwise," that they could "possibly have such a talk without the fact being known" was simply unrealistic until after the November elections. The risk of the appearance of "some betrayal of the principles which each of us hold so deeply" was grave. Wendell's letter would never be sent, however, and because of that fact the transformative potential of his and Roosevelt's political vision would survive as the speculative fodder of revisionist historians. Wendell filed his letter after it became obvious in early August that Roosevelt's document was common knowledge among the press corps. He might have excused the leak, until the letter's author, returned from his western inspection trip on July 18, blandly denied any knowledge of it when questioned in his press conference.

Prodded by Rosenman, Ickes, and his bigoted press secretary Steve Early to mollify Wendell, FDR made a "boneheaded" slip (Pearson's word) worse. He had been "caught off guard." The leak was inexplicable, he wrote Wendell on August 21. He was "awfully sorry that there was a leak on a silly thing like this," but he still hoped Wendell "will stop in . . . or run up to Hyde Park if you prefer. Always sincerely." Ellsworth Barnard, Wendell Willkie's early biographer, records his subject's final thoughts about Franklin Delano Roosevelt: "I've been lied to for the last time." Interestingly, when asked by Rexford Tugwell what she made of Rosenman's FDR-Willkie revelations in *Working with Roosevelt*, his 1952 memoir, Eleanor, sharp as ever in June 1957, expressed surprise. "It was all news to me he never spoke about that." She imagined her husband might have said something, "because no third party ever wins for some time." Still, to do Franklin justice, she added, "but it may well have been that he sighted that the swing was going to come."[65] Perhaps Mrs. Roosevelt's image of a "swing that was going to come" unwittingly explains her husband's ambivalent regard for the man on whose legs both of them had walked out of partisan hatreds into international understanding and on to the far final horizon where the parliament of humankind must be built.

Enfeebled to the point that he found it advisable not to accept his fourth renomination in person, Franklin Roosevelt, *sui generis* chief executive, leader of the free world, legatee, like Wendell Willkie, of Woodrow Wilson's trust, understood—even as he must deny recent medical findings—that death was bound to claim him before his great work as architect of the peace was finished. Of all those he would have deemed worthy of his baton (and surely not his new vice president), it was Wendell Willkie, "the swing that was going to come." Who else understood Stalin almost as well as he? Two years earlier, FDR had curtly ordered Churchill to leave the Russian dictator to himself. "Stalin hates the guts of all your top people," the president declared. "He thinks he likes me better, and I hope he will continue to do so." Roosevelt's and Willkie's last remaining months after the Chicago convention are a concatenation of hypotheticals: leaving for the Second Quebec Conference with Churchill, Roosevelt, again maladroitly, reached for the Rushville telephone number to propose that Wendell act as paramount US civil authority in soon-to-be defeated Germany; Wendell as special presidential representative at the United Nations conference in San Francisco was another plan.[66] FDR's other speech writer, the gifted Robert Sherwood, witnessed one of FDR's rare public displays of anger when Harry Hopkins demeaned the value of Wendell's contributions. Clearly, there was time for more *pas de deux*. And even a campaign endorsement?

Wendell had remained out of sight after the Wisconsin primary disappointment. He resurfaced at a party honoring Walter White for his years of service as executive secretary of the NAACP. He said nothing, donated five thousand dollars from *One World* proceeds to the civil rights organization, and was made to feel quite welcome. The two had discussed plans with a publisher to write a book together on the race problem as a world issue of prime importance. Wendell's essay in the October 7 *Collier's*, "Citizens of Negro Blood," was a forceful adumbration of the tenor of their book. It was an article written, declared the author, "with the deliberate intent of helping to arouse a public opinion that will require these candidates to put aside generalities, evasions and pious platitudes and deal in concise, concrete terms with this human, this national, this world problem." An earlier *Collier's* article, "Cowardice at Chicago," appearing September 16, castigated both national parties for proposals that required two-thirds approval by the US Senate of the United Nations Charter. "Both the Democratic and Republican parties propose to . . . prevent aggression and preserve peace, while this nation . . . maintains its traditional sovereignty." This was an article that channeled the League of Nations distress of Wendell's old idol Newton Baker.[67]

Wendell entered Manhattan's Lenox Hill Hospital suffering from acute arrhythmia two days after "Cowardice at Chicago" was published. He had ignored intermittent chest distress in Rushville, despite his property caretaker Mary Sleeth's urgings. The prognosis was guardedly positive. The last diary entry, September 21— "Eichelberger, as soon as I'm OK"—referred to Clark Eichelberger, director of the American Association for the United Nations. But there was to be no resumption of third-party planning with FDR. There were only notes for a book on race in the world with Walter White. Thomas Dewey was in a heated campaign contest with FDR. He reached out to Wendell for desperately wanted endorsement, hinting through John Foster Dulles of the position of secretary of state. Russell Davenport and Bartley Crum insisted that Wendell planned to join Republicans for Roosevelt and endorse his admired nemesis, which brought an adamant denial from Luce. "[Wendell] completely distrusted Franklin Roosevelt's statesmanship and had no intention of voting for him or supporting him." Roscoe Drummond vouchsafed a near-deathbed averral that as recently as September 30, Wendell "had not made up his mind." Ray Baldwin and the Cowleses believed he would wait until the week of the election before endorsing Dewey.[68]

Willkie died on the morning of October 8, age fifty-two. "It's all over. He went very fast," Lem Jones announced to the reporters waiting in the hospital lobby. "Citizens of Negro Blood" appeared the day before. The *New York Times* devoted its front page to his obituary, "WENDELL WILLKIE'S DEATH STUNS THE WORLD." A Roosevelt biographer offered a superb apostrophe to the fifty-two-year-old visionary "who ate too much, drank too much, smoked too much, and loved too much."[69] When news of his death reached the White House that day, the waspish Harry Hopkins upset Roosevelt by making a derisory remark. "Don't you ever say anything like that around here again," FDR exploded. "Don't even *think* it. You of all people ought to know that we might not have had Lend Lease or Selective Service or a lot of other things if it hadn't been for Wendell Willkie. He was a godsend to this country when we needed him most."[70] As a final judgment on his unique partner, the president's words were fitting. Left unsaid, however, must have been Roosevelt's awful realization that Wendell Willkie's wholly unexpected demise left their mutual vision of a reconstructed postwar world to his own ebbing mental and physical capacities and fast-approaching death. Harold Ickes's "barefoot Wall Street lawyer" and Clare Boothe Luce's "global Abraham Lincoln" doubtless would have wanted Americans to remember the admonition from his posthumous essay collection, *An American Program*: "Whatever we do at home constitutes foreign policy. And whatever we do abroad constitutes domestic policy. This is the great new political fact."[71] In tipping it off its solid isolationist base, Wendell started the Republican Party down a curious evolutionary path into an internationalism he hoped would fulfill the revised Wilsonian mission. The party's formal acceptance of foreign-policy bipartisanship, achieved by Wendell Willkie the year before his death, emerged as a controlling postwar doctrine—notably exemplified by Arthur Vandenberg's support of President Truman's Cold War foreign policy. Joseph Martin, soon Speaker of the House, judged this to be "Wendell Willkie's monument." The party that disavowed its maverick standard bearer entered the mid-twentieth century far better attuned to international challenges because of its temporary and unanticipated capture by an extraordinary internationalist.

Wendell's achievement represented a great double paradox, however. The Republican Party's internationalism was destined to swerve away from its optimistic Willkiean origins toward a steadily more belligerent anti-communism that became indistinguishable from imperialism in all but name. Instead of the ennobling One World ideal, the trajectory would end, *faute de mieux*, in Henry Luce's supremacist American Century. Vouchsafed the precious few years more that undoubtedly would have positioned him at the center of postwar international reconstruction and domestic politics, it risks no counterfactual sin on the part of an historian to suggest that Wendell's commitment to power-bloc understanding and coexistence—his firsthand familiarity with the dramatis personae of Russia, Eastern Europe, the Middle East, and Asia—would have expressed itself in vigorous counsels of moderation and reproach against the Cold War policies that rapidly displaced the Atlantic Charter ideals he and FDR had made the vivid vision of the possible world after V-E Day.

Sixty thousand people filed past Wendell's remains lying in the Fifth Avenue Presbyterian Church on Tuesday, October 10. Reverend John Sutherland Bonnell, DD, LLD, hung his memorial service sermon on a quotation from Wendell: "I have got to live with myself and what is most important is not that I attain office but that the principles I stand for should gain acceptance." Sumner Welles might have been thought to speak for FDR had he still possessed his position as undersecretary of state. He spoke movingly as a distinguished private citizen. Eleanor, accompanied by a general, represented Franklin. "His outspoken opinions on race relation were among his great contributions to the thinking world," she wrote of Wendell in her column. Walter White voiced identical sentiments. The tributes were all fine. Those who knew the story, sent simultaneous condolences to Irita and Edith. Once again, though, Walter Lippmann's tribute achieved incomparable saliency: "Second only to the Battle of Britain, the sudden rise of and nomination of Willkie was the decisive event, perhaps providential, which made it possible to rally the free world when it was almost conquered. Under any other leadership but his, the Republican party would in 1940 have turned its back on Great Britain, causing all who still resisted Hitler to feel that they were abandoned."[72]

Dead, in his prime, at fifty-two, Wendell's notable profile in Irving Stone's contemporaneous *They Also Ran* soon dwindled to that of a nearly forgotten, even improbable, public figure whose uncompromising liberalism had proved too quixotic for the neat political and ideological categories of public service of his day.

Unquestionably, the argument registers that he should have paid more attention to the care and feeding of his party's regulars. The end result, though, may not have been much different. His disappearance removed the only Republican presidential candidate who could have been elected in 1944 or 1948: himself. At the end of the day, as Reverend John Bonnell reminded them, what mattered most to Wendell Willkie and should matter even more to his fellow citizens in the disastrous second decade of their twenty-first century was not the attainment of office, "but that the principles I stand for should gain acceptance."

Wendell channeled responsible bipartisanship as the health of democracy. His corporate responsibilities confirmed insights of his Elwood upbringing that the health of the market economy was codependent with a just social contract. As Norman Thomas, perennial socialist presidential aspirant, scoffed in 1940, "[Willkie] agreed with Mr. Roosevelt's entire program of social reform and said it was leading to disaster."[73] His 1848 family heritage predisposed him to prize the positive impact of immigrants and rightness of the claims of the religiously and racially different. It predisposed him to a civil libertarian hardihood unusual in a businessman and greatly problematic in a politician. His evolving understanding of the meaning of white supremacy in his own country placed him in a rare category surpassed by no major future political leader to date, the judgment of the Obama presidency still unassessed.

No many years ago, the Wendell Willkie Memorial Building on Fortieth Street across from the New York Public Library housed the National Headquarters of the NAACP, Freedom House, and the since-retired American Committee for Protection of the Foreign Born, until its nocturnal unauthorized destruction to make way for a bank.[74] A plaque true to his likeness remains, bearing these covenanted words: "I believe in America because in it we are free—free to choose our government, to speak our minds, to observe our different religions."

ACKNOWLEDGMENTS

Because this book took far longer than its author would have thought possible, it will not be read by two persons to whom it owes an incommensurable debt: Ruth Ann Stewart, the author's best critic and spouse, and Carl Brandt, his sterling agent and friend. Had they lived, I believe they might have found the finished product worthy of their confidence. The personal support of the one and the professional dedication of the other I would wish for every historian/biographer.

As for many others whose special friendship, tested patience, professional expertise, and requisitioned hours of hearing about the book and reading chapters being written, their invaluable assistance affirmed the author's belief in the importance of his project, even as their advice and criticism made *The Improbable Wendell Willkie* better and longer. All shortcomings are mine alone, and, undoubtedly, there would be more but for the mnemonic prowess, computer dexterity, and delegated responsibilities of an extraordinarily capable NYU research assistant during this book's early years and now a PhD candidate in economics. Kelly Page Nelson has the author's eternal gratitude.

All books have several beginnings. One of them is a rewarding lunch seven years ago at New York University's faculty club with the distinguished corporate counselor Wendell L. Willkie II, Wendell Willkie's grandson. A biographer's invaluable opportunity: the afternoon was a feast of reminiscences, explanations, unresolved contradictions, good-humored candor, and subsequent introductions to the exuberant leftist Philip Willkie and the real estate entrepreneur Hall Willkie, respectively Wendell II's brother and cousin. Both gave liberally of their memories.

To Willkie grandson David, former senator Richard Lugar's campaign manager and generous Rushville, Indiana, host, I owe an unforgettable luncheon invitation to talk to local civic leaders together with Mayor Mike Pavey, Councilman Brian Sheehan, and Redevelopment Commissioner John McCane. Their questions and comments made me appreciate all the more why their native son's liberalism and internationalism held as little appeal almost seventy years later as they did for some Hoosiers in 1944. Rushville's courtly Paul Barada, of Barada Associates, drove me to the serene cemetery grove some miles outside Rushville where, phoenix-like, Wendell Willkie's memorial cross levitates above an open marble book whose two pages of poignant signature sayings arrest the visitor in contemplation of epic promise and cruel loss.

Wendell Willkie claimed his leadership of the Republican Party was due to the fact that he represented a spontaneous "movement." The "Willkie Clubs," created and organized by a self-propelled New York attorney without any political experience, young Oren Root Jr., were a catalyst new to Republican politics. Siblings Oren Root V and Dolores Root gamely agreed to a biographical third degree during an afternoon in which the rings of family history were collaboratively peeled away to recover their twenty-eight-year-old parent at the heart of one of the great possibilities of the US presidency. That the author also profited from Dolores Root's sustained interest and time reading portions of his book will remain two priceless occupational dividends.

Nonfiction books are assembled from folders arranged topically and chronologically box by box in places often distant but sometimes agreeably near. The Wendell L. Willkie Papers at Indiana University are housed in the Lilly Library, an accessible setting whose congenial, efficient staff made an entire summer and several additional research visits among the most rewarding sojourns of the author's career. Several eleventh-hour requests were accommodated not only expeditiously, but elicited a couple of follow-up suggestions by Sarah Mitchell and her associates that were bonanzas.

A similar reward was several weeks spent at atmospheric Soda House archives on the grounds of the Hagley Museum and Library outside Wilmington, Delaware, where an affable Lynn Catanese and her staff shepherded me through the endlessly fascinating du Pont and Pew family collections.

The daily drive from Rhinebeck to the FDR Presidential Library and Museum in Hyde Park, New York, like the Hagley Museum and Library, was a research journey into historic collections generated by an iconic family and the men and women in its service whose political beliefs and institutional achievements shaped the middle third of the American twentieth century. The benefit of former FDR archivist Bob Clark's expediting research prompts was providential.

Equally advantageous was now retired archivist John Haynes's well-known facilitation of time-constrained and multiple-topic research agendas of visiting researchers to the Manuscript Reading Room of the Library of Congress. Time constraints and competing exigencies were facilitated as well by Kelly Page Nelson's delegated and efficient follow-up retrievals from the Walter Lippmann Papers and Kenneth Farrand Simpson Papers in Yale University's Rare Books and Manuscripts Library and the David Lilienthal Papers held by Princeton University's Seeley G. Mudd Rare Books and Manuscripts Library.

What some refer to as the high gossip of history conserved by the Columbia Center for Oral History Archives inescapably draws us all to Director Mary Marshall Clark's sixth floor of Columbia University's Butler Library, where unvarnished opinions of those who played starring roles or merely bit parts in American history's previous century survive. On a vastly different scale of holdings, Elwood Public Library's Indiana Room yielded a trove of rare local Willkie news clippings and photographs as unsuspected by reference librarian Jordan Arehart as some of it was fabulously worthwhile to his New York visitor.

The Improbable Wendell Willkie owes special thanks to Irwin Gellman, a professional colleague of several decades whose forte of accuracy and bibliography were applied to every chapter. Blanche Wiesen Cook was present almost at the creation of the Willkie project, a fount of interpretive possibilities, biographical connections, and, above all, a collegial model of intellectual emancipation in all its virtues. Conrad Harper's legal services were priceless both in billable hours uncharged and Supreme Court decisions translated into plain English. I still shudder at the challenge of correctly and clearly summarizing *Tennessee Electric Power Co. et al. v. TVA* and *Schneiderman v. US* without his amicable initial guidance. Susan Butler Plum listened, suggested, and then applied a foundation executive's sharpness to inflated prose and unsubstantiated assertions.

John Rothmann, Harold Stassen scholar and recent professional associate, volunteered an encyclopedic memory of Wendell Willkie's friends, allies, and others. Patricia Bosworth shared vivid memories of her parents aboard the Willkie campaign train and of Willkie's reliance on her father's California political connections. Richard Moe, presidential counselor and preservationist, shared informed opinions about Wendell Willkie's large significance. Diplomatic historian David Mayers, a friend of years, seldom sees a historical judgment to be rushed. Hence, his friendship—professional and personal—is irreplaceable. Kenneth Wheeler listened over food and drink to talk of Wendell Willkie from year to year as though his interest in the subject was inexhaustible. Fellow historian that he is, he posed many caveats in service to friendship that fortunately survived the author's sometimes dogged singlemindedness.

The same may be said of Joni Maya Cherbo, of Manhattan, New York; Carol Ann Preece of Annapolis, Maryland; of my favorite science couple Sandra Masur and Victor Schuster, of New York's Upper West Side; and of Richard and Carolyn Thornell, Silver Spring, Maryland; and again David Mayers and Elizabeth Jones, Newton, Massachusetts, and London, UK. Comments and critiques of former graduate students William Jelani Cobb, Matthew Pratt Guterl, Khalil G. Muhammad, and Stacey Patton, now authorities in their respective fields, regularly provoked and stimulated their senior colleague.

This book owes a grateful great debt to my agent Gail Hochman of Brandt and Hochman, who has a solution to every book problem. Because I said it sincerely and so well when Robert Weil and I shaped together my last book, I repeat my esteem for him word for word: "The combination of critical enthusiasm and total engagement Bob Weil brings to manuscripts is matchless." Marie Pantojan, his calm, genial assistant, guards unerringly against the errors of an author's last-minute haste. Above all, I send a grateful salute to Allison Lewis and Michael Wilson of Washington, DC, whose daughters have afforded their grandfather the pleasure of dedicating a book to each.

NOTES

CHAPTER 1: Elwood, August 17, 1940

1 "Willkie Day" sources: An unexpected, excellent source for Willkie Day is found in Dave Cole, "They Wanted Willkie," *The Way of the Zephyr: Official Publication of the Lincoln-Zephyr Owners Club,* V. 31 (Jan.–Feb., 1998), pp. 4–14. In addition to exact data on planning, execution, and atmospherics of Willkie Day, this edition contains plausible speculations as to the model number (O6H56-26) and color (medium gray) of the 1940 Lincoln Continental Cabriolet in which Willkie rode into Elwood on August 17, 1940, p. 13. "The Crowd at Elwood," *Time,* V. 36 (Aug. 26, 1940), p. 16. Marcia Davenport, *Too Strong for Fantasy* (U. Pittsburgh, 1967), p. 275. Mary Earhart Dillon, *Wendell Willkie, 1892–1944* (Lippincott, 1952), p. 191, a rather unsympathetic biographer, notes mixed feelings of some Elwoodians on Willkie Day.

2 Joe Martin, as told to Robert J. Donovan, *My First Fifty Years in Politics* (McGraw-Hill, 1960), p. 112

3 The photo of Willkie in the Lincoln Continental is esteemed by many to be *sui generis*: "A Superb Campaign Picture," *The Zephyr,* pp. 14–16. Martin, *My First Fifty Years,* p. 112. Description of the cortege of Lincolns and occupants: *Zephyr,* pp. 9–11; "That Hat? It's a Luck Symbol to Mrs. Willkie," *Chicago Tribune,* Aug. 17, 1940, p. B5. "The First Tomato Festival," *History of Elwood,* Elwoodia.org. Dillon, *Willkie,* p. 191. An appreciation of Philip Willkie: Dorothy Dunbar Bromley, "The Education of Wendell Willkie," *Harper's,* Oct. 1940, 477–85, p. 480.

4 FDR's phrase from the second inauguration, quoted: H. W. Brands, *Traitor to His Class: The Privileged Life and Radical Presidency of Franklin Delano Roosevelt* (Doubleday, 2008), p. 457. Charles Peters, *Five Days*

in Philadelphia: Wendell Willkie, Franklin Roosevelt, and the 1940 Convention That Saved the Western World (Public Affairs, 2005), and Steve Neal, *Dark Horse: A Biography of Wendell Willkie* (U. Kansas, 1984), pp. 99–123. Ellsworth Barnard, *Wendell Willkie: Fighter for Freedom* (Northern Michigan U., 1966), pp. 164–66. On Willkie's national appeal: Harold Ickes quote, Neal, *Dark Horse*, p. 119, and 119–22; Barnard, *Willkie*, p. 164—"One myth can be dismissed at once. Willkie was not sold to the public by any group of public relations experts working either collectively or separately"; David Halberstam, *The Powers That Be* (U. Illinois, 1975)—"a Republican with sex appeal," p. 60; Warren Moscow, *Roosevelt and Willkie* (Prentice-Hall, 1968), pp. 25–51; Donald Bruce Johnson, *The Republican Party and Wendell Willkie* (U. Illinois, 1960), pp. 116–25. On GOP revival: Amity Shlaes, *The Forgotten Man: A New History of the Great Depression* (HarperPerennial, 2007), chaps. 14, 15; Raymond Moley, *After Seven Years* (Harper & Bros., 1939), pp. 352–84; Steve Fraser and Gary Gerstle, eds., *The Rise and Fall of the New Deal Order, 1930–1980* (Princeton, 1989), chap. 2.

5 Anti-FDR sentiment: Brands, *Traitor to His Class*, pp. 479–500; Herbert Parmet and Marie B. Hecht, *Never Again: A President Runs for a Third Term* (Macmillan, 1968); Ickes, quoted, Johnson, *Republican Party and Willkie*, pp. 125, 116; James T. Patterson, *Congressional Conservatism and the New Deal* (U. Kentucky, 1967), pp. 308–31. Gallup in early August revealed Willkie ahead of FDR in twenty-four states totaling an Electoral College majority: Johnson, *Republican Party*, p. 119.

6 John Kenneth Galbraith, *American Capitalism: The Concept of Countervailing Power* (Houghton Mifflin, 1952).

7 Willkie, "The True Meaning of 'Liberalism' ": Address at the University of Indiana on Foundation Day, Bloomington, Indiana, May 4, 1938: Wendell L. Willkie Papers, Manuscripts Department, Lilly Library, Indiana University. Booth Tarkington, quoted, Joseph Barnes, *Willkie: The Events He Was Part of—The Ideas He Fought For* (Simon & Schuster, 1952), p. 11.

8 Elwood politics: Dillon, *Willkie*, pp. 189–91; "Rushville Proud of a Son-in-Law—Named Willkie," *Chicago Daily Tribune*, July 4, 1940.

9 Frances Perkins Interview, "1940 Campaign": Oral History Research Office [OHRO], Columbia University Libraries, p. 696. Dillon, *Willkie*, p. 191.

10 William B. Pickett, *Homer E. Capehart: A Senator's Life, 1897–1979* (Indiana Historical Society, 1990), pp. 67–68. Dillon, *Willkie*, p. 190.

11 "45 Trains Pour Thousands into Willkie's Town," *Chicago Daily Tribune*, Aug. 7, 1940; "The Crowd at Elwood," *Time*, V. 36 (Aug. 26, 1940), p. 16; Hal Foust, "Traffic Hegira Handled with Hardly a Hitch," *Chicago Daily Tribune*, Aug. 17, 1940, p. B3; "They Wanted Willkie," *Zephyr*, pp. 8–10.

12 "Food By the Ton on Hand to Feed Elwood Crowds," *Chicago Tribune*, Aug. 17, 1940; "Sidwell Hotel," *Chicago Tribune*, Aug. 17, 1940.

13 Central High School backdrop said to be Russell Davenport idea, Dillon, *Willkie*, p. 174. Willkie Day crowds: Davenport, *Too Strong for Fantasy*, p. 275; Neal, *Dark Horse*, pp. 134–35; *Zephyr*, pp. 14–16.

14 Rationale for Elwood venue: Wendell Willkie, "Address Accepting the Presidential Nomination in Elwood," Gerhard Peters and John T. Woolley, *The American Presidency Project*. www.presidency.ucsb/ws/; Barnard, *Willkie*, pp. 199–200; Dillon, *Willkie*, pp. 173–74.

15 Colorful reports of the Central High School imbroglio: "Crowd at Elwood," *Time*; Martin, *First Fifty Years*, p. 113; Barnard, *Willkie*, p. 201; Dillon, *Willkie*, p. 174; Neal, *Dark Horse*, p. 134; *Zephyr*, pp. 14–16.

16 Willkie's Central High School remarks: "Accepting the Presidential Nomination"; Barnard, *Willkie*, p. 201.

17 Capehart's Elwood: "Guesses Vary on Elwood Crowd: 125,000 to 300,000," *Chicago Daily Tribune*, Aug. 18, 1940, p. B2; "Crowd at Elwood," *Time*, Aug. 26; *Zephyr*.

18 Photos of Willkie Day's mostly white crowd: "125,000 Crowd Elwood Park to Hear Willkie," *Chicago Daily Tribune*, Aug. 18, 1940; "The Story of Elwood Is the Story of America," *Life*, Aug. 12, 1940; "Elwood Kindles Torchlights for Her Famous Son," July 2, 1940. "Elwood, Ind., Gives GOP Big Welcome—All Color-Bars Down for Notification," *Chicago Defender*, Aug. 24, 1940; "Saw Willkie Accept," *Philadelphia Tribune*, Aug. 22, 1940; "Few Negroes in Elwood," New York *Amsterdam News*, Aug. 24, 1940. March on Washington for Jobs and Freedom: Juan Williams *Eyes on the Prize: America's Civil Rights Years, 1954–1965* (Penguin, 1987), p. 197; David Levering Lewis, *King: A Biography* (UIP, 2013, 3rd ed.), chap. 8; "250,000 Make History in Huge Washington March," *SCLC Newsletter* (Sept. 1963), p. 3; William P. Jones, *The March on Washington for Jobs and Freedom* (Norton, 2013).

19 "Crowd at Elwood," *Time*; "They Wanted Willkie," *Zephyr*. "The Story of Elwood Is the Story of America," *Life*, Aug. 12–26, 1940.

20 Taft description, quoted, Richard Norton Smith, *Thomas E. Dewey and His Times* (Simon & Schuster, 1982), p. 279. James T. Patterson, *Mr. Republican: A Biography of Robert A. Taft* (Houghton Mifflin, 1972), p. 20. On Taft and Willkie: "Party Leaders Look at Elwood and See Victory," *Chicago Daily Tribune*, Aug. 18, 1940, p. B5; Neal, *Dark Horse*, pp. 113, 221; Patterson, *Mr. Republican*, pp. 220–21; Charles Peters, *Five Days in Philadelphia* (Public Affairs, 2005), p. 195; Clarence E. Wunderlin Jr., *The Papers of Robert A. Taft, II (1939–1944)* (Kent State U., 2001), p. 294.

21 Halleck and Martin introductions: "Rep. Joe Martin Makes Address of Notification," *Chicago Daily Tribune*, Aug. 18, 1940, p. B6.

22 Willkie's forgotten acceptance speech: "Willkie Misplaces Something; He Was Almost Speechless," *Chicago Daily Tribune*, Aug. 18, 1949, p. B5; Martin, *First Fifty Years*, pp. 112–13; Barnard, *Willkie*, p. 203; Patricia Bosworth, *Anything Your Little Heart Desires: An American Family Story* (Doubleday, 2008), p. 75; Dillon, *Willkie*, p. 189; Neal, *Dark Horse*, p. 136.

23 "Martin Makes Address of Notification," *Chicago Tribune*, Aug. 18.

24 Willkie's disappointing address: Marcia Davenport, quoted, Bosworth, *Anything Your Little Heart Desires*, p. 75; Barnard, pp. 201–3; Dillon, pp. 193–94; Neal, p. 13; "Republicans: The Crowd at Elwood," *Time*, Aug. 26, 1940; "Party Leaders Look at Elwood and See Victory," *Tribune*, Aug. 18, 1940, p. B5.

25 Willkie debates Robert Jackson, Neal, *Dark Horse*, pp. 45, 135.

26 "Crowd at Elwood," *Time*, Aug. 26, 1940.

27 Clapper quoted, "Crowd at Elwood," *ibid.*

28 Willkie's opening remarks: "Address Accepting the Presidential Nomination in Elwood," Peters and Woolley, *The American Presidency Project*.

29 German forbears: "Address," *American Presidency Project*; Alden Hatch, *Young Willkie* (Harcourt, Brace, 1944), pp. 20–25; Barnard, *Willkie*, pp. 8–9; Martin, *Fifty Years*, pp. 112–13; Irwin F. Gellman, "The 'St. Louis' Tragedy," *American Jewish Historical Quarterly*, Vol. 61, No. 2 (Dec. 1971): 144–56.

30 The "Hardest Day": Stephen Bungay, *The Most Dangerous Enemy: A History of the Battle of Britain* (Aurum Press, 2000), pp. 224–25. On opposition to war participation: Wayne S. Cole, *America First: The Battle Against American Intervention in World War II* (U. Wisconsin, 1974); Michael G. Carew, "The Interaction Among National Newsmagazines and the Formulation of Foreign and Defense Policy in the Roosevelt Administration, 1939–1941" (NYU PhD diss., 2002), pp. 33–47; Justus D. Doenecke, *Storm on the Horizon: The Challenge to American Intervention, 1939–1941* (Krieger, 2000); Parmet and Hecht, *Never Again*, pp. 235–55.

31 Dillon, *Willkie*, p. 194. "Only the productive can be strong": "Address."

32 "Address."

33 "Address." David Levering Lewis, "The Implausible Wendell Willkie," *Profiles in Leadership: Historians on the Elusive Quality of Greatness*, ed. by Walter Isaacson (Norton, 2010), p. 241. Kenneally, *A Compassionate Conservative: A Biography of Joseph W. Martin, Speaker of the U.S. House of Representatives* (Lexington, 2003), pp. 24–25.

34 "Address." *Time*, Aug. 26, 1940. "A fight on our hands," quoted, Neal, *Dark Horse*, p. 122.

35 Dillon, *Willkie*, p. 201.

CHAPTER 2: "Grass-Roots Stuff"

1 Joseph Goebbels, *The Goebbels Diaries, 1931–1941*, translated and edited by Fred Taylor (G. P. Putnam, 1983), pp. 127–28, 268.

2 Joseph Barnes, *Willkie: The Events He Was Part Of—The Ideas He Fought For* (Simon & Schuster, 1952), p. 3.

3 "Nazis Cite Records in Reply to Willkie," *New York Times*, March 13, 1941, p. 22. Willkie claim for 1848 ancestral pedigree: Alden Hatch, *Young Willkie* (Harcourt, Brace 1944), p. 21.

4 Ludwig von Mises, "Grandfather Willcke," *New York Times*, March 22, 1941, p. 14. Mike Rapport, *1848: Year of Revolution* (Basic Books, 2008), p. 76.

5 Jonathan Sperber, *The European Revolutions, 1848–1851* (Cambridge, 2005), pp. 3–9. James J. Sheehan, *German History, 1770–1866* (Oxford, 1998), chap. XI, "Revolution and Reaction." Rapport, *1848*.

6 Priscilla Robertson, *Revolutions of 1848: A Social History* (Harper, 1960), p. 141. Rapport, *1848*; and Sperber, *The European Revolutions, 1848–1851*. James J. Sheehan, *German History*, chap. XI, "Revolution and Reaction."

7 Stephen Neal, *Dark Horse: A Biography of Wendell Willkie* (U. Kansas, 1984), p. 3, believes Joseph Willkie was a university student in the 1848 Revolution, an inference to be drawn from Alden Hatch, *Young Willkie* (Harcourt, Brace, 1944), p. 21. I take that inference to be most unlikely.

8 Willkie immigration history: Paul and Herman came to the United States with Wilhelm Joseph; Frank was born in the United States. Frank had run for mayor of Elwood and had served on the city council. He spelled his

name Wilkie. (Pearson and Allen, "The Washington Merry-Go-Round," published in the *Spokane Daily Chronicle*, Aug. 16, 1940.)

9 Alden Hatch, *Young Willkie*, p. 21. Ellsworth Barnard, *Willkie: Fighter for Freedom* (Northern Mich. U., 1966), pp. 8–9. The Prussian officer incident: Neal, *Dark Horse*, p. 3.

10 Joseph Willkie in Fort Wayne: Barnard, *Willkie*, p. 9.

11 Barnard, *Willkie*, p. 9.

12 Hatch, *Young Willkie*, p. 13; Barnard, *Willkie*, p. 8.

13 Sources for the Willkie and Trisch geneaologies and geographies often conflict and contradict. I've exercised a best judgment of the available sources as a blend: Barnard, *Willkie*, esp. pp. 9–10; Hatch, "A Passion for Freedom" *Young Willkie*, pp. 11–24; Mary Earhart Dillon, *Willkie, 1852–1982* (Lippincott, 1952), pp. 8–9; politicalfamilytrees.com; Drew Pearson and Allen, "The Washington Merry-Go-Round," *Spokane Daily Chronicle*, Aug. 6, 1940.

14 On the Trisches's antislavery beliefs, Barnes, *Willkie: The Events He Was Part Of*, p. 7. The Trisches in Kansas: Hatch, *Young Willkie*, pp. 18–19; Barnard, *Willkie*, p. 8.

15 Warsaw to Kansas and back: Barnard, *Willkie*, p. 8; Hatch, *Young Willkie*, pp. 16–17.

16 Circuit-riding Julia: Hatch, *Young Willkie*, p. 20; Dorothy Dunbar Bromley, "The Education of Wendell Willkie," *Harper's*, Oct. 1940, 477–85, p. 478.

17 Julia's daughters, Jennie, Henrietta: Barnard, *Willkie*, p. 20. Law practice: Barnard, *Willkie*, p. 16; Hatch, *Young Willkie*, pp. 19–20. "Elwood Has the Only Lady Attorney Central Indiana," *Daily Record*, April 15, 1897.

18 My research assistant, Kelly Page Nelson, assembled considerable useful fragmentary matter drawn from newsprint on Willkie early years. Indispensable for early years: Dorothy Dunbar Bromley, "The Education of Wendell Willkie," *Harper's*, Oct. 1940; as well, Janet Flanner, "Rushville's Renowned Son-in-Law," *New Yorker*, Oct. 12, 1940; and Alden Hatch, *Young Willkie* (Harcourt, Brace, 1944).

19 James A. Glass and David Kohman, *The Gas Boom of East Central Indiana* (Arcadia, 2005), pp. 9, 11, 96; David Montgomery, *The Fall of the House of Labor* (Cambridge, 1987), chap. 1. "History of Elwood," www.Elwoodiana.org.

20 Year 1887 in "History of Elwood," Elwoodiana.org; Glass and Kohman, *Gas Boom*, p. 91.

21 Barnard, *Willkie*, p. 10. Janet Flanner, "Profiles," *New Yorker*, Oct. 12, 1940: pp. 27–45, 28; Neal, *Dark Horse*, p. 2.

22 Barnard, *Willkie*, p. 13.

23 Origin of Wendell's name: Email from David Willkie to David Levering Lewis, June 25, 2015.

24 Elwoodiana.org; Glass and Kohrman, *Gas Boom*, chap. 2; Barnard, *Willkie*, p. 13; Dillon, p. 18.

25 Howard Zinn, *A People's History of the United States* (HarperPerennial, 1980, 2003), p. 277. Michael Kazin, *A Godly Hero: The Life of William Jennings Bryan* (Knopf, 2006), p. 37. Charles Hoffmann, "The Depression

of the Nineties," *Journal of Economic Hist.* XVI (June 1956): 137–64, esp. pp. 137–39.

26 Pivotal 1896 election: William R. Hal, *Realigning America: McKinley, Bryan, and the Remarkable Election of 1896* (U. Kansas, 2010); Martin J. Sklar, *The Corporate Reconstruction of American Capitalism, 1890–1916* (Cambridge, 1988); Richard Hofstadter, *The Age of Reform: From Bryan to FDR* (Greenwood, 1981); H. Wayne Morgan, *From Hayes to McKinley: National Party Politics, 1877–1896* (Syracuse, 1969).

27 Herman Willkie's debts: Barnard, *Willkie*, p. 14. News reports of debt, court action, Mississippi arrest in *Free Press*, June 29, 1894; Anderson *Herald*, July 20, 1894; Janet Flanner, "Profiles," *New Yorker*, Oct. 12, 1940, p. 28. Box 1, Fol. 50, "Elwood," L. Willkie Papers, Lilly Library, Indiana University. 1894 notes indicate that H. F. WILKIE (so spelled) and Henrietta involved in loan default action. Records show that for six months H. F. Willkie unable to pay. Court action.

28 Michael McGerr, *A Fierce Discontent: The Rise and Fall of the Progressive Movement in America* (Oxford, 2003), p. 3.

29 Stumping for Bryan: Hatch, *Young Willkie*, pp. 35–36.

30 Hatch, *ibid.*, p. 29.

31 Hatch, *ibid.*, p. 79.

32 Herman Willkie's household politics and the Bryan visit: Hatch, *ibid.*, pp. 41–43; Barnard, *Willkie*, p. 20. Bryan's imperialist equivocations: see Kazin, *A Godly Hero*, pp. 96–100; Stanley Karnow, *America's Empire in the Philippines* (Random House, 1989), p. 10.

33 Henrietta's character: "Lady Attorney," *Daily Record*, Mar. 15, 1897; George Davis, "They Knew Willkie," Palm Beach *Post-Times,* July 14, 1940. Barnard, *Willkie*, pp. 15–16; Dillon, *Willkie*, p. 17. Henrietta's epitaph: D. L. Lewis interview with Hall Willkie (Fred Willkie's son), July 26, 2012; D. L. Lewis with Wendell Willkie II (Wendell Willkie's grandson) Spring, 2012; Barnard, *Willkie*, p. 16.

34 "Crazy Willkies": George Davis, "They Knew Willkie," Palm Beach *Post-Times.* Barnard, *Willkie*, pp. 15–16. D. L. Lewis recorded interviews: David Willkie (Wendell Willkie grandson), June 25, 2012; Hall Willkie (Wendell Willkie's nephew), July 26, 2012; Wendell Willkie II (Wendell Willkie grandson), Spring 2012; Philip Willkie (Wendell Willkie grandson), Aug. 26, 2012.

35 Dillon, *Willkie*, p. 22. Janet Flanner, "Profiles," *New Yorker*, p. 28, gives 6,700 books as the Willkie household library size. Dorothy D. Bromley, "Education of Willkie," *Harper's*, p. 478.

36 Palm Beach *Post-Times.*

37 John Dewey's *The School and Society* appeared in 1899. His *Democracy and Education* (1916) could almost have been written by Herman Willkie. Similarly, Henrietta Willkie lived the precepts of Charlotte Perkins Gilman's foundational feminist text, *Women and Economics* (1898).

38 Photo of Wendell in uniform: Hatch, *Young Willkie*, p. 82. Barnard, *Willkie*, p. 17. Hatch, *Young Willkie*, p. 83. Neal, *Dark Horse*, p. 4.

39 Steve Neal, *Dark Horse*, p. 5. Hebert Parmet and Marie B. Hecht, *Never Again: A President Runs for a Third Time* (Macmillan, 1968), p. 5.

40 David Montgomery, *The Fall of the House of Labor* (Cambridge 1987), pp. 38–39; David Brody, *Steelworkers in America: The Nonunion Era* (Harper

Torchbooks, 1969); Melvyn Dubofsky and F. R. Dulles, *Labor in America: A History* (Harlan Davidson, 1999); Steve Fraser, *The Age of Acquiescence: The Life and Death of American Resistance to Organized Wealth and Power* (Little, Brown, 2015), esp. pp. 131–34.

41 Hatch, *Young Willkie*, p. 29.

42 "History of Elwood," Elwoodiana.org. Glass and Kohrman, *Gas Boom*, p. 91.

43 Barnard, *Willkie*, pp. 29–31.

44 The tin workers' strike: Dillon, *Willkie*, pp. 19–20; Barnard, *Willkie*, pp.29–31; Hatch, *Young Willkie*, pp. 134–36. Wendell Willkie's vivid account of the physical confrontation with the two strikebreakers recalled in Hatch, pp. 133–35.

45 For the early Indiana presence of the KKK and persistence of local racism in the state, see James H. Madison, *A Lynching in the Heartland: Race and Memory in America* (Macmillan, 2001).

46 In Elwood, the Welsh were factory workers: Hatch, *Young Willkie*, p. 112; Charles Peters, *Five Days in Philadelphia* (Public Affairs, 2005), pp. 26–27. On Herman and Henrietta Willkie's ongoing religious, political, and ethnic conflicts with Elwoodians, see Dillon, pp. 16–20; Barnard, *Willkie*, pp. 11–13; Steve Neal, *Dark Horse*; Hatch, *Young Willkie*.

47 On Willkie's Greek letter opposition and the Princeton eating clubs, see Hatch, *Young Willkie*, pp. 149–50; and John M. Blum, *Woodrow Wilson and the Politics of Morality* (Little, Brown, 1956), chap. 2.

48 See ironic treatment of Gwyneth and Wendell in Flanner, *New Yorker*, p. 29.

49 Barnard, *Willkie*, p. 32; Dillon, *Willkie*, p. 22; Neal, *Dark Horse*, p. 9.

50 On Willkie the Bloomington strategist: Neal, *Dark Horse*, p. 9; Barnard, *Willkie*, p. 36.

51 Barnard, *Willkie*, p. 36; Neal, *Dark Horse*, p. 9.

52 Barnard, *Willkie*, p. 37.

53 On Wendell Willkie and Gwyneth Harry: Hatch, p. 112; Dillon, *Willkie*, p. 28; Neal, *Dark Horse*, pp. 9–13; Barnard, *Willkie*, pp. 37–38.

54 Dillon, *Willkie*, p. 23. Lewis Wendell Willkie University of Indiana undergraduate transcript: Folder—Biographical, 1929. Date of Matriculation (Jan. 4. 1910). Major Subject: Law. Graduated June 18, 1913. A. B.—Grades: Latin B+s English A, B, A.

CHAPTER 3: Puerto Rico to Commonwealth & Southern

1 Mary Earhart Dillon, *Wendell Willkie, 1892–1944*, p. 23. Barnard, *Willkie*, pp. 39–40.

2 Ellsworth Barnard, *Wendell Willkie: Fighter for Freedom*, p. 42. Alden Hatch, *Young Willkie*, pp. 190–91.

3 Willkie on Puerto Ricans: Hatch, *Young Willkie*, pp. 193–95. Barnard, *Willkie*, p. 42. Cesar J. Ayala, *American Sugar Kingdom: The Plantation Economy of the Spanish Caribbean, 1898–1934* (UNC 1999), p. 2. Ayala and Rafael Barnabe, *Puerto Rico in the American Century: A History Since 1898* (UNC, 1999), pp. 33–51.

4 Henry Cabot Lodge quote: Ayala and Rafael Barnabe, *Puerto Rico in the American Century: A History Since 1898*, p. 14. Ivan Musicant, *Empire by Default: The Spanish-American War and the Dawn of the American*

Century (Holt, 1998), chap. 15. Sidney W. Mintz, *Worker in the Cane: A Puerto Rican Life History* (Yale, 1960).

5 Ayala, *American Sugar Kingdom*, p. 2.

6 Ayala, *ibid.*, pp. 107–11. Mintz, *Worker in the Cane*, p. 23.

7 Dillon, *Willkie*, p. 24. Hatch, *Young Willkie*, pp. 192–93.

8 Sidney Mintz, *Worker in the Cane*, p. 41.

9 Joseph Barnes, *Willkie: The Events He Was Part Of—The Idea He Fought For* (Simon & Schuster, 1952), p. 28; Neal, *Dark Horse*, p. 12.

10 Barnard, *Willkie*, p. 43. Dillon, *Willkie*, p. 24.

11 Neal, *Dark Horse*, says the book a night discipline occurred at Phi Delta Phi, p. 13. Barnard locates Willkie at Beta Theta Pi, p. 44.

12 Barnard, *Willkie*, pp. 45–46; Neal, *Dark Horse*, p. 13.

13 Barnard, *Willkie*, p. 46; Neal, *Dark Horse*, p. 13.

14 A. Scott Berg, *Wilson* (Putnam, 2013), pp. 239–40, 264–65, 400–402. John Milton Cooper Jr., *Woodrow Wilson: A Biography* (Random House, 2009), pp. 348–52, 221–24. Melvin Urofsky, *Louis D. Brandeis: A Life* (Pantheon, 2009), pp. 324–25; 343–47. Dillon, *Willkie*, p. 25.

15 "A Willkie Speech That Rocked the Roof, Back in '16," *Chicago Tribune*, July 5, 1940, p. 8. IU president's quote: Barnard, *Willkie*, p. 46; Dillon, *Willkie*, pp. 24–25, contains most complete contemporary account of the Class Day speech.

16 Barnard, *Willkie*, p. 46; Neal, *Dark Horse*, p. 13.

17 Barnard, *Willkie*, p. 46. Apparently, a Democrat-GOP standoff made possible a 1917 reform Socialist ticket headed by John Lewis. See Indiana University Oral History Research Center: Lillian Pritchard Interview, Sept. 1, 1976, 66 pages, esp. p. 44.

18 Dillon, *Willkie*, p. 24. Barnard, *Willkie*, p. 48.

19 Dillon, *Willkie*, p. 26.

20 Barnard, *Willkie*, p. 50. On Willkie's official name change: Neal, *Dark Horse*, p. 14.

21 Barnard, *Willkie*, p. 44.

22 Neal, *Dark Horse*, p. 15; Barnard, *Willkie*, pp. 50–51.

23 Cooper, *Woodrow Wilson*, pp. 370–71. Justus D. Doenecke, *Nothing Less Than War: A New History of America's Entry into World War I* (U. Press of Kentucky, 2011), pp. 242–45.

24 Cooper, *Wilson*, pp. 312–13, 374. Howard Zinn, *A People's History of the United States: 1492–Present* (HarperCollins, 1998), esp. pp. 361–62. Doenecke, *Nothing Less Than War*, p. 164.

25 Bryan's resignation: John Milton Cooper, *Woodrow Wilson: A Biography* (Knopf, 2009), pp. 287–88, 292–93. Zinn, *People's History*, p. 362.

26 Quoted in Doenecke, *Nothing Less Than War*, p. 21.

27 Doenecke, *ibid.*, pp. 16–20.

28 David Levering Lewis, *When Harlem Was in Vogue* (Knopf, 1979), p. 10; *W.E.B. Du Bois: The Biography of a Race, 1868–1919* (Holt, 1993), pp. 515–16.

29 John Higham, *Strangers in the Land: Patterns of American Nativism, 1860–1925* (Rutgers, 1988, 2nd ed.), pp. 208–9; Bob Guernsey and Jane Hedeen, *The Effect of World War I on German Americans: You Are There 1914, The Violin Maker Upstairs* (Indiana Historical Society, 2010). Murray Levin, *Political Hysteria in America* (Basic Books,

1971). Erik Kirschbaum, *Burning Beethoven: The Eradication of German Culture in the United States during World War I* (Berlinica, 2014), chaps. 1, 6.

30 "Willkie on German Tyranny," *Call Leader*, Oct. 17, 1917.

31 Linda Gordon, *The Second Coming of the KKK: The Ku Klux Klan of the 1920s and the American Political Tradition* (Liveright, 2017), chap. 9.

32 Barnard, *Willkie*, p. 57; Dillon, *Willkie*, p. 27.

33 Barnard, *Willkie*, p. 57.

34 Neal, *Dark Horse*, p. 18.

35 Irvin Stone, *They Also Ran: The Story of the Men Who Were Defeated for the Presidency* (New American Library, 1943; rev. ed., 1966), pp. 42–43. Geoffrey Ward, *A First-Class Temperament: The Emergence of Franklin Roosevelt* (Harper & Row, 1989), pp. 510–11. H. W. Brands, *Traitor to His Class: The Privileged Life and Radical Presidency of Franklin Delano Roosevelt* (Doubleday 2008), pp. 135–37.

36 Irving Stone, *They Also Ran*, p. 46.

37 Eliot's "The Hollow Men" cited in John Milton Cooper Jr., *Breaking the Heart of the World: Woodrow Wilson and the Fight for the League of Nations* (Cambridge, 2001), p. 376.

38 Neal, *Dark Horse*, p. 18.

39 Barnard, *Willkie*, p. 64.

40 Florette Henri, *Black Migration: Movement North, 1900–1920* (Anchor, 1976), chap. 9, p. 284; Bernard C. Nalty, *Strength for the Fight: A History of Black Americans in the Military* (Free Press, 1986), pp. 110–11; Chad L. Williams, *Torchbearers of Democracy: African American Soldiers in the World War I Era* (UNC, 2010), p. 72.

41 Jules Witcover, *The Year the Dream Died: Revisiting 1968 in America* (Warner Books, 1997), chap. 9. Neal, *Dark Horse*, p. 19; Dillon, *Willkie*, p. 32; Barnard, *Willkie*, pp. 62–65.

42 *Official Report of the Proceedings of the Democratic National Convention held in Madison Square Garden, New York City, June 24, 25, 26, 27, 28, 30, July 1, 2, 3, 4, 5, 7, 8, & 9* (Scanned by Google, 2009); Dillon, *Willkie*, pp. 32–33.

43 Four years later, Governor Smith would ask the NAACP's Walter White to manage a parallel campaign. Walter White, *A Man Called White: The Autobiography of Walter White* (U. Georgia, 1995; orig. pub., 1948), pp. 99–100; Kenneth Robert Janken, *White: The Biography of Walter White, Mr. NAACP* (New Press, 2003), esp. chap. 5; David Levering Lewis, *When Harlem Was in Vogue* (Penguin, 1997), pp. 207–8.

44 Quoted: Robert A. Slayton, *Empire Statesman: The Rise and Redemption of Al Smith* (Free Press, 2001), p. 215.

45 John Higham, *Strangers in the Land: Patterns of American*, pp. 323–24.

46 McAdoo on segregating the federal bureaucracy: Joel Williamson, *The Crucible of Race: Black-White Relations in the American South* (Oxford, 1984), pp. 366–67. Reception before the convention: Slayton, *Empire Statesman*, p. 208.

47 FDR's "Happy Warrior" speech: Ward, *A First-Class Temperament*, pp. 695–96; Barnard, *Willkie*, pp. 65–66. Slayton, *Empire Statesman*, p. 210.

48 Neal, *Dark Horse*, on Willkie's blaming FDR, pp. 20–21.

49 Newton Baker quote, Barnes, *Willkie*, p. 151; Neal, *Dark Horse*, p. 20.

50 Ku Klux Klan: Williamson, *The Crucible of Race*, pp. 472–75; Higham, *Strangers in the Land*, pp. 286–99; Gordon, *The Second Coming of the KKK*.

51 Vivid description of the KKK convention debate: Slayton, *Empire Statesman*, pp. 212–13; Gordon, *The Second Coming of the KKK*, chap. 9. On Bryan's decline, Richard Hofstadter, *The Age of Reform: From Bryan to FDR* (Random House, 1955), pp. 288–89.

52 Willkie quoted: "Ohio Delegates Part in Selecting Davis Is Related, Wendell Willkie Gave Masterful Address on Convention Before Kiwanis Club," Akron *Beacon Journal*, July 17, 1924, p. 1. Neal, *Dark Horse*, p. 21.

53 "The Democratic Convention of 1924": Digital History ID 3393. 2014 Copyright. Digital History.

54 Balloting details: "Ohio Delegates Part in Selecting Davis . . . ," Akron *Beacon Journal*, July 14, 1924. Barnard, *Willkie*, p. 65; Dillon, *Willkie*, pp. 32–33.

55 Wendell on Davis and Coolidge: Barnard, *Willkie*, p. 66.

56 Davis and *Briggs v. Elliott*: Richard Kluger, *Simple Justice: The History of Brown v. Board of Education . . .* (Vintage, 1977), pp. 670–73.

57 Wendell quoted as recalling, "[Herman] practically dropped his law practice for almost a year to make speeches against them . . .": Barnard, *Willkie*, p. 66.

58 Neal, *Dark Horse*, pp. 21–22; Barnard, *Willkie*, p. 67.

59 Dillon, *Willkie*, pp. 31–32.

60 Upturned car story: Neal, *Dark Horse*, p. 22. Descriptions of Wendell in Akron Affairs: Barnard, *Willkie*, pp. 66–67; Dillon, *Willkie*, p. 34.

61 Barnard Interview of Edith Willkie, Aug, 23, 1972.

62 Dillon, *Willkie*, pp. 33–34.

63 Ernest Freeberg, *The Age of Edison: Electric Light and the Invention of Modern America* (Penguin, 2012), pp. 1–3, 113–16, 189–94. John F. Wasik, *The Merchants of Power: Sam Insull, Thomas Edison, and the Creation of the Modern Metropolis* (Palgrave, 2003), pp. 45–51. Charles R. Morris, *A Rabble of Dead Money, The Great Crash and the Global Depression: 1929–1939* (Public Affairs), chap. 2.

64 On Cobb's biography and Commonwealth & Southern: Barnes, *Willkie*, p. 51; Barnard, *Willkie*, pp. 80–83; Dillon, *Willkie*, pp. 36–37; James C. Bonbright and Gardiner C. Means, *The Holding Company: Its Public Significance and Its Regulation* (McGraw-Hill, 1932), pp. 130–31, 186; "Willkie Ruses Duplicated in Ike's Buildup," *Chicago Tribune*, May 5, 1952, pp. 1, 10. Freeberg, *The Age of Edison*, p. 113.

65 Barnard Interview with Edith Willkie, Aug. 25, 1972. Neal, *Dark Horse*, p. 23.

66 Wendell telegram to Julia, Oct. 29, 1929; Wendell letter to Julia, Oct. 29, 1929. Willkie Papers, Lilly Library, Indiana University, Fol. 9, Correspondence, Family, 1921–1936.

67 Liaquat Ahamed, *Lords Finance: The Bankers Who Broke the World* (Penguin, 2009), esp. Part 4.

CHAPTER 4: Willkie v. FDR: The Politics of Business, the Business of Politics

1 On Insull's utility empire: James C. Bonbright and Gardiner C. Means, *The Holding Company: Its Public Significance and Its Regulation* (McGraw-

Hill, 1932), esp. pp. 108–11; M. L. Ramsay, *Pyramids of Power: The Story of Roosevelt, Insull, and the Utility Wars* (Bobbs-Merrill, 1937); Charles R. Morris, *A Rabble of Dead Money, the Great Crash and the Global Depression: 1929–1939* (PublicAffairs, 2017), p. 155; In one estimation, Insull's holding company (an octopus-like financial instrument of New Jersey origin) controlled assets valued in hundreds of millions of dollars with a capitalization of merely $25 million: John F. Wasik, *The Merchant of Power: Sam Insull, Thomas Edison, and the Creation of the Modern Metropolis* (Palgrave, 2006), p. 201. See Amity Shlaes, *The Forgotten Man: A New History of the Great Depression* (HarperPerennial, 2007), chap. 4. On Ickes and Insull, T. H. Watkins, *Righteous Pilgrim: The Life and Times of Harold L. Ickes, 1874–1952* (Holt, 1990), esp. pp. 242–48.

2 Joseph Barnes, *Willkie: The Events He Was Part Of—The Ideas He Fought For* (Simon & Schuster, 1952), pp. 89, 51. A recent, much kinder appraisal of Insull, Morris, *A Rabble of Dead Money*, pp. 164–65.

3 Willkie's defiance of Insull: Mary Earhart Dillon, *Wendell Willkie* (Lippincott, 1950), p. 39. Insull quote: Steve Neal, *Dark Horse: A Biography of Wendell Willkie* (U. Kansas, 1984), p. 21.

4 On the FDR-Hearst convention dynamic, see David Nasaw, *The Chief: The Life of William Randolph Hearst* (Houghton Mifflin, 2000), pp. 454–55. Willkie on the convention's third ballot politics: Fol. 34. 1932 Democratic Convention—June 27–July 2, Chicago. Willkie Papers, Lilly Library, Indiana University. Neal, *Dark Horse*, p. 27.

5 FDR quoted: H. W. Brands, *Traitor to His Class: The Privileged Life and Radical Presidency of Franklin Delano Roosevelt* (Doubleday, 2000), p. 253. Adam Cohen, *Nothing to Fear: FDR's Inner Circle and the Hundred Days That Created Modern America* (Penguin, 2009), p. 10.

6 FDR in Portland, Oregon: Richard A. Colignon, *Power Plays: Critical Events in the Institutionalization of the Tennessee Valley Authority* (SUNY, 1997), p. 105; FDR in Portland: Dillon, *Wendell Willkie*, p. 41.

7 FDR on Insull: Amity Shlaes, *The Forgotten Man*, p. 136.

8 M. L. Ramsay, *Pyramids of Power*, pp. 36–37.

9 Irving Stone, *They Also Ran* (New American Library, 1943, rev. ed., 1966), pp. 374, 379–80.

10 Willkie to Walter Carpenter, Aug. 9, 1933: Fol. 11, Corr, Misc., 1929–33, Willkie Papers. C & S stock value: Irving Stone, *They Also Ran*, p. 379; Barnard, *Willkie*, p. 81.

11 Dillon, *Willkie*, p. 67. Barnard, *Willkie*, pp. 94–95.

12 Bonbright and Means, *The Holding Company*, p. 186; and Dillon, *Willkie*, pp. 80–81.

13 Preston J. Hubbard, *Origins of the TVA: The Muscle Shoals Controversy, 1920–1932* (Vanderbilt U. Press, 1961). Colignon, *Power Plays*, pp. 50–52.

14 FDR TVA quote: Brands, *Traitor to His Class*, p. 338.

15 Kelly Nelson, "The Tennessee Valley Authority's 'Yardstick' Electrical Rates and Consumer Welfare," North Carolina State University, 2015. Willkie TVA quote: Herbert Parmet and Marie B. Hecht, *Never Again: A President Runs for a Third Term* (Macmillan, 1968), p. 61. Dillon, *Willkie*, p. 90, notes that in 1946, the General Accounting Office conducted the first external audit of TVA, revealing that TVA had drawn money from public treasury each year and made no repayments. Of the total $718 million of government money spent on TVA, more than half went for power facilities

rather than flood control. "This colossal expenditure of federal funds had been devoted to the direct benefit of only 3.8 per cent of the population of the country."

16 Thomas K. McCraw, *Morgan vs. Lilienthal: The Feud within the TVA* (Loyola U. Press, 1970), p. ix. David Lilienthal, *Democracy on the March* (Harper Bros., 1944).

17 Arthur Meier Schlesinger Jr., *The Age of Roosevelt: The Politics of Upheaval* (Houghton Mifflin, 1960), Vol. 3, p. 373. A more restrained TVA appreciation, Watkins, *Righteous Pilgrim*, pp. 378–81. Also, James MacGregor Burns and Susan Dunn, *The Three Roosevelts: Patrician Leaders Who Transformed America* (Atlantic Monthly Press, 2001), pp. 402–4.

18 Willkie's Military Affairs testimony: Dillon, *Willkie*, pp. 44–45; Neal, *Dark Horse*, p. 29.

19 Dillon, *Willkie*, p. 45.

20 Morgan on meeting FDR: Aaron D. Purcell, *Arthur Morgan: A Progressive Vision for American Reform* (U. Tenn., 2014), pp. 135–36. Arthur E. Morgan, *The Making of TVA* (Prometheus Books, 1974), pp. 6–7. McCraw, *Morgan vs. Lilienthal*, pp. 1–12.

21 Farley quote: McCraw, *Morgan vs. Lilienthal*, p. 25. FDR recommendations declined: McCraw, *Morgan vs. Lilienthal*, p. 17. See Morgan's own account of the Farley dispute: Morgan, *Making of TVA*, pp. 14–17.

22 McCraw, *Morgan vs. Lilienthal*, pp. 38–39. Colignon, *Power Plays*, p. 122.

23 Steven Neuse, *David E. Lilienthal: The Journey of an American Liberal* (U. Tennessee, 1996), chap. 3; Norris quoted: McCraw, *Morgan vs. Lilienthal*, p. 23.

24 Neuse, *David E. Lilienthal*, p. 37; Colignon, *Power Plays*, p. 69.

25 Lilienthal critics, Morgan, *Making of TVA*, p. 22; McCraw, *Morgan vs. Lilienthal*, p. 30; Neuse, *David E. Lilienthal*, p. 68; Colignon, *Power Plays*, p. 138.

26 Morgan, *Making of TVA*, p. 79. Aaron D. Purcell, *Arthur E. Morgan: A Progressive Vision of American Reform* (Tennessee, 2014), esp. pp. 163–64.

27 Neuse, *David E. Lilienthal*, p. 68. On Morgan's holistic plans: A. Morgan, *The Making of TVA*, pp. 56–60; Schlesinger, *Politics of Upheaval*, p. 372.

28 Richard Colignon, *Power Plays*, p. 106.

29 Colignon, *Power Plays*, p. 132; McCraw, *Morgan vs. Lilienthal*, p. 27.

30 McCraw, *Morgan vs. Lilienthal*, p. 28. Neuse, *David E. Lilienthal*, p. 68. A somewhat more objective reading of early tensions among the TVA directorate, Matthew L. Downs, *Transforming the South: Federal Development in the Tennessee Valley, 1915–1960* (LSU, 2014), pp. 97–98.

31 Barnard, *Willkie*, p. 363.

32 Colignon, *Power Plays*, p. 135. McCraw, *Morgan vs. Lilienthal*, pp. 28–29, 32.

33 Melvin I. Urofsky, *Louis D. Brandeis: A Life* (Pantheon, 2009), pp. 344, 691.

34 Brandeisian critics: Colignon, *Power Plays*, pp. 90–96, 126; Urofsky, *Louis D. Brandeis*, p. 691. Adam Cohen, *Nothing to Fear*, p. 10.

35 Neuse, *David E. Lilienthal*, p. 78. On back channel assurances: McCraw, *Morgan vs. Lilienthal*, p. 42. MacGregor Burns and Dunn, *The Three Roosevelts*, p. 403.

36 Willkie-Lilienthal meeting: Neal, *Dark Horse*, p. 29; Shlaes, *The Forgotten Man*, p. 183; Colignon, *Power Plays*, pp. 148, 151; McCraw, *Morgan vs. Lilienthal*, p. 43.

37 McCraw, *Morgan vs. Lilienthal*, p. 43. Shlaes, *Forgotten Man*, p. 192.

38 Barnard, *Willkie*, p. 88. Nelson, "The Tennessee Valley Authority's 'Yardstick' Electricity." Unpublished article shared by K. Nelson.

39 McCraw, *Morgan vs. Lilienthal*, p. 45.

40 Barnard, *Willkie*, p. 88. Nelson, "The Tennessee Valley Authority's 'Yardstick' Electricity."

41 Donald Bruce Johnson, *The Republican Party and Wendell Willkie* (U. Illinois, 1960), p. 54. Appliances sales; Barnes, *Willkie*, p. 65.

42 Stone, *They Also Ran*, p. 381.

43 Willkie-Lilienthal correspondence: Box 63, Willkie, Wendell: Mar. 31, 1934; Willkie to Lilienthal, Jun. 7, 1934; Willkie-Lilienthal, Jun. 18, 1934; Lilienthal-Willkie, July 14, 1934, David E. Lilienthal Papers, Seeley Mudd Library, Princeton University.

44 FDR to Lilienthal, July 9, 1934; Lilienthal to FDR, Aug. 9, 1934, Lilienthal Papers, Princeton. Robert E. Sherwood, *Roosevelt and Hopkins: An Intimate History* (Harper & Bros., 1948), p. 1.

45 Wasik, *Merchant of Power*, p. 260. Colignon, *Power Plays*, p. 80.

46 FDR to Baker, quoted, Joseph Barnes, *Willkie: The Events He Was Part Of*, p. 77.

47 McCraw, *Morgan vs. Lilienthal*, p. 30; Neal, *Dark Horse*, p. 43. Lilienthal quote: Barnard, *Willkie*, p. 92.

48 FDR meets Willkie: James MacGregor Burns, *Roosevelt: The Lion and the Fox, 1882–1940* (Harcourt, 1956, 1984), p. 433; Neal, *Dark Horse*, p. 31; Frances Perkins, *The Roosevelt I Knew* (Viking, 1946), p. 111. Wendell to Edith: Barnard, *Willkie*, p. 77.

49 Barnes, *Willkie: The Events He Was Part Of*, p. 75.

50 Dillon, *Willkie*, p. 60. Colignon, *Power Plays*, pp. 180–83.

51 Barnes, *Willkie*, pp. 84, 92–93.

52 Barnard, *Willkie*, p. 92.

53 *Ibid*, pp. 90–93.

54 Willkie quote: David Lilienthal Diary, Jan. 24, 1935, David Lilienthal Papers, Mudd Manuscript Library, Princeton University. See, as well, Joseph P. Lash, *Dealers and Dreamers: A New Look at the New Deal* (Doubleday, 1988), pp. 197–98.

55 Wendell's demands that TVA comply with same accounting system as that of private utilities; charge a rate that would bring a "fair return on the property devoted to this business"; "stand on its own bottom" in borrowing money; and file its rate with the Fed Power Commission were rejected. The House committee amended TVA bill to have TVA accounts audited by Comptroller Gen and also that TVA not sell power under cost, which was dropped in reconciliation: Barnard, *Willkie*, pp. 92–93, 100; Dillon, *Willkie*, p. 98.

56 Dillon, *Willkie*, pp. 62–63: The Holding Company Act with its Section XI provided that by Jan. 1, 1940, every holding company must dispose of its securities and be dissolved unless it could show that continuance was necessary for the operation of a geographically integrated system serving an economic district extending into two or more contiguous states. Barnard,

Willkie, p. 94. On Farley's alienation: Daniel Scroop, *Mr. Democrat: Jim Farley, the New Deal, and the Making of Modern American Politics* (U. Michigan, 2006), p. 146.

57 Colignon, *Power Plays*, p. 184.

58 Irving Stone, *They Also Ran*, p. 373.

59 Barnard, *Willkie*, p. 99.

60 Burns, *Roosevelt: The Lion and the Fox*, pp. 180–81; David M. Kennedy, *Freedom from Fear: The American People in Depression and War, 1929–1945* (Oxford, 1999), p. 273; Frank Freidel, *FDR: Launching the New Deal* (Little, Brown, 1973), esp. chap. 25.

61 Dillon, *Willkie*, p. 71.

62 Indiana University commencement address: Irving Stone, "Wendell L. Willkie," *They Also Ran*, p. 382.

63 Cohen to Willkie and Willkie to Cohen regarding delay in filing C & S until US Supreme Court rules on constitutionality of act: Willkie Papers, Box—Willkie, MSS: 1921–1940 (A-O), Fol. 7, Cohen, Ben V 1937–38.

64 Michael Beschloss, *Kennedy and Roosevelt: The Uneasy Alliance* (Norton, 1980), pp. 88, 102. Ronald Kessler, *The Sins of the Father: Joseph P. Kennedy and the Dynasty He Founded* (Warner Books, 1996), pp. 117–19, 122. David Nasaw, *The Patriarch: The Remarkable Life and Turbulent Times of Joseph P. Kennedy* (Penguin, 2012), esp. pp. 208–11, 489.

65 Purcell, *Arthur Morgan*, p. 169.

66 Schlesinger, *Politics of Upheaval*, p. 372. On Arthurdale, see H. W. Brands, *Traitor to His Class: The Privileged Life and Radical Presidency of Franklin Delano Roosevelt* (Doubleday, 2008), pp. 460–61.

67 Morgan, *Making of TVA*, pp. 56, 60. Lilienthal, quoted: Barnes, *Willkie*, pp. 132–33. Downs, *Transforming the South*, p. 98. Morgan aligns with Willkie: in late Sept. 1936, Morgan gave Wendell a two-page memorandum outlining methods of cooperation, mutual confidence, reasonableness, recognition of both public and private interests: Purcell, *Arthur Morgan*, pp. 187–88. Lilienthal's "basket-weaving" quote: Purcell, *ibid.*, p. 183, and McCraw, *Morgan vs. Lilienthal*, pp. 51–52. Morgan's complaint of TVA colleagues: Morgan, *Making of TVA*, p. 56. Senator Norris praise of Morgan: McCraw, *Morgan vs. Lilienthal*, p. 49. Memphis *Press Scimitar*, July 13, 1936. C & S–TVA truce: Purcell, *Arthur Morgan*, p. 134.

68 FDR's retention of Lilienthal and placating of Arthur Morgan: McCraw, *Morgan vs. Lilienthal*, pp. 56–59. McCraw, *Morgan vs. Lilienthal*, pp. 51–52; Norris quote, p. 49. Matthew L. Downs, *Transforming the South: Federal Development in the Tennessee Valley, 1915–1960* (LSU, 2014). FDR's retention of Lilienthal and placating of Arthur Morgan: McCraw, *Morgan vs. Lilienthal*, p. 56.

69 Pierre S. du Pont to Wendell Willkie, June 12, 1936: Wendell L. Willkie Papers, Fol [No #] Corr-Misc, 1936, April–June. Fraser and Gerstle, *Rise and Fall of the New Deal Order*, pp. 3–4.

70 *Alabama Power Co. v. Ickes*, 302 US 464-Supreme Court 1938. *Business Week*, Aug. 29, 1936; "TV-Utilities Setup Will Be Continued," *Atlanta Constitution*, Aug. 26, 1936, both in Lilienthal Papers, Box 74, Norris, George W., 1936. Willkie to Walter Lippmann, Mar. 9, 1936, Lilienthal Papers.

71 David Halberstam, *The Powers That Be* (U. Illinois, 1975). On restructuring national business interests during the Depression: M. L. Lilienthal,

Pyramids of Power: The Story of Roosevelt, Insull and the Utility Wars (Bobbs-Merrill, 1937), p. 39; Fraser and Gerstle, *The Rise and Fall of the New Deal Order*, esp. pp. 10–15.

72 Nervous businessmen in Barnard, *Willkie*, pp. 97–98.

73 Wendell to Robert, Aug. 17, 1936: Willkie Papers, Fol. 9 Corr., Family, 1921–1936. Neal, *Dark Horse*, p. 33.

74 Wendell Willkie to Franklin Roosevelt, May 21, 1936, in Barnard, *Willkie*, p. 111.

75 On Alexander Sachs [Sax]: McCraw, *Morgan vs. Lilienthal*, p. 68; Joy Hakim, *A History of Us: War, Peace and All That Jazz* (Oxford, 1998).

76 McCraw, *Morgan vs. Lilienthal*, pp. 68–69.

77 FDR's power pool directive, September 17, 1936: McCraw, *Morgan vs. Lilienthal*, p. 70. According to Milton, Wendell and Morgan not only challenged FDR in the heated deliberations, but Morgan covertly passed to Wendell his "Memorandum of a Proposed TVA and Commonwealth and Southern Co., Transmission Pool," prepared for the president's exclusive consideration: George Fort Milton to Norris, Nov. 4, 1936, Box 74, Norris, George W., 1936. Lilienthal Papers. Neuse, *David E. Lilienthal*, pp. 90–91; Colignon, *Power Plays*, pp. 195–96, 207.

78 On Willkie's alternating position vis-à-vis the power pool: Lilienthal to Norris, Oct. 19, 1936, Box 74, Norris, George W., 1936. Lilienthal Papers. Unofficial odds on the election: Brands, *Traitor to His Class*, p. 454; Kennedy, *Freedom from Fear*, p. 286. Willkie and Lilienthal on GOP prospects: Neal, *Dark Horse*, p. 33.

79 La Follette and Norris warnings: McCraw, *Morgan vs. Lilienthal*, p. 74. FDR to La Follette: Barnard, *Willkie*, p. 116.

80 Stone, *They Also Ran*, pp. 382–83. Robert A. Slayton, *Empire Statesman: The Rise and Redemption of Al Smith* (Free Press, 2001), p. 385.

81 Daniel Scroop, M. *Democrat: Jim Farley, the New Deal, and the Making of Modern American Politics* (U. Michigan, 2006), p. 131. Willkie votes Landon: Parmet, *Never Again*, p. 62.

82 Moley, *Seven Years*, p. 352. Amity Shlaes, *Forgotten Man: A New History of the Great Depression* (HarperPerennial, 2007), p. 197. Brands, *Traitor to His Class*, p. 453.

83 Willkie as Abe Lincoln of Wall Street: Stone, *They Also Ran*, p. 373.

84 Barnes, *Willkie*, p. 105.

85 Barnes, *ibid.*, pp. 118–20.

86 Willkie memorandum to FDR, Nov. 23, 1937: Willkie Papers, Manuscripts Department, Lilly Library, Indiana U.; Barnard, *Willkie*, pp. 119–20.

87 Harold L. Ickes, *The Secret Diary of Harold L. Ickes: The Inside Struggle, 1936–1939* (Simon & Schuster, 1954), p. 60. Morgan's reactions: McCraw, *Morgan vs. Lilienthal*, pp. 85–87.

88 Arthur Morgan, "Public Ownership of Power," *Atlantic Monthly,* September 1937: 339–46. McCraw, *Morgan vs. Lilienthal*, p. 102, incorrectly identifies the *New Republic* as the locus of Morgan's *Atlantic Monthly* article. FDR's regret: McCraw, *ibid.*, p. 102.

89 Barnard, *Willkie*, p. 110; Stone, *They Also Ran*, p. 382.

90 Dillon, *Willkie*, pp. 108–9, 130. Althschul to Bricker, Feb. 14, 1939: Frank Altschul Papers 1884–1986 (1884–1974), Series I: Correspondence. Rare Books and Manuscripts Library, Columbia University.

91 Dillon, *Willkie*, pp. 108–9. Neal, *Dark Horse*, p. 45.
92 Barnes, *Willkie*, p. 140. Neal, *Dark Horse*, p. 46.
93 Stone, *They Also Ran*, p. 383.
94 Stone, *ibid.*, p. 384. Henrietta to Wendell, Jan. 9, 1939: Willkie Papers, Lilly Library, Indiana University.
95 Alan Brinkley, *The Publisher: Henry Luce and His American Century* (Knopf, 2010), pp. 252–53.

CHAPTER 5: 1940: Political Science and Serendipity

1 Kenneth Simpson quote, Neal, *Dark* Horse, pp. 53–54.
2 Farley quote: Daniel Scroop, *Mr. Democrat: Jim Farley, the New Deal, and the Making of Modern American Politics* (U. Michigan, 2006), p. 131.
3 Joseph Proskauer Transcripts, interviewed by J. Auerbach, Jan. 25, 1961: Columbia Oral History Project, pp. 36–37. Scroop, *Mr. Democrat: Jim Farley, the New Deal, and the Making of Modern American Politics*, p. 146. Arthur Schlesinger Jr., *The Politics of Upheaval* (Houghton Mifflin, 1960), Vol. III, pp. 604–6.
4 Letter to Frank Altschul, Sept. 26, 1938: Frank Altschul Papers, Columbia Rare Book & Manuscript Library, Butler Library.
5 Sam Pryor III, *Make It Happen: The Fascinating Life of Sam Pryor, Jr.* (Sam Pryor III, 2008), pp. 72–73.
6 The Waterbury, Connecticut, Beefsteak Club: Morton Tenzer interviews Raymond E. Baldwin, Raymond E. Baldwin Transcripts, Vol. 2, Pt. 1, Feb. 6, 1970, p. 488, Columbia Oral History Project. Biographical sources in Mary Dillon, *Wendell Willkie*: Raymond Baldwin (pp. 123–24, 144–45, 147, 149 *et passim*); Samuel Pryor Jr. (p. 123). Sources in Ellsworth Barnard, *Willkie*: Frank Altschul (pp. 159, 330); Pryor (pp. 139, 159, 176, 181 *et passim*). Sources in Neal, *Dark Horse*: Baldwin (pp. 53, 87, 91, 94, 97 *et passim*); Pryor (pp. 46, 53, 77, 102, 105, 109 *et passim*). Information on J. Kenneth Bradley extremely spotty: Baldwin Transcripts, Vol. 2, Pt. 1, p. 482; no record of death, burial; spotty correspondence exists in Frank Altschul Papers, Rare Book & Manuscript Library, Butler Library, Columbia University.
7 Raymond E. Baldwin Transcripts, Vol. 1, Pt. 1, Oct. 23, 1969, pp. 59, 170–73.
8 On ethnic class: Baldwin Transcripts, Vol. 1, Pt. 1, Oct. 23, 1969, pp. 30–31.
9 On race relations: Baldwin Transcripts, Vol. 2, Pt. 2, Feb. 7, 1970 pp. 789–93.
10 Joseph Proskauer interviewed by J. Auerbach, Jan. 25, 1961, Columbia Oral History Project.
11 Second inaugural: H. W. Brands, *The Traitor to His Class: The Privileged Life and Radical Presidency of Franklin Delano Roosevelt* (Doubleday, 2008), pp. 456–57; Susan Dunn, *Roosevelt's Purge: How FDR Fought to Change the Democratic Party* (Harvard, 2010), p. 3.
12 H. W. Brands, *The Traitor to His Class*, chap. 34. Dunn, *Roosevelt's Purge*, chap. 1. Warren Moscow, *Roosevelt and Willkie* (Prentice-Hall, 1968), p. 40.
13 Kennedy, *Freedom from Fear*, pp. 318–19; Ira Katznelson, *Fear Itself: The New Deal and the Origins of Our Time* (Liveright, 2013), esp. pp. 176–79; Nancy J. Weiss, *The National Urban League: 1910–1940* (Oxford, 1974), esp. pp. 274–80.
14 Profile of John Henry Rorbeck: Roger P. Plaskett, "Welcome to Harwinton's History: The 'Jason Skinner House,'" *Harwinton Historian*, 2 pp;

Pryor, *Make It Happen*, pp. 63–65; Baldwin on Rorbeck: Baldwin Transcripts, Interview Jan. 16, 1970, Vol. 2, Pt. 1, p. 389. Columbia Oral Hist. Project.

15 Joseph Proskauer interviewed by J. Auerbach, Jan. 25, 1961, Columbia Oral History Project, p. 37.

16 Herbert Hoover quote: Richard Norton Smith, *Thomas E. Dewey and His Times* (Simon & Schuster, 1982), p. 277; Gallup GOP poll: Smith, *Thomas Dewey*, p. 280.

17 Charles Halleck to Frank Altschul, Nov. 10, 1938, Frank Altschul Papers, Rare Book & Manuscript Library, Columbia University.

18 Baldwin Transcripts, interview, Feb. 6, 1970, Vol. 2, Pt. 2, pp. 577–80, Columbia Oral Hist. Project. On Lowell Thomas: Lowell Thomas, Wikipedia, pp. 1–10. Michael Korda, *Hero: The Life and Legend of Lawrence of Arabia* (Harper, 2010), pp. 353–54, 525–26; Scott Anderson, *Lawrence in Arabia: War, Deceit, Imperial Folly and the Making of the Modern Middle East* (Doubleday, 2013), p. 486.

19 Baldwin Transcripts, Vol. 2, Pt. 2, pp. 577–80.

20 Smith, *Thomas Dewey*, p. 250.

21 Smith, *ibid.*, pp. 236, 173–206, 269.

22 Baldwin Transcripts, Vol. 2, Pt. 2, pp. 582–83.

23 Arthur Schlesinger Jr., quoted: Lynne Olsen, *Those Angry Days: Roosevelt, Lindbergh, and America's Fight Over World War II, 1939–1941* (Random House, 2013), p. xvii. Justus D. Doenecke, *The Battle Against Intervention, 1939–1941* (Krieger, 1997), chap. 1.

24 "Frank Altschul, A Banker and Noted Philanthropist," *New York Times*, May 30, 1981.

25 Olsen, *Those Angry Days*, esp. chap. 5. Doenecke, *Battle Against Intervention*, chap. 1. Wayne S. Cole, *Roosevelt and the Isolationists, 1932–1945* (U. Nebraska P., 1983).

26 Henry Wallace at Atlantic City, Feb. 28, 1935, quote: Dillon, *Willkie*, p. 98. "Idle Men. Idle Money," *Saturday Evening Post*, June 1937: Stone, *They Also Ran*, p. 383.

27 Warren Moscow, *Roosevelt and Willkie* (Prentice-Hall, 1968), pp. 49–51.

28 Altschul to John Bricker, February 14, 1939: Altschul Papers.

29 Altschul to Dorothy Thompson, 6 pages, Mar. 3, 1939: Altschul Papers.

30 Neal, *Willkie*, p. 47.

31 Willkie, Christ Church of Greenwich—200 Anniversary, 12 pages, May 2, 1939: Speeches & Writings, Box 172, Willkie mss. Lilly Library. 12 pp. Pryor, *Make It Happen*, p. 86. Dillon, *Willkie*, p. 123. Baldwin and Willkie: Raymond E. Baldwin Papers, pp. 836–38, Columbia Oral History Project.

32 Citations found *passim*: Dillion; Neal, Barnard, Stone, and most accessibly, Charles Peters, *Five Days*, pp. 23–25.

33 Willkie demurral: Neal, *Dark Horse*, p. 47; Hugh Johnson on Willkie: Stone, *Also Ran*, p. 384.

34 A Tammany Democrat: Barnard, *Willkie*, p. 143; Farley on Willkie, James A. Farley Interview, pp. 397–99: James A. Farley Interview: Columbia Oral History Project. Daniel Scroop, *Mr. Democrat: Jim Farley, The New Deal, and the Making of Modern American Politics* (U. Michigan, 2006). Peters, *Five Days in Philadelphia*, p. 25.

35 Barnard, *Willkie*, pp. 121–22. George Fort Milton, Memorandum to the

President, Oct. 13, 1938, Ellsworth Barnard Collection: Willkie Papers, Manuscripts Department, Lilly Library, IU.

36 Willkie, quoted, *Time*, July 31, 1939, p. 45.

37 Barnes, *Willkie*, pp. 146–47. Barnard, *Willkie*, pp. 122–24.

38 Lilienthal, Diary, Aug. 15, 1939, David Lilienthal Papers, Mudd Manuscript Library, Princeton.

39 Herbert Parmet and Marie B. Hecht, *Never Again: A President Runs for a Third Term* (Macmillan, 1968), p. 83. Marcia Davenport, *Too Strong for Fantasy* (U. Pittsburgh, 1967), pp. 261–62. Neal, *Willkie*, p. 38. A perceptive Frenchmen's Willkie observations: Raoul de Roussy de Sales, *The Making of Yesterday* (Reynal & Hitchcock, 1947), p. 154.

40 On Irita Van Doren's family history and Colonel William M. Brooks: U.S. War Dept., *The War of the Rebellion*, Vol. 39, Pt. 2 (Govt. Printing Office, 1892), p. 887. Barnard, *Willkie*, p. 136; Neal, *Dark Horse*, pp. 40–41.

41 Recording capacity revealed: R. J. Butow, "The FDR Tapes," *American Heritage*, Feb/Mar. 1982, pp. 20–22.

42 William Shirer quoted, Neal, *Willkie*, p. 38. Edith Willkie interviewed, Aug. 29, 1972: Barnard, Ellsworth, Interviews, Manuscripts Department, Lilly Library, Indiana U.

43 Willkie, "Evening Star of the Great Day of the Whigs," *New York Herald Tribune*, Aug. 27, 1939. W. Ball to Willkie, Jan. 29, Willkie to W. Ball, Feb. 2, 1940; Julia Peterkin to Willkie, Mar. 6, 1940: Folder 32, Corr., Misc 1940: Willkie Papers, Lilly Library.

44 Willkie, *The Young Melbourne*—review, April 27, 1939: Speeches & Writings, Box 107, Lilly Library.

45 Barnes quote: Peters, *Five Days in Philadelphia*. Willkie quoted on Irita Van Doren: Neal, *Dark Horse*, pp. 43–44.

46 Davenport, *Too Strong for Fantasy*, pp. 259–62.

47 Halberstam, *The Powers That Be*, p. 68; also, opinion expressed that the Eastern Establishment "had compelled the Party to nominate Wendell Willkie . . . by a combination of every kind of pressure the publishers, broadcasters and bankers could collectively exert around the country," of Theodore White, *The Making of the President 1964*, cited by Marcia Davenport, *Too Strong for Fantasy*, p. 263. Luce on Wendell, Alan Brinkley, *The Publisher: Henry Luce and His American Century* (Knopf, 2010), pp. 254–55; Neal, *Dark Horse*, p. 49. James L. Baughman, *Henry Luce and the Rise of the American Media* (Johns Hopkins, 1987), p. 119.

48 "We the People," Stone, *They Also Ran*, p. 385; Neal, *Dark Horse*, p. 68; Moscow, *Roosevelt and Willkie*, p. 63.

49 Stone, *They Also Ran*, p. 385.

50 Neal, *Dark Horse*, p. 68. James McGregor Burns, *Leadership* (Harper & Row, 1978), p. 281.

51 Neal, *Dark Horse*, pp. 72–73.

52 John Fitzgerald Kennedy, *Why England Slept* (W. Funk, 1940). Foreword by Henry Luce.

53 Peters, *Five Days in Philadelphia*, pp. 39–41.

54 Barnard, *Willkie*, pp. 155–57.

55 Oren Root to Wendell Willkie, April 9, 1940, Oren Root Jr. (IV) Papers, Archives, Hamilton College. Mrs. Root's role: Stone, *They Also Ran*, p. 385.

56 Oren Root, *Persons and Persuasions* (Norton, 1974), p. 22. Barnard, *Willkie*, p. 156; Neal, *Dark Horse*, p. 69. Despite his proactive role in launching

the Willkie campaign, Oren and Dolores Root remember their father as extremely reserved and predictable. Oren Root IV and Dolores Root interview with David Levering Lewis, March 28, 2014.

57 Root, *Persons and Persuasions*, pp. 28–30.

58 Lynne Olson, *Those Angry Days: Roosevelt, Lindbergh, and America's Fight over World War II* (Random House, 2013), p. xvi. Cole, *Roosevelt and the Isolationists*, p. 7, chap. 19. Doenecke, *The Battle Against Intervention*, pp. 11–15. Robert Dallek, *Franklin D. Roosevelt and American Foreign Policy, 1932–1945* (Oxford, 1979), Part 3. Harvard Sitkoff, *A New Deal for Blacks: The Emergence of Civil Rights as a National Issue: The Depression Decade* (Oxford, 1978), pp. 304–8.

59 Kenneth D. Durr, *Life of the Party: Kenneth F. Simpson and the Survival of the Republicans in 1930s New York* (Montrose, 2009), chap. 1; Neal, *Dark Horse*, p. 54; Smith, *Dewey and His Times*, p. 293.

60 Smith, *Dewey and His Times*, p. 332.

61 Peters, *Five Days in Philadelphia*, p. 37. Warren Moscow, *Roosevelt and Willkie* (Prentice-Hall, 1968), p. 38. Barnard, *Willkie*, pp. 131–32.

62 Micro-politics of the Willkie cadre: Harold Talbott, Hill School and Yale alum, notable polo player, Chrysler Corporation director, and future air force secretary under Dwight Eisenhower committed to Willkie. Sinclair Weeks, Harvard and AEF service, who had worried about raising money for a winning nominee as new chair of the GOP Finance Committee, now had such a candidate. Henry Breckenridge, Princeton and Harvard Law, Olympics fencing champion, and Woodrow Wilson's assistant secretary of war and FDR's most significant Democratic challenger in the 1932 primaries, became a major Democrat for Willkie activist, as did John Hanes II, Yale, Reynolds Tobacco director and FDR's treasury undersecretary. Hanes's voluntary service to British secret service agents would remain unrevealed until the following century. Ernest T. Weir, president of the National Steel Corporation, began a one-man campaign to raise funds for a Willkie boom. Sources: Barnard, *Willkie*; Joseph Barnes, *Willkie: The Events He Was Part Of—The Ideas He Fought For* (Simon & Schuster, 1952); Dillon, *Willkie*; Neal, *Dark Horse*.

63 Barnard, *Willkie*, p. 159; Dillon, *Willkie*, p. 124. Moscow, *Roosevelt and Willkie*, p. 63. Thomas E. Mahl, *Desperate Deception: British Covert Operations in the United States, 1939–44* (Brassey's, 1998), p. 169.

64 Thomas Lamont: Edward M. Lamont, *The Ambassador from Wall Street: The Story of Thomas W. Lamont, J.P. Morgan's Chief Executive* (Madison Books, 1994), p. 453. Oren Root, *Persons and Persuasians*, p. 35.

65 James H. Madison, ed., "Fair Trial," *Wendell Willkie: Hoosier Internationalist* (Indiana UP, 1992), pp. 71–87, p. 73. Parmet and Hecht, *Never Again*, p. 82; Richard M. Ketchum, *Borrowed Years, 1938–1941*, p. 417, p. 76.

66 Bruce Barton to Thomas Dewey, June 13, 1940: Kenneth Farrand Simpson Papers, Series 1, Corr., Yale University Rare Books and Manuscripts Library. Ickes quote: Neal, *Dark Horse*, p. 59. Willkie-Baldwin convention entente: Baldwin Interview, pp. 853–55, Columbia Oral History Project. Peters, *Five Days*, pp. 49–50.

67 Neal, *Dark Horse*, pp. 75–78; Olsen, *Angry Days*, p. 270.

68 Drew Pearson Papers, Lyndon B. Johnson Library and Museum; and Peters, *Five Days*, p. 24. Gallup polling: Neal, *Dark Horse*, p. 78.

69 National Press Club announcement: Neal, *Dark Horse*, p. 77.

CHAPTER 6: The Philadelphia Story

1 Credible source for Longworth-Borah affair: Gore Vidal, *The Golden Age* (Vintage, 2000), pp. 13–14; Donald Bruce Johnson, *Republican Party and Wendell Willkie*, p. 76.

2 Edward Lamont, *The Ambassador from Wall Street*, pp. 454–5. Halberstam, *The Powers That Be*, p. 68; Theodore White, *The Making of the President 1964* (Atheneum, 1964), p. 263; Vidal, *The Golden Age*, pp. 99–100. Thomas Mahl, *Desperate Deception: British Covert Operations in the United States, 1939–44* (Brassey's, 1998), p. 156.

3 Anthony Beevor, *The Second World War* (Little, Brown, 2012), p. 117; Ronald C. Rosbottom, *When Paris Went Dark: The City of Light Under German Occupation, 1940–1944* (Little, Brown, 2014), p. 43.

4 Mahl, *Desperate Deception*, pp. x–xi.

5 Pryor quoted: Johnson, *The Republican Party*, p. 91. Alsop and Longworth on "grass roots": Neal, *Dark Horse*, pp. 86, 99.

6 Pryor III, *Make It Happen*, p. 94.

7 Booth Tarkington quote: Barnes, *Willkie*, p. 11.

8 Mahl, *Desperate Deception*, chap. 6. Neal, *Dark Horse*, pp. 83–84.

9 Peters, *Five Days*, pp. 64–65; Neal, *Dark Horse*, pp. 85–86.

10 Peters, *Five Days*, p. 65. Stone, *They Also Ran*.

11 Neal, *Dark Horse*, p. 91; Peters, *Five Days*, p. 67.

12 John Hamilton's address: Dillion, *Willkie*, p. 156; James J. Kenneally, *A Compassionate Conservative: A Political Biography of Joseph Martin, Jr.*, p. 59.

13 Vidal, *Golden Age*, p. 111. Peters, *Five Days*, p. 62.

14 J. A. Gregg was the author's godfather. *Official Report of the Proceedings of the Twenty-Second Republican National Convention, held in Philadelphia, June 24, 25, 26, 27 and 28, 1940* (Judd & Detweiler, 1940), p. 114.

15 Pryor, *Make It Happen*, p. 93; Peters, *Five Days*, p. 83.

16 *Official Report of the Proceedings*, p. 147. Peters, *Five Days*, p. 91.

17 Peters, *Five Days*, p. 81. Neal, *Dark Horse*, pp. 159–61.

18 Dillon, *Willkie*, p. 143; Brands, *Traitor to His Class*, p. 552.

19 *Official Report*, pp. 209, 211; Dillon, *Willkie*, p. 160; Parmet, *Never Again*, pp. 160–61; Peters, *Five Days*, pp. 73–74.

20 *Official Report of the Proceedings*, p. 209.

21 Peters, *Five Days*, pp. 98–99. Arthur H. Vandenberg Jr., ed., *The Private Papers of Senator Vandenberg* (Houghton Mifflin, 1952), p. 2; Lawrence S. Kaplan, *The Conversion of Senator Arthur H. Vandenberg* (U. Kentucky, 2015), pp. 68, 80–83; Neal, *Dark Horse*, p. 58; Mahl, *Desperate Deception*, chap. 7, pp. 138–39.

22 1940 Republican National Convention Balloting: Wikipedia.org, "1940 Republican National Convention."

23 Dillon, *Willkie*, p. 161; Neal, *Dark Horse*, p. 109; Baldwin Interview, Oral History Project, Columbia, pp. 859–60, 857.

24 Drew Pearson, "Merry Go-Round Goes to Philadelphia," June 24, 1940: United Features Syndicate.

25 Neal, *Dark Horse*, p. 111.

26 Steve Neal, *McNary of Oregon: A Political Biography* (Western Imprints, 1985), p. 203; McNary ticket "an obvious trick": Parmet, *Never Again*, p.

171; Peters, *Five Days*, p. 110. Ralph Cake Oral Interviews, Columbia University, p. 111.

27 *Official Report of the Proceedings.* Neal, *Dark Horse*, p. 116.

28 Mencken quote: Mahl, *Desperate Deception*, p. 156. Still, outcomes of American political conventions often have no more predictive certainty than weather forecasts. Dewey's lead was still considerable. Ohio's Taft and Michigan's Vandenberg each had enough pledged votes to determine the path to victory. Probably 80 percent of delegates claimed to be noninterventionists. The perennial Dutchess County GOP congressional representative, Hamilton Fish III (FDR's own congressman), arrived in Philadelphia with fifty like-minded isolationist delegates whose expenses were provided by a German operative.

29 J. Roscoe Drummond, "What Nominated Wendell Willkie?," *Christian Science Monitor*, July 1, 1940.

CHAPTER 7: Saving the GOP to Save Freedom

1 C & S resignation and son Philip, Dillon, *Willkie*, p. 175.

2 Ralph Cake Oral Interviews, Columbia OHP; McNary quote, Neal, *Dark Horse*, p. 126; Neal, *McNary of Oregon: A Political Biography* (Oregon Historical Society, 1985). For minor discordances of dates and factoids, see Barnard, *Wendell Willkie*, pp. 191–93.

3 Barnard, *Willkie*, pp. 191–93; Neal, *Dark Horse*, p. 123. Altschul to Hamilton, June 13, 1938, Hamilton to Altschul, Sept. 12, 1938, Frank Altschul Papers, Manuscripts Library, Columbia University.

4 "Principled stubbornness": Dillon, *Willkie*, p. 178

5 Dillon, *Willkie*, pp. 179–80; James J. Kenneally, *A Compassionate Conservative: A Political Biography of Joseph W. Martin, Jr., Speaker of the House of Representatives* (Lexington, 2003), pp. 59–60; Neal, *Dark Horse*, p. 123.

6 Pew quoted: Dillon, *Willkie*, p. 176. Hamilton dismissal: Barnard, *Willkie*, pp. 191–93; Neal, *Dark Horse*, p. 123. Cf. John D. M. Hamilton, "Willkie's First Trip—An Offering of the Chairmanship," nineteen-page typescript, John D. M. Hamilton Papers, Library of Congress.

7 Pierre du Pont to William Z. Ripley, Dec. 19, 1936. The Longwood Manuscripts—Group 10, series A: Papers of P. S. du Pont, Box 1286. Hagley Museum and Library, Wilmington, DE. Hamilton in England: Dillon, *Willkie*, p. 176.

8 Hamilton in England: Dillon, *Willkie*, p. 176. Du Pont stipend: Pierre du Pont to James P. Selvage, July 22, 1941, Box 1286, Hagley Museum and Library.

9 Willkie, in H. W. Brands, *The Traitor to His Class: The Privileged Life and Radical Presidency of Franklin Delano Roosevelt* (Doubleday, 2008), p. 573.

10 Chicago Convention, in Susan Dunn, *1940: FDR, Willkie, Lindbergh, Hitler—the Election amid the Storm* (Yale, 2013), chap. 10. Richard Moe, *Roosevelt's Second Act: The Election of 1940 and the Politics of* War (Oxford, 2013), see chap. 2. On a Hopkin's candidacy, see David L. Roll, *The Hopkins Touch: Harry Hopkins and the Forging of the Alliance to Defeat Hitler* (Oxford, 2013), p. 45; Robert E. Sherwood, *Roosevelt and Hopkins: An Intimate History* (Harper & Bros., 1948), p. 99.

11 Lynne Olson, *Those Angry Days: Roosevelt, Lindbergh, and America's Fight over World War II* (Random House, 2013), p. 189.

12 Dunn, *1940*, pp. 137–45. H. L. Mencken quote: Mahl, *Desperate Deception*, p. 156. Steve Neal, *Dark Horse*.

13 Willkie on FDR nomination: Neal, *Dark Horse*, p. 128. W. O. Douglas on Willkie, p. 119.

14 FDR on Willkie: Neal, *Dark Horse*, p. 122; and Barnard, *Willkie*, p. 219.

15 Drew Pearson, "Covering Willkie," The Washington Merry-Go-Round, syndicated column, Aug. 13, 1940, Pared Down Collection, LBJ Library.

16 Willkie loyalist, Lamoyne Jones: Neal, *Dark Horse*, p. 132. Herbert and Marie B. Hecht Parmet, *Never Again: A President Runs for a Third Term* (Macmillan, 1968), pp. 213–14; Norman Thomas, quoted: James H. Madison, ed., *Wendell Willkie, Hoosier Internationalist* (Indiana UP, 1992), p. 62.

17 Vandenberg article: Neal, *Dark Horse*, p. 58. Walter Lippmann to Willkie, July 30, 1940: The Papers of Kenneth Simpson, Manuscripts Collection, Yale.

18 Crum at Colorado Springs: Patricia Bosworth, *Anything Your Little Heart Desires: An American Family Story* (Simon & Schuster, 1997), pp. 72, 33; Marcia Davenport, *Too Strong for Fantasy* (U. Pittsburgh, 1967). p. 278.

19 On internecine tensions, see Drew Pearson, "Broken Promises," Drew Pearson Papers, LBJ Library; Oren Root Jr., to Wendell Willkie, Sept. 3, 1940, Oren Root Papers, Archives of Hamilton College Library; Barnard, *Willkie*, p. 214; Dillon, *Willkie*, p. 185.

20 Janet Flanner, "Profiles," *New Yorker*, Oct. 12, 1940, p. 27. The eleventh-hour federal judgeship deal: Warren Moscow, *Roosevelt and Willkie*, p. 106.

21 Monetary limits: Dillon, *Willkie*, pp. 178, 186. Neal, *Dark Horse*, p. 165; especially Barnard, *Willkie*, pp. 212–13.

22 Percy Wood, "WILLKIE TELLS POLICY TODAY." Elwood Ready: "Great Throngs Begin Moving In," *Chicago Daily Tribune*, Aug. 17, 1940, p, 1.

23 Elwood Nomination: Mary Earhart Dillon, *Wendell Willkie, 1892–1944* (Lippincott, 1952), pp. 193–95; Ellsworth Barnard, *Wendell Willkie: Fighter for Freedom* (Northern Mich. U., 1966), pp. 199–201; Steve Neal, *Dark Horse*, pp. 134–36.

24 Philip Kinsley, "Willkie Sounds the Battle Cry: Challenges Roosevelt to Debate," *Chicago Tribune*, Aug. 18, 1940, p. 1. "Candidate Maps His Principles in Keynote Speech," *Chicago Daily Tribune*, Aug. 18, 1940, p. 1. On Elwood address: "The speech was intelligent, forthright, and, in some respects, courageous, Susan Dunn, *1940*, p. 157; "No speech could have satisfied them": Stone, *They Also Ran*, p. 389.

25 Michael Fullilove, *Rendezvous with Destiny: How Franklin D. Roosevelt and Five Extraordinary Men Took America Into War and Into the World* (Penguin, 2013), p. 155.

26 Johnson, *The Republican Party*, pp. 119, 129.

27 Lynn Olson, *Those Angry Days*, chap. 10.

28 Mahl, *Desperate Deception*, p. 167.

29 Century Club influence: Ketchum, *The Borrowed Years*, p. 474; Olson, *Those Angry Days*, chap. 10; Parmet, *Never Again*, p. 61. Democratic Platform: William Langer and S. Everett Gleason, *The Undeclared War, 1940–*

1941 (Harper Bros., 1953), p. 204. On Roper Survey figures: Robert E. Sherwood, *Roosevelt and Hopkins: An Intimate History* (Harper & Bros., 1948), pp. 127–28.

30 Destroyers for bases: Richard M. Ketchum, *The Borrowed Years, 1938–1941: America on the Way to War* (Random House, 1989), pp. 474–77; Barnard, *Willkie*, p. 228; David Roll, *The Hopkins Touch*, p. 61; Joseph Barnes, *Willkie: The Events He Was Part Of—The Ideas He Fought For* (Simon & Schuster, 1952), p. 201. Olson, *Those Angry Days*, pp. 190–91; Willkie denounces: Neal, *Dark Horse*, p. 140.

31 McNary Assistant, Ralph Cake Oral Interview, Columbia Univ., pp. 8–9.

32 Neal, *Dark Horse*, pp. 140–41.

33 Willkie to Lothian: Mahl, *Desperate Deception*, p. 165; Neal, *Dark Horse*, p. 120.

34 Edith Willkie interview, Aug. 29, 1972: Ellsworth Barnard Interviews. Willkie Papers, Lilly Library, Indiana University.

35 Selective Service: Parmet, *Never Again,* p., 224. Senator Capper: Justus D. Doenecke, *The Battle Against Intervention*, p. 31; Senator Wheeler: Neal, *Dark Horse*, p. 130.

36 According to Ellsworth Barnard, who gives no exact date, the Willkie Special arrived at its first stop, Chicago's Union Station, at 8:30 a.m. on Sept. 13: Barnard, *Willkie*, p. 230.

37 Marcia Davenport, *Too Strong for Fantasy*, p. 276.

38 Dillon, *Willkie*, pp. 214–15.

39 I. F. Stone, "The Lewis-Willkie Pact," *Nation*, Nov. 2, 1940: 413–14. Dillon, *Willkie*, p. 271. Barnard, *Willkie*, p. 232.

40 Stone, *They Also Ran*, pp. 388–91.

41 Parmet, *Never Again*, p. 219.

42 Doeneck, *Battle Against Interventionism*, pp. 9–18. Dunn, *FDR, Willkie, Lindbergh, Hitler*, p. 65. Olson, *Those Angry Days*, pp. 67–70.

43 Moe, *Roosevelt's Second Act*, pp. 54–61.

44 Newspapers for Willkie: Justus Doenecke, *Battle Against Intervention*, pp. 6–7. Gallup poll: Johnson, *The Republican Party and Wendell Willkie*, p. 147. Neal, *Dark Horse*, p. 151.

45 Wendell Willkie II to David Levering Lewis: interview at NYU Torch Club, June 2012.

46 Stone, *They Also Ran*, p. 390.

47 Neal, *Dark Horse*, p. 160; Langer and Gleason, *The Undeclared War*, pp. 205–6.

48 British Comfort with Willkie win as well: Mahl, *Desperate Deception*, p. 165.

49 Barnard, *Willkie*, p. 259.

50 The First Lady: Eleanor Roosevelt, *This I Remember* (Harper & Bros., 1949), p. 220; Blanche Wiesen Cook, *Eleanor Roosevelt: The War Years and After* (Viking, 2016), pp. 345–46. Stone, *They Also Ran*, p. 395.

51 "The FDR Tapes," Introduction by Arthur Schlesinger Jr., *American Heritage*, Feb/Mar. 1982: 18–21. Langer and Gleason, *Undeclared War*, pp. 207–10.

52 I. F. Stone, "The Lewis-Willkie Pact," *Nation*, Nov. 2, 1940: 413–14. Lee Pressman Oral Interview, Vol. I, pp. 96–110, Columbia University. Dillon, *Willkie*, p. 213. Hugh Ross, "John L. Lewis and the Election of 1940,"

Labor History (2001): 160–90. Cf. John D. M. Hamilton, "John L. Lewis in the Campaign of 1940," John D. M. Hamilton Papers, Library of Congress.

53 Robert Sherwood, *Roosevelt and Hopkins*, pp. 189–90. David Nasaw, *The Patriarch: The Remarkable Life and Turbulent Times of Joseph P. Kennedy* (Penguin, 2012), p. 494.

54 Kennedy quote: Nasaw, *The Patriarch*, p. 432. Ronald Kessler, *The Sins of the Father: Joseph Kennedy and the Dynasty He Founded* (Warner Books, 1996), pp. 161, 207, 213, 223. Joseph Kennedy to Charles Lindbergh, Dec. 8, 1938: Amanda Smith, ed., *Hostage to Fortune: The Letters of Joseph P. Kennedy* (Viking, 2001), p. 305.

55 Smith, *Hostage to Fortune*, p. xxi.

56 On C. B. Luce and J. P. Kennedy: Sylvia Jukes Morris, *Rage for Fame: The Ascent of Clare Boothe Luce* (Random House, 1997), pp. 340–41, 383; Nasaw, *The Patriarch*, pp. 379–80, 482–90; Alan Brinkley, *The Publisher: Henry Luce and the American Century* (Knopf, 2010), pp. 253–60, 303–4; Kessler, *The Sins of the Father*, pp. 161, 207, 210–11.

57 LBJ recollection: Kessler, *The Sins of the Father*, p. 224. Michael Beschloss, *Kennedy and Roosevelt: The Uneasy Alliance* (Norton, 1980), p. 221. Kennedy radio endorsement: Smith, ed., *Hostage to Fortune*, epigraph. For Kennedy's account of the FDR-Willkie outcome: Arthur Krock, "Private Memorandum," 12-1940: Arthur Krock Papers, Princeton University Library. Moe, *Roosevelt's Second Act*, pp. 296–98.

58 Sherwood, *Roosevelt and Hopkins*, pp. 19–90.

59 "Son-of-a-bitch" quote: Barnard, *Willkie*, p. 258. Richard J. Whalen, *The Founding Father: The Story of Joseph P. Kennedy* (New American Library, 1964), p. 337.

60 Stone, *They Also Ran*, pp. 396–97.

61 Ross, *John L. Lewis and the Election of 1940*, p. 188.

62 Joe Martin, as told to Robert J. Donavan, *My First Fifty Years in Politics* (McGraw-Hill, 1960), p. 120.

63 Samuel Lubell, quoted: Neal, *Dark Horse*, p. 177.

64 Marcia Davenport, *Too Strong for Fantasy*, pp. 283–84. See Olson, *Those Angry Days*, p. 263.

65 Willkie, "Loyal Opposition," Series VII: Speeches & Writings, Box 106, Willkie Papers, Lilly Library, IU. Dillon, *Willkie*, pp. 229–30. Barnard, *Willkie*, pp. 270–71. Neal, *Dark Horse*, p. 182.

66 On entente Willkie and Root on Willkie Clubs' reinvention: Wendell Willkie to Oren Root Jr., Nov. 6, and Nov. 22, 1940; Oren Root Jr., to Russell Davenport, Dec. 12, 1941, Oren Root Jr. (IV) Papers, Hamilton College Library. Willkie Clubs were reconstituted as The Independent Clubs of America in December 1940; they ceased existence after December 7, 1941.

67 Sam Pryor III, *Make It Happen: The Fascinating Life of Sam Pryor, Jr.* (Sam Pyor III, 2008), p. 99. Sam Pryor remonstrance: Dillon, *Willkie*, p. 227. Arthur Krock: Arthur Krock Papers, Princeton University Library. Burns and Dunn, *Three Roosevelts*, p. 436.

CHAPTER 8: *Pas de Deux*: Willkie and Roosevelt

1 Joe Martin, as told to Robert J. Donovan, *My First Fifty Years in Politics* (McGraw-Hill, 1960), p. 129.

2 Joseph Barnes, *Willkie: The Events He Was Part Of—The Ideas He Fought*

For (Simon & Schuster, 1952), p. 244. Mary Earhart Dillon, *Willkie*, pp. 232–33.

3 Doenecke, *Battle Against Interventionism*, pp. 8–15. Interventionist percentiles: Burns and Dunn, *The Three Roosevelts*, p. 429. Olson, *Those Angry Days*, chap. 15. Parrish, *Anxious Decades*, p. 470. A. Scott Berg, *Lindbergh* (Berkeley Group, 1998), pp. 408–12.

4 Virginia Durr to Ellsworth Barnard, Interview, Oct. 6, 1977, E. Barnard Papers, Lilly Library, Indiana U. Neal, *Dark Horse*, p. 186.

5 Barnes, *Willkie*, p. 188.

6 On Hobe Sound exclusivity: Cleveland Amory, *The Last Resorts* (Harper & Bros., 1948), p. 145. Barnard, *Willkie*, pp. 273, 277. Dillon, *Willkie*, p. 232. Felix Frankfurter, "Memorandum," January, 16, 1941, pp. 1–7. Frankfurter Papers, 1921–1949, Box 1, PSF, Franklin D. Roosevelt Presidential Library.

7 Dillon, *Willkie*, p. 283; Dunn, *1940*, p. 280; Olson, *Those Angry Days*, p. 281. Martin, *My First Fifty Years*, p. 121. Frankfurter, "Memorandum," p. 5, FDR Library.

8 Frankfurter, "Memorandum," p. 7.

9 Eleanor Roosevelt, *This I Remember* (Harper & Bros.), p. 222. Joseph Barnes, *Willkie: Events He Was Part Of*, p. 245.

10 Robert E. Sherwood, *Roosevelt and Hopkins: An Intimate History* (Harper & Bros., 1948), pp. 3–4. David L. Roll, *The Hopkins Touch: Harry Hopkins and the Forging of the Alliance to Defeat Hitler* (Oxford, 2013), p. 54.

11 Most informed background account of Willkie UK trip: "Willkie-Frankfurter Document," 1-16-1941, PSF: Willkie, FDR Library, Hyde Park. Roy Howard at LAG: Barnes, *Willkie*, chap. 14.

12 Longfellow puzzle: Joseph Barnes, *Willkie: The Events He Was Part Of*, p. 246. Ellsworth Barnard, *Willkie*, pp. 279–82.

13 Liaquat Ahamed, *Lords of Finance: The Bankers Who Broke the World* (Penguin, 2009), p. 5. Barnard, *Willkie*, p. 282. Mollie Panter Downes, *London War Notes: 1939–1945* (Farrar, Straus and Giroux, 1971), pp. 128–29.

14 Harrison Salisbury: David Roll, *The Hopkins Touch*, pp. 93–94; Rebecca West: Steve Neal, *Dark Horse*, p. 38. Barnes, *Willkie*, pp. 245–46.

15 London ubiquity: Barnard, *Willkie*, p. 279; Barnes, *Willkie*, pp. 235–36; Dillon, *Willkie*, p. 282; Olson, *Those Angry Days*, p. 282; Neal, *Willkie*, pp. 200–201.

16 Champagne toast: Barnard, *Willkie*, p. 282.

17 Barnes, *Willkie*, p. 236.

18 Berg, *Lindbergh*, pp. 413–14. Nasaw, *The Patriarch*, pp. 518–19.

19 Barnard, *Willkie*, p. 285. Barnes, *Willkie*, p. 189. Neal, *Willkie*, p. 187.

20 Wendell Willkie, "Statement of Wendell Willkie Before Senate Foreign Relations Committee," Feb. 11, 1941, 12 Pages, Willkie MSS, Manuscripts Dept., Lilly Library, IU.

21 Barnard, *Willkie*, p. 288.

22 Dillon, *Willkie*, p. 248. Neal, *Dark Horse*, p. 205.

23 Neal, *Dark Horse*, p. 209.

24 Willkie, "Americans, Stop Being Afraid," *Collier's*, May 10, 1941.

25 Gerald Nye, "Our Madness Increases as Our Emergency Shrinks," Radio

Address, delivered in St. Louis, Aug. 1, 1941. *Vital Speeches of the Day*, Vol. VII, pp. 720–23.

26 Joseph Kennedy's warning: Neal Gabler, *An Empire of Their Own: How the Jews Invented Hollywood* (Random House, 1989), p. 344. Clayton R. Koppes and Gregory D. Black, *Hollywood Goes to War: How Politics, Profits, and Propaganda Shaped World War II Movies* (Free Press, 1987), pp. 37–39.

27 Barnard, *Willkie*, p. 312.

28 Wendell Willkie to D. Worth Clark, Sept. 8, 1941, Willkie Papers; Willkie, "For Release to Morning Papers," Sept. 11, 1941, Willkie Papers; Willkie, Statement by Wendell L. Willkie, "For Immediate Release," Sept. 15, 1941, Willkie Papers, Lilly Library, Indiana U. "Willkie Charges Clark with Falsehood, Senator Later Offers Apology," Baltimore *Sun*, Sept. 26, 1941, p. 1. Koppes and Black, *Hollywood Goes to War*, p. 45. For colorful give-and-take between studio representatives and the committee: Gabler, *An Empire of Their Own*, pp. 344–47.

29 Berg, *Lindbergh*, p. 426.

30 *The Wave of the Future*: Berg, *Lindbergh*, pp. 405–7. Dunn, *1940: FDR, Willkie, Hitler—the Election amid the Storm*, pp. 242–44, 281–82. Dillon, *Willkie*, p. 253; David Roll, *The Hopkins Touch*, p. 148.

31 Berg, *Lindbergh*, p. 426. Barnard, *Wilkie*, p. 306.

32 Thomas G. Patterson, Garry Clifford, et al., eds., *American Foreign Relations: A History Since 1895* (Wadsworth, 2010), p. 181. Roll, *Hopkins Touch*, pp. 138–45. Brands, *Traitor to His Class*, pp. 605–6.

33 Antony Beevor, *The Second World War* (Little, Brown, 2012), pp. 174–91.

34 Roll, *The Hopkins Touch*, p. 77.

35 Roll, *ibid.*, p. 111.

36 Dorothy Thompson to Wendell Willkie, Oct. 14, 1941: Ellsworth Barnard, Interview Notes, Lilly Library, Indiana U.

37 Barnard, *Willkie*, pp. 310–11.

38 Barnard, *ibid.*, p. 316.

39 Wendell Willkie telegram to Republican Members of the House and Senate, Oct. 20, 1941, Manuscripts Division, Library of Congress.

40 Barnard, *Willkie*, p. 319.

41 Dillon, *Willkie*, pp. 257–59. FDR's Willkie compliment: Neal, *Dark Horse*, p. 214.

42 Barnes, *Willkie*, p. 272.

43 Frances Perkins, *The Roosevelt I Knew* (Penguin, 2011), p. 113. FDR to Wendell Willkie, Dec. 7, 1941: Barnard Willkie Notes, Barnard Manuscript, Lilly Library, IU.

44 On Admiral Richardson's advice: Roll, *The Hopkins Touch*, pp. 70–71. Willkie to FDR, Dec. 12, 1941: Barnard Manuscript, Lilly Library, IU.

45 Grace Tully on Willkie: Barnard Manuscript. Lamoyne Jones on FDR: Barnard Manuscript. Neal, *Dark Horse*, pp. 219–20.

46 Barnard, *Willkie*, p. 324. Neal, *Dark Horse*, p. 220.

47 Edith Willkie: Barnard Manuscript Interviews, Aug. 23, 1972, Lilly Library. Drew Pearson Papers, LBJ Library and Museum. Nathan Miller: Barnard, *Willkie*, p. 330.

48 Wendell Willkie, "Fair Trial," *New Republic* (Mar. 18, 1940): 370–72; See "Willkie as a Liberal: Civil Liberties and Civil Rights," Harvard Sitkoff,

Toward Freedom Land: The Long Struggle for Racial Equality in America (U.P. Kentucky, 2010), pp. 131–32, 136.

49 William Schneiderman and Harry Bridges, "Wendell Willkie," *Dissent on Trial: The Story of a Political Life* (MEP, 1983), p. 79; Harvard Sitkoff, *Toward Freedom Land: The Long Struggle for Racial Equality in America* (U. Kentucky, 2010), p. 134.

50 Arthur M. Schlesinger, "Can Willkie Save His Party?," *Nation* (Dec. 6, 1942): 561–64; Wendell Willkie, "The Future of the Republican Party," *Nation* (Dec. 13, 1942): 609–10.

51 Neal, *Willkie*, p. 207.

52 Johnson, *The Republican Party and Wendell Willkie*, p. 204.

53 Taft quote: Clarence E. Wunderlin Jr. ed., *The Papers of Robert A. Taft, II* (Kent State U., 2001), p. 354. Wendell Willkie, "Speech of the Month," *Republican*, June–July, 1942. Barnes, *Willkie*, p. 238. Willkie's dream: Barnard, *Willkie*, p. 326.

54 Willkie quote: Neal, *Dark Horse*, p. 221.

55 Joe Martin, as told to Robert J. Donovan, *My First Fifty Years in Politics* (McGraw-Hill, 1960), p. 129.

56 Max Lerner, *America as a Civilization: Life and Thought in the United States Today* (Simon & Schuster, 1957), p. 63.

57 James J. Kenneally, "Black Republicans During the New Deal: The Role of Joseph W. Martin, Jr.," *The Review of Politics* (2001): 117–39, 133–34. Nancy J. Weiss, *Farewell to the Party of Lincoln: Black Politics in the Age of FDR* (Princeton, 1983), pp. 21, 205 (footnote 90). Harvard Sitkoff, *A New Deal for Blacks: The Emergence of Civil Rights as a National Issue; The Depression Decade* (Oxford, 1978), pp. 90–91. Willkie on Negro advancement: Levi Jolley, "Square Deal Is Pledged by Willkie," *Baltimore Afro-American*, July 6, 1940, p. 1; Barnard, *Willkie*, pp. 328–29.

58 See Cleveland Amory, *The Last Resorts* (Harper Bros., 1948), p. 145.

59 Barnes, *Willkie*, p. 341.

CHAPTER 9: Exceptionalism at Work

1 Wendell Willkie, "The Case for Minorities," *Saturday Review* (June 28, 1942). David F. Krugler, *1919, the Year of Racial Violence: How African Americans Fought Back* (Cambridge, 2015), p. 213; David Levering Lewis, *When Harlem Was in Vogue* (Penguin, 1997, orig. published 1981), pp. 18–24. American Hebrew Award: text of award, signed by Joseph H. Biben, publisher of *American Hebrew*, Oct. 14, 1942; Speeches and Writings, Box 6, Fol. 1942, Dec. 17, 1942, Willkie Papers. Barnard, *Willkie*, p. 338; Dillon, *Willkie*, p. 303.

2 Proposed Resolution for the Republican National Committee, April 17, 1942, 4 pp., Willkie Papers. Kenneally, "Black Republicans During the New Deal."

3 Jervis Anderson, *A. Philip Randolph: A Biographical Portrait* (Harcourt, Brace 1972), pp. 262–63. Lester Granger to Wendell Willkie, Mar. 28, 1942, Willkie Papers. "Wendell L. Willkie Launches Match Campaign for Negro Workers," NUL Publicity Service, Mar. 31, 1942, Willkie Papers.

4 Ira Katznelson, *Fear Itself: The New Deal and the Origins of Our Time* (Liveright, 2013), pp. 182–86.

5 Harvard Sitkoff, *A New Deal for Blacks: The Emergence of Civil Rights*

as a National Issue: The Depression Decade (Oxford, 1978), pp. 288–92. Robert L. Zangrando, *The NAACP Crusade Against Lynching, 1909–1950* (Temple, 1980). On FDR's silence: cf. Kenneth O'Reilly, *Nixon's Piano: Presidents and Racial Politics from Washington to Clinton* (Free Press, 1995), pp. 120–21.

6 See Kenneth Robert Janken, *White: The Biography of Walter White, Mr. NAACP* (New Press, 2003), Chaps 1–4. Lewis, *When Harlem Was in Vogue,* esp. Chap 5.

7 Walter White, *A Man Called White: The Autobiography of Walter White* (U. Georgia, 1995; orig. pub., 1948), pp. 190–91, 198. Jervis Anderson, *A. Philip Randolph: A Biographical Portrait* (Harcourt, Brace, 1972), pp. 255–60. Janken, *White,* pp. 256–58, 267. Neal, *Dark Horse,* pp. 273–74.

8 Dillon, *Willkie,* p. 303. Thomas J. Knock, " 'History with Lightning': The Forgotten Film *Wilson,*" *American Quarterly* Vol. 28 (Winter 1976): 523–43. "An expensive fiasco," in the considered judgment of historians Koppes and Black, *Hollywood Goes to War,* pp. 317, 319.

9 OWI wartime propaganda: Thomas Cripps, *Slow Fade to Black: The Negro in American Film, 1900–1942* (Oxford, 1977), pp. 379–80. White's failure to improve *Birth of a Nation*: Cripps, *ibid.,* p. 374. Detailed critique in Koppes and Black, *Hollywood Goes to War,* pp. 178–81.

10 White, *A Man Called White,* p. 199. On assisting Walter White: Walter White to Walter Wanger, Oct. 22, 1940, Walter F. Wanger Papers; Wanger to Willkie, June 13, 1942, Walter Wanger Papers, Univ. of Wisconsin. Janken, *A Man Called White,* pp. 267–68.

11 Walter Wanger to Walter White, June 16, 1941, Walter F. Wanger Papers, Wisconsin Center for Film and Theater Research, U. of Wisconsin.

12 White quoted: Thomas Cripps, *Slow Fade to Black,* pp. 375–76. On studio heads' resistance: Koppes and Black, *Hollywood Goes to War,* p. 181.

13 Oscar speech: "Wendell L. Willkie at the Annual Awards Dinner of the Academy of Motion Picture Arts and Sciences," Feb. 26, 1942, 9 pages, Willkie MSS, Lilly Library, IU.

14 Freedom House dedication: "Willkie Speaks at Dedication of Freedom House," *New York Herald Tribune,* Jan. 22, 1942, p. 1. Freedom House inaugural dinner: "The Board of Directors of Freedom House, March 19, 1942, Willkie Papers, Lilly Library, Indiana U. Hebert Agar: Olson, *Those Angry Days,* pp. 139–45.

15 Wendell Willkie "Opening Remarks," 3 pp., Box 5, Fol. 1942, Mar. 19, Speeches and Writings, Willkie Papers. See Ethan Michaeli, *The Defender: How the Legendary Black Newspaper Changed America* (Houghton Mifflin, 2016), p. 243.

16 Walter White to Harry Warner, May 25, 1942; Walter White to Olivia de Havilland, May 25, 1942, Walter White Papers; NAACP Collection, Library of Congress. OWI pressure: Cripps, *Slow Fade to Black. Tennessee Johnson* (aka *The Man on America's Conscience*) controversy: Koppes and Black, *Hollywood Goes to War,* pp. 84–89.

17 Elmo Roper's warning: Neal, *Dark Horse,* p. 276. Walter White's Hollywood gambit: Cripps, *Slow Fade to Black,* p 376; Janken, *A Man Called White,* pp. 266–67. On black dissent in Hollywood: Thomas Dyja, *Walter White: The Dilemma of Black Identity in America* (Ivan R. Dee, 2008), p. 159.

18 Walter Wanger to Willkie, June 14, Wanger telegram to Willkie, July 16,

1942, Wanger Papers. White, *A Man Called White*, pp. 200–201; Janken, *White*, pp. 268–69.

19 Barnard, *Willkie*, pp 340–41; White, *A Man Called White*, p. 201.

20 White, *A Man Called White*, p. 202. Janken, *White*, p. 269. Ronald Brownstein, *The Power and the Glitter: The Hollywood-Washington Connection* (Vintage, 1992), pp. 167–74. Opratios: Thomas Dyja, *Walter White*, p. 160. Coppes and Black, *Hollywood Goes to War*, p. 182.

21 Alonzo L. Hanby, *Man of the People: A Life of Harry Truman* (Oxford, 1995), p. 433; David McCullough, *Truman* (Simon & Schuster, 1992), pp. 369–70. Neal, *Dark Horse*, p. 273.

22 "Wendell Willkie Speech to 33rd NAACP Annual Conference," July 19, 8 pp., appended to Walter White to Wendell Willkie, July 2, 1942, Walter White Collection, NAACP Papers, LOC. "Wendell Willkie's Speech Before NAACP Convention," *Pittsburgh Courier*, July 25, 1942, p. 1. Neal, *Dark Horse*, p. 273.

23 Wendell Willkie to Drew Pearson, June 26, 1942, Drew Pearson Collection, LBJ Library. Barnes, *Willkie*, pp. 285–87. Neal, *Dark Horse*, p. 223.

CHAPTER 10: One World or Nothing

1 "Interview with Major R.T. Knight, AC," Oct. 23, 1942—PSF Willkie, FDR Library, Hyde Park. Wendell Willkie, *One World: The Photographic Album Edition* (The Limited Edition Club, 1944), I. Barnes, *Willkie: The Events He Was Part Of*, pp. 289, 294.

2 Wendell quoted: Neal, *Dark Horse*, p. 229; Walter White, *A Man Called White*, pp. 203–4. Smith, *Dewey and His Times*, pp. 349–50.

3 Ben Robertson to Wendell Willkie, Sept. 9, 1942: Van Doren, Irita, Willkie File, LOC. Barnes, *Willkie*, p. 289. Herbert Strentz, "Compatriots: Wendell Willkie, the Press and the Cowles Brothers, an Introductory Survey, Including Willkie's One World Trip with Publisher, Gardner (Mike) Cowles": School of Journalism & Mass Communications, Drake University. Presented July, 1988, p. 33. Wendell Willkie to FDR, "Personal and Confidential," July 29—PSF Willkie, FDR Library. FDR Memorandum to General Marshall, July 31; Office of the Chief of Staff Memorandum to the President, July 31, 1942—PSF Willkie, FDR Library.

4 FDR quoted: Barnard, *Willkie*, pp. 347–48. Antony Beevor, *The Second World War* (Little, Brown, 2012), p. 331.

5 Barnard, *Willkie*, p. 348. FDR to General Chiang Kai-shek, Aug. 21, 1942, PSF Willkie, FDR Library. Garry Clifford et al., eds., *American Foreign Relations: A History since 1895* (Wadsworth, 2010), pp. 191–92; Roll, *The Hopkins Touch*, p. 203.

6 "Edith Willkie Interview," Aug. 23, 1972, Barnard Interviews MS.

7 Barnes, *Willkie*, p. 293; "Interview with Maj. Knight." Gardner Cowles, *Mike Looks Back: The Memoirs of Gardner Cowles, the Founder of Look Magazine* (Gardner Cowles, 1985), p. 71. Roll, *The Hopkins Touch*, pp. 209–10. Neal, *Dark Horse*, p. 230.

8 Willkie, *One World: The Photographic Album Edition*, p. 2.

9 "Britain and Egypt," *The Voice of Free Arabism*, Sept. 3, 1942. Wendell L. Willkie, *One World*, with an introduction by Donald Bruce Johnson (U. Illinois, 1966; orig. pub., 1943), p. 13. Barnard, *Willkie*, pp. 350–52.

10 Frank Gervasi, "Willkie at the Front," *Collier's*, Sept. 1942. "Willkie in

Cairo," *Egyptian Mail*, Sept. 3, p. 1; "Willkie in the Middle East," *Egyptian Mail*, Sept. 4, 1942, p. 1; Neal, *Dark Horse*, pp. 234–37.

11 Willkie, *One World: Photo Edition*, pp. 4–6. Barnard, *Willkie*, pp. 350–51.

12 "M. Wendell Willkie a Apporte a la Turquie un Message d'Optimisme Raisonne," *La Syrie et L'Orient*, Sept. 10, 1942. Cowles, *Mike Looks Back*, pp. 76–77. Neal, *Dark Horse*, p. 239. Ray Brock, "End of Soviet Rift with Turkey," *New York Times*, Dec. 11, 1942. "Mr. Willkie's Stay in Ankara," *The Eastern Times*, Sept. 10, 1942.

13 Robert E. Sherwood, *Roosevelt and Hopkins: An Intimate History* (Harper & Bros., 1948), p. 657. Emir Dr. Kamuran Aali Bedir-Khan, "Memorandum on the Kurdish Question," Beirut, Sept. 10, 1942, 8 pages.

14 Robert E. Sherwood, *Roosevelt and Hopkins: An Intimate History* (Harper & Bros., 1948), p. 657. Emir Dr. Kamuran Aali Bedir-Khan, "Memorandum on the Kurdish Question," Beirut, Sept. 10, 1942, 8 pages.

15 "M. Wendell Willkie a Beyrouth," *La Syrie et L'Orient*, Sept. 11, 1942, p. 1; Neal, *Dark Horse*, p. 239.

16 Cowles, *Mike Looks* Back, p. 73. Willkie's de Gaulle dramatization: Irita Van Doren Papers, Library of Congress.

17 Cowles, *Mike Looks Back*, pp. 74–75.

18 "Mr. Willkie in Jerusalem," Extract, *Iraq Times*, Sept. 14, 1942.

19 Albert Hourani, *A History of the Arab Peoples* (Harvard, 2002), chap. 21.

20 Barnard, *Willkie*, p. 353; Neal, *Dark Horse*, p. 241. Interestingly, Bartley Crum came to a more partisan opinion on the subject in a book dedicated to Willkie: Bartley C. Crum, *Behind the Silken Curtain* (Simon & Schuster, 1947), p. 291. Secret Minutes: "Notes for Mr. Wendell Willkie's Visit, 'Jewish Army,'" Library of Congress.

21 Georgina Howell, *Gertrude Bell: Queen of the Desert, Shaper of Nations* (Frarrar, Straus and Giroux, 2006). David Anderson, "Iraqi Siege Broken by British Assault," *New York Times*, June 2, 1941.

22 "Mr. Wendell Willkie's Visit to Baghdad," *Iraq Times*, Sept. 12, 1942, p. 1. Cowles, *Mike Looks Back*, pp. 76–78.

23 Cowles, *ibid.*

24 "Roosevelt's Envoy in Iraq," *Iraq Times*, Sept. 14, 1942, p. 1. Neal, *Dark Horse*, p. 243.

25 Willkie, *One World*, p. 30.

26 Barnard, *Willkie*, p. 352.

27 "M. Willkie a Tehran," *Journal de Tehran*, Sept. 15, 1942, p. 1; A. P, Saleh to Minister Dreyfus, "Press Items on Mr. Willkie's Visit to Tehran": Library of Congress. Cowles, *Mike Looks Back*, p. 78. Neal, *Dark Horse*, p. 244.

28 "Major Knight Interview," p. 13: Library of Congress. Sherwood, *Roosevelt and Hopkins*, p. 637.

29 Ahmad Qavam telegram to Willkie, American Legation, Sept. 22, 1942; Mohammad Said telegram to Willkie, American Legation, Sept. 24, 1942: Library of Congress. Barnard, *Willkie*, p. 354; Edmund Stevens to Wendell Willkie, Sept. 26, 1942: Library of Congress.

30 William Standley to Teheran Ministry, Sept. 13, 1942: LOC. David Mayers, *FDR's Ambassadors and the Diplomacy of Crisis* (Cambridge, 2013), pp. 225–26. Roll, *The Hopkins Touch*, p. 395. Mary Earhart Dillon, *Willkie*, p. 270.

31 Willkie, *One World*, chap. 4; Barnard, *Willkie*, p. 357. Different version of Ballerina incident: Dillon, *Willkie*, pp. 273–74.

32 Robert Conquest, *The Great Terror* (Oxford, 2008, 40th anniv. ed.), p. 15.

33 Cowles, *Mike Looks Back*, p. 80. Willkie, *One World: Photographic Edition*, pp. 68–69; Willkie, *One World*, p. 85.

34 Willkie, *One World*, p. 68.

35 Willkie, *ibid.*, p. 97.

36 Eisenhower, quoted: Thomas G. Paterson, Garry Clifford, Shane J. Maddock, Deborah Kistatsky, Kenneth J. Hagan, eds. *American Foreign Relations since 1895* (Wadsworth, 2010), p. 191. Beevor, *Second World War*, p. 282. Roll, *The Hopkins Touch*, pp. 15, 226–27.

37 Sherwood, *Roosevelt and Hopkins*, p. 635. Roll, *The Hopkins Touch*, pp. 216–21.

38 Beevor, *Second World War*, chap. 24.

39 Willkie, *One World*, p. 83; *One World: Photographic Album Edition*, p. 102. Cowles, *Mike Looks Back*, p. 81. Willkie, *One World*, p. 100. Mayers, *FDR's Ambassadors*, p. 226.

40 *American Foreign Relations since 1895*, p. 192. Drew Pearson, "Proposed Book on Russia," p. 5: Drew Pearson Papers, LBJ Library and Museum, p. 5.

41 Sherwood, *Roosevelt and Hopkins*, pp. 639–40.

42 Willkie, *One World Photographic*, pp. 72–74; *One World*, pp. 55–58. Cowles, *Mike Looks Back*, p. 80. Beevor, *Second World War*, p. 233.

43 Willkie, *One World Photographic*, p. 72.

44 Willkie, *One World*, pp. 58–59. Barnard, *Willkie*, p. 360. Sherwood, *Roosevelt and Hopkins*, pp. 634–35. Cook, *Eleanor Roosevelt*, p. 439. Barnes, *Willkie*, p. 303.

45 Cowles, *Mike Looks Back*, pp. 82–83. Drew Pearson, "Proposed Book on Russia," chap. III, pp. 3–4, Box G315; and "Willkie, Wendell (1940–1944)," Box G247: Drew Pearson Papers, LBJ Library & Museum. Barnard, *Willkie*, pp. 359–60.

46 Willkie, *One World*, pp. 85–86.

47 Willkie, *One World: Photographic*, chap. 5; *One World*, chap. 5.

48 Rana Mitter, *Forgotten Ally: China's World War II, 1937–1945* (Houghton Mifflin Harcourt, 2013), p. 173.

49 Willkie, *One World*, p. 123. Cowles, *Mike Looks Back*, p. 86. Russell Davenport, "Secret and Personal," Memorandum, 8 pages, LOC. Theodore H. White to Wendell Willkie, Oct. 2, 1942: LOC. Hannah Pakula, *The Last Empress: Madame Chiang Kai-shek and the Birth of Modern China* (Simon & Schuster, 2009), p. 383.

50 Willkie, *One World*, p. 112.

51 John Service was a "China Hand," disgraced in the McCarthy frenzy over "who lost China": E. J. Kahn Jr., *The China Hands: America's Foreign Service Officers and What Befell Them* (Viking, 1972), pp. 115–16.

52 Willkie, *One World*, p. 129.

53 "Subject: Visit to China of Mr. Wendell L. Willkie as a Special Representative of the President," to the Secretary of State, Chungking, Oct. 8, 1942, Enclosure No. 3, Irita Van Doren Papers, Library of Congress. Willkie, *One World*, pp. 126–27 et passim.

54 "Visit to China of Mr. Wendell L. Willkie," Enclosure No. 4: LOC. Han-

nah Pakula, *The Last Empress*, pp. 386–89. John Paton Davies Jr., *China Hand: An Autobiography* (U. Penn., 2012), pp. 194–209.

55 Cowles, *Mike Looks Back*, p. 86. Willkie, *One* World, p. 128. Hannah Pakula, *The Last Empress*, p. 407, pp. 390–95.

56 Pakula, *The Last Empress*, p. 417.

57 John Paton Davies Jr., *China Hand: An Autobiography*, pp. 95–96. Rana Mitter, *Forgotten Ally: China's World War II, 1937–1945*, pp. 13, 328. E. J. Kahn Jr., *The China Hands*, p. 110.

58 "Visit to China of Mr. Wendell L. Willkie," Enclosure No. 5. Davies, *China Hand*, p. 96. Pakula, *The Last Empress*, chap. 5. Barnard, *Willkie*, p. 369.

59 Cowles, *Mike Looks Back*, pp. 88–89. Pakula, *The Last Empress*, pp. 410–11.

60 Willkie, *One World*, p. 130. "Visit to China . . . Willkie," October 4: State Dept.

61 Willkie, *One World*, p. 132.

62 Willkie, *ibid.*, p. 150.

63 "Visit to China . . . Willkie," Enclosure No. 13, 5 pages.

64 Pakula, *Last Empress*, p. 408, pp. 403–4. Willkie, *One World*, pp. 142–44. Stilwell, quoted: Barnard, *Willkie*, p. 360.

65 "Visit to China . . . Willkie," Enclosure No. 10: State Dept.

66 "Visit to China . . . Willkie," Enclosure No. 12: State Dept.

67 Willkie, *One World*, p. 141.

68 Mitter, *Forgotten Ally*, p. 280.

69 Willkie, *One World*, pp. 137–38. Davies, *China Hand*.

70 Pakula, *Last Empress*, pp. 407–8.

71 "Visit to China . . . Willkie," Enclosure No. 13: State Dept. Willkie, *One World*, pp. 147–8. Barnard, *Willkie*, p. 373. Neal, *Dark Horse*, pp. 257–58.

72 Pakula, *Last Empress*, p. 412.

73 "Visit to China . . . Willkie," Enclosure No. 15, State Dept. Pakula, *Last Empress*, chaps. 35–36. Cook, *Eleanor Roosevelt*, pp. 460–63, esp. pp. 433–44. Neal, *Dark Horse*, pp. 256–57.

CHAPTER 11: 1944—Not This Time

1 Wendell Willkie typescript statement, Edmonton, Oct. 12, 1942, Willkie Papers, Lilly Library, IU.

2 Ellsworth Barnard, *Willkie*, p. 378. Willkie, "Draft Notes for Conversation with President Roosevelt," Oct. 14, 1942, Willkie Papers, Lilly Library, IU.

3 Willkie, "Draft for the Press in Washington," Oct. 14, 1942, Willkie Papers, Lilly Library, IU.

4 Willkie, "Wendell L. Willkie's REPORT TO THE PEOPLE," Oct. 26, 1942, Willkie Papers, Lilly Library, IU. "Around the World with Willkie," *Christian Science Monitor*, Oct. 27, 1942; "On Mr. Willkie," *New York Post*, Oct. 27, 1942; Barnard, *Willkie*, pp. 378–79. FDR reaction to Willkie radio address: Barnard, *Willkie*, p. 381; Barnes, *Willkie*, p. 310.

5 FDR to Willkie, April 15, Willkie to FDR, April 21, 1942. FDR Papers, Hyde Park. Barnard, *Willkie*, p. 325. GOP member quote: Johnson, *The Republican Party*, pp. 216–18.

6 The Willkie Japanese relocation comment at Frankfurter event: Harvard Sitkoff, *Toward Freedom Land: The Long Struggle for Racial Equality in America* (U. Kentucky, 2010), p. 136.

7 Jeffrey F. Liss, "The Schneiderman Case: An Inside View of the Roosevelt Court," *Michigan Law Review*, Vol. 74, No. 3 (Jan. 1976), pp. 500–523, pp. 500–502.

8 Carol King, Introduction, "The Schneiderman Case. US Supreme Court Opinion, with an introduction" (published by American Committee for Protection of the Foreign Born, 1943), p. 9.

9 Carol King, "The Willkie I Knew," *NM* (Oct. 24, 1944): 10–27, p. 10.

10 Joseph P. Lash, ed., *From the Diaries of Felix Frankfurter: With a Biographical Essay and Notes* (Norton, 1975), esp. pp. 211–14.

11 Warren Moscow, *Roosevelt and Willkie* (Prentice-Hall, 1968), p. 174.

12 King, "The Willkie I Knew," pp. 10–11.

13 King, Introduction, *The Schneiderman Case*, pp. 10–11. Jeffrey Liss, "The Schneiderman Case," pp. 503–5.

14 Neal, *Dark Horse*, pp. 270–71. Liss, "Schneiderman Case," pp. 516–17.

15 Robert Aron, *Histoire de Vichy, 1940–1944* (Fayard, 1954), IIIe Periode, esp. chap. III.

16 Willkie to Drew Pearson, Jan. 7, 1943, Drew Pearson Papers, LBJ Library.

17 Barnes, *Willkie*, pp. 311–12. Neal, *Dark Horse*, p. 262. Robert Gildea, *Fighters in the Shadows: A New History of the French Resistance* (Harvard, 2015), pp. 249–56.

18 James MacGreggor Burns, *Roosevelt: The Lion and the Fox* (Harcourt, 1956), p. 467. Eleanor Roosevelt, *This I Remember* (Harper & Bros., 1949), p. 220.

19 Neal, *Dark Horse*, pp. 279–80. "Wendell Willkie Calls on Madame Chiang Kai-shek," *Look*, Dec. 29, 1942. Pakula, *The Last Empress*, pp. 412–13.

20 On the socioeconomics and geography of the national plutocracy: Thomas Ferguson, "Industrial Conflict and the Coming of the New Deal: The Triumph of Multinational Liberalism in America," in Steve Fraser and Gary Gerstle, eds., *The Rise and Fall of the New Deal Order, 1930–1980* (Princeton, 1989), esp. pp. 10–16.

21 Bronson Batchelor to Joseph Newton Pew, Mar. 19, 1942; Joseph Pew Jr., to Bronson Batchelor, Mar. 27, 1942, J. N. Pew Papers, Hagley Museum & Library. Johnson, *The Republican Party*, pp. 222–23. Neal, *Dark Horse*, p. 278.

22 Donald Bruce Johnson, *The Republican Party and Wendell Willkie*, pp. 222–26; Spangler quote: Johnson, *ibid.*, p. 226. Barnard, *Willkie*, pp. 382–84. Neal, *Dark Horse*, p. 278.

23 Homer Capehart cited: Neal, *Dark Horse*, p. 279. Raymond Moley, cited: Johnson, *The Republican Party*, p. 222.

24 Jouette Shouse, "Memorandum," to Lammot du Pont, Mar. 4, 1943, Du Pont Papers, Manuscripts and Archives Dept., Hagley Library Hagley Museum and Library.

25 Johnson, *Republican Party and Willkie*, p. 240.

26 Simon & Schuster Press Release: "Questions and Answers about Wendell Willkie's Book, *One World*," Willkie Papers. Barnes, *Willkie*, p. 313.

27 Willkie, *One World*, ix. Barnes, *Willkie*, pp. 313–17.

28 Willkie, *One World*, p. 30.

29 Willkie, *ibid.*, pp. 86, 133. Wendell Willkie, Diary 1943, May 19: Diaries, Willkie Papers, IU.

30 Stalin and Chiang Kai-shek: Willkie, *One World*, pp. 86, 133. Harold Stassen, "Report on a Wakening World," *New York Times Sunday Book*

Review, April 11, 1943; Alec Irby, David G. Dalin, John F. Rothmann, Harold E. Stassen: *The Life and Perennial Candidacy of the Progressive Republican* (McFarland, 2013), pp. 18–20.

31 Willkie, *One World*, p. 19.

32 Willkie, *ibid.*, pp. 19, 190, 195. Alexis De Tocqueville, *Democracy in America* (The Folio Society, London, 2002; orig. pub. 1835), pp. 239, 326.

33 Robert E. Sherwood, *Roosevelt and Hopkins: An Intimate History* (Harper & Bros., 1948), pp. 830–31.

34 Madame Chiang's opinion of FDR and Willkie: Barnes, *Willkie*, p. 353. Pakula, *The Last Empress*, pp. 430–31. Cowles, *Mike Looks Back*, p. 90.

35 Franklin Roosevelt to Wendell Willkie, Mar. 6, 1943, Willkie Papers, Lilly Library, IU.

36 Source of misremembered Crum anecdote: Tex McCrary and Jinx Falkenberg, "New York Close Up," *New York Herald Tribune*, Sept. 10, 1951; Ellsworth Barnard, "Interviews," Willkie Papers, Lilly Library.

37 Thomas J. Sugrue, *The Origins of the Urban Crisis: Race and Inequality in Postwar Detroit* (U. Michigan, 1997). "Riots More Costly to War Than Strikes," *Detroit Free Press*, June 26." Tragedy in Detroit," *New York Times*, June 22, 1943. "Hoover Urges Curb on Incipient Riots, Blames Hoodlums," *New York Times*, Aug. 10, 1943. Harvard Sitkoff, "The Detroit Race Riot of 1943," *Toward Freedom Land: The Long Struggle for Racial Equality in America* (U. Kentucky, 2010), p. 43.

38 White, *A Man Called White*, pp. 231–32. Janken, *White*, p. 274. Wendell Willkie, "Open Letter," CBS Radio, June 24, 1943: The Paley Center for Media, New York, NY. Neal, *Dark Horse*, p. 275.

39 Johnson, *The Republican Party*, pp. 241–43. Barnard, *Willkie*, p. 427. Neal, *Dark Horse*, pp. 280–81.

40 Willkie's boast: Robert T. Elson, *The World of Time Inc.: The Intimate History of a Publishing Enterprise, Volume Two: 1941–1960* (Atheneum, 1973), p. 71. Joseph N. Pew to Harlan J. Bushfield, July 22, 1943, J. N. Pew Jr., Collection: Manuscripts and Archives Department, Hagley Museum and Library. Neal, *Dark Horse*, pp. 280–81.

41 Wendell Willkie to Drew Pearson, July 4, 1943, Box G 247, Willkie, Wendell 32 (1943–1963), Drew Pearson Papers: LBJ Library.

42 Barnard, *Willkie*, p. 428. Johnson, *The Republican Party*, p. 246. Smith, *Dewey*, p. 386.

43 Willkie's "free enterprise system" quoted: Barnard, *Willkie*, p. 429. Johnson, *The Republican Party*, pp. 246–47.

44 S. K. Nelson, "Willkie as Candidate," *New Republic*, Oct. 4, 1943. Joseph N. Pew to Frank Gannett, Sept. 7, 1943, Pew–Du Pont Papers, Hagley Library. Barnes, *Willkie*, p. 341.

45 Milburn P. Akers, "Missouri Republican Czar Still Doesn't Like Willkie," *Chicago Star*, Oct. 16, 1943. Barnes, *Willkie*, p. 342. Johnson, *The Republican Party*, p. 251.

46 Ring Lardner Jr., to Walter White, Aug. 27, 1943. "Now's the Time to Insure Decent World, Social Leader Says," Los Angeles, *Daily News*, Sept. 30, 1943. "Must Defeat Ideas as Well as Armies of Foe, Willkie Warns in War Chest Talk," Los Angeles *Daily News*, Sept. 30, 1943.

47 Marc Connelly to Walter White, Sept. 11, 1943, Walter White Collection, NAACP Papers, LOC.

48 Comfortable California lead: Neal, *Dark Horse*, p. 287. Barnard, *Willkie*, p 436. G. Edward White, *Earl Warren: A Public Life* (Oxford, 1982), pp. 127–28.

49 Patricia Bosworth, *Anything Your Little Heart Desires* (Simon & Schuster, 1997), pp. 96–97.

50 White, *A Man Called White*, p. 204.

51 "Has Wendell Willkie Lost?," *New Republic*, Nov. 29, 1943; S. K. Nelson, "Willkie as Candidate," *New Republic*, Oct. 4, 1943: 442–43. Milton P. Akers, "Hamilton Tries to Hide Willkie Behind Smokescreen of Favorite Sons," *Pittsburgh Courier*, Nov. 7, 1943. Joseph N. Pew to Edgar Queeny, Nov. 16, 1943, Pew Collection, Hagley Library.

52 John Hamilton to Joseph Pew, Nov. 10, Nov. 12, 1943, Pew Collection, Hagley Library. Barnes, *Willkie*, p. 355.

53 Wendell Willkie, "Don't Stir Distrust of Russia," *New York Times Magazine*, Jan. 2, 1944. Barnard, *Willkie*, p. 438.

54 Barnes, *Willkie*, p. 346.

55 William H. Wills, "Will the Republican Party Commit Suicide in 1944?," CBS Radio address, Jan. 8, 1944, pp. 3198–3202, esp. 3202, John D. M. Hamilton Papers, Library of Congress. John Hamilton, "In Answer to a Republican Governor," Jan. 15, 1944, Pew Collection, Hagley Library. Barnes, *Willkie*, p. 355.

56 Johnson, *The Republican Party*, pp. 246–47, 264–65.

57 Neal, *Dark Horse*, pp. 290–91. Alan Brinkley, *The Publisher: Henry Luce and His American Century* (Knopf, 2010), p. 304.

58 Barnes, *Willkie*, p. 359. Johnson, *The Republican Party*, p. 274.

59 Johnson, *The Republican Party*, pp. 279–80.

60 Lippmann consolation, quoted: Neal, *Dark Horse*, p. 306. Edith Willkie reminiscence: Barnard "Interviews," Willkie Papers.

61 Rosenman on FDR's poor condition: Map Room, Small Collections, FDR Papers. "Rosenman on Wallace," p. 203: [FDR]. Joseph Lelyveld, *His Final Battle: The Last Months of Franklin Roosevelt* (Knopf, 2016), p. 188. Neal, *Dark Horse*, p. 314. Graham White and John Maze, *Henry A. Wallace: His Search for a New World Order* (UNC, 1995), p. 199. Joseph Lelyveld, *His Final Battle: The Last Months of Franklin Roosevelt* (Knopf, 2016), p. 188. Brands, *Traitor to His Class*, pp. 768–70, Wallace scrape with RFC's Jesse Jones: Steven Feinberg, *Unprecedented Power: Jesse Jones, Capitalism, and the Common Good* (Texas A&M, 2011), pp. 454–61. Rosenman quote: Small Collections, Oral History, Interviews, P.Z. Fol. Rosenman, Samuel, "Reminiscences of Samuel Rosenman," 1960, p. 195, FDR Library.

62 Samuel I. Rosenman, *Working with Roosevelt* (Harper & Bros., 1952), pp. 463–44. Smith, *Thomas E. Dewey*, p. 411.

63 Rosenman, *Working with Roosevelt*, chap. 24, esp. pp. 463–68. Barnard, *Willkie*, pp. 482–83. Neal, *Dark Horse*, pp. 317–18. White and Maze, *Henry A. Wallace*, pp. 199–200. Watkins, *Righteous Pilgrim: Life and Times of Harold Ickes*, pp. 810–11.

64 Drew Pearson to Wendell Willkie, Aug. 1, 1944; Drew Pearson to Bartley Crum, June 19, 1944: Drew Pearson Papers, LBJ Library.

65 Rosenman, *Working with Roosevelt*, pp. 463–64. Rexford G. Tugwell, "Interview with Eleanor Roosevelt," FDR Library.

66 Rosenman on FDR's poor health: "The Fall Campaign," Small Collections.

Fol. Rosenman, Sam, p. P. 203. See Lelyveld, *His Final Battle*, pp. 12–13, 60–61, 93, 97. Drew Pearson Papers, Box G 24747, Willkie, Wendell #2 (1943–1963), pp. 2–4: LBJ Library. Johnson, *The Republican Party*, pp. 301–3. Neal, *Dark Horse*, pp. 318, 320. FDR to Churchill re handling of Stalin: FDR to Stalin telegram, April 18, 1942.

67 Wendell Willkie, "Citizens of Negro Blood," *Collier's*, Oct. 7, 1944; "Cowardice at Chicago," *Collier's*, Sept. 16, 1944.

68 Pearson opinion: Drew Pearson Papers, Box G247, Willkie, Wendell #2 (1943–1963) p. 4. On Crum and Davenport opinions: Neal, *Dark Horse*, p. 314. On Baldwin, Luce, Drummond opinions: Barnard, *Willkie*, pp. 499, 500. Crum to Drew Pearson, Oct. 11, 1944, telegram, Pearson Collection, LBJ Library.

69 Apostrophe quote: Cook, *Eleanor Roosevelt*, p. 522.

70 FDR's anger at Hopkins: Neal, citing Sherwood, *Roosevelt and Hopkins*, p. 314.

71 Willkie, "Foreign Policy," *An American Program* (Simon & Schuster, 1944), pp. 22–23.

72 Lippmann, quoted: Neal, *Dark Horse*, p. viii.

73 Willkie loyalist, Lamoyne Jones: Neal, *Dark Horse*, p. 132. Herbert and Marie B. Hecht Parmet, *Never Again: A President Runs for a Third Term* (Macmillan, 1968), pp. 213–14. Norman Thomas, quoted: James H. Madison, ed., *Wendell Willkie, Hoosier Internationalist* (U. Indiana, 1992), p. 62.

74 Christopher Gray, "Demolished Club Casts a Long Shadow," *New York Times*, April 13, 2014, p. 12.

BIBLIOGRAPHY

Ayala, Cesar J. *American Sugar Kingdom: The Plantation Economy of the Spanish Caribbean, 1898–1934.* UNC, 1999.

Ayala, Caesar J., and Rafael Bernabe. *Puerto Rico in the American Century: A History Since 1898.* UNC, 2007.

Baughman, James L. *Henry Luce and the Rise of the American News Media.* Johns Hopkins, 1987.

Barnard, Ellsworth. *Wendell Willkie: Fighter for Freedom.* Northern Michigan U., 1966.

Barnes, Joseph. *Willkie: The Events He Was Part Of—The Ideas He Fought For.* Simon & Schuster, 1952.

Beevor, Antony. *The Second World War.* Little, Brown, 2012.

Berg, A. Scott. *Lindbergh.* Berkley Group, 1998.

Berg, A. Scott. *Wilson.* Putnam, 2013.

Beschloss, Michael R. *Kennedy And Roosevelt: The Uneasy Alliance.* Norton, 1980.

Billingsley, Kenneth Lloyd. *Hollywood Party: How Communism Seduced the American Film Industry in the 1930s and 1940s.* Forum, 1998.

Bishop, Jim. *FDR's Last Year: April 1944–April 1945.* Morrow, 1974.

Bonbright, James C., and Gardiner C. Means, *The Holding Company: Its Public Significance and Its Regulation.* McGraw-Hill, 1932.

Bosworth, Patricia. *Anything Your Little Heart Desires: An American Family Story.* Simon & Schuster, 1997.

Brands, H. W. *The Traitor to His Class: The Privileged Life and Radical Presidency of Franklin Delano Roosevelt.* Doubleday, 2008.

Brinkley, Alan. *The Publisher: Henry Luce and His American Century.* Knopf, 2010.

Burns, James Macgregor. *Leadership.* Harper & Row, 1978.

Bungay, Stephen. *The Most Dangerous Enemy: A History of the Battle of Britain.* Aurum Press, 2000.

Carew, Michael G. "The Interaction Among National Newsmagazines and the Formulation of Foreign and Defense Policy in the Roosevelt Administration, 1939–1941." NYU PhD diss., 2002.

Caro, Robert A. *The Years of Lyndon Johnson: The Path to Power.* Knopf, 1982.

Cohen, Adam. *Nothing to Fear: FDR's Inner Circle and the Hundred Days That Created Modern America.* Penguin, 2009.

Cole, Wayne S. *Roosevelt and the Isolationists, 1932–1945.* U. Nebraska Press, 1983.

Colignon, Richard A. *Power Plays: Critical Events in the Institutionalization of the Tennessee Valley Authority.* SUNY Press, 1997.

Conquest, Robert. *The Great Terror.* Oxford, 2008, 40th anniv. ed.

Cook, Blanche Wiesen. *Eleanor Roosevelt: The War Years and Beyond, 1939–1962.* Viking, 2016.

Cooper, John Milton, Jr. *Breaking the Heart of the World: Woodrow Wilson and the Fight for the League of Nations.* Cambridge, 2001.

———. *Woodrow Wilson: A Biography.* Random House, 2009.

Cowles, Gardner. *Mike Looks Back: The Memoirs Of Gardner Cowles, Founder of Look Magazine.* Gardner Cowles, 1985.

Cripps, Thomas. *Slow Fade to Black: The Negro in American Film, 1900–1942.* Oxford, 1993.

Culver, John C., and John Hyde. *American Dreamer: A Life of Henry A. Wallace.* Norton, 2000.

Davenport, Marcia. *Too Strong for Fantasy.* U. Pittsburgh, 1967.

Davies, John Paton, Jr., *China Hand: An Autobiography.* U. Penn., 2010.

Dillon, Mary Earhart. *Wendell Willkie, 1892–1944.* Lippincott, 1952.

Doenecke, Justus D. *The Battle Against Intervention, 1939–1941.* Krieger, 1997.

———. *Nothing Less Than War: A New History of America's Entry into World War I.* U. Press of Kentucky, 2011.

Dunn, Susan. *1940: FDR, Willkie, Lindbergh, Hitler—The Election of 1940.* Yale, 2013.

———. *Roosevelt's Purge: How FDR Fought to Change the Democratic Party.* Harvard, 2013.

Durr, Kenneth D. *Life of the Party: Kenneth F. Simpson and the Survival of the Republicans in 1930s New York.* Montrose, 2009.

Dyja, Thomas. *Walter White: The Dilemma of Black Identity in America.* Ivan R. Dee, 2008.

Fraser, Steve, and Gary Gerstle, eds. *The Rise and Fall of the New Deal Order, 1930–1980.* Princeton, 1989.

Freeberg, Ernest. *The Age of Edison: Electric Light and the Invention of Modern America.* Penguin, 2013.

Fullilove, Michael. *Rendezvous with Destiny: How Franklin D. Roosevelt and Five Extraordinary Men Took America into War and into the World.* Penguin, 2013.

Gabler, Neal. *An Empire of Their Own: How the Jews Invented Hollywood.* Random House, 1988.

Gellman, Irwin F. *Secret Affairs: FDR, Cordell Hull, and Sumner Welles.* Enigma Books, 1995.

Halberstam, David. *The Powers That Be.* U. Illinois, 1975.

Hatch, Alden. *Young Willkie.* Harcourt, Brace, 1944.

Ickes, Harold L. *The Secret Diary of Harold L. Ickes: The Inside Struggle, 1936–1939.* Simon & Schuster, 1954.

Janken, Kenneth Robert. *White: The Biography of Walter White, Mr. NAACP.* New Press, 2003.

Johnson, Donald Bruce. *The Republican Party and Wendell Willkie.* U. Illinois, 1960.

Jordan, David M. *FDR, Dewey, and the Election of 1944.* Indiana U., 2011.

Kahn, E. J. *The China Hands: America's Foreign Service Officers and What Befell Them.* Viking, 1972.

Kaplan, Lawrence S. *The Conversion of Senator Arthur G. Vandenberg: From Isolationism to International Engagement.* U. Press Of Kentucky, 2015.

Kenneally, James J. *A Compassionate Conservative: A Political Biography of Joseph W. Martin, Jr., Speaker of the U.S. House of Representatives.* Lexington, 2003.

Kennedy, David M. *Freedom from Fear: The American People in Depression and War, 1929–1945.* Oxford, 1999.

Kessler, Ronald. *The Sins of the Father: Joseph P. Kennedy and the Dynasty He Founded.* Warner Books, 1996.

Ketchum, Richard M. *The Borrowed Years, 1938–1941: America on the Way to War.* Random House, 1989.

Kimball, Warren F. *Franklin Roosevelt as Wartime Statesman.* Princeton, 1991.

Koppes, Clayton R., and Gregory D. Black. *Hollywood Goes to War: How Politics, Profits, And Propaganda Shaped World War II Movies.* Free Press, 1987.

Krugler, David F. *1919, the Year of Racial Violence: How African Americans Fought Back.* Cambridge, 2015.

Lamont, Edward M. *The Ambassador from Wall Street: The Story of Thomas W. Lamont, J.P. Morgan's Chief Executive.* Madison Books, 1994.

Langer, William L., and S. Everett Gleason. *The Undeclared War, 1940–1941.* Harper & Bros., 1952.

Lash, Joseph P. *Dealers and Dreamers: A New Look at the New Deal.* Doubleday, 1988.

Lawrence, Bill. *Six Presidents, Too Many Wars.* Sat. Rev. Press, 1972.

Lelyveld ,Joseph. *His Final Battle: The Last Months Of Franklin Roosevelt.* Knopf, 2016.

Lewis, David Levering. *W.E.B. Du Bois: The Fight for Equality and the American Century, 1919–1963.* Holt, 2000.

Mahl, Thomas E. *Desperate Deception: British Covert Operations in the United States, 1939–44.* Brassey's, 1998.

Martin, Joe, as told to Robert J. Donovan. *My First Fifty Years in Politics.* McGraw-Hill 1960.

Mayers, David. *FDR's Ambassadors and the Diplomacy of Crisis: From the Rise of Hitler to the End of World War II.* Cambridge, 2013.

McCraw, Thomas K. *Morgan vs. Lilienthal: The Feud Within the TVA.* Loyola U. Press, 1970.

McCullough, David. *Truman.* Simon & Schuster, 1992.

McGeer, Michael. *A Fierce Discontent: The Rise and Fall of the Progressive Movement in America.* Oxford, 2003.

Mintz, Sidney W. *Worker in the Cane: A Puerto Rican Life History.* Yale, 1960.

Mitter, Rana. *Forgotten Ally: China's World War II, 1937–1945.* Houghton Mifflin Harcourt, 2013.

Moe, Richard. *Roosevelt's Second Act: The Election of 1940 and the Politics of War.* Oxford, 2013.

Moley, Raymond. *After Seven Years.* Harper & Bros, 1939.

Moscow, Warren. *Roosevelt and Willkie.* Prentice-Hall, 1968.

Morris, Sylvia Jukes. *Rage for Fame: The Ascent of Clare Boothe Luce.* Random House, 1997.

Neal, Steve. *Dark Horse: A Biography of Wendell Willkie.* U. Kansas, 1984.

Neuse, Steven M. *David E. Lilienthal: The Journey of an American Liberal.* U. Tennessee, 1996.

Newman, Robert P. *Owen Lattimore and the "Loss" of China.* U. Cal., 1992.

Official Report of the Proceedings of the Twenty-Second Republican National Convention, Held in Philadelphia, Pennsylvania, June 24, 25, 26, 27 and 28, 1940. Judd & Detweiler, 1940.

Olson, Lynne. *Citizens Of London: The American Who Stood with Britain in Its Darkest, Finest Hour.* Random House, 2010.

———. *Those Angry Days: Roosevelt, Lindbergh, and America's Fight over World War II.* Random House, 2013.

O'Reilly, Kenneth. *Nixon's Piano: Presidents and Racial Politics from Washington to Clinton.* Free Press, 1995.

Pakula, Hannah. *The Last Empress: Madame Chiang Kai-Shek and the Birth of Modern China.* Simon & Schuster, 2009.

Panter-Downes, Mollie. *London War Notes, 1939–1945.* Edited by William Shawn. Farrar, Straus and Giroux, 1971.

Parmet, Herbert, Marie B. Hecht. *Never Again: A President Runs for a Third Term.* Macmillan, 1968.

Paterson, Thomas G., J. Garry Clifford, Shane J. Maddock, Deborah Kistatsky, and Kenneth J. Hagan, eds. *American Foreign Relations: A History Since 1895.* 7th ed. Wadsworth, 2010.

Patterson, James T. *Congressional Conservatism and the New Deal, 1933–1939.* U. Kentucky, 1967.

———. *Mr. Republican: A Biography of Robert A. Taft.* Houghton Mifflin, 1972.

Peters, Charles. *Five Days in Philadelphia: Wendell Willkie, Franklin Roosevelt, and the 1940 Convention That Saved the Western World.* Public Affairs, 2005.

Perkins, Frances. *The Roosevelt I Knew.* Viking, 1946.

Propaganda in Motion Pictures: Hearings before a Subcommittee of the Committee on Interstate Commerce. United States Senate. Seventy-Seventh Congress. First Session On S. Res. 152. A Resolution Authorizing an Investigation of War Propaganda Disseminated by the Motion Picture Industry and Any Monopoly in Production, Distribution, or Exhibition on Motion Pictures: September 9 to 26, 1941. US Govt. Printing Office, 1942.

Pryor, Sam, III. *Make It Happen: The Fascinating Life of Sam Pryor, Jr.* Sam Pryor III, 2008.

Purcell, Aaron D. *Arthur Morgan: A Progressive Vision for American Reform.* U. Tennessee, 2014.

Radosh, Ronald, and Allis Radoch. *Red Star over Hollywood: The Film Colony's Long Romance with the Left.* Encounter Books, 2006.

Ramsay, M. L. *Pyramids of Power: The Story of Roosevelt, Insull, and the Utility Wars.* Bobbs-Merrill, 1937.

Rapport, Mike. *1848, Year of Revolution.* Basic Books, 2008.

Reynolds, David. *Summits: Six Meetings That Shaped the Twentieth Century.* Basic Books, 2007.

Roll, David L. *The Hopkins Touch: Harry Hopkins and the Forging of the Alliance to Defeat Hitler.* Oxford, 2013.

Root, Oren. *Persons and Persuasions.* Norton, 1974.

Roosevelt, Eleanor. *My Day: The Best of Eleanor Roosevelt's Acclaimed Newspaper Columns, 1936–1962.* Da Capo, 2000.

———. *This I Remember.* Harper & Bros., 1949.

Roosevelt, Elliott, and James Brough. *A Rendezvous with Destiny: The Roosevelts of the White House.* Putnam, 1975.

Rosenman, Samuel I. *Working with Roosevelt.* Harper & Bros., 1952.

Schlesinger, Arthur M., Jr. *The Politics of Upheaval.* Vol. III. Houghton Mifflin, 1960.

Scroop, Daniel. *Mr. Democrat: Jim Farley, the New Deal, and the Making of Modern American Politics.* U. Michigan, 2006.

Sherwood, Robert E. *Roosevelt and Hopkins: An Intimate History.* Harper & Bros., 1948.

Shlaes, Amity. *The Forgotten Man: A New History of the Great Depression.* HarperPerennial, 2007.

Sitkoff, Harvard. *Toward Freedom Land: The Long Struggle for Racial Equality in America.* U. Kentucky, 2010.

Slayton, Robert A., *Empire Statesman: The Rise and Redemption of Al Smith.* Free Press, 2001.

Smith, Amanda, ed. *Hostage to Fortune: The Letters of Joseph P. Kennedy.* Viking, 2001.

Smith, Richard Norton. *Thomas E. Dewey and His Times.* Simon & Schuster, 1982.

Sperber, Jonathan. *The European Revolutions, 1848–1851.* Cambridge, 2005.

Stone, Irving. *They Also Ran.* New American Library, 1943; revised ed., 1966.

Swanberg, W. A. *Luce and His Empire.* Scribner, 1972.

Urofsky, Melvin I. *Louis D. Brandeis: A Life.* Pantheon, 2009.

Vandenberg, Arthur H., Jr., ed. *The Private Papers of Senator Vandenberg.* Houghton Mifflin, 1952.

Van Doren, Carl. *Benjamin Franklin.* Viking, 1938.

Ward, Geoffrey C. *A First-Class Temperament: The Emergence of Franklin Roosevelt.* HarperCollins, 1989.

Wasik, John F. *The Merchant of Power: Sam Insull, Thomas Edison, and the Creation of the Modern Metropolis.* Palgrave, 2006.

Whalen, Richard J. *The Founding Father: The Story of Joseph P. Kennedy.* New American Library, 1964.

White, G. Edward. *Earl Warren: A Public Life.* Oxford, 1982.

White, Graham, and John Maze. *Henry A. Wallace: His Search for a New World Order.* UNC, 1995.

White, Walter. *A Man Called White: The Autobiography of Walter White.* U. Georgia, 1995; orig. pub., 1948.

Willkie, Wendell L. *An American Program.* Simon & Schuster, 1944.

————. *Free Enterprise: The Philosophy of Wendell L. Willkie as Found in His Speeches, Messages and Other Papers.* Nat. Home Library Assoc., 1940.

————. *Hoosier Internationalist.* Edited By James H. Madison. U. Indiana, 1992.

————. *One World,* with an introduction by Donald Bruce Johnson. U. Illinois, 1966; org. pub., 1943.

Wunderlin, Clarence E., Jr., ed. *The Papers of Robert A. Taft, II (1939–1944).* Kent State U., 2001.

INDEX

Page numbers in *italics* refer to illustrations.

ABOUT THE AUTHOR

David Levering Lewis was born into a family of academics in Little Rock, Arkansas. He grew up in Wilberforce, Ohio, and Atlanta, Georgia. He graduated Phi Beta Kappa from Fisk University at age nineteen and received a master's in US history from Columbia University the following year. He was awarded a PhD in modern French history from the London School of Economics and Political Science and has taught at the University of Ghana, the University of California at San Diego, Rutgers University, Harvard University, and New York University. He is the author and editor of ten books of history and biography. His research and writing have garnered fellowships from the Woodrow Wilson International Center for Scholars, Guggenheim Foundation, Center for Advanced Study in the Behavioral Sciences, National Humanities Center, and the John D. and Catherine T. MacArthur Foundation.

Lewis describes himself as a student of comparative history, a characterization borne out by a range of subjects that includes a history of anti-Semitism in France (*Prisoners of Honor: The Dreyfus Affair*), an exploration of late-nineteenth-century conflict between British imperialism and Islamic fundamentalism (*The Race to Fashoda: European Colonialism and African Resistance in the Scramble for Africa*), a biography of Martin Luther King Jr. (*King: A Biography*), and *God's Crucible: Islam and the Making of Europe, 570–1215*.

A two-time winner of the Pulitzer Prize for his two-volume biography of W. E. B. Du Bois, Lewis gained further distinction when he was recognized by the history field with two of its most prestigious awards, the Bancroft Prize and the Francis Parkman Prize. Lewis has served as president of the Society of American Historians and is a member of the Academy of Arts and Sciences and the American Philosophical Society. He was awarded the 2010 National Humanities Medal by President Barack Obama. In 2013, Lewis became the Julius Silver University Professor and a professor of history, emeritus, at New York University. The author is the father of two daughters and two sons, and resides on Manhattan's Upper West Side and near Stanfordville, New York.

Read More from
DAVID LEVERING LEWIS

God's Crucible:
Islam and the Making of Europe, 570–1215

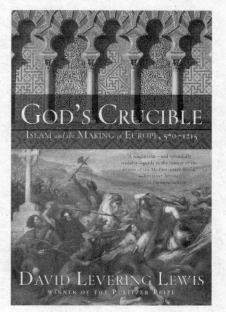

"A magisterial work by one of America's greatest historians. . . . The same wit, acuity, and awe-inspiring authority we have come to expect from David Levering Lewis."
> —Reza Aslan, author of *God: A Human History* and
> *Zealot: The Life and Times of Jesus of Nazareth*

"Lewis has made an important contribution to the growing body of literature on Muslim-Christian relations that has emerged after 9/11."
> —James Reston Jr., *Washington Post*

"A furiously complex age; a powerful narrative."
> —*New York Times Book Review*, Editors' Choice